FIVE HISTORIC SHIPS
From Plan to Model

Lexington: **the author's model. Photo by Mark Convertito.**

FIVE HISTORIC SHIPS
From Plan to Model

George S. Parker

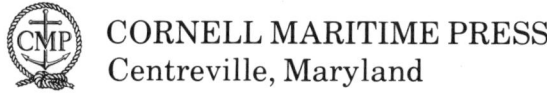
CORNELL MARITIME PRESS
Centreville, Maryland

Copyright © 1980 by Cornell Maritime Press, Inc.

No part of this book may be used or reproduced in any manner whatsoever without written permission except in the case of brief quotations embodied in critical articles and reviews. For information, address Cornell Maritime Press, Inc., Centreville, Maryland 21617.

> **Note:** Full-scale hull plans, sail plans, and detail sheets for each of the five models described in this book are available through your supplier or from the publisher at a nominal cost.

Library of Congress Cataloging in Publication Data

Parker, George S 1924-
     Five historic ships.

     Bibliography: p.
     Includes index.
     1. Ship models. I. Title.
VM298.P35   623.8'201   80-22137
ISBN 0-87033-258-9

Manufactured in the United States of America

First edition

CONTENTS

	Acknowledgments ix
	Foreword xi
I	Shaping the Hull 3
II	Square Rig Design 58
III	Fore-&-Aft Rig Design 79
IV	Finishing the Hull 91
V	Deck Structures 136
VI	Ground Tackle 146
VII	Guns & Gunports 155
VIII	Boats & Davits 166
IX	Ironwork 175
X	Blocks, Bull's-Eyes Deadeyes, Hearts, & Rigging Screws 194
XI	Rigging Square-Rigged Models 199
XII	Rigging Fore-&-Aft Models 221
XIII	Model Mountings & Display Cases 230
XIV	Lexington 237
XV	Wasp 257
XVI	Isaac Webb 277
XVII	Helen B. Thomas 297
XVIII	Margaret Haskell 313
XIX	Tools for Model Builders 331
XX	Materials 334
	Plates 338
	Bibliography 355
	Index 359

ILLUSTRATIONS

Lexington: the author's model		*Frontispiece*
The Five Ships		
Lexington		238
Wasp		256
Isaac Webb		276
Helen B. Thomas		296
Margaret Haskell		314
Sail Plans and Hull Plans of Models		
Isaac Webb	Following page	178
Margaret Haskell		210
Lexington		242
Wasp		274
Helen B. Thomas		306
Plates		338

Figures, Tables, Photographs of models in construction, and Plans appear throughout the book.

FOREWORD

The intent and purpose of this book is to set forth as carefully and as accurately as possible the methods and operations required to build five ship models, along with pertinent information concerning model building in general.

I was prompted to write the book by coming to realize what a large portion of time, in model building, is spent doing preliminary research and preparing working drawings—all before the actual model building can begin.

I have been building models, as time and conditions have permitted, since 1948. As I worked on each model, I kept a log of time spent doing the required research, redrawing plans to the desired scale, and building the model itself.

Since no one book contains all the necessary information the model maker needs, the modeler must pour over many volumes to obtain all the details of a given construction and rig. Then, by sorting the array of information, he can catalog the details so that a particular model can be built. This research can be a laborious, time-consuming, and frequently frustrating task. By the same token, plans customarily found in books are frequently reduced to some small arbitrary scale, not entirely suited to the needs of the model maker, and must be adapted. My log showed that a very large portion of my total model-building time was spent on research, and a lesser but substantial portion on drawings. I thus wanted to provide potential model makers with appropriate drawings and step-by-step instructions, from hull block to mast truck, for five specific models.

The ships selected represent those used in five types of important marine activity from the Revolution into the twentieth century. *Lexington* was a British merchant brig which was purchased for service in the Continental Navy and renamed. She was armed and sent to sea against British shipping. *Wasp* was an American sloop-of-war built as a war vessel and saw service in the War of 1812. *Isaac Webb* was built for the North Atlantic packet service and was designed according to the principles used in the last stages of packet ship development. *Helen B. Thomas* was the first fishing schooner built without a bowsprit and, along with her contemporaries, represents the final development of the Grand Banks fishing vessels. *Margaret Haskell* was built during the last years of development and use of large sailing colliers.

These five models will be works which the builder will be proud to own. They will not have plastic counterparts. They are not currently sold in kit form and they do not have sister ships on display in several maritime museums. The scales of the drawings were selected so the models can be accommodated in the average home for display purposes. Yet they will be large enough to permit accurate, detailed reproductions by any tyro with normal mechanical ability.

A good starting point for the novice in building square-rigged models is *Lexington*, which is where I started. The scale is large, and, with only three yards crossed on each of the two masts, the modeler must perform all the necessary operations to build a square rigger. However, he does not have to labor through the many repetitive, time-consuming operations such as those required on a three-masted model with four or five yards on each mast. Having built *Lexington* the modeler can apply the lessons learned, and patience acquired, to *Wasp*. *Wasp*'s rigging was somewhat more developed, but she was built when vessels were still using rawhide, rope, and wood as the principle rigging components.

After *Wasp* the modeler will be ready to build *Isaac Webb* whose rigging is smaller in scale, and on which ironwork was used extensively. The modeler will then become a ship's blacksmith for miniature vessels.

Isaac Webb's rig was the highest development in square-rig design. Any changes made thereafter were introduced to save labor costs and did not improve the basic idea of the rig. The relative profusion of deckhouses and other appurtenances were characteristic of later deep-water sailing merchantmen and gives the modeler good exercise in ship model joinery. Once all three models have been built the modeler is ready to tackle the model of any square-rigged vessel.

Although *Helen B. Thomas* and *Margaret Haskell* were fore-and-afters with substantially less rigging and less complicated concepts in rigging, they were built during the last stage of the development of commercial sail when steel wire was used almost exclusively for standing rigging and very sophisticated ironwork was used extensively above the deck and in the rigging. This demands a further development in the modeler's art as a ship's smith to manufacture these fittings.

The chapters are organized into three groups. The first thirteen deal with those operations common to several or all types of models—hull carving, concepts of rig, anchor tackle, ship's boats, and guns. These are followed by a separate chapter on each of the five vessels, describing the major work, in sequence, from shaping the hull through to rigging, with a listing of rigging for models without sails—the step-by-step operations needed to complete each model. The concluding chapters deal with materials and tools, and include a short discussion about woods most suitable for model work. No description of such operations as wood working, soldering, or the use of tools is included since these topics are beyond the scope of this book. The bibliography, however, cites excellent references for those desiring such information.

The book as a whole is arranged to introduce concepts, terminology, and methods of construction without inundating or overwhelming the reader.

In the chapters devoted to the five specific models, for example, I had originally intended to list the sequential steps from template making to completion, but found that such lists were subject to error and omission and the listing too inflexible to allow modelers any freedom by way of omissions or alternate procedures. Consequently these chapters are presented as *guides* for the sequence of operations rather than as absolute directives.

There is a whole new vocabulary for novices to learn. It is hoped that the introduction of new words has been gradual enough to allow comfortable assimilation. The reader should be aware that some parts of rigging on the schooners are not designated by the names commonly used. This was done because the proper names are different than those used on the square riggers and, since the terminology for square riggers was learned first, those designations are carried through on the schooners. Furthermore, there are a few words used in this book according to antiquated usage. Although incorrect by modern standards, they have been retained because they are used in most reference books.

Little mention has been made relative to the painting of these models because the sequence of applying it relative to other work must be governed to some extent by the order used for construction. All paint must have a flat or matte finish. Each coat should only be thick enough to cover and no more should be applied than is necessary to obtain a reasonably smooth finish. Color schemes are indicated in the detail sheets. When these vessels were built paint (except bottom paint) was made by adding color to linseed oil. Pastel shades must not be used. Most colors are quite clearly understood, but when selecting the paint for the bulwarks interiors and gun carriages on the war vessels, consider that the red color was used to hide blood. The bottoms of the war vessels were painted with white paint because anti-fouling paint was unknown. *Isaac Webb*'s bottom was probably sheathed with sheet copper and should properly be mottled green to look like tarnished copper. Anti-fouling paint on the two schooners should be a dark maroon.

Acceptable omissions and alternate equipment or methods have been indicated in several places. It is not intended for readers to believe those cited to be the only ones possible. The criterion model builders should use is to consider whether the omission or alternative will make the model look like a toy or retain the appearance of a miniature vessel.

There are innumerable parts and details on each model that are almost impossible to remember in proper sequence. It is recommended that, before starting work on any model, a listing of the major categories be made. As each category is finished the next is outlined and thoroughly detailed. Time spent on this planning is well spent because false starts are avoided, and the work progresses in an orderly manner.

Because some accuracy is lost in reducing, reproducing, and the subsequent enlargement of drawings, models built from the reduced scale drawings may not be exactly as designed. However, no two actual vessels built from the same set of plans by the same yard perform identically, proving that full-sized craft are not always shaped exactly as designed. It is important though that the finished hull be fair and symmetrical about the vertical, longitudinal center line. Readers who use these plans will have to enlarge the plans for hulls and boats so that molds can be made for carving their shapes. Other dimensions can be simply scaled-up and the parts made accordingly. Readers who do not want to bother with this extra work can obtain from the publisher the full scale, highly-detailed plans in sets of three sheets for each model consisting of a hull plan, sail plan, and detail sheet.

Scale ship model building is a very rewarding pastime. The builder not only produces a beautiful miniature replica of a vessel with all of its historical implications, but many very pleasant restful hours are spent during its construction. There need be no deadlines, the work is easy and very different from most reader's vocational pursuits, and the builder can exercise his or her inclination toward miniaturization and perfection without limit.

It is my hope that this book will instill confidence and provide the know-how for those who heretofore have considered the concepts and work too complicated, yet would like to try their hands at this hobby.

ACKNOWLEDGMENTS

Since all the square riggers of the type described in this book were gone and most of the schooner's contemporaries had either disappeared or been altered extensively before I was born, most of my information has come from books, models, paintings, and photographs. Fortunately there have been enough writers, model makers, artists, and photographers interested in marine affairs to record the model of hull and rigging schemes of by-gone vessels. To these people I am deeply indebted.

My quest for this information has led me to most maritime museums from Maine to Virginia. Without exception, the staffs were most helpful and I wish to thank them for their assistance.

By the nature of this work, a considerable portion must be devoted to giving directions. To break up an otherwise large book of unending directives, a balance was established by inserting sections containing historical and other relevant information. Much credit must go to Mrs. Patricia Flemming for reviewing drafts of the first chapters and making suggestions concerning the extent of these sections to set the tone of the book.

My writing for the past twenty-five years has consisted of contract specifications. In terms of grammar and readability, this form of writing is one of the poorest. Consequently, I had lost the writing skills I had learned as far back as elementary school, and assistance in recapturing them came from Dr. Phyllis Cantor, who took an active interest in the work and the quality of presentation. Through her comments and suggestions on the text of the first four chapters, this book has been substantially improved.

Many of the descriptions in Chapter I, particularly those dealing with reading and using the plans, were especially difficult to write. These descriptions are important, not only for their intrinsic value, but because they are the introduction for many readers to the use of plans and to woodworking. I want to thank Messrs. Alan Brightman and Harold Whittle for their comments and suggestions concerning the clarity of the chapter. I wish, also, to thank both Mr. and Mrs. Brightman for checking punctuation, spelling, and readability of the final draft of the book.

Few books would ever be published without typists who decipher less-than-fully-legible author's handwriting. In this regard I want to record my thanks to Mrs. Judith Moretti and Mrs. Patricia Donnelly for their efforts in typing what must have seemed to be an endless succession of alien words.

Considerable credit must go to my wife for the original idea of writing this book, for tolerating the lack of companionship, for commenting on varied versions of difficult passages, and for listening patiently to the same information reiterated in several ways over the three years it has been in preparation.

George S. Parker

Cos Cob, Connecticut
May, 1980

FIVE HISTORIC SHIPS
From Plan to Model

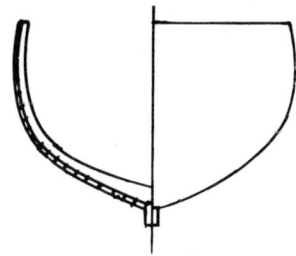

Chapter I
SHAPING THE HULL

Addressed to the ship model builder, this book shows and describes detailed as well as general methods and tools required to build a selection of five historic ships (described in the Introduction) not available in kits and representing important maritime activity from American Revolution days into the 20th Century. The graphic range of guide-line detailing is presented in plates, plans and photographs coinciding with text descriptions and instructions using the colorful terminology peculiar to the history of sailing and ships.

TYPES OF HULLS

There are two types of hulls commonly used in building ship models. The more exotic type is the built-up model while the other more common type is the carved hull model.

Built-Up Models

In particular, the multi-decked war vessel fascinates the novice who in trying to build them is usually frustrated and failure results before framing is completed. Construction of even single-decked hulls requires an expertise in woodworking and an advanced knowledge of old-time wooden ship construction far beyond the capacities of the average neophyte. Without such elementary information as timber and planking sizes, much estimating must be done because plans do not show them.

Carved Hull Models

Plans are simple, accurate representations containing all information needed to carve the hull. Given the know-how to use simple woodworking tools and the ability to read ships' plans, any novice can produce a carved hull. For this reason carved hulls are the selection for the models in this book.

BUILT-UP HULL HISTORY

Not only are carved hulls easier to construct, but they have a much longer and more interesting history. Built-up hulls generally were not made until about three hundred years ago. For the first hundred years designers built them to use as visual aids while trying to sell their new designs to royalty or Admiralty officials who were not schooled in reading naval drawings. Frequently these models were adorned with symbolic carvings and moldings, often executed by outstanding artists of the day.

These "Admiralty" models were excellent examples of modeler's art and are priceless collectors' items preserved in museums or private collections. They are usually devoid of rigging, probably because time-honored, proven rules governed spar sizes and rigging practices. Although the need for these models has disappeared, skilled and knowledgeable builders have continued to construct them. So as not to detract from the excellent workmanship revealed when some decking and outside planking is omitted, models are frequently not rigged.

CARVED HULL HISTORY

Carved hull models date back for at least four thousand years; substantiating artifacts have been found in ancient Egyptian tombs. It is quite certain that these had a religious connotation. It has been speculated that they were miniature replicas of the dead man's vessel, provided to transport his soul into the hereafter or, perhaps, to be used as an example of another vessel to be built after he arrived there.

A relatively recent example of models used for religious purposes, and probably the last in western culture, is the "Church Ship." These were built by seamen and contributed to their churches instead of a monetary offering because their pay scale was so low. The popularity of this practice dwindled by the time of the Reformation. Since then carved hull models have been built for many other reasons.

Colonial builders carved models of one side of their proposed hulls, called half models. Builders took off dimensions from their shape to build their vessels. By the end of the nineteenth century American naval architects had learned how to draw ship plans without the aid of half models. From then on the use of half models dwindled, but there still exists an older generation of country boatbuilders who use them. Modern naval architects build hull forms of their latest creations for testing in towing tanks. Youngsters build them to sail and race in ponds and sheltered harbors. Shipping companies have models built of their prize vessels for display in their office windows, and amateur builders construct fully finished and rigged models as a pastime.

SHIP'S PLANS

To build a model's hull, the modeler must have a rudimentary knowledge of ship's plans and be able to work with them. Without presuming to give a course in naval drafting, enough information is presented here to enable a novice to make the hull block and templates to carve the hull. With this information and step-by-step instructions for the work, the model builder can transform a wooden block into an accurate representation of the drawings.

HULL PLAN PARTS—"MERCHANT VESSEL OF 1800"

A vessel's hull plan, like any other, is a graphic representation of the designer's idea. Unlike most other plans, few if any dimensions are given, so the modeler must take measurements from either full-size drawings or expand those taken from drawings of reduced scale. Builders of the models described in this book can either enlarge portions of the reduced scale drawings included or use the full-sized drawings obtainable separately.

In this chapter a set of hull plans will be studied which could have been used for a merchant ship of about 1800. Methods for making the forms or templates required to shape the hull will be examined, followed by a description of how hulls are built by two separate methods. This particular hull type was selected from many types available because it requires most of the operations on any type hull. After these concepts are grasped, the modeler will be able to produce any hull likely to be found on suitable plans.

The upper plan on any drawing is the hull as viewed from its side. This profile plan is called the sheer plan. Below it there is another full-length plan which shows one side of the hull as viewed from below and is called the half-breadth plan. A third plan, which may appear in various locations in the drawing (below the half-breadth of those in this book) is a double plan called the body plan. One side shows half of the forward end as viewed from in front, the other half, the rear end, as viewed from behind. Half views from below and from the ends are sufficient because the side not shown is a mirror image of the other. Plate I, displaying the three plans, is a drawing of the "Merchant Vessel of 1800." Readers who study other plans will note lines and projections which are used by the architect during original drawing work but are not required by model builders. Hull drawings of the five models discussed here include a top view of half the deck with side views of deck structures and fittings on the sheer plan.

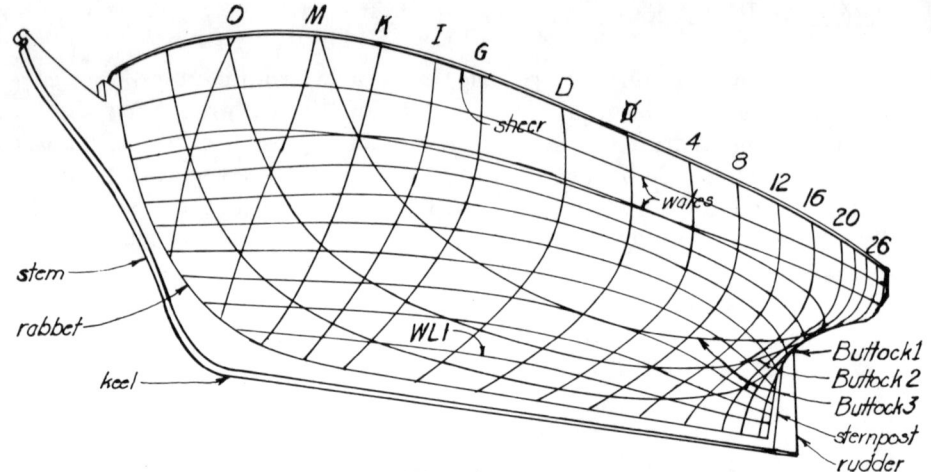

Fig. 1
Perspective drawing of hull for
Merchant Vessel of 1800 – PLATE I

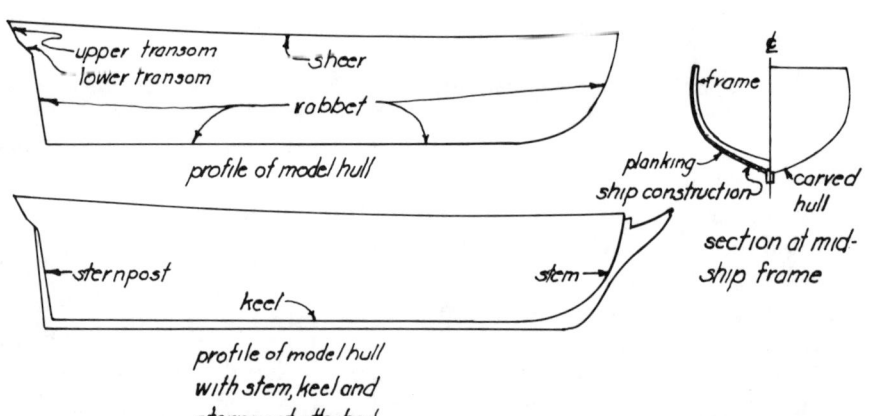

Fig. 2
Side and end profiles

Sheer Plan (Profile)

Plate I is a standard drawing of these plans. The sheer plan is drawn as if every point is on a visual ray exactly perpendicular to the vertical, fore-and-aft center line plane. Half-breadth and body plans are drawn on the same principle with rays which are exactly perpendicular to those in the sheer plan and to each other. By this scheme of projection, known as orthographic, all measurements in the plane of the drawing are true length. But, to those untrained in the use of these drawings, they are difficult to understand. There is a tendency to visualize shapes as they are seen rather than from three vantage points, all 90° apart.

As an example, consider a finicky house purchaser looking over a building with two sides of equal height and a standard gable roof between. No judgment of its lines would be made by viewing it from directly in front or at an end. Instead, these surfaces would be viewed on an angle to obtain a comprehensive picture of how they relate. It is evident from this vantage point that the nearest corner will appear higher than the other two, even though intuition gained through experience indicates they are equal. Drawings constructed from this vantage point are called perspectives. They are easy to visualize, but measurements of the same distances vary with location on the drawing. Perspectives of ships' hulls share the same fault, so it would be impossible to use them for construction. For comparison, because objects are visualized in perspective, see the hull (shown in Plate I) drawn in perspective in Fig. 1.

Sheer plans show many things other than the hull's profile. To simplify this plan for the reader, some items normally shown are omitted; they are not relevant to this discussion and vary from vessel to vessel. On the very top of this plan there are two closely and evenly spaced curved lines. They show the thickness of the rail, a continuous timber fastened to the top of the hull. It provides a neat finish and ties the top of the frames together. The curve at its underside is called the sheer. There are two continuous, closely spaced, nearly equidistant dotted lines below the rail from one end of the hull to the other. They show the height of the highest deck. The lower is along the side and the higher at the center line. Frequently, partial-length higher decks were used in either or both ends. If so, other dotted lines on the sheer plan show their elevations. There are two more curved lines lengthwise, nearly equidistant above and below the deck. They are farthest apart near the middle, close at the right end and closer on the left. These show the upper and lower edges of an extra thick belt of planking, called wales.

Before going on it is important to designate the ends of the hull properly. Note the arrows above the sheer plan. Both originate at a vertical line labeled "⓪" below the keel. This line is in the center of the widest frame in the hull, called the midship frame, regardless of its position along the keel.

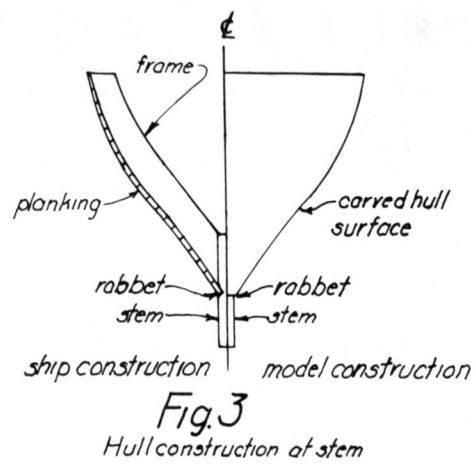

Fig. 3
Hull construction at stem

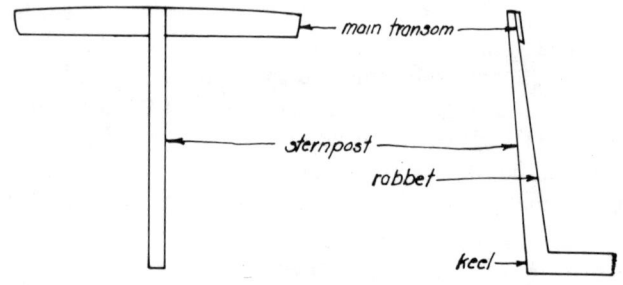

Fig. 4
Main transom construction

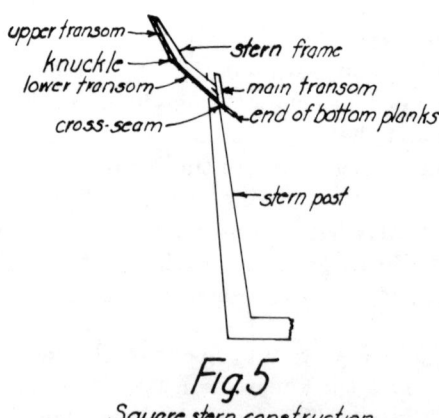

Fig. 5
Square stern construction

All to the right is the forward part; all to the left is the after part. The forward end is the bow; the after end the stern.

There are three views in Fig. 2. The upper left-hand view is the hull in profile; the upper curve is the sheer. The two lines labeled upper and lower transoms show the stern's profile stripped of the ornamentation board shown in the sheer plan on Plate I. The other line below the lower transom and the line on the bottom and up the bow is called the rabbet. It is the line where planking intersects the stem, keel, and sternpost. Refer to the plate and figure. The right-hand view is a section at the midship frame as if the hull has been sawed in two at that point to reveal the cut surface from one end. Its left side shows real ship construction; that on the right, carved hull construction. The lower left-hand profile shows the model's hull with the stem, keel, and sternpost in place.

In ship construction the stem, keel, and sternpost form the backbone of the hull. These parts project into the hull to allow frames to be fastened to their interior faces, to their sides or a combination of both. Note that Fig. 3 was drawn to show construction at the stem where the frame bolts to the side of the stem as opposed to being bolted to the top of the keel. Also note that in ship construction the rabbet is a notch cut in the sides of the backbone members to receive the ends and sides of planking. Carved hulls need no backbone, so the hull is shaped in profile, the sides carved up to the rabbets, and the backbone members are fastened to the narrow intervening space.

Shape of sterns is not clearly shown by orthographic projection when dealing with square-sterned vessels like the example or the three square-rigged models. To better understand the shape of these surfaces it will help to find out how they were built. The sternpost penetrated the hull to nearly weather deck level as shown in Fig. 4. A heavy crosswise timber called a main transom was fastened to its upper forward face. The lower and outboard surfaces of the timber were shaped like a main frame so that planking could be fastened to it. Stern frames, fore-and-aft frames bolted to the after face, formed the stern's shape and provided fastening points for the crosswise transom planking, as shown in Fig. 5.

The lower transom was dead flat. At its lower edge and coincident with the lower beveled face of the main transom there was a junction between the crosswise planking of the lower transom and the fore-and-aft hull planking, aptly named the cross seam. It was absolutely level and straight throughout on this hull although there was more or less upturning at the ends on some models. Planking on the upper transom was also run crosswise. Planking on the sides above the cross seam passed over the ends of transom planking and was sawed off flush.

The point of this discussion is to demonstrate that there is a very subtle change from curved hull to dead flat at the cross seam. Without this knowledge novices would shape the lower transom as if the bottom planking terminated at the knuckle. Shaping this area will be covered later in this chapter under "Shaping the Outside." Elliptically-shaped sterns, such as those on the fore-and-afters, were an integral part of hull construction with only one transom, so modelers do not have to concern themselves with cross seams and lower transoms on these hulls.

Upper transoms on the "Merchant Vessel of 1800," upper and some lower transoms on the square-sterned models, and the one transom on the fore-and-afters are all curved surfaces. The method of generating these surfaces will also be discussed later in this chapter under "Shaping the Outside."

Half-breadth Plan (Full-length) & Body Plan (Double)

The entire hull profile, deck elevations, and wales in the sheer plan have been covered. Attention, therefore, can be turned to the other two plans. On the half-breadth plan there are two long horizontal parallel lines. The lower is the center line; the upper shows the half-width of the stem, keel, and sternpost along with the overall extent of these parts lengthwise of the hull. The other line labeled sheer is a curved line which shows the outside shape of the hull at its sheer as viewed from above. Although it has been learned that half-breadth plans are views from below, it is better to visualize this from above since a long section of the hull is wider below the rail and would obstruct viewing this shape. At the stern there are three lines somewhat perpendicular to the center line. The aftermost one is the stern at the sheer, the next one forward is the knuckle, and the third is the cross seam. Just aft of the cross seam there is a radial-shaped opening which is the rudder port.

The right side of the body plan shows half-widths of the stem and keel; on the left side half-widths of sternpost and keel. Upper and lower transoms and cross seam are shown as viewed from behind. Also, an indication of the stern ornamentation is drawn on the transoms. Highest lines on both sides are the sheer as viewed from each end.

Grid System Lines (Curves Hull Shape)

All other lines in each of the three plans are parts of a three-dimensional grid system used to show the curved hull shape. This sounds formidable but is quite simple and is the only way an ever-changing, non-mathematical, curved surface can be described. Now, it is imperative to use both Plate I and Fig. 1 in following the next four paragraphs.

In the sheer plan there are two sets of mutually perpendicular lines. Horizontal ones are called waterlines. Vertical ones are called stations. The midship station is labeled ⌽, as cited before. Those forward are labeled with uppercase letters; those aft with arabic numerals.

Each station and waterline is an edge view of a plane perpendicular to the center line which pierces the exterior hull surface. The curves formed where these planes pierce the hull surface are shown in perspective in Fig. 1. Actual shapes of these curves are shown in the body and half-breadth plans, respectively, as labeled.

There are two sets of mutually perpendicular lines on the half-breadth plan. The vertical ones are station planes viewed from below. The other set are planes called buttocks and are labeled Buttock 1, etc. The actual shape of their intersections with the hull surface is shown in the sheer plan.

In the body plan there are two sets of mutually perpendicular lines. By close examination it is discovered that the horizontal ones are exactly the same distances above the keel as the waterlines in the sheer plan. After a little thought it becomes evident that these lines represent the same waterline planes. With similar reasoning it is evident that the vertical ones are buttocks as shown in the half-breadth plan, the only difference being that those in the body plan are end views while those in the other plans are longitudinal edge views of the same planes. Now the hull's shape is known and a method will be devised to transfer these lines to the hull block.

MEASUREMENTS

Before proceeding, consider the matter of scale of the five historic ship models and how measurements are handled. These craft were designed while the English system of measurement was used exclusively. Therefore, both construction and body-shape plans were drawn using feet and inches.

Full-Scale Plans

If the modeler wishes to work also with the full-sized, full-scale drawings, shown reduced for this text, the sets of plans may be purchased either through a bookshop or by order to the publisher. The full-scale plan figures for *Lexington, Wasp,* and *Helen B. Thomas* are drawn to a scale of 1/4" to the foot. Hence, 1/4" in the plan represents one foot on the real vessel. In other words, these models will be one forty-eighth as long as their seagoing counterparts. The *Isaac Webb* and *Margaret Haskell* plans are drawn to a scale of 1/8" to the foot for a reduction of one ninety-sixth.

Unless the modeler has an architects' scale from which measurements can be read directly, conversions must be made occasionally to check dimensions. As a simple example, check the width of the *Margaret Haskell* keel which measures 3/16″ in the plan. Multiply 3/16″ by 96 for a result of 18″ or 1 1/2′. Although this system is cumbersome it must be used. In other instances the model maker may have to scale-down from actual sizes.

Conversions

To somewhat confuse matters, many suppliers are buying items in increasing quantities from foreign sources where the metric system is used, so conversions may have to be made to obtain the size to purchase. Use Table I to make these conversions. The left-hand column shows various fractional sizes as measured on the model or calculated. Each fraction is converted horizontally to decimal size in inches and metric size in millimeters in center and right-hand columns respectively.

As an example, the fore shrouds on the *Margaret Haskell* are of 4 1/2″ diameter twisted wire, so what size standard (twisted electrical conductor) copper wire must be used? Divide 4 1/2″ by 96 to obtain a quotient of .047″. By using Table I, this wire is 3/64″ or 1.2 mm in diameter.

TABLE I
Conversion Between English and Metric Sizes

Fractional Size Inches	Decimal Equivalent Inches	Metric Size Millimeters
1/64	0.016	0.40
1/32	0.031	0.80
3/64	0.047	1.20
1/16	0.063	1.58
3/32	0.094	2.38
1/8	0.125	3.18
3/16	0.188	4.76
1/4	0.250	6.35
3/8	0.375	9.52
1/2	0.500	12.80
1	1.000	25.40

ENLARGING REDUCED-DRAWINGS

There is a special type of scale frequently used in ships drawings; it is included here in every plan within the set for each model. This scale is essential for the modeler who wishes to build from the reduced plans included in this book. Since the scales *reduced* simultaneously with the drawings, they therefore can be used to *enlarge* to the required size.

Establishing Dimensions by Scale

These scales are graduated to match the vessels as designed. Those for quarter-scale models have seven horizontal lines. Feet and multiples are indicated and labeled starting at zero one foot from the right-hand end. The foot to the right of zero has two diagonals which pass through the ends of the lowest line and the center of the highest. Measuring horizontally from zero, the diagonals cross the second line at 1" and 11", the second at 2" and 10", and so on.

Scales for eighth-scale models have a similar configuration, but there are only four horizontal lines, so the diagonals cross the second line at 2" and 10", the third at 4" and 8", and the fourth at 6". This coincides with the divisions on an architects' scale which is divided in inches on the quarter scale and every two inches on the eighth scale.

To use these scales a good divider is necessary. The dimension under consideration is spanned with dividers and transferred to the scale in the drawing. Set the left leg on a foot division mark to the left of zero so the right leg falls in the divided foot. The only requirement is that the measurement be taken along a horizontal line, and it is the sum of the feet to the left of zero plus the inches to the right. When scales are shorter than the dimension desired to be scaled, some convenient length such as 10' can be set on the dividers and stepped off along the line being measured until the balance is within the range of the scale. Dimensions obtained from these scales can be used to construct templates at the desired scale, along with obtaining dimensions of spars, etc. See the next section for the method of making templates from the reduced plans.

Scales in detail sheets included in the chapters for each model are drawn for use with a standard rule graduated in sixteenths. Due to space limitations all drawings in the sheets are not reduced equally, so use the appropriate scale. Where unimportant, drawings do not have an associated scale but proportions are maintained.

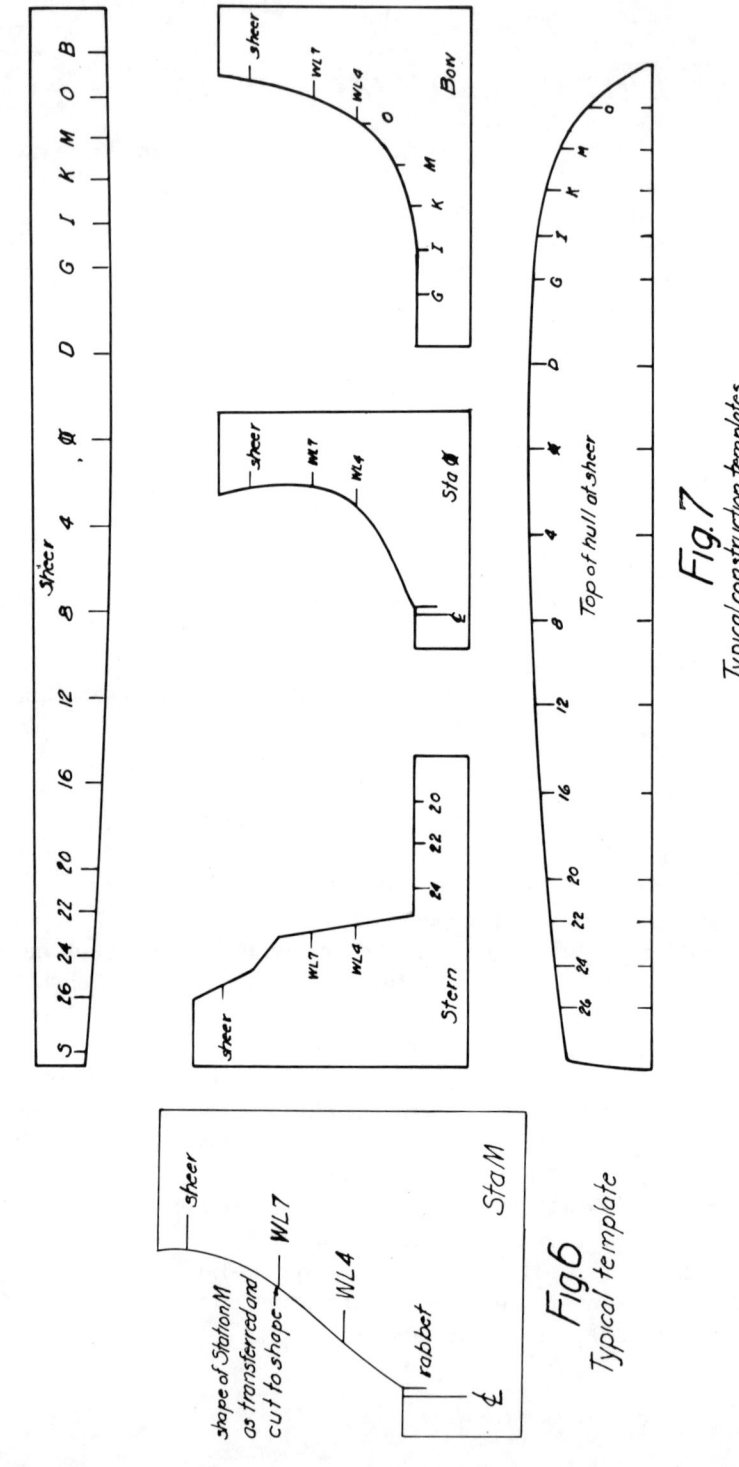

TEMPLATES

Templates are transfer mechanisms between plans and hull blocks. They are molds made from plans used to draw shapes on the hull block and/or check shapes being carved.

Drawing & Shaping

They are made from some relatively stiff, durable material such as poster board. Fig. 6 is a typical example. The easiest way to make them is to lay the plan on poster board with carbon paper between. With a small pointed stylus trace the shape on the plan. In addition, tick off and label desired references. Station templates should be drawn so the hull curve continues about 1/2" above hull with tick marks at vertical center line, at rabbet offset, at sheer elevation, and at least two waterlines spaced some distance apart. Bow templates must be long enough to show at least three stations, sheer elevations, and two waterlines with the curve continued 1/2" above.

Where bowsprits cut through the hull below the rail, a cut back is shown in the sheer plan. Neglect it when drawing the templates; these shapes will come automatically when bowsprits are fitted. Templates for the sterns must fulfill the same requirements as those for the bow. Where stern ornamentation is shown in sheer plans, it must be omitted, so draw the upper transom line from the bottom edge or knuckle on the center line profile and continue in a straight line up through the ornamentation. Stern templates should be drawn with a straightedge. Bow, stern, station, and sheer templates must all fit outside the hull. The shape of the sheer over the midship portion of the hull may be confused with one or more waterlines because they are close by on the inside or outside of the sheer line. Its width at a confused station can be verified by measuring the half-width of the station at the sheer directly from the body plan.

Helpful Hints. When making bow, stern, and station templates allow enough size to obtain a reasonable degree of rigidity. Cut them to shape with sharp shears. Some bending of the cardboard is unavoidable but can be corrected with a dry, medium hot iron. After flattening, check each template for true form against the drawing. Slight deviations from truth can be cut away with medium-fine sandpaper. If errors are major, make new templates. When all templates are correctly shaped, transfer all reference lines to the other side of each one and identify them. Templates drawn in Fig. 7 are for the "Merchant Vessel of 1800."

Some modelers prefer to make templates of sheet aluminum 1/32" thick. Though stiffer than poster board, it is harder to cut and more difficult to mark clearly. Excellent sheer templates can be made from thin boards. Wood takes reference marks well and shapes easily with the grain.

Techniques for Enlarging

Modelers who want to build from the reduced-scale drawings have to increase parts of the drawings to original size. Generally those required are for each station, profile of the bow, profile of the stern, profile of the sheer, and shape of the hull at the sheer as viewed from above. Rather than drawing these enlarged plans and copying their forms on template stock as described before, it is easier to draw the shapes directly onto the stock. Tools required are a 12" architects' scale with eighth and quarter scales, sharp pencils, and irregular curves designated #5, #20, and #26 by K&E Co.

Methods of drawing station templates are typical of those to make all but the sheer templates. Reference lines are the vertical center line, half-width of the keel, waterlines, height of sheer, and buttock lines. Spacing is obtained in feet and inches as described in the last section. Dimensions transferred to the template stock are measured off by using the appropriate scale on the architects' scale. Accuracy in measuring cannot be overstressed and each set of lines must be exactly perpendicular with each other.

After the grid is drawn, transfer enlarged measurements of widths of the section curve on each waterline and at the sheer, plus heighths on the buttocks. Then connect these points using one or more irregular curves. A little practice using light lines is in order for those unfamiliar with the use of curves. When drawing the first part of the line the curve should match at least three adjacent points. Successive settings should match at least two points on the curve being extended. After the complete curve has been lightly drawn, compare it visually with the plan, and check it for any unfairness. After making any corrections, redraw the curve to shape with a soft, sharp pencil and cut it to shape following previous instructions. Bow and stern profiles are drawn using end stations and waterlines as reference lines.

Sheer curves are too straight to be drawn with irregular curves except around the bow and stern if the ends are blunt as viewed from above. Carefully measure the spacing of the stations and the distance the bow and stern is displaced from the end stations which are ticked off on a reference line. Reference for the profile is the highest continuous waterline and for the view from above the center line. Distances above and off the reference lines are ticked off on the stations. Then the template stock is placed over a board and brads driven at each point through the stock into the board.

Check for fairness by sighting along the brad line and correct as necessary. Then spring a thin batten around the line of brads and draw the curve. Careful layout work is required to draw sterns of all models and to draw around the bows on the square-riggers. If stock other than poster board is desired for these templates, the shapes can be transferred after the original has been cut to shape.

HULL BLOCK MATERIAL

Stock for hulls must be the best pine available. It must be knot-free, pitch-free, and straight-grained. Lumber described as clear, free of knots, or select is not necessarily suitable as purchased. Neither is kiln-dried lumber; it may have been rained on or stored in a damp area since drying. Pattern maker's grade white or sugar pine thoroughly air-dried is preferable. If this or equal quality lumber is not procurable, then clear, straight-grained white pine can be cured.

This is done by *sticking* the lumber. Saw the boards slightly oversize on both length and width for the hull. Then lay narrow strips of the same thickness lumber on a flat surface crosswise to and under the first board. Three strips, one in the middle and one under each end, will suffice. Three similarly located strips are placed under each board as the pile is made. Weights on the top board minimize warpage. Two months' drying time undercover in a dry place is usually sufficient.

TWO BUILDING METHODS

There are two viable methods of building a carved hull—by carving a rectangular prism of wood or by gluing preshaped boards together to partially shape the hull before carving. Each method has advantages and disadvantages but both produce identical results. The method of construction is usually governed by the amount of power machinery available.

In order to carve a hull from a rectangular prism of wood, it is necessary to obtain a knot-free solid block. Blocks large enough to make hulls are generally not available, so the builder must make them. Therefore, both methods require boards to be glued together to form each block. The boards, or lifts, are finished to the same thickness as the distance between waterlines.

The available plans of the five historic ship models described in this book are drawn so standard thickness lumber can be used. All boards must be of equal width and exactly parallel-sided to avoid layout problems later. The boards are glued together, one on top of the other, to produce a block with a

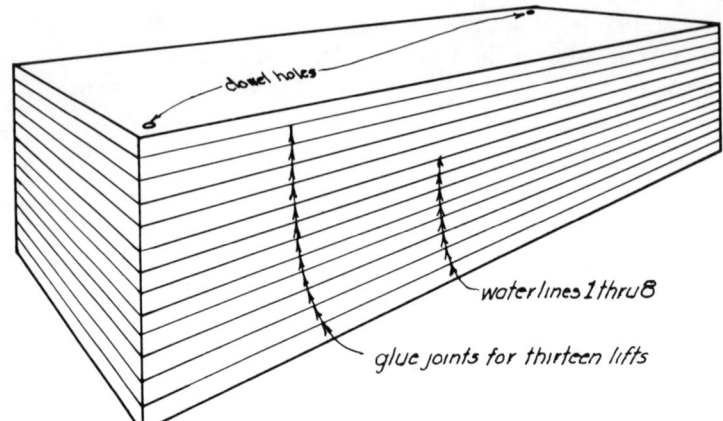

Fig. 8
Ideal hull block for our model with each lift in perfect alignment

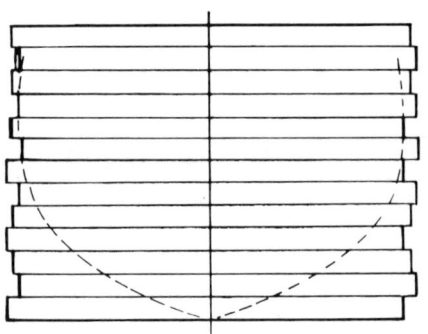

Fig. 9
End view of hull block showing effect of slippage

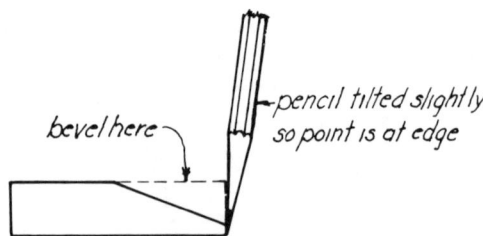

Fig 10
Cross-section of a home-made straightedge

depth equal to the distance from the keel's top to the highest point on the sheer.

Glue joints have a finite thickness of about 1/64". As will be seen while shaping the hull, it is better that these glue joints nearly coincide with waterlines. Therefore, standard thickness boards frequently have to be slightly milled to allow for joint thickness. When gluing blocks, suitable equipment such as C-clamps must be used to apply heavy pressure during the drying period. Weights are not adequate for this purpose. Glue must be a good quality brand such as Weldwood Plastic Resin, Elmer's Glue-All, or Carpenter's Wood Glue. Follow manufacturer's directions exactly.

Method 1 (Using Hand Tools Only)

Estimating Lifts—Making the Block. A rectangular prism is the easiest block for the builder to make without power tools. It is simply several boards of suitable length, width, and thickness glued together as shown in Fig. 8. Each board or lift must be slightly longer and wider than the overall length and width of the hull. The number of lifts is determined by dividing the maximum depth by the distances between waterlines. If the result is even, that is the number; if there is a remainder, add one. The example in the figure needs thirteen. The number and dimensions of lifts for each of the five models is given in Chapters XIV through XVIII.

Large flat surfaces covered with glue are very slippery and will not stay in place while clamping. To overcome this problem, dowels are located in opposite corners outside the finished hull. Select one lift for the top and lightly mark its center lengthwise. Then, with the half profile of the top hull aligned along the center line, locate one hole outside the bow. Turn the template over, align it with the center line, and locate the other hole well outside the side of the hull near the stern. Stack lifts with edges and ends in perfect vertical alignment. The previously marked lift has to be set on top. Before proceeding, check depth of the stack against the hull plan to make sure none of the lifts was accidentally omitted. When depth checks, clamp the whole with C-clamps or place in a vise and bore a 5/16" hole at each location all the way through with an auger bit and brace. Do not mix the order or orientation of these pieces after boring.

Gluing Technique. Now the lifts are ready to glue together. If powdered glue is used, mix a very liberal quantity so there will be enough to complete the work. Each freshly-mixed batch should be allowed to set for about ten minutes to allow any unmixed particles to become water-soaked. Previously applied glue will start setting up between batches, therefore, it is recommended that the builder use premixed glue and start with no less

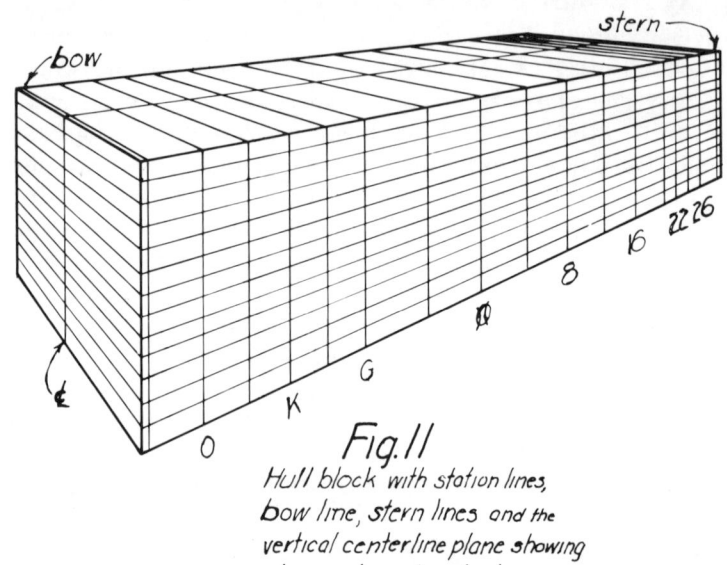

Fig. 11
Hull block with station lines, bow line, stern lines and the vertical centerline plane showing glue joints and waterlines

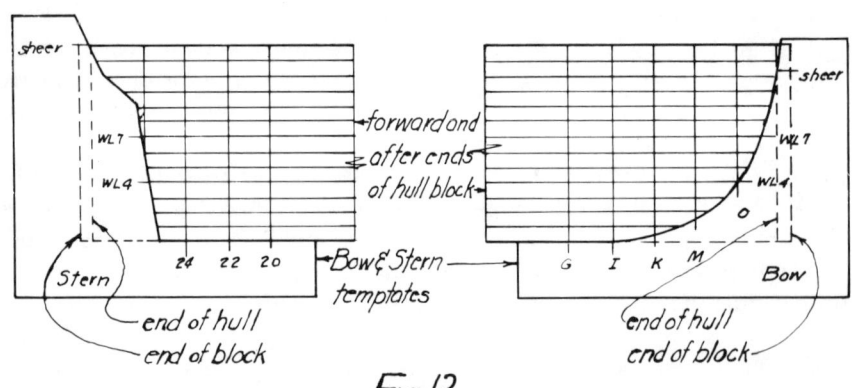

Fig. 12
Templates applied to draw profiles

than a pint in reserve. Enlist the aid of a helper, if possible, to accelerate the work. Once started, work rapidly and continuously until the last clamp has been tightened. Apply glue as evenly as possible to each surface. Use an old table knife or paint stirrer to spread it. Start by applying glue to the top of the lowest lift and to both surfaces of the next. Lay the second on the lowest and insert a 5/16" dowel from the bottom up in each hole. Continue applying glue to successive pieces, setting them in place and feeding the dowels up into the highest pieces.

Remember that the top surface of the highest lift is not covered with glue. When the last piece is in place, set C-clamps at about 6" intervals along each side and in the middle of each end. Set each clamp lightly with scrap blocks under the clamp to minimize crushing the wood fiber.

Then apply heavy pressure, starting in the center and working toward each end. This sequence tends to force entrapped air out through the ends. After glue is dry, remove clamps and saw dowels flush. The block should look approximately like Fig. 8.

Even though dowels are used, there will be some slippage. See Fig. 9 for end view of block showing exaggerated slippage with the form of the midship station drawn in. It shows how excessive slippage renders the block useless unless very wide lifts are used. The drawing in Fig. 8 shows an ideal situation in which lifts are in perfect alignment. This is seldom realized, but normal slippage is of little consequence if all layout work is done on and from the top surface.

Layout Work. All layout must be done with a soft, black, sharp pencil. Lines must be sharp and indelible. Tools for this work are a suitable straightedge and an accurate try square. Steel straightedges can be quite heavy and may be expensive. Years ago the author made one from well-seasoned pine. One edge was planed perfectly straight and the upper corner beveled, as shown in Fig. 10. Suitable stock size is 3/8" thick, 2" wide and, for these models, 40" long. A hole in one end permits hanging it on a nail to preserve its shape. The bevel not only identifies the perfect edge but also allows the user to see the line being drawn. Try squares, a mandatory item to purchase, should be of top quality with a fixed blade or a machinist's quality, adjustable-blade square.

Start to lay out by accurately locating the center of the top lift on each end and draw a line between marks. Continue this line down each end by using the square, and connect the lower ends across the bottom. Once done, this establishes the vertical fore-and-aft center line. It is exactly central and square with the top lift. Now lay the top profile template on the upper surface with its center line aligned with the one on the block and centered to allow equal waste on each end. Then transfer the location of each station, the extreme bow and extreme stern to the block. With the square,

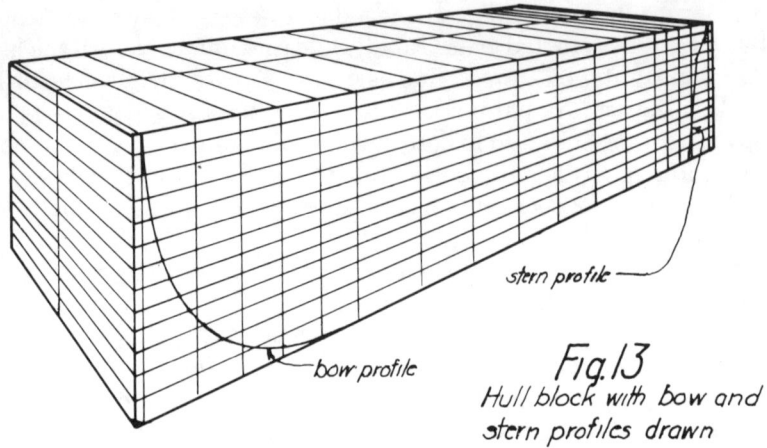

Fig. 13
Hull block with bow and stern profiles drawn

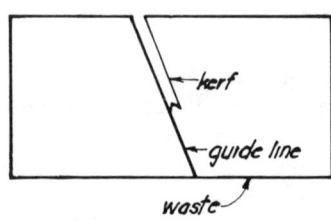

Fig. 14
Proper location of kerf at guide or profile line

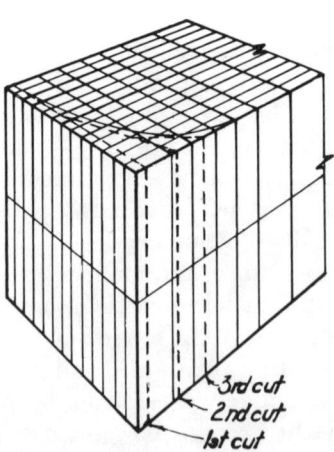

Fig. 15
Partial view of bow showing sequence for sawing profile

draw each line across the top and down each side. Finish the layout work by connecting each set across the bottom. While drawing the station and end lines across the top and all lines down the sides or ends, make sure the beam is held firmly against the block. By following this method, all lines refer back to the top, thereby eliminating errors due to slippage between lifts. While doing this layout work proceed carefully and accurately; errors made here are permanently built into the hull. At this point the block should look like Fig. 11.

A partial view of this block, as seen in Fig. 12, shows how bow and stern templates are applied to draw on their contours. Do not confuse ends. Apply templates and draw profiles on each side, making certain that station lines on the block are lined up with those on templates. The block should look like Fig. 13 and is now ready to start shaping.

Shaping. Much of the excess wood on the bow can be removed with a handsaw. Lay the block on its bottom and saw off the excess material outside the bow profile. This cut must follow Fig. 14. Adjust the saw cut to and outside the line or, as older carpenters express it, "save the line." Lay the block on its side and saw down outside the curve, as shown in Fig. 15. Several cuts are made perpendicular to the center line plane. After the excess has been removed, finish shaping to the lines with a block plane, spokeshave or rasp. While shaping, check the surface by holding the blade of a square along several glue joints. When the surface has been cut down to the profile on each side and no light can be seen between blade and surface, it is completed.

Stern profile shaping is a short job but requires an element of sawing skill. Refer to Fig. 16 for the sequence of cutting, and remember that every cut must be made to "save the line." There is no easily-handled alternative for shaping this type stern because all cuts are nearly perpendicular to the grain, and a saw is the only tool which will make smooth, straight cuts without excessive work. Practice with three or four trial cuts on a piece of scrap lumber using methods outlined in appropriate references in the Bibliography.

The cut must match the line on the top, it must match the line on the side, and it must be perfectly flat. When sawing, keep the arm aligned with the saw, move the arm in a reciprocating motion, and allow the saw's weight to force the teeth into the cut. After the knack is learned, the stern can be tackled. The suggested sequence, indicated in Fig. 16, avoids the necessity of starting a cut on a sharp angle. As an example, if the upper transom were cut first, it would be very difficult to start the saw in a cut for the lower transom.

Start work by extending the lower transom profile lines to the end of the block. Connect these lines across the end to provide a saw guideline. Stand

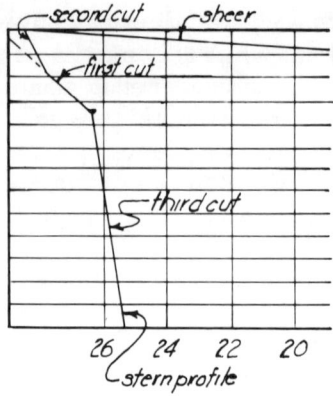

Fig. 16
Stern end of hull block
showing sequence of saw cuts

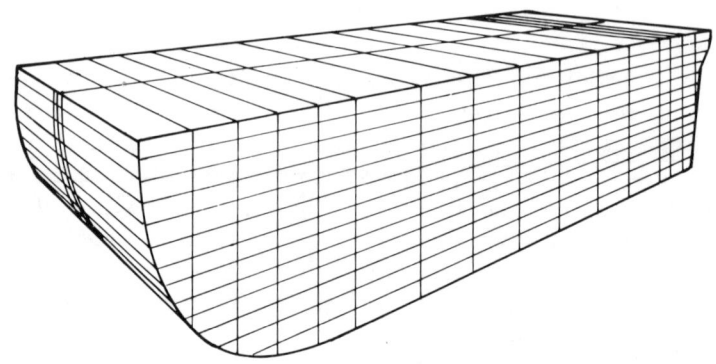

Fig. 17
Hull block with bow and stern
profiles shaped

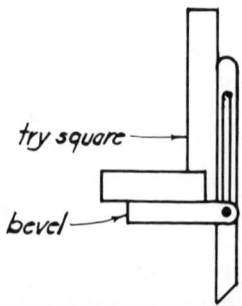

Fig. 18
Setting bevel with trysquare

the block on end in a vise and start sawing in the normal position. When the cut is about an inch deep on the far side, start lowering the sawing hand on each stroke until the kerf is level. Continue sawing to, but not beyond, the cross seam. During the progress of this operation check each side to be certain the approach to the rabbet at the top of the sternpost, or cross seam, is at an even rate. Do not rock the saw, or the bottom of the kerf will be bowed. When this cut is completed, lay the block on its top and saw up the rabbet to the cross seam using the same technique. Finish the work by sawing down the upper transom from the top of the block. There will probably be evident a slight rocking when the saw touches where the two cuts meet at the cross seam. This can be straightened out with a chisel, using the flat side against each surface in turn. Make light cuts crosswise of the block, producing a straight, clean corner at the cross seam.

Before proceeding, refer to Fig. 17, which shows the correct shape of the block. Note that the center line and rabbet offsets are drawn on the bow profile. These lines must be drawn on the hull for the entire length of the rabbet. The center line is already drawn along the bottom. Lay off the half-width of the keel on each side at both ends on the bottom and draw a line through these tick marks. Extend each of these lines up the sternpost rabbet profile to the cross seam. It is easy if an adjustable blade square is available. If not, set a bevel against a square, as shown, with the blade projecting just enough to reach the cross seam while the bevel beam rests on the bottom. Setting bevels square is demonstrated in Fig. 18. It helps later to extend the center line over each transom. Draw it down the upper transom with a square from the sheer. Connect the center line at the cross seam with that on the upper transom. Center and rabbet offset lines over the bow profile are started by ticking off their locations on its upper end. These tick marks are connected to the lines on the bottom by drawing along a straight side of a piece of poster board bent over the profile. Finish the work by reconnecting the station lines across the newly cut surfaces both forward and aft.

The next operation consists of cutting the sheer profile. Refer to Fig. 12. Fit the bow and stern templates carefully, as before, and tick mark the sheer on both sides on each end. Then draw the sheer curve on each side with the aid of the sheer profile template. Make sure the proper ends of the template are used and that ends are not reversed when shifting sides. If either are in error and go undetected until after the cutting has been started, the damage is irreparable and a new block must be built. Finish this lay out work by connecting the sheer lines across each end as shown in Fig. 19.

Usually sheer curves are relatively shallow and can be readily cut with a spokeshave. However, if the sheer is a substantial curve, such as in *Margaret Haskell*, make a series of saw cuts across the block in the deepest

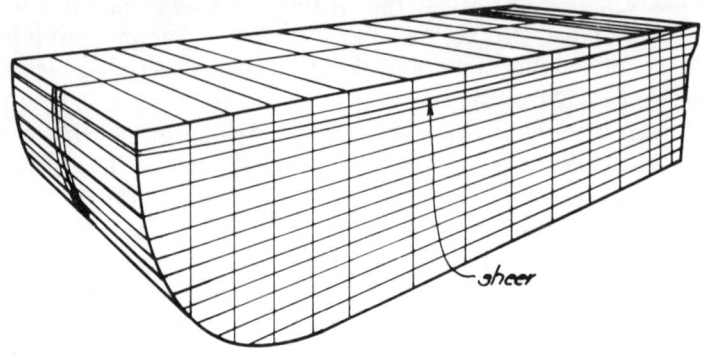

Fig. 19
Hull block with bow and stern
profiles shaped, sheer drawn

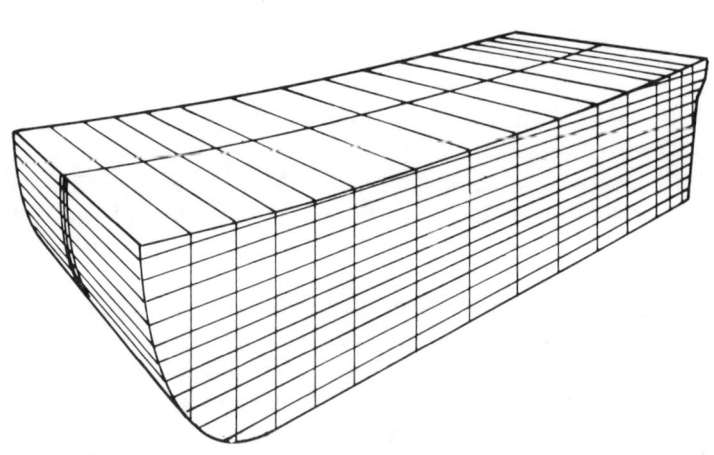

Fig. 20
Hull block with sheer plane shaped
and center and station lines redrawn

portion down to within 1/8" of the sheer curves. Then cut out the material above the kerf bottoms with a chisel. Clamp the block in a vise and cut the sheer. Start at each end with a spokeshave and work toward the low point. While cutting, check for flatness across the block as described for the bow profile. When nearing completion, check the surface for fairness and deviation from a continuous smooth curve. This is done by sighting along the block lengthwise at sheer level. Any dips or humps are very obvious from this vantage point. After a continuous curve is obtained at or slightly above the sheer curve, finish the surface with sandpaper on a block. Use coarse paper and sand lengthwise of the hull until all tool marks are removed, the sheer is down to its mark on each side, and the surface is fair. Now the block looks like Fig. 20.

Restore the center line and station lines on top of the hull. After this is done, align the top view template with the center line and stations. Draw its shape on that side, turn it over, realign and draw the other side so the hull block looks like Fig. 21.

The last step before carving the hull is cutting down the sides. Care must be exercised in this operation so the hull surface is not cut into.

Refer to the half-breadth and body plans in Plate I. These show that all parts of the hull from Station G forward are narrower below than at the sheer. Between Stations G and 16, the hull is substantially wider below the sheer. In many types, this swelling continues in some degree to the transom. Because of this swelling, the sides have to be cut. Taper as shown for the midship station in Fig. 22. The shape on each side must be fair and perfectly shaped where it intersects the sheer. After the hull has been cut down to the lines all around, tick each station on the sides for aligning station templates while carving. The hull block with perfectly shaped sides is shown in Fig. 23. There is little to be gained, however, from making the cuts too perfect, except at the sheer, because all below will have to be removed anyway.

Summary

Now the block is ready for carving, so review what has been done to make sure it is understood. A block was built of suitable length and width composed of lifts, equal in thickness to the distance between waterlines, and in sufficient quantity to obtain the required depth. The side profile was worked into the block. This shape consists of the sheer at the top, both transom profiles in the center line plane at the upper stern, and the rabbet at both sternpost and stem. Then the shape of the hull at the sheer as viewed from above was carved. All the while, the work was done from a vertical center line plane and stations clearly marked on the original block

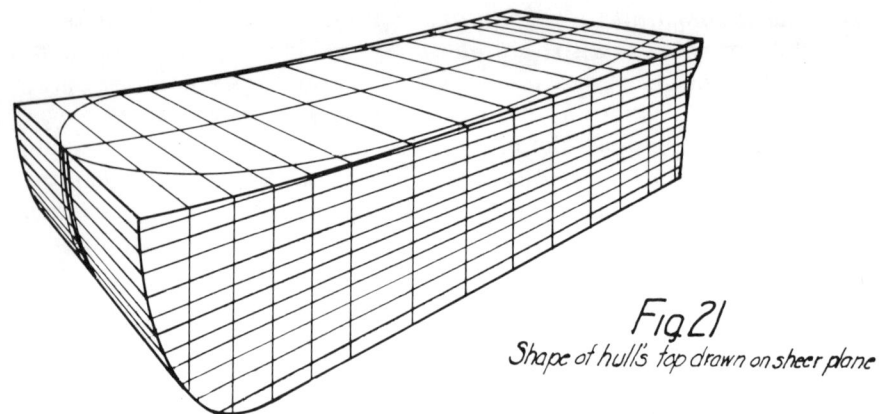

Fig. 21
Shape of hull's top drawn on sheer plane

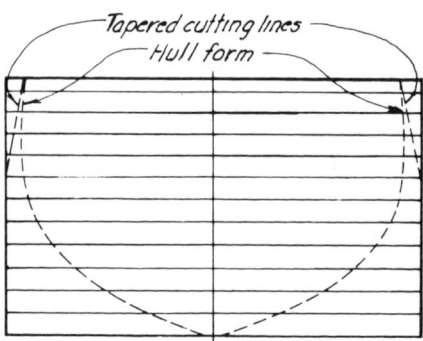

Fig. 22
Sectional view of hull block showing tapered cuts on sides at Station ⋈

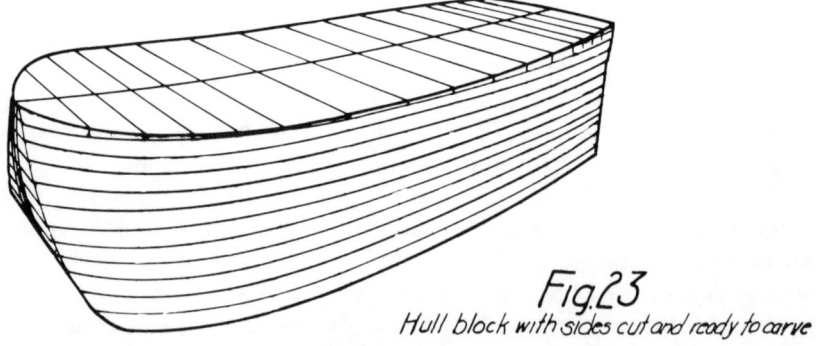

Fig. 23
Hull block with sides cut and ready to carve

and carried along by redrawing them on each newly carved surface. In addition, the rabbet offset, or half the keel width, was clearly marked on each side at the stem, keel, and sternpost to define the athwartship extent of the rabbet profile.

As mentioned before, there is another method of making and shaping a hull block which produces identical results except that there is a lot less wood to remove. That method will be explored before carving operations are described. Carving is identical, however, regardless of how the hull block is built. Following are the processes required to produce a hull block with carved profiles composed of preshaped lifts.

Method 2 (Using Selective Power Tools)

This method consists of preshaping most of the lifts, gluing all together and shaping the sheer, the end profiles, and the upper part of the hull at the sides to bring the hull block up to an equivalent condition to that done under Method 1. Method 2 is probably better for the builder who has access to a band saw, jigsaw, or saber saw. There is more layout work required here but far less carving later on.

Lift Selection, Lay Out, and Preshaping. Start work by selecting enough lifts to contain the entire sheer curve. On this hull, two are sufficient but it would be advisable to add another for strength. Glue these together as described for the whole block under Method 1. After the glue has dried, lay out the fore-and-aft center line, bow line, stern line, and each station line on this assembly and on each of the ten other lifts. Continue these lines down each end or side and across the bottom. Identify each crosswise line to avoid confusion later. Each single lift should look like that shown in Fig. 24a.

The single lifts are now ready for lay out work before sawing to shape. To minimize chance of error, it is strongly recommended that a compass be used for this lay out work as opposed to a rule. The compass joint must be reasonably stiff and the pencil holder adjustable. Fit it up with a soft, sharp pencil adjusted to the same length as the steel point. Now the lowest lift can be laid out. Step off the distances; WL1 intersects the rabbet forward of Station K and aft of Station 24, as measured on the sheer or body plans. Draw a crosswise line through each point and step off the keel's half-width on each side of the center line. Then step off the half-width of WL1 on Station K as measured from the center line in the half-breadth plan and transfer it to the lift. Step this measurement off on each side of the center line and repeat for each station all the way back to Station 24. Clearly mark these points as shown in Fig. 24b.

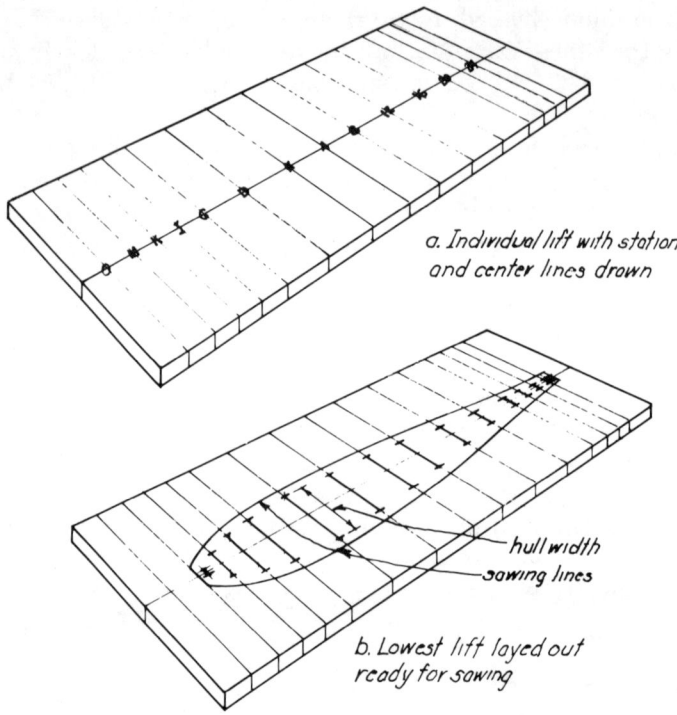

a. Individual lift with station and center lines drawn

b. Lowest lift layed out ready for sawing

— hull width
— sawing lines

Fig. 24
Sawn lift layout

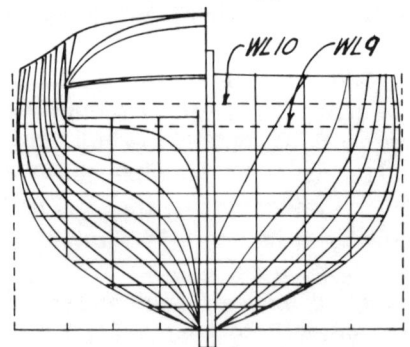

WL 10   WL 9

Fig. 25
Body plan with WL9 & WL10 drawn in dotted lines

Because some slippage may occur, add extra stock to allow for it. Where waterlines cross sections or rabbets at less than 45°, add 1/4". On higher lifts, where the sides and ends are more plumb, 1/8" will be sufficient. Where intersecting angles fall in between, the amount added should be about 3/16". It is preferable to add 1" in length to lifts which cut the rabbet forward of the sternpost. This prevents splitting of the waste while sawing down the rabbet line. After the excess allowance has been ticked off at the ends and each station, connect the tick marks with a freehand curve similar in shape to WL1 on the half-breadth plan. The lowest lift should look like the one shown in Fig. 24b. It is ready for sawing. Repeat the same lay out operation on each of the remaining nine lifts.

If the modeler wishes, some lumber can be saved on the lower lifts. Fig. 24b shows considerable excess in both length and width. Careful measuring beforehand allows use of shorter and narrower lumber. However, it is suggested that lumber be left the full length and width for the first hull. Above WL7, the actual shape of any specific waterline curve on the half-breadth plan between Stations D and 12 is confusing. Also, as the drawing stands, the shape of the lifts above WL8 are not shown. They are not shown on the plans because more waterlines would only add to the confusion. Lift widths can be obtained readily from the body plan. Step off the lift thickness in the body plan above WL8 for waterlines 9 and 10, and draw lines parallel to those below to represent these planes shown as dotted lines in Fig. 25. Hull widths at the stations for these lifts and for the confused waterlines below can be measured directly by stepping off from the center line along the waterline to points where stations cross it. Transfer these to the lifts as was done before from the half-breadth plan. Similar construction lines drawn in the sheer plan show locations of fore and aft ends of lifts.

When all lifts are completely laid out, saw them to shape and restore all lines cut away on both sides and ends.

Alignment and Gluing. Lift alignment is more critical on this type hull block than one made of parallel-sided lifts. The best method for maintaining alignment is by screwing the lifts together before gluing with round-head screws long enough to pass through the upper lift and half-way through the one below. This precludes gluing more than one lift on at a time but produces excellent results. The round heads prevent gluing another on without removing the aligning screws from the next lift below.

Start gluing work by aligning the center and station lines of the first and second lifts. Clamp them together and recheck alignment. At this point the builder will realize the value of station and center lines girdling each lift. Now insert a screw toward each end on the center line but far enough inside so it does not break through the hull's surface. On this hull, Stations

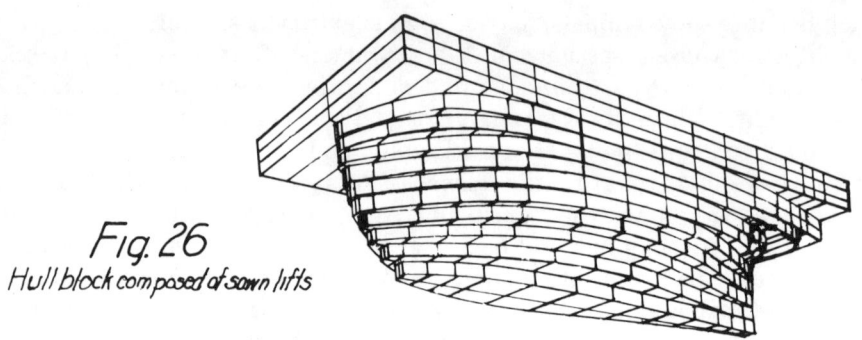

Fig. 26
Hull block composed of sawn lifts

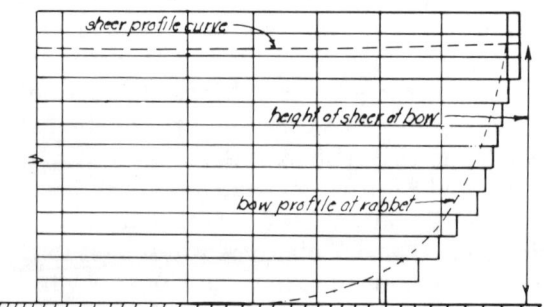

Fig. 27
Partial view of forward end of block showing measuring height at bow

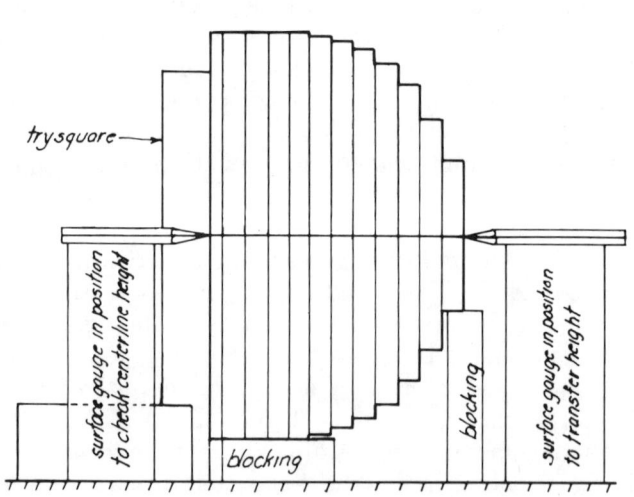

Fig. 28
Set-up for checking center line on bottom of block against centerline on sheer plane

I and 24 would be appropriate. Withdraw the screws, apply glue to the mating surfaces, reset the screws and apply clamps. Before setting the screws tightly, check alignment again and adjust if necessary. After the glue is dry remove clamps and screws. Repeat the process for each of the sawed lifts. Remember to shift screw locations a quarter inch or so along the center line on each new lift so they will be in solid wood in the lift below. After all ten lifts have been glued together, prepare the top three lifts for gluing onto the block.

These three lifts were left parallel-sided for specific reasons. This configuration allows the center line to be established easily, it allows drawing the sheer curve with a template, and it allows the upper stern profile to be drawn more easily. Drawing sheer and stern profiles on curved, irregular surfaces is difficult and, unless carefully done, errors tend to creep in. The parallel edges also provide reference base surfaces when checking or reestablishing the center line on the bottom, as will be seen.

The block in perspective is shown in Fig. 26 with the three upper lifts set in place. From observation it is evident that bow and stern templates cannot be used to locate points where the sheer cuts through the rabbet forward, and where it cuts through the upper transom at the stern (described under Method 1). The easiest way to establish the points is by direct measurement transferred from the plan. Extend the rabbet line horizontally at the keel both forward and aft to points under the hull extremities. Draw perpendiculars from the rabbet extensions to the sheer at the extremities and measure these distances. Now lay the hull block on a flat smooth surface with the three-lift assembly in place. The distances taken from the plan can then be measured vertically from the flat surface. Locate the points on each side at both ends. Finish the lay out work by drawing the sheer on each side with the template and lines across each end at the ends of the sheer curves. A view of the forward end of the block indicating the method of measuring the height at the bow is shown in Fig. 27.

Shaping the Sheer. There are three ways to shape the sheer. The safest is the first, described under Method 1. The second is to smooth and square up one edge and saw the curve only slightly oversize with a large industrial quality band saw (one with a capacity of more than a 6'' cut). The third consists of slitting the three-lift assembly up lengthwise into strips between 2'' to 3'' wide. Each outer strip can then be sawed on a smaller band saw. Inner pieces can be marked and sawed. The smaller varieties of band saws do not possess the required rigidity to saw accurately at or close to full capacity except in expert hands, if indeed the capacity is adequate. This method is not recommended for the beginner because the strips must be glued to the block before the sheer is finished and alignment both crosswise and lengthwise is difficult to maintain. However, where the hull has a deep sheer curve, this method may be advantageous to the experienced woodworker. Finish the sheer plane with a spokeshave and sandpaper as described under Method 1.

Regardless of which method is followed for shaping the sheer, the center line, bow line, stern line, and all stations must be redrawn on the top of the hull and the three-lift assembly glued onto the tenth lift in perfect alignment.

After all this has been done, the block must be checked for even limited misalignment both lengthwise and crosswise between stations and center lines on the top and bottom surfaces of the block. Again, undetected errors made here are permanently built into the hull. The center lines top and bottom must be exactly parallel with each other in the center line plane and both must lie on a plane perpendicular to the sheer. Also, the station lines on the sheer must be exactly above those on the bottom. Fig. 28 shows a good setup for checking alignment of center lines.

Select two short pieces of wood with equal thickness. Set these crosswise on the workbench spaced slightly less than the model's length and set the model on its side on the block. It is very handy now to have the parallel-sided three-lift assembly. Block up under the lowest lift so the sheer plane is perpendicular to the bench top, as checked with a square. If necessary, shim up with a thin wedge-shaped piece or pieces of wood under each end until the center line on the sheer plane is exactly parallel with the bench top, and readjust blocking accordingly under the lowest lift. Now make a surface gauge of scrap lumber the right height so the point of a pencil on its top surface will match the center line. Now shift the surface gauge to the other side and check the center line on the hull's bottom.

If it checks at each end, aligning and gluing was done well. If it does not, then slide the surface gauge along the bottom from one end to the other to draw a new center line with the pencil contacting the hull. Label it to prevent confusion with other lines. This work could have been done by direct measurement with a rule from the bench top and the new center line drawn with the straightedge, but accuracy is diminished somewhat and, even so, the surface gauge will be needed later to scribe the waterline.

Whether or not a new center line was drawn, lay off keel half-widths on the bottom and draw them in at this point. Redraw the center line with a fine, felt-tipped pen and also mark where stations cross the center line, using the designated letter or number as shown on the plan.

As stated before, stations must be checked on the bottom for alignment with those above. This is done simply by setting the model right side up on the bench. Place a square against the bow, with its beam on the bench top. Measure above the hull from its blade to Station ⌀. Now measure from the blade to the same station at bench top level on one side. If the line on the side of the lowest lift is not in proper location, tick mark its proper location. Repeat the same operation on the other side. If one or both do not jibe, correct the tick marks across the bottom and, using the template for the top of the hull, relocate each station along the bottom. Mark their locations between rabbet offsets. Use the felt-tipped pen to make them indelible. Turn the hull over, draw on the shape of the hull at the sheer and saw off excess wood forward of the bow line. Now the hull is ready to cut the end profiles followed by cutting down the sides.

Cutting End Profiles and Sides. Set the hull upside down in a vise, with bow upward at an angle. Try the bow template and cut the bow profile to shape, as described under Method 1. The method is identical except there is far less to remove, and cutting is done while using a template for form instead of previously scribed lines. Fig. 29 shows the bow profile during shaping, with its template in place for checking. Work the profile down until the shape matches the template when its station and other reference lines match those on the block. While the template is properly fitted, tick off the location of Stations K through O on the center line.

Sterns are somewhat difficult to lay out on this type block. Start work on the rabbet. Set a bevel from the template at the obtuse angle between the rabbets at the top of the keel and forward edge of the sternpost. Adjust the blade so it extends between half and two-thirds the way up to the cross seam. This foreshortened distance is used so the bevel when applied will not stand at too large an angle with the center line plane, which will be very evident after it is applied. Mark the location of the intersection of the rabbets (astern of Station 24 on this hull) and line up the bevel with this mark. Draw the forward edge of the sternpost up at least half way to the cross seam. Saw down the line carefully, as described before.

As the sawing progresses, measure the depth of cut as taken directly from the sheer plan. When the height of the cross seam has been reached, stop sawing, and break away the waste wood. Turn the hull right side up on the workbench. Set the bevel at the angle between the keel rabbet and the upper transom from the sheer plan. Set the bevel, as shown in Fig. 30, and draw the upper transom profile on each side. Saw down these lines until well below the knuckle. Now turn the hull over, locate the knuckle on the newly cut upper transom plane at the center line and draw a line through it across the hull. Finish the lower transom (or transoms) with a chisel by working beveled side up from each side toward the center. Check progress with the stern template. Cut until the template fits perfectly—when all reference lines check.

Now that the profile is complete, set the hull up, as described for checking the center line, and draw the center line over all surfaces of each end profile. The rabbet offsets should also be drawn at this time, as described

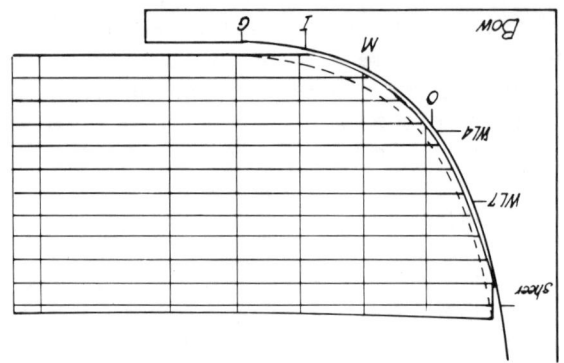

Fig. 29
Partially shaped bow profile being checked against its template

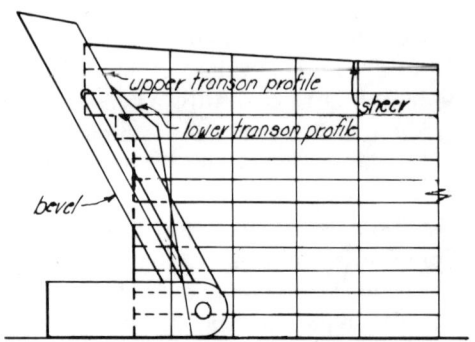

Fig. 30
Laying out upper transom

under Method 1. Cut down the sides, remembering to taper the cuts, as also described in Method 1, and tick stations on the sides.

Summary

As before, review what has been done under *this* method. An adequate number of lifts was selected, equivalent in thickness to the distance between waterlines of suitable length and width. An assembly was made of parallel-sided lifts deep enough to contain the sheer curve, with one additional for strength. All other lifts plus this assembly were accurately marked with center line, bow line, stern line and all station lines. Each separate lift was laid out according to the shape of its waterline and sawed to shape with excess stock allowed for slippage. These sawed lifts were glued together with center and station lines in reasonably close alignment. The sheer curve was laid out on the three-lift assembly and was cut before gluing to other lifts. End profiles were formed and sides cut down. It should be noted that center line and station line locations were checked and adjusted, as necessary, so that the hull should be symmetrical about its center line and stations perpendicular to the keel rabbet. As reference lines were cut away they were carried along by redrawing them on each newly carved surface. In addition, the rabbet offset is thus clearly marked from the cross seam to the bow, and the center line girdles the entire hull profile. The block is now ready to carve on its outside surfaces.

Two methods of producing hull blocks have been described. Each is viable, depending upon the builder's access to power machinery. All the following operations are identical except that in Method 1 the amount of material required to be removed from the produced hull is substantially greater.

Regardless of how the hull was produced, it is a good time to clean up the work area and organize the station templates in preparation to carve the hull. Check cutting edges of the spokeshave, drawknife, gouges and other tools to be used. Remember, clean sharp tools are easier to work with and produce predictable results. Dull tools, on the other hand, are erratic in behavior and often unsafe.

While speaking of safety, consider that during the outside shaping operation to come, one can be ankle deep in shavings which are dry as tinder within half an hour. Refrain from smoking and keep extension cords off the floor, out of the way, along with any tool cords. Minimize chances of fire! Keep a pressurized water- or carbon dioxide-type extinguisher nearby, just in case.

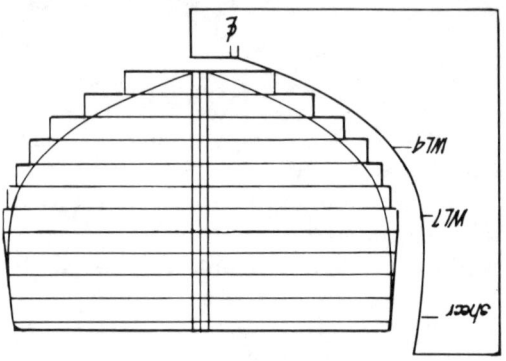

Fig. 31
Section at Station ⚓ with template fitted

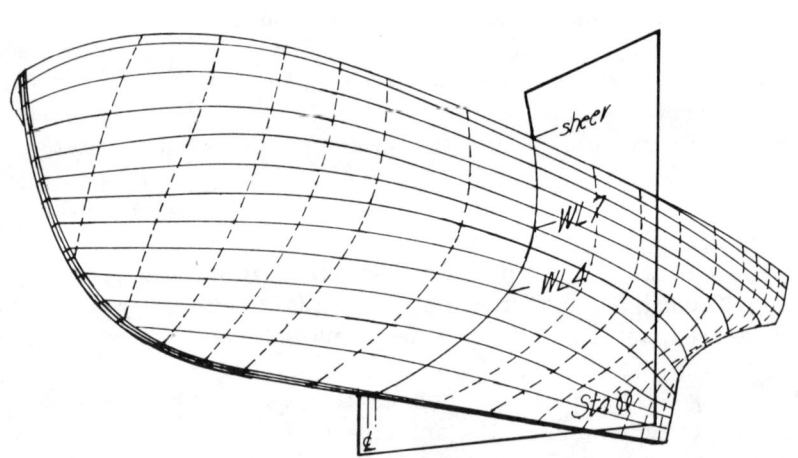

Fig. 32
Completed hull block with Station ⚓ template fitted

CARVING THE BLOCK'S OUTSIDE SURFACE

Screw a piece of scrap lumber, about 1' long by 2" wide and 3/4" thick, edge-down and centrally located on the center line. While shaping, this block is set in the vise so that the whole hull is above the jaws. It makes little difference which end is done first. For purposes of this discussion, shaping will be started at the bow.

Clamp the block in a vise on the sheer plane so the bow is tilted upwards at an angle of about 15°. Arrange templates for Stations ⌽ through 0 in order on the bench. The idea behind using templates for the outside is slightly different than at the bow profile. When setting templates against the hull block hold them with their center lines parallel to the center line plane, as shown in Fig. 31. They also must be perpendicular to the bottom of the hull and center line plane. When held in this fashion, each template is displaced both upward and outward. The idea while carving is to reduce these displacements simultaneously until neither exceeds 1/16". Final removal work is done with successively finer grades of sandpaper until displacements have diminished to zero, as shown in Fig. 32.

When carving, never try to carve from templates on an individual basis. Rather, work over an area covering at least three stations. With these simple concepts in mind, carve one side of the model's hull.

Now fit Station ⌽ template to determine where the first excess material must be removed. Make long cuts with a plane, spokeshave or drawknife somewhat parallel to the hull's center line plane. If the hull was built following Method 1, this cut will obviously be at the outside square corner (refer to Fig. 23); if it was made following Method 2, the point for the first cut is not so obvious and the template must be used. Remember that Station ⌽ is the widest section of the hull and that adjacent stations will be somewhat smaller when completed. Therefore, stock is removed until each displacement is 1/4" or less. After this excess has been removed, try templates at Stations D and G. At this point hold the templates in place and draw lines wherever they touch the hull's surface. These lines show the modeler where the next material must be removed and the direction to cut with the spokeshave.

When displacements of the template at Station ⌽ do not exceed 3/16", add more stations to the number of working templates. Try to arrange work so that the displacement of each succeeding template forward of Station ⌽ will not exceed 1/16" of the next one aft. Soon after achieving this point in carving work, the displacement of Station ⌽ will diminish to 1/16". Stop work in this area and keep shifting work forward one station until displacements do not exceed 1/16" for all forward templates.

While working at or close to the rabbets and the sheer be careful not to cut too deeply. After one side of the bow is done, reverse the tilt of the hull and repeat the process at stations aft of Station ⓪. In general, the process is identical but there are stations forward of the cross seam with an "S" shape requiring that the stock on the lower ends be removed with curved tools such as gouges, rasps and curved-sole planes.

After each side has been completed with tools, sand them with #80 sandpaper to remove irregularities and tool marks. Check with templates to govern the extent of stock removal. When sanding at rabbets and sheer, take precautions that edges are not rounded off. This sanding operation should remove stock to a point where all templates fit to within 1/32" of the finished surface. Final sanding is held in abeyance until after the hull has been hollowed out.

There is one chore left before going on—shaping the curve of the upper transom. This surface, a small portion of a large cylinder, has a slight curve. Its shape at rail level is shown on the half-breadth plan and was reproduced on the sheer plane when the hull's shape was drawn. If it is not clearly drawn, reset the template and darken it up. Tick mark the outside of the hull at ends of this curve. As shown in Fig. 30, reset a bevel for the angle at the outer edge of the transom as taken off the sheer plan, and draw this angle through the tick marks on each side. Turn the hull upside down and form this surface with a rasp. Work from each side with a rolling motion. When nearly down to the lines, finish with sandpaper on a block. Use the same rolling motion. When completed, the knuckle should be a fair curve when viewed from both astern or the side. Sand the lower transom dead flat to remove marks left by the saw.

Sterns on *Lexington* and *Wasp* will be formed the same as described. *Isaac Webb*'s stern was built with every transom curved, and when fashioning these surfaces on her model the modeler should start with the highest, in the manner just described, and work down through successive transoms to the cross seam, and finish each one before moving to the next one below.

Summary

Before starting with hollowing out work consider what has been done. Surfaces have been carved between the rabbets below and the sheer at the top, according to the prescribed shape defined by the templates located at set intervals along the hull. Tool work brought the hull shape down so each template was displaced no more than 1/16" from final form. Rough sanding removed tool marks and irregularities on the surfaces to allow template displacement not exceeding 1/32". Outside work was finished by forming the curve on the upper transom and sanding both transoms smooth. All that remains is the sanding of outside hull surfaces.

HOLLOWING OUT THE HULL BLOCK

Hollowing out the center of the hull block is the last rough work on the model. This is done to decrease the hull's weight, to weaken the structural strength of the individual lifts reducing any tendency to warp, and allowing the wood to establish water-content equilibrium with the surrounding air. The bottom is left thick to increase the hull's stability which helps offset weight of the rigging. One third of the hull depth at the sheer's low point is sufficient for any hull.

The end result should be to hollow out the hull to the point that the upper part of the sides is about 3/8" thick, which blends into the surface of the bottom. To establish to what extent to carve the interior, draw a line around each side 3/8" in from the outside on the sheer plane. Allow somewhat more at the stern so the finished thickness there will be equal to that at the sides.

Set the hull upright in the vise. Place terry cloth or some other heavy and soft material between the vise jaws and the hull. This will minimize scarring the sides when under medium clamping pressure. Remove the block from the top of the hull so the sheer plane is free to work on. Using a gouge, start at the middle by gouging into the surface. Make the hole deeper, longer, and wider. The finished depth, in order to conform with the predetermined results, should be at the glue joint between the fourth and fifth lifts. Finished thickness at the sides can be gauged by using the thumb and forefinger on one hand as a caliper.

There is a way to reduce the amount of hollowing out gouge work on hulls. Called honeycombing, it is making a series of holes bored with a bit and brace. It is important to establish the extent of boring, to prevent breaking through the outside. This is done by laying out the waterline on the sheer plane which will ultimately be the bottom of the hollowed out portion.

To allow for excess stock, move the curve in about 3/8" along the side, and foreshorten the ends. Curves drawn through the inner marks define the outboard extent of boring. Fig. 33 shows a top view of the sheer plane, including the boring curve and gouging curve. It has not been analyzed whether it is better to just go at it with a gouge or to go through the lay out and boring work beforehand. The latter method certainly reduces the size of blisters on one's palm.

Before boring any holes, set a depth gauge on the auger or mark it so the end of the worm will just reach the selected waterline (WL4 on this hull) when boring at the lowest point in the sheer. After the boring is done, gouge out the inside as already described. Fig. 34 shows a cross section of the hull hollowed out.

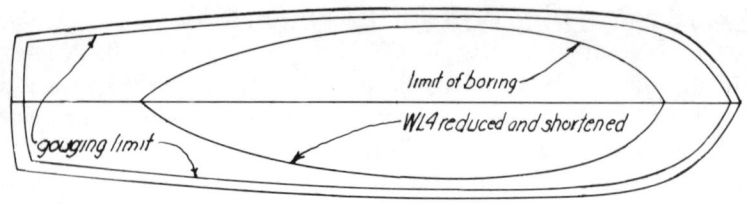

Fig. 33
Top view of sheer plane layed out for removal of stock inside

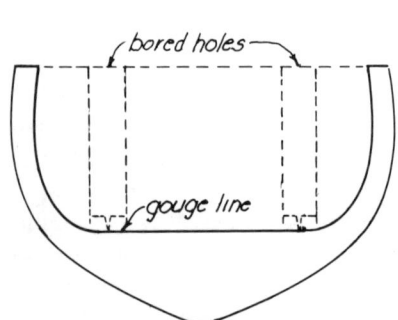

Fig. 34
Cross section of hollowed out hull at Sta. 4

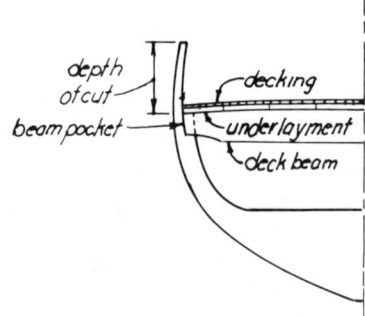

Fig. 35
Model deck installation arrangement

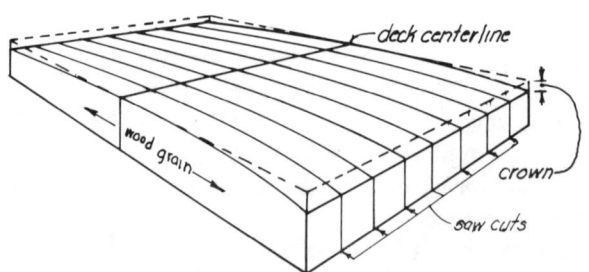

Fig. 36
Model deck beams shaped at crown and sawn, ready to fit

While gouging out the inside, do not use hammers or mallets on chisels; use sharp tools small enough to be easily handled and controlled. However, accidents do occur and there is always a possibility of pitch pockets, hidden knots or other defects being encountered when shaping the hull. Handle them by making two parallel lines in the direction of the grain on each side of the flaw. Cut down the sides and square off the ends with a chisel so the slot is about 1/4" deep. Shape a piece of pine to fit snugly in the slot and deep enough to protrude about 1/8" above surrounding surfaces. Glue this "dutchman" in place and when dry, continue shaping. If a tool is accidentally driven through the hull while gouging out the interior, set in a dutchman sufficiently wide and long to remove every trace of splintered wood; it should be thick enough to extend above both inside and outside surfaces and finished to match adjacent surfaces.

GENERAL BULWARKS & DECK CONSTRUCTION

Forming the inside of the bulwarks varies somewhat from model to model, but the method is common to all. For this description, assume the bulwarks are planked up on the inside like contemporary war vessels.

A cross section of one side of the hull with the model's deck installation arrangement is shown in Fig. 35. Bulwarks thickness is obtained from the plan (not shown in Plate I) and drawn on the top of the hull, using the outside as reference. This must be done very accurately so bulwarks thickness will be uniform. After thickness of deck and underlayment has been selected, it is added to the plan's measurement between the underside of the rail and the deck at the side. This dimension is calculated for each station and transferred to the inside of the hull on a station-by-station basis. Points are connected in a fair curve which defines the depth of the cut shown in Fig. 35. The best tool for cutting out this notch is a square-bitted, inside-beveled, curved-shank chisel sold in carving sets. The bit is about 3/8" wide and, when honed to a fine edge, vertical plunge cuts can be made without splitting the wood. Completed bulwarks must be absolutely uniform in thickness from top to bottom of the cut and throughout its length. At the bow the bulwarks must meet in a perfect "V." The bottom of the cut is finished clean and smooth in a fair curve to provide a bed for the edges of the deck underlayment.

In models, deck beams support the underlayment and form the deck shape. Decks curve slightly upward so water runs readily to the sides where scuppers direct it overboard. Crown is the vertical distance from the deck at the side to the deck amidships. Top surfaces of deck beams are curved in a small arc of a large circle to provide a crown of about 1/8" in a deck beam length of 6".

Deck beams are preferably made of one piece of wood. The piece of wood should be long enough with the grain to span the widest part of the hull and wide enough to make all required beams. Locate its center, and scribe on the center line. Establish the crown and mark this distance down from the top across each end. Then by eye form the curved surfaces on the top. See Fig. 36. Deck beams should be spaced about 6" apart throughout the length of the hull. Strip the deck beam block up into beams of appropriate thickness.

Pockets for deck beams must be carefully located so the beams run perpendicular to the center line. Each pocket must provide a snug fit, with no force, for its beam. It is preferable to make the pockets slightly less in depth than their beam end. Then the beam is cut on its lower side to adjust its height so its top surface matches the land for the underlayment exactly as shown in Fig. 35. When fitting beams for length, saw equal amounts from each end so the center of the beam is in the middle of the hull. Set each end of the beams in a liberal application of glue so each pocket is completely filled. After the glue is thoroughly dry, drive a short brad vertically down through each beam end into the hull. Finish the job by laying the deck underlayment. Usually, strips of pine 3/4" wide by 1/8" thick are adequate. These strips must be long enough to span the length of the hull; glue them to each beam and to bedding areas after the ends or sides have been cut to make a snug fit at the bulwarks. Set the strips in place with short brads at every bearing point and edge-glue each to its neighbor. After the glue is dry, set each brad so its head is about 1/32" below the surface and sand to remove all irregularities.

The foregoing description covers that work which, in general, is common to all models in terms of building from solid wood blocks. Beyond this point each model has unique features which cannot be covered in a general description.

A MODIFIED APPROACH—PICTORIAL "HOW-TO"

Parts of this chapter may be difficult for the novice to understand. Therefore, it is hoped the novice will gain a better understanding by following a pictorial step-by-step process. Building a model of the *Margaret Haskell* hull, as explained, follows that described under Method 2. Certain deviations were made to accommodate the materials which were at hand. These will be pointed out in the following work progress explanations, matching photo sequence.

The lumber was old excellent pine, rough-sawed, about 1 1/4" thick. Its length and width was slightly less than adequate to allow much excess when using 1" thick lifts; rather than plane it down to 1/2" thickness and

SHAPING THE HULL   45

finish out the compliment of lifts with lesser quality lumber, double-thick lifts were used, set with extreme care while gluing.

Before milling this lumber, it was noted that the hull depth at the extreme stern was 1/16" more than 4", thus the stock was finished a little thick to make up the difference. Also, the sheer curve cut through the top of the highest full-length lift at Station 5, so a short piece on the bow provided enough material forward. Sheer and top of hull curves were drawn on the hull block directly. Templates were made for bow, stern, and stations.

Sequence for Building the Hull

Photo 1 shows these templates and the tick stick used to locate bow, stations, and stern on the lift center lines and finished block. Also refer to Fig. 7.

Photo 2 shows the five lifts with center, station, and end lines drawn along with the cutting lines for the lowest three lifts. Refer to Fig. 24 for the drawing and accompanying description of this layout. Because the lifts were of marginal width, no stock had to be cut away along the sides. Also, since the lifts were only slightly over the finished width, extreme care was exercised to minimize slippage which did not exceed 1/32" for any lift either fore and aft or athwartships.

Photo 3 shows the third lift being glued to the lower two. Note the number and location of the C-clamps and the waste wood under their jaws. As thick lifts like these are quite stiff, fewer clamps are needed, but, if thinner lifts had been used, at least one more pair would have been required to obtain uniform clamping pressure.

Photo 4 shows the method of establishing the height of sheer at the bow. Also see Fig. 27. The blade of the square rests firmly on the bench top, and the height, as measured in the plan, was ticked on the block. After bow and stern heights were ticked off on each side, the square was moved from the positions shown to one of alignment with the bow line on the side of the fifth lift. The distance from the blade to one station (#10 was used here) was checked at both sheer and bench top levels to establish the amount of slippage. Fortunately, it checked the same for all four measurements; no adjustment had to be made.

Photo 5 shows how the vertical center line is checked or reestablished on the bottom of the block. Refer to Fig. 28. Note the center and station lines redrawn on the newly cut and finished sheer plane. The block is resting on two equal-depth wood strips so the center line is parallel with the bench top. Squareness of the sheer plane to the bench top is attested to by the square. The surface gauge is adjusted to the center line as shown. Then the gauge is moved, without changing the adjustment, to both bow and stern of the lowest lift. Again, the existing center line was at the correct height which shows how accurately the screws held all lifts in alignment during gluing operations.

Photo 6 shows the hull block slightly farther advanced than that drawn in Fig. 26. Note the weight of the construction lines as opposed to the shape of the hull drawn on the sheer plane. The dark construction lines were deliberately drawn with a felt-tipped pen so they would stand out in a photo. The cutting line is drawn in with the normal weight of a sharp pencil to retain accuracy.

Photo 7 shows a nearly-formed bow profile being checked with its template. Refer to Fig. 29. Note that the station lines do not quite match. At this point, tool work was stopped and the small amount of remaining material was removed with sandpaper.

Photo 8 shows the saw in its cut while forming the rabbet; note the single surface transom sawed square (across the hull). Also note that the saw teeth are cutting parallel to the surfaces of the lifts. Both *Helen B. Thomas* and *Margaret Haskell* did not have multiple transoms, cross seams, nor light framing aft of the sternpost. They were built with a heavy full-width timber bolted to the top of the keel construction within the hull which protruded aft to the lower part of the transom. This formed a backbone to which full-sized athwartship frames were fitted like those forward. These frames were then planked-over, the same as other portions of the hull. Therefore, the after end was an integral part of the hull construction as opposed to being the light-weight appendage on the square-riggers.

Photo 9 shows the profile between the sternpost rabbet and the lower extremity of the transom being shaped with a chisel. Note the horizontal line defining the lower point of the transom's surface. This method of cutting was used because it seemed easier than with a rip saw. The profile is a curve at the head of the sternpost and blends into adjacent profiles. This profile was roughed out with a gouge and finished with a round rasp.

Photo 10 shows the hull being carved on its outside at the port side of the bow. It shows the side of the hull from Station 8 aft. It has been roughed down with a plane and more work will be done over the portion from Station 8 to the bow. This hull differs from the other four in that there is no midship or widest frame. Instead, the hull from Station 10 through 14 is of a constant shape. This was the designer's method of obtaining a long, burdensome hull without increasing beam. The portion with constant cross section is tricky to form properly, particularly at the ends. If done with a spokeshave, there is a tendency to form heavier unsightly sections at the ends.

The best way to handle this portion of the hull is with a plane. By reducing the depth of cut when approaching the final shape, it can be cut down to 1/16" from the final shape. Then the curved surfaces forward and aft can be blended with it at each end. In spite of these precautions and method, there will appear to be a slightly bulbous area at Stations 10 and 14 down low on the hull when viewed from certain angles. This is an optical illusion which appeared on the vessel.

The photo shows pencil lines where each of the eight forward templates touch the hull (described previously). Too much stock has been cut away at mid-height of Stations 4, 5, and 6; this demonstrates how not to form a hull. Note that Stations 7 and 8 have been worked down so that when the templates are applied they match the hull over a long portion in their middle. Now if stock is removed only where the templates touch, the distance over which they touch will increase. By successive fitting, marking, and cutting operations the displacement of each template will be reduced until final form is obtained. Since the middle portion at Stations 4 through 6 had been cut too deeply, the area just astern and both above and below were worked carefully until the "error" was removed. Then the marks on the hull formed a continuous belt about midway between top and bottom so that long passes with the spokeshave could be used to remove the lines. On this hull the upper part of Stations 1 and 2 curve outward too much to use a spokeshave. It was cut down with a rasp and followed by coarse sandpaper, but remember that sanding tends to round off edges unless care is exercised.

Photo 11 shows the hull ready for final sanding and marked on the sheer plane for boring out the inside. The continuous curve shown on the hull block is the shape of the third waterline (1 1/2" from the bottom) reduced by 3/8" on each side and with foreshortened ends. This line defines the extent of boring. Note the auger bit and brace with a depth stop fitted so the bit worm cannot go deeper than the third waterline. Also refer to Fig. 33.

Photo 12 shows the hull thoroughly honeycombed inside the curve. Note the suitable tools for marking and hollowing out the hull.

Photo 13 shows the hull completely hollowed out. Note that with few exceptions all evidence of the bored holes has been removed and the bottom is relatively smooth. A smooth bottom is important, particularly on this model, because five masts will set on this surface. Deep ripples make it difficult to set masts properly and these five have to be in perfect alignment.

This photo also shows the hull marked with the cut for the underlayment and decking. Although not very evident, slightly more stock was left across the stern and over the flare in the bow to prevent breaking through. These lines were made with a marking gauge and cut deeper with a knife. Tools for cutting down are shown. This hull has no bulwarks. Therefore, it is cut down to the total depth of the underlayment plus deck planking so that when completed the deck will be flush with the sheer plane.

Photo 14 shows the cut made for the underlayment and decking; refer to Fig. 35.

Photo 15 shows the deck beam stock marked up with the center line, crown, and curve shape. Refer to Fig. 36.

Photo 16 shows the hull with all deck beams installed. Note that the forward beam is deeper than the others and has a hole low on the center line. Unlike any of the other hulls described in this book, the *Margaret Haskell* bowsprit enters the hull and buries below the highest continuous deck. Hence, the bowsprit bed must be made before the underlayment is installed. Regardless of how the bowsprint is fitted, it should be replaceable because it is one of the most vulnerable spars on the model. The hole in the deck beam receives a stud on the bowsprit's inboard end.

Photo 17 shows the bowsprit piercing the hull. Layout technique and fitting of the bowsprit is described in Chapter XVIII.

Photo 18 shows the hull with its deck underlayment installed. This point brings this pictorial presentation of hull construction up to where the text left off for the "Merchant Vessel of 1800," in the previous sections of this chapter.

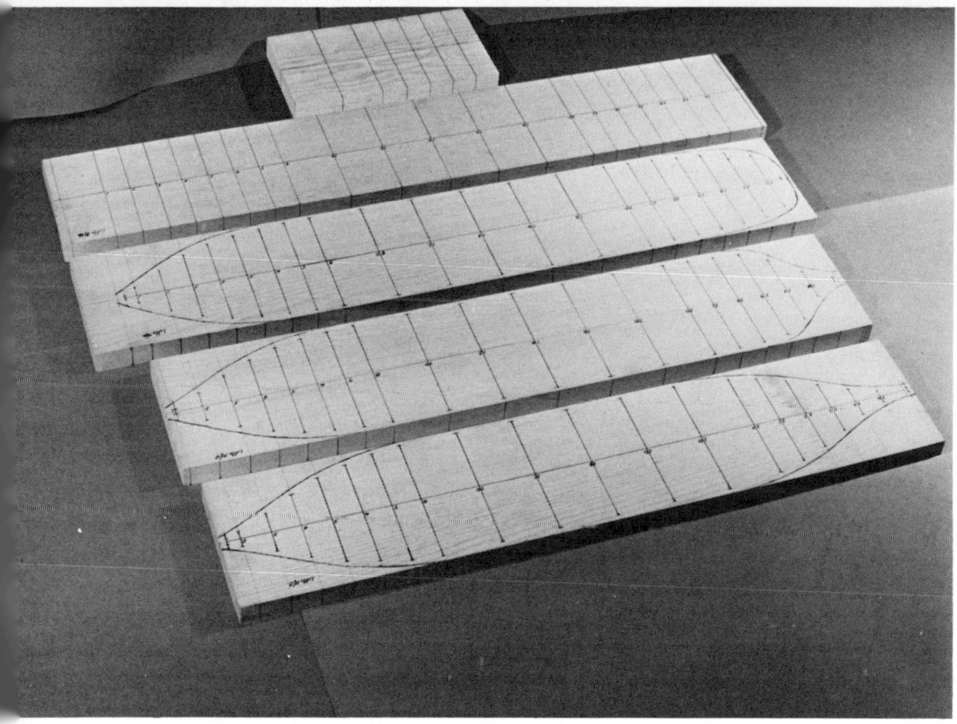

1—Tick stick and templates for hull construction. Photo 2—Five lifts ready for
g, followed by gluing together.

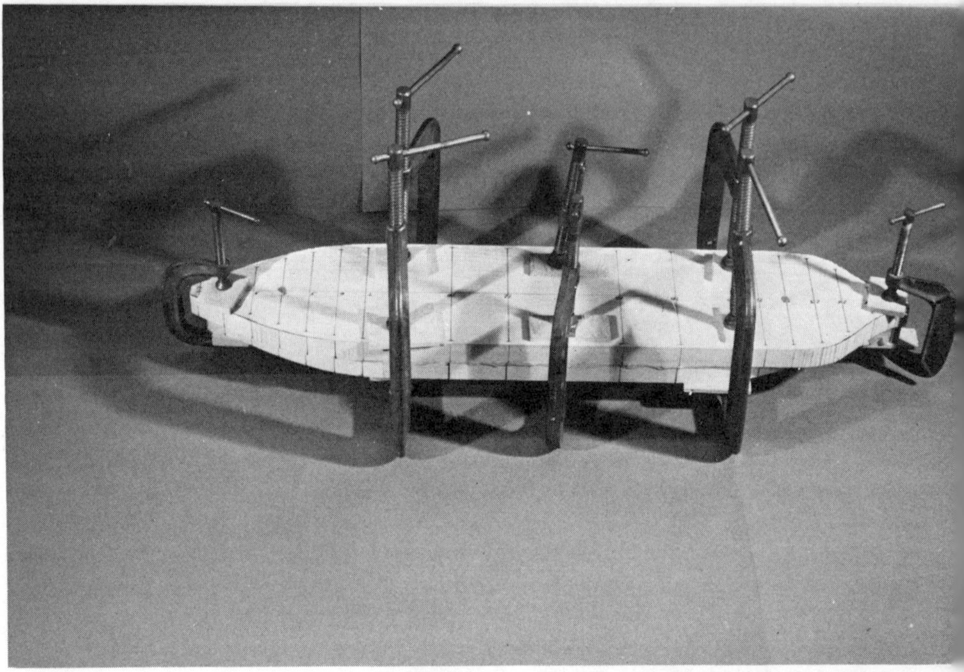

Photo 3—Gluing the third lift to the lower two. Photo 4—Establishing height of she the bow.

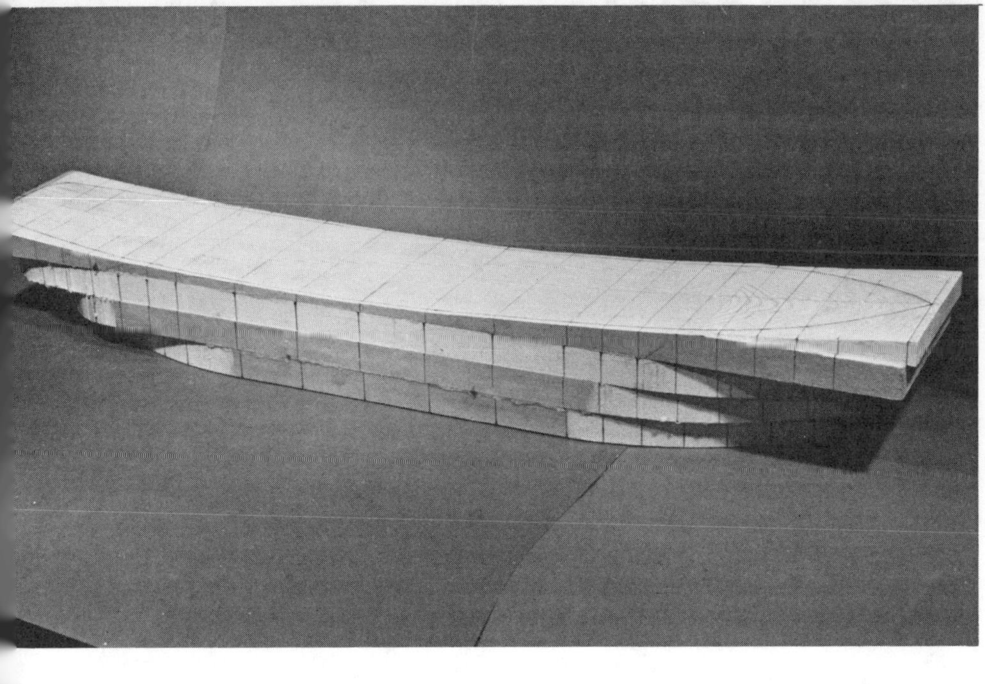

oto 5—Checking center line plane for squareness with sheer. Photo 6—Hull block
dy to start shaping.

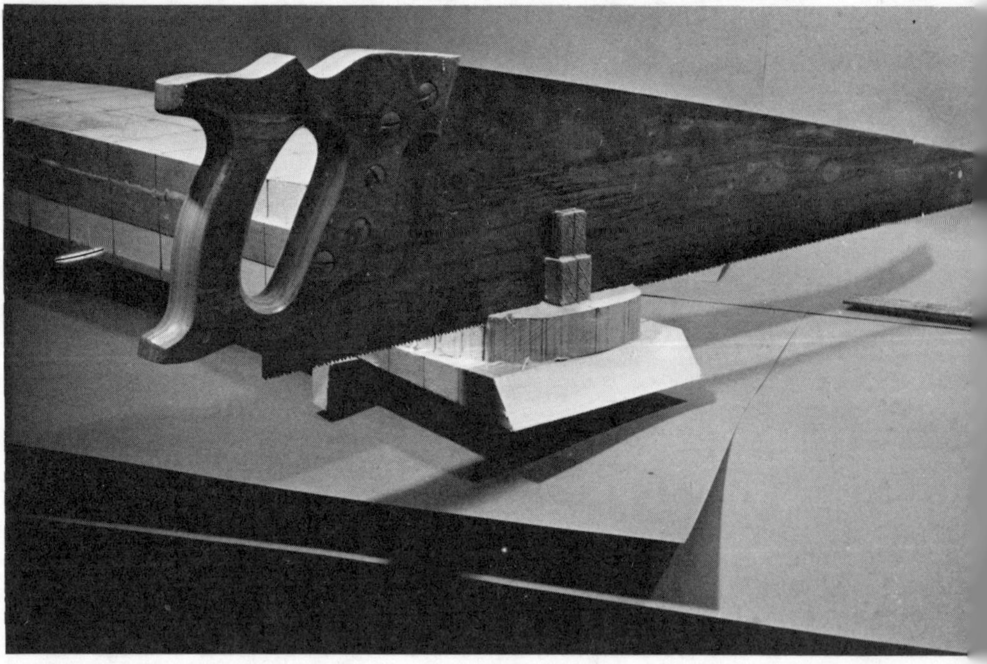

Photo 7—Checking bow profile with its template. Photo 8—Sawing stern profile at t rabbet.

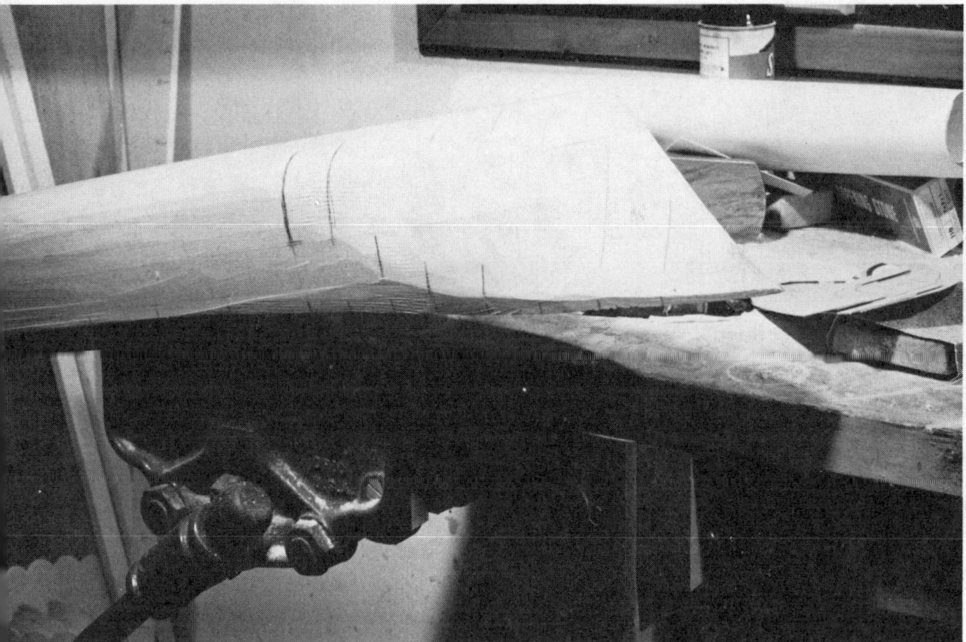

Photo 9—Forming stern profile below the transom. Photo 10—Carving the port bow.

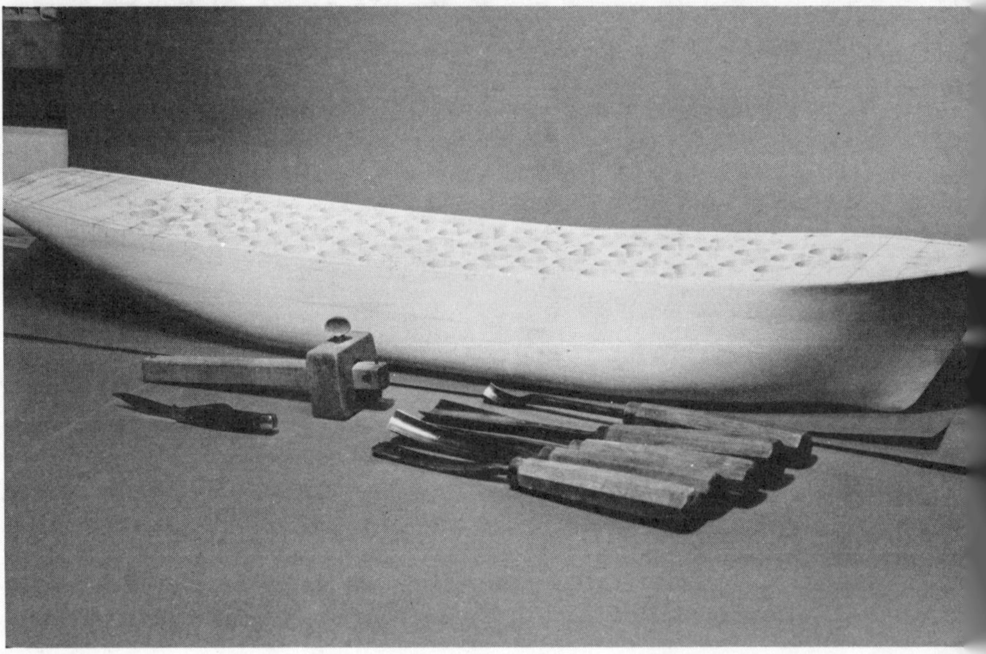

Photo 11—Carved hull with outline of boring area drawn on the sheer plane. Ph 12—Hull with inside bored out.

Photo 13—Hull completely hollowed out. Photo 14—Inside cut down to receive underlayment.

Photo 15—Deck beam stock marked for cutting crown. Photo 16—Deck beams instal
Note deep forward beam with a hole to receive the bowsprit's heel.

Photo 17—Bowsprit fitted in hull. Photo 18—Underlayment installed.

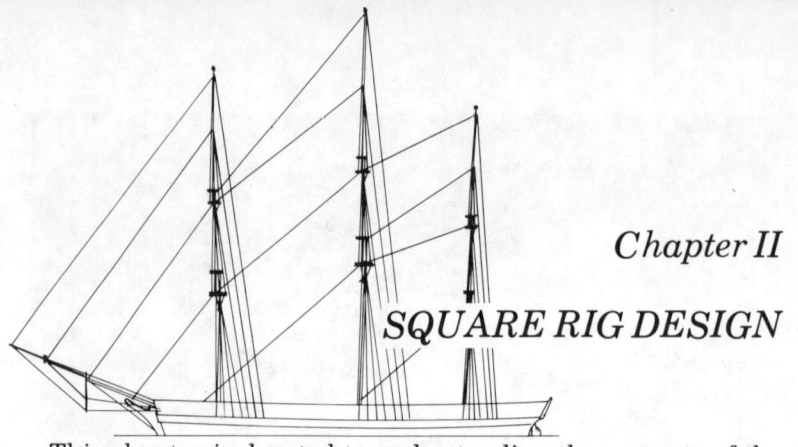

Chapter II
SQUARE RIG DESIGN

This chapter is devoted to understanding the concepts of the square rig. This was the traditional rig used by the colonists and by their seagoing European forebears on the sailing merchant and war vessels of the day and was the type rig used on the *Lexington, Wasp,* and *Isaac Webb.*

The square rig was probably first used on primitive small craft. The history of its sophistication runs parallel to the technological advancement of mankind from a small craft with one sail capable of traveling short distances to large commercial vessels and warships capable of traversing the world's oceans with relative ease. By the time *Lexington* was built, the concepts of the square rig were almost fully developed. Most changes made thereafter served to simplify the rigging and improve the parts but did not alter the overall design concept. Therefore, a general description of each facet of this rig will suffice to explain design principles for each square-rigger in this book.

These descriptions will cover those aspects of sparring and rigging necessary to understand the principles of the square rig. Chapters IX and X cover hardware and fittings. Chapter XI describes rigging of square-rig models. Because rigging was being refined over the time span covered by these models, Chapters XIV, XV, and XVI cover those items not covered previously and which differ from model to model. Included are tables showing sizes of components and descriptions of lead for each piece of rigging.

Basic concepts are developed here for a single-masted craft rigged with all parts basic to the principles. These elements are expanded by multiplication to include three-mast assemblies with several spars in each. Each assembly with its own rigging and spars is integrated into a unit called a sailing ship. The end result is the rig for the "Merchant Vessel of 1800."

The mechanics of the rigging system are quite simple, although the rig appears to be a complex maze of canvas, rope, and spars. The arrangement was developed to be as economical of material and weight as possible, yet be able to withstand stress created by the severest weather. Sails were divided on mast assemblies according to the number of masts in each. By dividing up the sail area in this manner, individual sails could be handled by manpower alone and the number which were set could be governed by the wind velocity at the time.

MASTS & STANDING RIGGING

The spars and rigging covered here are not normally moved or adjusted while handling the vessel at sea. Masts are the vertical spars. The term "standing rigging" is a general term covering elements of the rig which support masts and other fixed spars.

Refer to Fig. 37; it is the basic model with a single mast and simple rigging in place. The mast is supported with one guy to the bow and two to either side, all from the top of the mast. Now an explanation of the need for this equipment is valuable.

Natural Forces Affect Design

The object of sails is to extract at least part of the wind's energy which is imparted via the mast to the hull, propelling the vessel forward. Except in the special case of the wind being directly astern, the balance of its energy acts to force the mast sidewise. Hence, all sailing craft tilt away from the wind. Due to the vessel's motion in a seaway, other forces act on the mast. Under any condition at sea other than a flat calm, waves roll a vessel sidewise and pitch it lengthwise. When waves are high, these motions set up tremendous forces against the mast's own weight, momentum, and the top-hamper attached thereto.

The resultant of these complex forces changes in both magnitude and direction constantly and acts radially outward. No mast, except in small craft, can withstand these forces by itself; so a system of guys was devised for support and to still allow the sails to be worked effectively. Forces acting toward the stern are constrained by the stay. Those acting sidewise are counteracted by the shrouds. Those acting forward could not be handled by a rope to the stern, as it would interfere with other rigging and sails, so the shrouds are shifted aft at the rail to provide the required counterforce. This set of one stay and two shrouds is collectively called standing rigging and is the basic building block of the scheme used on all sailing craft regardless of complexity.

Developing the Scheme—"Merchant Vessel of 1800"

With these concepts in mind, the masting and standing rigging scheme for the "Merchant Vessel of 1800" can be developed. Under all conditions, history proves, there is a limit to the size of sails that can be handled by a vessel and her crew. In the past, individual sail dimensions were reduced to a manageable size by dividing the vessel's length with a series of mast

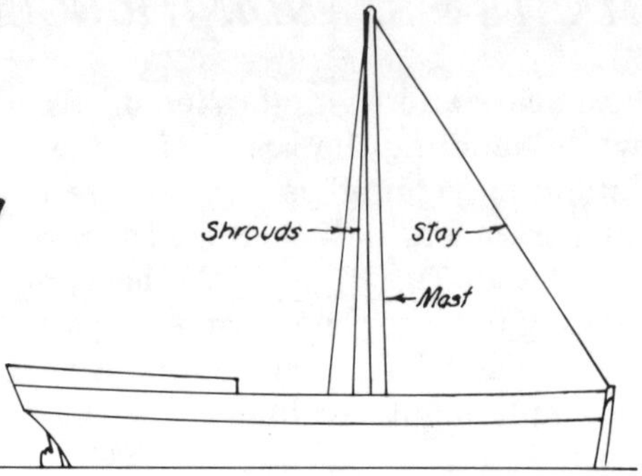

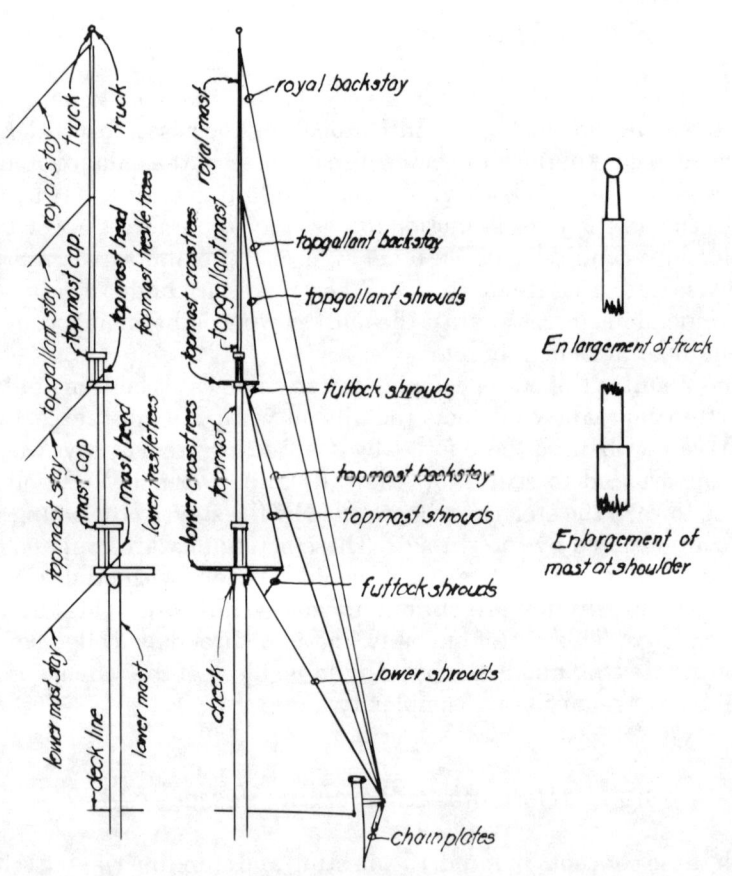

Fig. 37
Basic model with single mast and standing rigging in place ready to finish rigging

Fig. 38
End and side views of a typical mast assembly with runs of standing rigging drawn.

assemblies and each assembly arranged to contain several spars over their length with one sail per spar.

Three mast assemblies were in keeping with the then contemporary practice. Working from forward, they were named fore-, main- and mizzenmasts. The mainmast assembly was the largest. Its diameter, height, and rigging size was greater than the others, with the foremast assembly next and the mizzenmast assembly the smallest. Over the period from 1776 to 1850 there were an equal number of masts in each assembly, although this was not always common practice. Mast assemblies in vessels over this period varied from having three masts to five in each.

Lexington had three masts in each assembly which was common on smaller merchant ships with two masts. *Isaac Webb* and *Wasp* had four, which was standard on war vessels and large merchantmen. Only large clippers and similar fast carriers were fitted with five masts in each assembly.

Refer to Fig. 38 for a drawing of a typical mast assembly with four masts. Regardless of the number of masts in the assembly, each was made of three pieces, or spars. Although grammatically incorrect, the lowest spar was called the lower mast. The next mast up was called the topmast. Topmast heels overlapped the heads of lower masts, and topmasts were supported by fore and aft timbers called trestletrees on the lower masthead. Lower mast trestletrees were supported by blocking called cheeks bolted to the mast. Crosswise timbers were halved into upper surfaces of the trestletrees, called crosstrees.

An oak pin through the heels of topmasts rested on the trestletrees to support the topmasts. Upper ends of lower mastheads were fitted with caps which embraced both masthead and topmast. This construction at each end of the heads prevented any movement between spars. Topmasts and topgallant masts were similarly fitted except that cheeks were omitted; there were generally fewer crosstrees, and the whole assembly was substantially smaller. Topgallant masts changed to royal masts at an abrupt change in diameter (called a shoulder) which prevented standing rigging from sliding down. Royal masts (or any upper mast) terminated with a shoulder and a tapered section (called a pole) surmounted by a ball (called a truck).

The view of the mast from one end of the hull, as in Fig. 38, includes standing rigging on one side. The lower shrouds run from just above the lower trestletrees to the outboard edge of a heavy timber on the hull's surface. This timber was called a channel. Topmast shrouds ran from just above the topmast trestletrees to the outboard ends of the lower crosstrees, and topgallant shrouds ran from topgallant masthead to topmast crosstrees. An elongated link chain ran from the lower end of each lower shroud to the side of the hull below, called chain plates. Topmast and topgallant

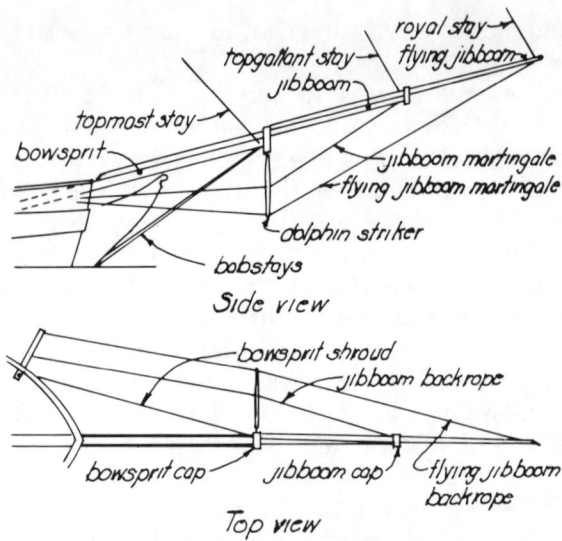

Fig. 39
Two views of bowsprit assembly

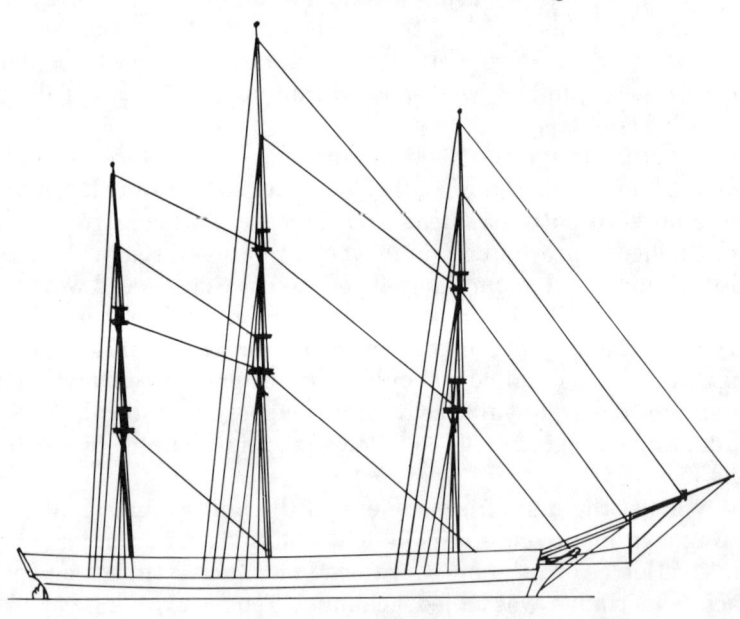

Fig. 40
"Merchant Ship of 1800 with standing rigging in place

shrouds were supported on their lower ends in a similar manner, with a rope from the crosstrees' ends to a rod in the shrouds below, or to a band around the mast. The number of shrouds on these masts varied according to their size.

It was impossible to fit crosstrees so that they provided enough support for their masts and for those above. Therefore, ropes (called backstays) were led from upper mastheads to the channels. Topmast backstays were attached astern of the lower shrouds, topgallant backstays were aft of topmast backstays, and so on for any upper mast backstays. They provided the necessary force, acting aft and sidewise, to assist the shrouds on topmast and topgallant masts. Topgallant and higher masts were light with smaller sails so they did not require massive support given those below. It must also be remembered that lower masts had to support not only their own sails but the weight and some of the forces in all the masts above. Hence, higher masts were relatively light with minimal rigging. Rather than rig trestletrees and crosstrees with shrouds, a single backstay was run to the channels for this light duty.

All square-riggers carried a similar spar assembly forward. It was fitted in the hull at an angle somewhat higher than the sheer at the bow. Steeve, the angle measured upward from horizontal, was greater in older vessels. This spar assembly's purpose was to provide a better supporting angle for stays on topmasts and higher masts in foremast assemblies.

Fig. 39 is a drawing of side and top views of this assembly with its standing rigging for the "Merchant Vessel of 1800." The bedded spar projecting from the bow is called the bowsprit. Its outboard end was fitted with a cap similar to masthead caps. The cap supported a lighter projecting spar called a jibboom. The cap was supported by two chocks called bees which also contained holes through which the fore-topmast stays were rove. Larger vessels like *Isaac Webb* and *Wasp* had caps on their jibboom ends to steady a second light spar called a flying jibboom. Stays from the upper spars in the foremast assembly rove over sheaves in the outer ends of the lighter spars. The ends of these stays and fore-topmast stays led in to the bow where they were secured.

Bowsprits were stayed against the upward pull of the stays by a rope called bobstay which led from the outboard end to the stem near the waterline. Sidewise forces were counteracted by bowsprit shrouds which led to the bow with suitable spread. Jibbooms and flying jibbooms were stayed against upward-acting forces by a stay of rope called martingale. They rove through a vertical spar called a dolphin striker under the bowsprit cap and then led upward to the bow near the bowsprit shrouds. This appeared to be an awkward arrangement but it kept those cables clear of anchor rope when moored and out of the way when anchors were stowed. Jibbooms and flying jibbooms were stayed sidewise with back-

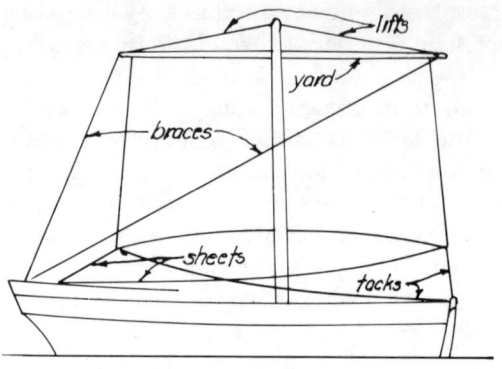

Fig. 41
Basic model with square sail set

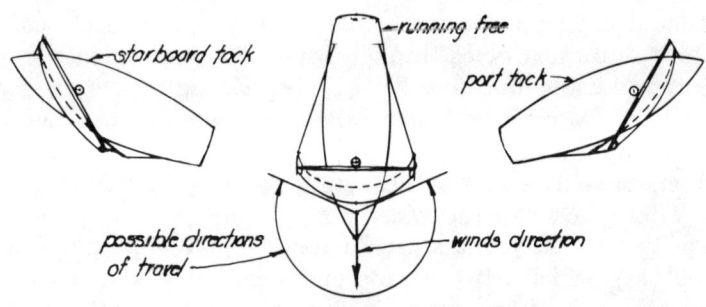

Fig. 42
Basic model with square sail trimmed for three directions of travel

ropes which led from their outboard ends through a small spar on each side of the bowsprit cap (called a whisker boom) and secured outboard of the bowsprit shrouds.

Fig. 40 is a side view of the "Merchant Vessel of 1800" with all rigging in place. Martingales are not shown because their leads nearly parallel those of the ends of fore-topgallant and royal stays. Note the large quantity and spread of lower mast shrouds, in keeping with the tremendous forces they had to counteract. Topmast shrouds were fewer and smaller. Rigging for upper masts was further reduced in both size and quantity, in keeping with substantially reduced forces.

Before 1800, bowsprit steeves were quite high, a carry-over from the days when bowsprits were fitted with yards and sails beneath them. By 1800 these sails had nearly disappeared. However, some vessels carried yards to spread backropes, and war vessels did so to support the lower part of a triangular (boarding) net under the jibboom. At that time the yard was being downgraded to small spars on each side of the bowsprit cap. By 1850 the steeve had been reduced so that the bowsprit was almost an extension of the sheer.

Staying of masts also was changed over this period to reduce the interdependence of mast assemblies. The object was to reduce the possibility of loosing upper masts on other assemblies when an upper mast on any assembly broke and came down. For example, in 1775 mainstays led to the bow. Main-topmast stays led to foremast heads. Higher mainmast stays led to the heads of the next lower masts in the foremast assembly. Refer to Fig. 40.

If the main-topgallant mast was carried away at its heel in heavy weather, the fore-topgallant and royal masts were also carried away along with the fore-topmast and possibly with some upper mizzen masts and jibbooms. Later vessels carried main and main-topmast stays to the foot of the foremast, and all upper mainmast stays led to the foot of the next lower mast in the foremast assembly. Stays from mizzen masts could not be lowered to the same degree, however, but some advantage was obtained and the lighter, upper masts were stayed to the heavier forward masts.

SPARS & RUNNING RIGGING

The spars and rigging covered here are those which supported the sails and controlled them when the vessel was handled at sea. Spars, as now, were then called yards, booms, and gaffs and the rigging called running rigging.

Refer to Fig. 41 to see the basic model with its square sail fitted. Note that lifts (from the masthead to each end of the yard) support and hold it horizontally; braces (leading aft from each yard end) control the yard in the horizontal plane; the sail is lashed to an iron rod on the top of the yard and hangs down the yard's forward side, similar to a window shade on its rod; the lower corners of the sail are held in place by ropes, called sheets and tacks.

Yards were constrained at the mast by several different types of mechanisms and held close to their mast's forward sides, preventing endwise sliding yet allowing them to swing in the horizontal plane. Adjustable braces, tacks, and sheets permit positioning sail properly for the course with respect to the wind's direction. Fig. 42 shows the basic model sailing on three courses. The left drawing shows the model on a starboard tack, i.e., the wind is blowing over the right or starboard bow. The center drawing is the model with the wind directly astern, and at right it is illustrated close-hauled on a port (left) tack.

Yards, as drawn, on the starboard and port tacks are hauled to the smallest angle possible with the center line without interfering with shrouds and stays. Because the wind must blow on the after surface of the sail to provide a forward-acting force on the mast, the model here is sailing as closely as possible to the wind on each tack. A vessel has to use these courses when destination is directly to windward. By alternating between port and starboard tacks, a vessel crisscrosses the direct path to her destination until reached.

Sheets are ropes used to control the lower or after corners of sails. Those for lower sails are secured to the vessel's sides aft of the sail when beating to windward.

Tacks (no connection to the course of a vessel sailing to windward) are ropes used to control the lower forward corners of sails. Tacks were used only on the lower sails when the wind was blowing toward the sails' forward, windward edges; they were secured to deck at the vessel's side just forward of the fore end of the yard when hauled for beating to windward. Tacks hauled the windward edge of the sails rigidly taut, preventing trembling and flapping edges from wind blowing directly on them. Lower corners of topsails and higher sails had no tacks; they were sheeted to the ends of the next yard below and swung with it. Sailing with a good breeze dead astern is the ideal course for a square-rigger. Tacks were not rigged while on this course because sheets controlled them perfectly. All sails billow forward and the vessel drives forward easily before the following waves.

Fig. 43 demonstrates how a typical vessel's mast assembly was rigged. This rigging is applicable to both the "Merchant Vessel of 1800" and the *Wasp* since both were of the same era. Note that standing rigging and one part of running rigging are drawn on the left side. Yards and sails along with their running rigging are drawn on the right side.

Lower yards were not normally raised or lowered at sea. They were approximately twice as long as the vessel's beam which made them too heavy to handle. Consequently, permanently installed heavy ropes which hung from the mast were secured to the yard's center to hold them in place. *Lifts* were adjustable so the yard could be adjusted to make the topsail set properly, but, in general, their function was to support the yard ends. There was a block and tackle arrangement between the yard near its center and the lower corner of the sail. When furling the sail, this tackle, called a *clew garnet*, was used to hoist the sail's corner up on the after side of the sail. Other ropes led down the forward side attached to lower and outer edges. When hauled in, these lines drew the parts aloft.

Furling is completed by the seamen who work their way out on ropes abaft the yard, as described in Chapter XI. From this position they pulled the sail up over the forward side of the yard and stowed it in neat rolled folds on the yard's upper surface. Rope was then passed from the yard's center around both yard and sail in a helical fashion toward each end to hold the sail in place. In heavy weather when the vessel could no longer carry all sail, highest sails were furled. Upon further increases in wind velocity, the next to the highest sails were furled down to the topsails. Third to be removed were the lowers but, because they were so large, such removal of whole sails could possibly be too much of a sail area reduction. To overcome this problem, a scheme called reefs was designed and built into the sails.

The band of vertical lines shown in Fig. 43 represents short pieces of rope, *reef points*; they reeve through holes in the sail and hang down on each side. Reef tackle were used to haul sail up, so the reef band was just under the yard. Then the reef points were passed around the upper part of the sail and the iron rod, mentioned before, where they were tied and secured the upper portion of the sail. By this device the area of sails was reduced.

Topsail and higher yards were lowered to just clear the next lower mast head, when their sails were furled. In the same illustration, note lines called tyes for topsail, topgallant, and royal yards. They were secured to the middle of the yards and were rove over a sheave just below the mast heads. They led from the sheave to deck at the waterways abaft the masts. Lower ends of topsail and topgallant yard tyes were hooked to block and tackle purchases called halyards which assisted in hoisting the yards when setting sail.

Lifts illustrated for these yards were adjustable to the extent of their travel on the masts. A transition in lifts for hoisting yards started in the early 1800s whereby standing lifts were introduced and used thereafter. These standing lifts were secured to the ends of the yards and their mast heads with sufficient length to just allow the yard to be lowered to its furled position.

Clews (the term garnet was left off when applied to the sails above the lower sails) for topsails and higher sails were normally single ropes, except

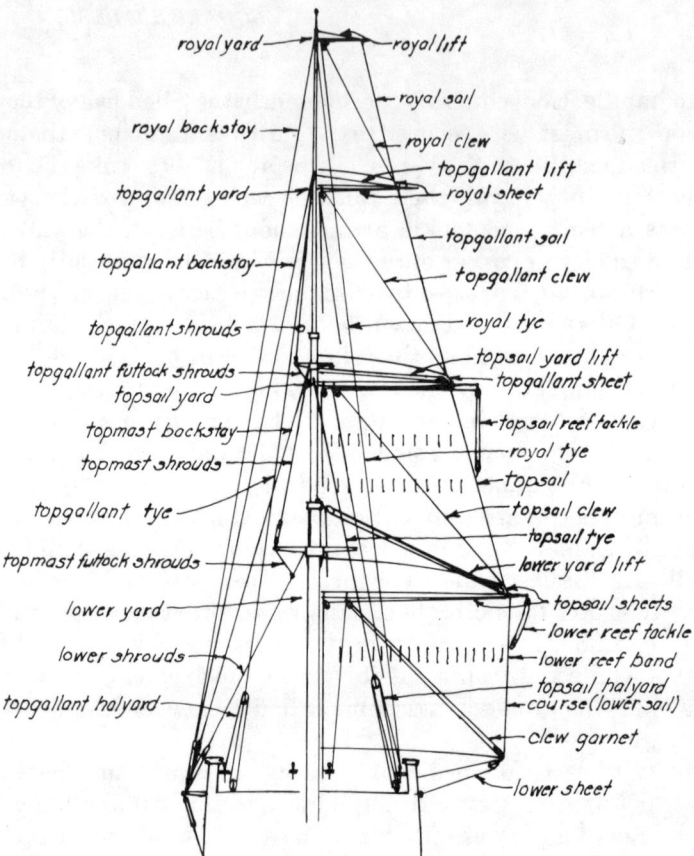

Fig. 43
Typical mast rigging with sails set on one side as viewed from aft.

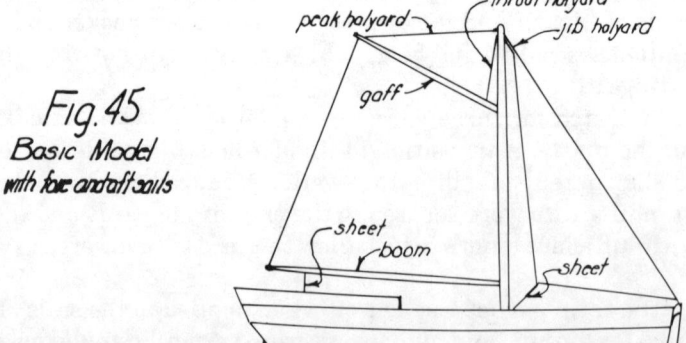

Fig. 45
Basic Model with fore and aft sails

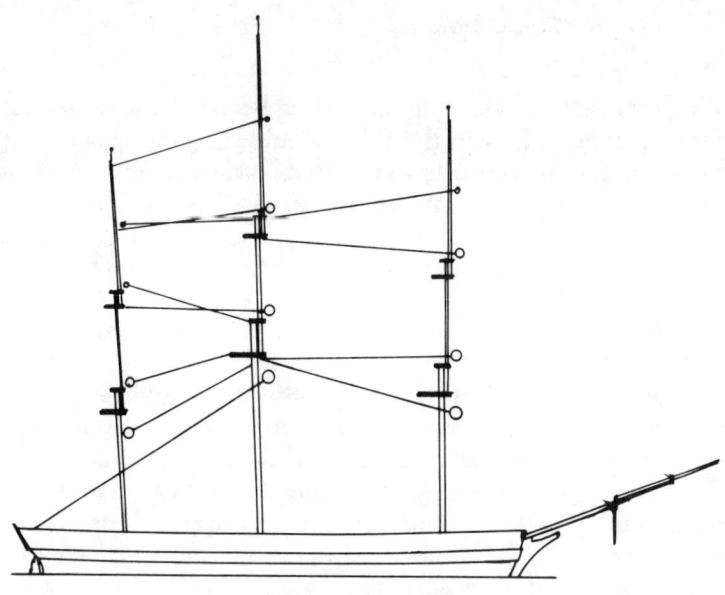

Fig. 44
Line diagram showing leads of braces on
"Merchant Ship of 1800"

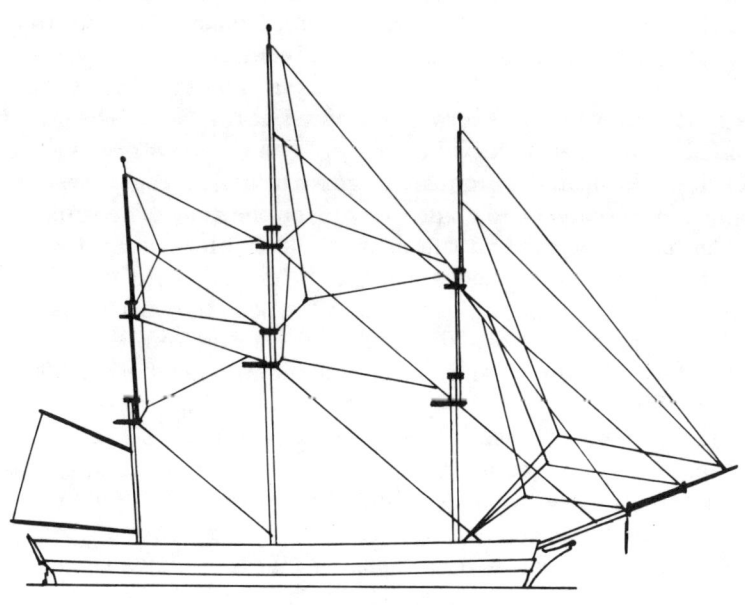

Fig. 46
"Merchant Ship of 1800" with
fore-and-aft sails in place

when on very large vessels or on those ships headed for areas where severe weather was expected; then they were doubled up on topsails and sometimes on topgallants. Topsails were fitted with two and sometimes three rows of reef points. They were reefed after all other square sails were furled, and under the severest weather and only while the vessel could maintain course. The lowest reef was used when the vessel had to heave to, a condition of weather so bad that the vessel would be steered on a course allowing her to ride out the storm more easily without regard to the direction of the next landfall.

A *brace* on the end of every yard controlled the angle between the yard and the wind. On fore- and mainmasts, braces for yards led aft. Main yard braces always led to the hull near its stern. Sometimes foreyard braces led to the hull near the main shrouds. At other times they led to the mainstay at or close to the mainmast head. All other braces led to the mast behind. Mizzenmast yard braces led forward to the mainmast. Refer to Fig. 44. Mainmast yard braces of brigs led to the foremast. Large vessels built or rerigged after the 1850s had as many as seven yards per mast. These vessels were those which carried skysail yards. Yards were permanently mounted on mast caps and topmast caps to divide the size of topsails and topgallant sails. This development reduced the power required to hoist topsail and topgallant yards and reduced the amount of reefing which had to be done, thereby cutting the crew size necessary to handle these vessels.

All square-riggers carried *fore-and-aft sails* supported on the stays, plus another supported by spars on the lower aftermast. Both types are shown on the basic model in Fig. 45. The forward sail is hoisted on the stay by its halyard. Its lower forward corner is secured at the foot of the stay and is controlled by a sheet at its other corner. The quadrilateral sail is more complicated. Its top and bottom are laced to the gaff and boom respectively. Both gaffs and booms were made to swing on the mast. The sail's forward edge, the luff, is secured to the mast at close intervals by loose fitting wooden rings called mast hoops. The gaff is hoisted along with the sail on its mast end by the throat halyard and by the peak halyard on its outboard end. The sail is controlled by its sheet which leads from the boom to the deck's center line. Fig. 46 shows the fore-and-aft sails for the "Merchant Vessel of 1800."

Names for some of these sails, particularly staysails on the foremast, were apparently changed from time to time. The names used in this book may not always agree with those found in other books. Instead of using different names for the same sail to conform with practice at the time, the names used in this book will be consistent for the square-rigged models. They will be called staysails preceded by the name of the stay, similar to that done for square sails. The quadrilateral sail on mizzenmasts will be called a spanker.

Sheets were fitted on both sides where staysails were set over or outboard of other stays. Leeward sheets controlled the sails while windward sheets hung slack. When the vessel tacked, the role of each sheet was reversed. This double sheet arrangement allowed sails to be sheeted from deck.

Summary

Now review what has been learned about square-riggers in terms of their spars and rigging. Vessels are equipped with mast assemblies spaced appropriately on their center lines each of which is composed of three or more sticks or spars. Those emanating from the deck are called lower masts, those higher are called topmasts and the highest contain from one or two masts, even though one piece. Depending on the number of masts in this spar, their names, from bottom to top, are topgallant and royal masts with the highest mast surmounted by a pole and truck. Topmasts and topgallant masts overlap the one below and are secured in place at each end of the overlap. Lower masts are supported against forces acting forward and sidewise by several shrouds, each of which originates at the masthead and fans out in a fore-and-aft direction as they lead to channels. At the channels they are connected to chain plates which anchor to the vessel's sides. Topmasts are similarly supported by shrouds leading from topmast heads to crosswise timbers in the lower masthead, called crosstrees, where the shrouds connect to futtocks or futtock shrouds anchored to either the lower shroud or to a band around the lower mast. Topgallant mast shrouds lead from the head to topmast crosstrees where futtocks lead to topmast shrouds or to a band around the topmast. To further support topmasts and higher masts, backstays lead from their heads down to channels abaft lower shrouds and thence to chain plates. If royal masts are used, these light-duty spars are not fitted with shrouds but depend solely on backstays.

Another assembly is fitted which projects from the bow. Its inboard spar is called a bowsprit, that farther out a jibboom, and the third a flying jibboom. This assembly provides the leverage necessary for the stays which run from each masthead in the foremast assembly. Bowsprits and other spars in the assembly are supported against forces acting upward and sidewise by bobstays, martingale stays, shrouds and back ropes. Stays from masts behind the foremast run from their heads down to the next lower masthead, in general, with after lower-mast stays running to the deck at or near the next forward mast.

Each mast is fitted with a yard to support a square sail. All yards, except lower yards, are hoisted to a point just below the mastheads when their sails are set and are lowered to a point just above the next lower masthead when their sails are furled. Yards swing in a horizontal plane from the forward side of the masts to obtain an appropriate angle between the sail and the wind's direction. Braces from yard ends lead aft (or forward) to adjust this angle and to hold them in place after adjustments are made. Lower sails are controlled at their corners by ropes, called sheets, and tacks which attach to hull sides. All other square sails are sheeted to the end of the next lower yard. Most stays are fitted with triangular sails that hoist on the stay and are controlled by sheets which lead down and aft from their lower after corners. A quadrilateral sail is fitted to the lower aftermast called a spanker which secures to the gaff above, to the mast on its forward edge, and to the boom below. It is controlled by a sheet and is hoisted by throat and peak halyards.

SAILS—FITTING

This section is for those who desire to fit sails; many models are so rigged. Before deciding whether or not to fit sails, it is best to become familiar with the advantages and disadvantages.

Choosing Cloth

It is virtually impossible to make a model's sails "stand" as they would appear on a sailing vessel at sea. Schemes have been tried to make them billow, as they do in a good breeze, by using such devices as soaking with starch or some heavy sizing and drying them before a fan in their position. The billowing effect can be obtained but the sails sag unnaturally as soon as the fan is removed. The only other time a vessel would have her sails set would be either at anchor or at a wharf to dry them out. This has to be done when there is little or no wind and the sails just hang like sheets on a clothesline.

Some builders display models with sails furled, as when vessels were going to be in port for a short stay. The customary way is to fit them up with bare yards. When vessels were to stay in port for a longer period, all sails with associated rigging were removed and stowed below until made ready to sail again. Usually the yards were squared, i.e., braced so they were perpendicular to the center line.

The only way a model of a square-rigger can be fully rigged is to fit sails. As will be seen later in this section, there is rigging associated with sails which cannot be fitted without them. If the model is rigged with furled sails, most of the rigging is left in place. Models rigged with bare yards and no fore-and-aft sails carry the least rigging of all. In general, the rigging carried on a model without sails consists of all standing rigging, all yard rigging, and sheets for staysails on the head stays.

On square-riggers from 1775 to 1850 sails were made of heavy flax. This material does not hold its shape well. Because of this poor quality, sails were baggy, such as those shown to billow with beautiful curves, depicted in artists' works.

Cloth that is thin enough to even come close to proper scale is unobtainable, but that obtainable from model supply houses for sailing models will be reasonably satisfactory. If the model is to be rigged with furled sails, make them about half-depth so the amount of cloth to be rolled up on the yards will not be bulky. All sails seem to discolor and become dirty with age. Unfortunately, model sails turn a dirty brown instead of grey as did sails on vessels. Also, slanting edges of sails tend to turn inward so their outer edges become misshapen. It is the author's opinion that sails, even if furled, tend to hide and detract from the fine and delicate work of the builder.

Sail Construction Features

Fig. 47 shows construction of typical sails suitable for any square-riggers. Note the curve in the lower edge of the square sail; it varied according to the sail's location. Lower sails had only enough to clear deckhouses or other encumbrances. Topsails had a substantial curve because they had to clear the lower masthead appendages and stays. Higher sails required less because there was less in the way to clear. Clearance of sails and rigging with other parts was very important because it eliminated the chance of chafe. Chafing is extremely detrimental to sails and rigging, so they were arranged in such a manner that ropes did not rub together; sails had as little contact as possible with spars and rigging. Topsails and topgallant sails unavoidably rubbed on parts of the mastheads when executing some maneuvers and they were reinforced as indicated by sewing a second layer of canvas to them in the form of an inverted "T."

Edges of all sails were turned inward on themselves and sewed fast. A continuous rope, called a boltrope, was sewn all the way around the sail with loops called earings worked in at each corner. Material for sails came in bolts 24" wide. One width of this material was called a cloth. These cloths were sewn to each other; seams between adjacent cloths are represented by parallel lines in Fig. 47. Reinforcing in the form of additional layers of sailcloth was sewn to sails at reef bands and other areas where excessive stress was placed on the sail. Earings were worked into the boltropes at all points where rigging lines were attached (loops spliced into

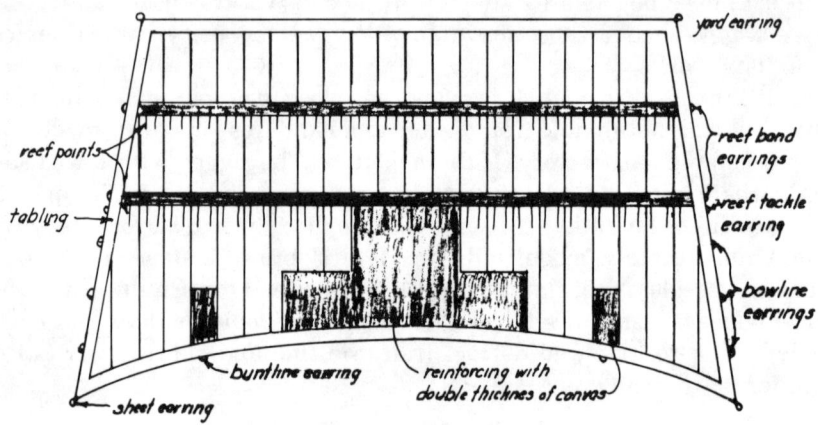

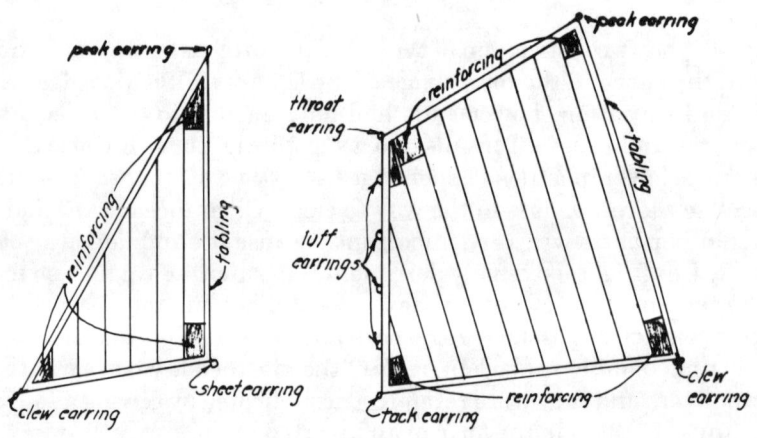

Fig. 47
Typical sails

the boltrope). Upper corner earings on square sails were used to lash the sail to the yard ends. Lower ones were connected to sheets and tacks. Those on the end of each reef band were lashed to the ends of the yard, while sails were reefed and those just below the reef band earings were for the reef tackles. Bowline earings and others are explained in Chapter XI. Earings at the corners of triangular and quadrilateral sails were used for either securing ropes to the sail, such as halyards and sheets, or to secure each end to the boom or gaff. Mast hoops were normally secured to earings, but square sails were secured to the iron rod on the yard by several turns of small rope through finished holes in the head of the sails. In the same manner, spankers were secured to gaffs and booms. Staysails were secured to their stays by horseshoe-shaped pieces of iron called hanks. The hanks had an eye in each side of the open end and the sail was seized to these through finished holes in the sail. Finished holes were sewed around their edges like a buttonhole but were round instead of being a slit.

The square sail in Fig. 47 is typical. Each sail has reef bands and earings according to location and rigging. The triangular sail is typical of staysails used on head stays of *Lexington* and *Wasp* and of all of the staysails on *Isaac Webb*. Staysails between the masts on *Lexington* and *Wasp* were quadrilateral, requiring special stays and rigging. This equipment is described in Chapter XI. Each square-rigged model here carries quadrilateral sails on her lower aftermast. *Lexington*'s was different, a carry-over from older practice. Her rigging is described in Chapter XIV. Types, shapes, and sizes of sails are shown dotted in each vessel's sail plan.

Preparations, Patterns, & Details

If the modeler decides to make sails, work should be started by making patterns. Since cloth tends to stretch with handling, each pattern must be reduced slightly in its overall size. The exact amount of reduction depends on the type of cloth, its weight and the quantity of work which must be done. The model sailmaker will have to find the related total requirements by trial and error.

The following descriptions cover sails built on a scale of 1/4" to the foot, such as those for *Lexington* and *Wasp*. Fix sail patterns to the cloth so the seams between cloths align with the weave. Cut the sail 1/4" oversize on each edge. Fold the excess over in a double fold to make the tabling (a broad hem) and iron it flat. Cut away the excess folds in each corner so they lie flat. Then with a sewing machine set for fine stitches sew these folds down on their inner edges. Finish the machine work by stitching from tabling to tabling in parallel lines 1/2" apart to simulate seams between cloths and along the top and bottom of each reef band.

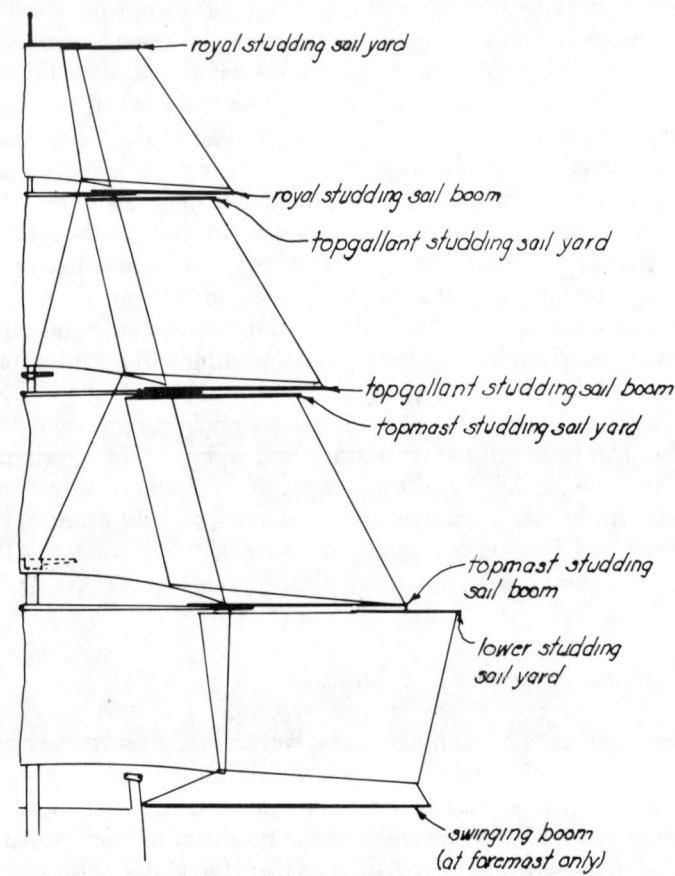

Fig. 48
Typical studding sail spars and rigging

Here the builder must decide the degree of miniaturization to be attempted. If the attempt is going to be maximum, boltropes will have to be sewn around the outside edges of the sail. They should be relatively heavy three-stranded cord (four-stranded on the original vessel) sewn to the sail with stitches no more than 1/16'' apart; pass the needle between strands of the cord to encircle one strand and the very edge of the tabling with each stitch. Corner earings are loops in the boltropes and are seized together at their throat. Other earings are short pieces of rope spliced into the boltrope on both ends to form a small loop. Boltropes may be too much for the modeler and, indeed, will not be faulted for their omission and, even if they are sewn on, fitting the earings can be very tedious and may also be omitted.

Sails for smaller scale models must have their cloth and tabling widths reduced accordingly. Scales of 1/8'' to the foot, as for *Isaac Webb*, make the inclusion of much detail almost impossible.

Since no rigging is connected to furled sails where it would show, very little detail is required. Normally when headsails were doused, they were rolled up and secured along the spars in the bowsprit assembly and those between masts were removed altogether, but their halyards and sheets were left in place. Probably the easiest way to handle sails on models is to furl them. As stated earlier, sails to be furled should be half-depth. This is a reasonable guide for large-scale models, but the smaller the scale the less sail that can be made into a nice, tight, small roll because the cloth is the same thickness regardless of scale. Therefore, sails on small-scale models must be cut shorter.

When furling square sails, the clews or clew garnets haul the lower corners up abaft the sail. Leech lines on the outboard edges and buntlines on the bottom haul these edges up on the forward side of the sail. These lines all haul the sail toward the yard's center which makes a large bundle in the middle with less toward the yard's end. Crew on the yard then hauled a large fold over the yard, and the balance was arranged in neat, small folds. Then the large fold was pushed up over the smaller folds and tucked in under the forward side so it appeared to be a neat, smooth-tapering roll of cloth. This roll started with nearly nothing at the earing and gradually increased in diameter until it was equal to the yard's diameter, about three-quarters the way in where it increased in size rapidly to the large bundle at the yard's center.

Triangular staysails on the head stays were lowered so they stretched along the jibboom or flying jibboom aft of their stay. They were rolled as described for the square sails. Spankers on *Wasp* and *Isaac Webb* were furled by lowering the gaff and folding the sail on the boom. When the gaff was down and resting on these folds, excess cloth was pulled out and arranged to hide edges of the folds on each side so this too appeared as a roll. The spanker (more properly a lateen sail) on *Lexington* had ropes from points along the upper spar leading to the after and lower edges of this sail; these hauled the sail up under the spar, and then the spar was lowered to a point where crew could roll up sail and secure it to the yard.

Sails were secured to their spars after furling by ropes which were called gaskets. Gaskets were attached to the spar at the larger portion of the furled sail and wound around both spar and sail in an open helical fashion toward the spar's end. The heavy part of square sails, particularly lower sails, could not be swung up over the yard by the crew without the mechanical leverage provided by a net in the form of an equilateral triangle, with one edge lashed under the sail to the iron rod above the yard. The opposite corner was fitted with a rope which was passed ahead of the sail and up to the masthead where it was connected to a portable tackle. By hauling on the tackle, the large bundle was swung up to the top of the yard. This net and rope was called a bunt gasket and tail rope.

All war vessels and most merchantmen carried another set of sails to extend the area of their square sails. None of their rigging was fitted except in favorable weather because both spars and sails were light. The sails were called studding sails and were arranged as drawn in Fig. 48. Their combined areas nearly doubled that of working sails. Because light canvas in light airs is more effective than heavy working canvas, studding sails were of great assistance in lower latitudes where calm or near calm was frequently encountered and in trade-wind belts where steady, moderate winds blow almost constantly. They are almost impossible to rig on a model unless of very large scale, but fittings for their yards should be included on models of *Wasp* and *Isaac Webb*. These fittings are described in Chapter IX.

Chapter III
FORE-&-AFT RIG DESIGN

To develop the concepts of the fore-and-aft rig as it was used on American schooners, it helps to fully comprehend that this was the traditional rig of larger fishing vessels and of most coastwise traders from the early nineteenth century onward.

The fore-and-aft rig, used in some form for many centuries, was particularly advantageous in warmer climates where heavy weather was the exception to normal weather patterns. Examples of these historical craft are the Arabian dhows, Chinese junks, Greek luggers and a host of others used in the Mediterranean Sea and Indian Ocean. Their sails were quite different from those on American schooners but their rest positions were fore-and-aft. However, different as they were, the sails of American schooners were modifications of the sails of those earlier craft. The overall rigging scheme, though, was developed and perfected along the American Atlantic seaboard and in the Maritime Provinces of Canada.

Schooner rig is far simpler in all respects than square rig. There are fewer spars in each mast assembly with correspondingly fewer sails and less rigging. Because of this, construction and maintenance costs were less than for a square-rigger of comparable size. Schooners were more weatherly, i.e., fore-and-aft sails could be trimmed so they would sail closer to the wind and, therefore, travel fewer miles to make a windward port. Since there were fewer sails and less running rigging there was less work required to get under way and to handle sails at sea. Hence, fewer seamen were required.

At this point the reader may very well ask why were square-riggers put into service after the large advantageous schooners were built. Ease of handling and small crews do not necessarily qualify a vessel for deep-sea work where heavy weather exists much of the time. As was pointed out in the previous chapter, square-riggers could remove sails until only topsails were left. Since these sails were high above the deck, they were exposed to the wind when the hull was either in the trough or on the crest of the waves and the wind force was nearly constant. Not so on a schooner which, by necessity, reefed by lowering the gaff part way, securing an equal height of sail on the boom. This lowered the sails to a point where they were becalmed in the trough of high seas, but when the vessel climbed over the

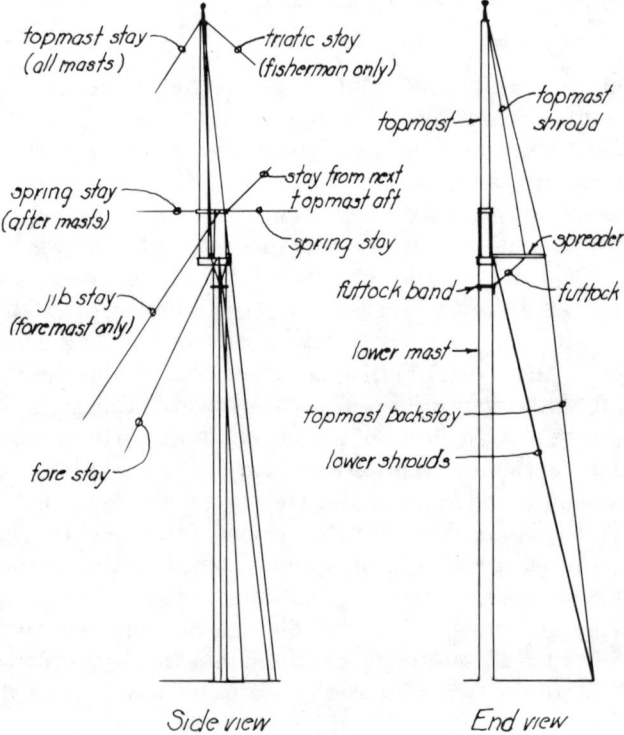

Fig. 49
Typical fore-and-aft mast

crest the sails were almost instantaneously subjected to the full blast of the wind. Frequently sails were blown away leaving the vessel helpless or, even if they held, severe stresses would have been delivered to hull, spars and rigging.

Weatherliness, though, was not an overriding factor for later ocean carriers. By the middle of the nineteenth century, Matthew F. Maury, associated with the U.S. Hydrographic Office, authored several works on the geography, tidal currents and sailing routes of world bodies of water. His documents were based on data he collected from log books and reliable sources. These pages demonstrated for seamen the best courses to sail on the most traveled world trade routes at various times of the year. With this information, captains could select routes where fair winds could be expected or strong head winds could be avoided. So the inability of a square-rigger to sail close to the wind was not as detrimental as one may assume.

Because schooners had limitations on their usefulness, they were built for services where their qualities could be used to advantage. *Helen B. Thomas* was built to work on shoal fishing banks in the open ocean during winter and summer. While most of the crew manned the dories to fish, this relatively large vessel under reduced sail was handled by as few as two men. When gale winds rolled the seas into the short, high breakers, typical on the fishing banks, these vessels had to claw off to windward for deeper and smoother water. Speed in getting from the banks to market was essential, particularly with a catch of fresh fish on ice during warm weather. To avoid spoilage, if the discharging port was to windward, the vessel had to be weatherly and fast. *Margaret Haskell* was built to carry massive cargoes of coal from the Delaware River and Chesapeake Bay ports to cities in New England. Prevailing westerlies made many trips south a beat to windward as did northeast storms on the way back. Part of each trip to ports in Massachusetts and Maine was along the south and east coasts of Cape Cod, treacherous as any in the world. To successfully make these trips and avoid disaster on the Cape with a profitable degree of speed, the vessel had to be weatherly, reasonably fast and easily handled. During her life, manning costs eventually became a substantial part of operating costs and rigging was designed so she could be handled by a very small crew aided by steam winches.

STANDING RIGGING

Schooners were multi-masted, fore-and-aft rigged vessels with masts of nearly equal height. Two-masters, like *Helen B. Thomas*, had slightly higher aftermasts. Five-masters, like *Margaret Haskell*, had masts of equal height. Mast names on two-masters were fore- and mainmasts.

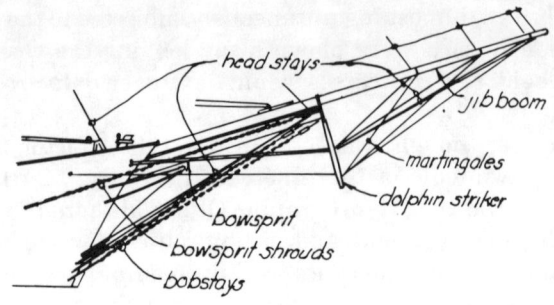

Fig. 50
Typical bowsprit rigging

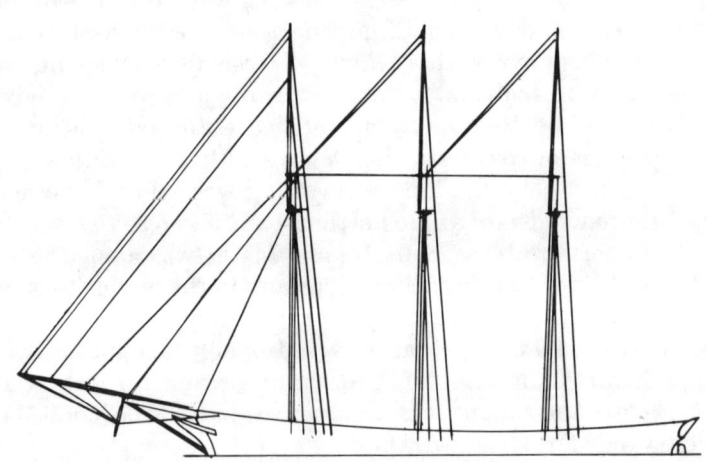

Fig. 51
Typical three-masted
schooner's standing rigging

Names of masts of five-masters varied but one popular scheme will be used consistently in this book, namely, foremast, mainmast, mizzenmast, jiggermast, and spanker mast.

The mast and rigging depicted in Fig. 37 is applicable as a basic model for developing a fore-and-aft rig. The reasoning covering the need and function of this equipment is exactly the same whether applied to a square-rigger or a schooner. Mast assemblies in larger schooners built during and after the latter part of the nineteenth century were standard in principle if not in detail. Normally each assembly consisted of a relatively tall lower mast with a short, overlapping topmast. In general, the number of mast assemblies was governed by the length of the hull so lower sails could be of manageable size.

Fig. 49 is a schematic drawing of a typical schooner's mast assembly. Each lower mast has three or more shrouds per side, and topmasts have one backstay. Fishing schooners did not normally carry topmast shrouds, but coal schooners had two. Head stays ran to the bow and bowsprit assembly. Stays on other masts and topmasts ran to the next masthead forward. Stays, as drawn in the side view, were fitted where indicated. No single mast carried all of these stays, but points of attachment and leads are clearly indicated along with designation of which masts were fitted with each. There were many variations to the leads of stays; those which apply to these schooners are covered in Chapter XII.

Bowsprit assemblies on coal-carrying schooners were similar to those for square-riggers except that flying jibbooms were never fitted; refer to Fig. 50. Note the chain bobstays and bowsprit shrouds. The number of head stays shown in Fig. 49 is consistent with fishing schooner rig. The number of head stays in Fig. 50 is typical of the large schooners. The large number of head stays on coal schooners were used to divide up the area into a series of several overlapping staysails, each small enough for one or two crewmen to handle while tacking. Bowsprit shrouds and jibboom backropes were fitted similarly to those on square-riggers; refer to Fig. 39.

Helen B. Thomas was rigged without a bowsprit; instead, her bow was abnormally long and her foremast shifted a short way aft. By this means the forestay attached to the deck nearly halfway between the stem and foremast. The other two head stays fastened directly to the stem which extended slightly above the rail.

Fig. 51 is a line drawing of the standing rigging on a typical three-masted schooner. This rig was common on coastwise trading schooners. As vessels were built larger and longer, more masts were added and therefore the distance between masts seldom exceeded 40' or 50'.

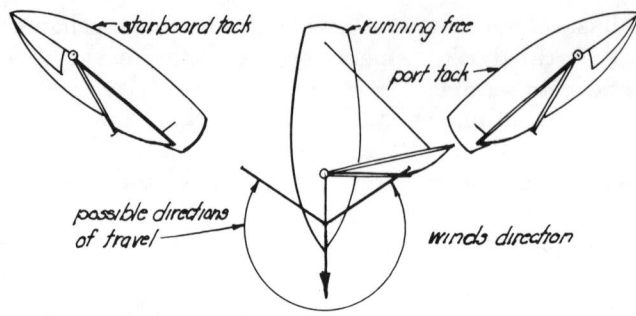

Fig. 52
Basic model with fore-and-aft sails trimmed
for three directions of travel

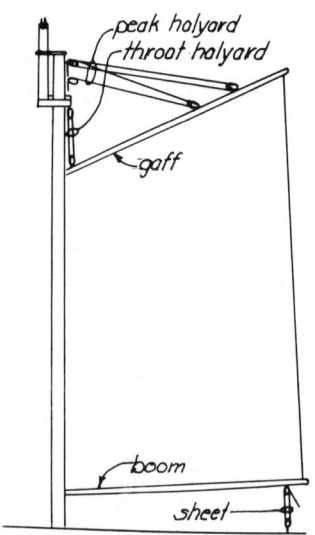

Fig. 53
Typical lower sail

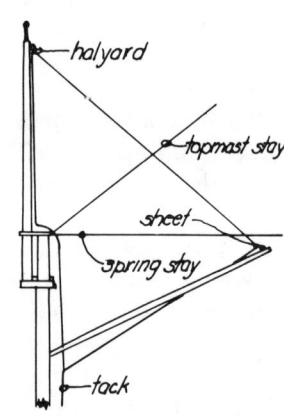

Fig. 54
Typical topsail

RUNNING RIGGING

Running rigging on a schooner was very simple as compared to that of a square-rigger. Each mast was fitted with a quadrilateral sail. These sails were named foresail, mainsail, etc., according to the mast to which it was fitted. Their heads were hoisted by and seized to gaffs. Forward edges were secured to hoops on the masts and lower edges were seized to booms. Booms and gaffs were built so they could swing about the masts while still connected to them. Their rest positions were abaft the mast over the hull's center line. However, when sailing, they could be swung from the topmast backstay on one side to its mate on the other. When beating to windward, the sails were hauled closely to the center line. As the course was altered away from the wind they were eased off the center line. When sailing with the wind they were eased off until the gaff nearly touched the backstay. Fig. 52 is a diagram showing the basic model (as in Fig. 45) beating to windward on both tacks and running before the wind.

Fig. 53 is a drawing of a typical mast with the lower sail set and fitted with its running rigging. Sails between masts were cut so the gaff could swing under the spring stay. Those on the aftermast were usually peaked up higher since there was no standing rigging in the way. Also, booms and gaffs were longer on these sails.

Fig. 54 is a drawing of a typical topsail. Topsails were basically triangular sails cutaway sufficiently to clear the lower masthead. Upper forward edges were secured to topmasts with hoops similar to lower sails. Halyards hoisted them up, and sheets on their after corner held them to the end of the gaff. Tacks held the lower corner down. When topsails were being set, the tack was led down on one side of the peak halyard and on the other side of the gaff to make the sail set as flat as possible.

Topsails on all masts except after ones were set on the leeward side of the stays between masts. Those on aftermasts had no stays to interfere with their swing from side to side during tacking, but topsails between masts had to be reset each time the vessel tacked. They were hauled in to the mast and both sheets and tacks had to be swung over the spring stays before resetting the sails to leeward on the new heading. This was a miserable chore, so topsails on forward masts were set only when the vessel was going to be on one tack for a long run.

Fig. 55 is a drawing of the two typical staysails used on schooners. Those on coasters were hanked to the stay and were shaped so their sheet earing was above the spring stay which allowed these sails to swing over to the other side while tacking. Those on fishing schooners were quadrilateral and hung below the topmast stay. When tacking, these sails were lowered to deck by halyards on each upper corner and rehoisted to leeward after the vessel was on her new course. Because this mode of handling precluded

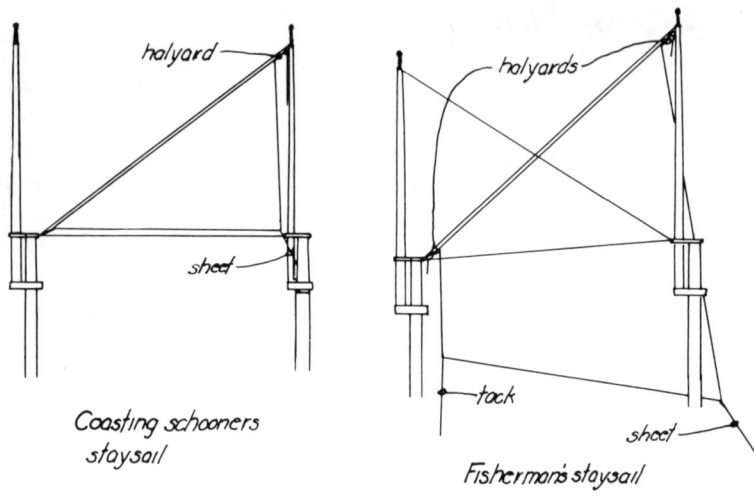

Fig. 55
Typical staysails between masts

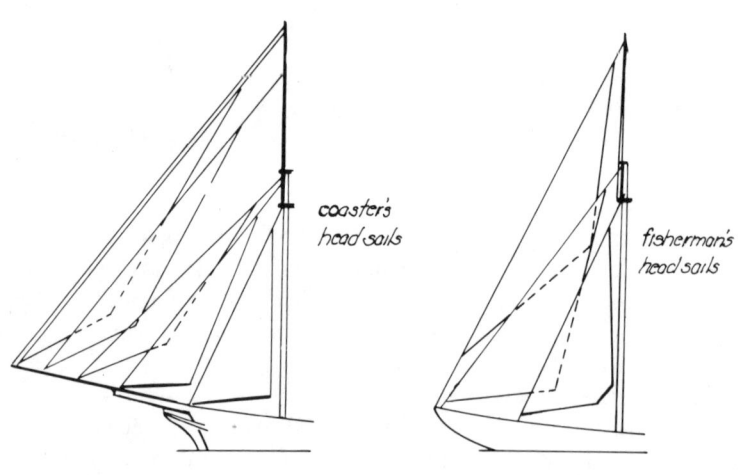

Fig. 56
Typical head sails

hanking the staysail to the stay, the boltrope along the upper edge was wire rope instead of hemp to prevent excessive stretching.

Fig. 56 shows headsail arrangements. Names for headsails on coasters varied like the names of the masts on five-, six-, and seven-masters. Names used in this book will be as follows, starting from inboard: forestaysail, jib, flying jib, outer jib, and jib topsail. This was the actual number used on *Margaret Haskell*. Forestaysails and jibs had booms on their lower edges and were fitted with single sheets. The three outer jibs overlapped so a sheet was rigged on each side. The other headsail arrangement was that used on *Helen B. Thomas*. These sails were called jumbo, jib, and balloon (ballooner) from inboard out, which was an odd assortment of names but they are a carry-over from previous arrangements and were more appropriate at that time. The jumbo's lower, after corner was cut off diagonally and fitted with a small boom called a sprit. All headsails had double sheets.

It was common practice to remove topmasts on fishing schooners during colder weather. Because the air is heavier when cold and winds blow harder, topsails and other light sails could be used infrequently anyway. By removing these spars and their rigging, considerable weight and windage was removed. When these spars were sent down, only that standing and running rigging directly connected with the spars and their sails was removed in anticipation of sending them up again the next spring. Sometimes only the fore-topmast was sent down, allowing setting main topsails and fisherman's staysails.

Summary

It is important now to review the fore-and-aft rig as applied to *Helen B. Thomas* and *Margaret Haskell*. Vessels were equipped with mast assemblies on their center lines, each of which was composed of two spars. Those emanating from the deck were called lower masts, those above were called topmasts. Topmasts overlapped lower masts the same as those on square-riggers and were finished off on their top by trucks. Several shrouds supported masts against forces acting forward and sidewise. Topmasts were similarly supported by backstays and those on *Margaret Haskell* had shrouds.

Margaret Haskell had a bowsprit and a jibboom which was stayed against upward- and sidewise-acting forces by bobstays, martingales, shrouds, and backropes.

Helen B. Thomas did not have a bowsprit, so her head stays anchored to the hull. Between masts the stays secured to the head of the next forward mast. Those on foremasts led forward to the hull or bowsprit assembly.

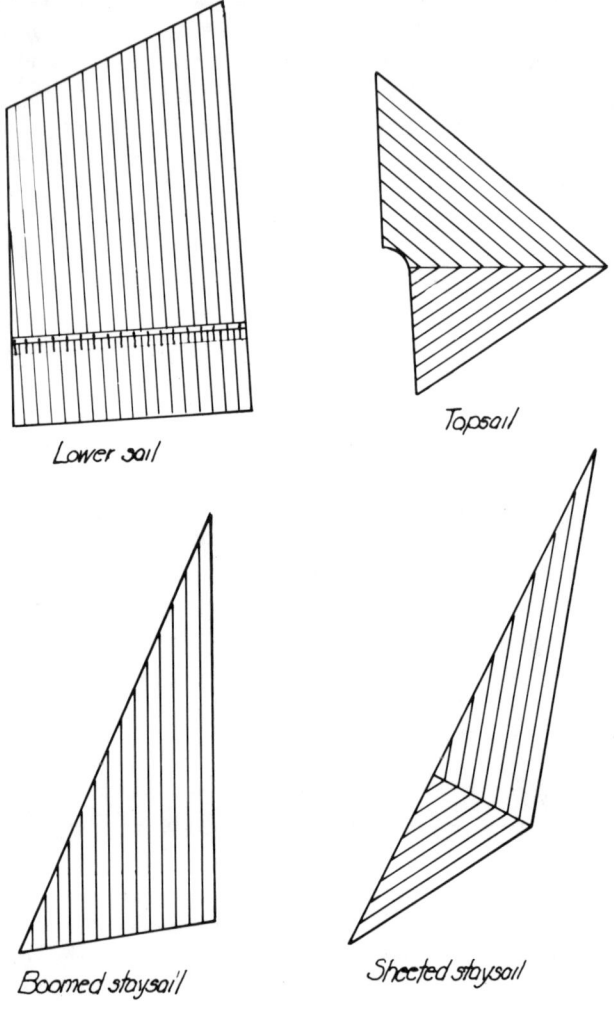

Fig. 57
Typical schooner's sails

Each lower mast was fitted with a quadrilateral sail which was hoisted by a gaff and controlled below by a boom. Gaffs were hoisted by throat and peak halyards and booms were controlled by sheets. Topmasts were fitted with triangular sails which were sheeted to the end of the gaffs and held down by their tacks. Staysails were fitted to head stays and topmast stays between masts, and they were fitted with sheets.

Descriptions in this chapter have covered only those aspects of a schooner rig which can readily be understood. Details of masting and rigging are covered in Chapters IX, X, and XII. Rigging schemes for each model are in Chapters XVII and XVIII.

SAILS, FITTING, & RIGGING

This section is for those who desire to fit sails and for novices to better understand how the rig actually worked. Except for sheets and tacks on topsails and topmast staysails, schooners were fully rigged whether sails were fitted or not. Sails are far easier to fit on the model schooner than on the square-rigger because a large portion of the work can be done off the schooner, and that which must be done on board is relatively easy since there is a minimum of rigging in the way.

Model schooner sails must be constructed more carefully than square-rigger sails. The most difficult part is stitching the parallel seams lengthwise to represent cloths in quadrilateral sails. These series of closely-spaced seams tend to pucker the sails' central areas, and, consequently, sails so made have edges that hang slack. Sails with such a fault would not stand on a vessel and would be detrimental to her weatherliness.

Fig. 57 is a drawing of the four types of sail used on these schooners. No drawing was made of a fisherman's staysail since it was identical to the lower sail if the reef band was removed. Boltropes did not have earings as was earlier described for square-riggers. Where connections were made along booms and gaffs or for mast hoops and hanks, metal grommets were fitted in the tabling and, instead of finished loops in the boltropes at the corners of sails, the boltropes were spliced to a hand-forged ring or similar fitting. Note the direction of the seams between cloths in topsails and sheeted staysails. These strong seams between the ends of the cloths make the sails set better and resist stretching due to pull of the sheets.

Tablings are not shown on these sails; they were very narrow on the vessel and when scaled down are seemingly of insignificant width, so they must be as narrow as possible.

When making sails it is important to orient the patterns properly with the cloth weave. The after edges of quadrilateral sails and boomed staysails should be parallel with the selvage. If the builder is not too fussy, the selvage can be used as the edge of the sail and thus eliminate sewing one tabling. Topsails are made with the forward edge parallel to the selvage; triangular staysails are made with the longest edge parallel to the selvage but tablings should be sewn into these sails.

Start work on the sails by sewing interior seams first. This includes seams between cloths, seams where cloths meet, and reef bands. Adjust the sewing machine thread tension so stitches are not tight to minimize puckering. Iron the cloth as smooth as possible before cutting the sails to shape. Tablings must be turned twice before sewing so the cut edge is hidden and ironed flat before stitching. Check after ironing to make sure that all edges are perfectly straight. Since boltropes tend to make sails baggy, it is recommended that they be omitted and the small metal earings be sewn to the tabling in each corner of the sail.

When completed, the lower sails are attached to the booms and gaffs off the model. At about 2' scaled-down intervals run a thread through the tabling about 2" long. After this has been done, secure the corner earing irons to the ends of the boom and gaff. Then tie the short threads in square knots above the gaff and below the boom so the sail is snug to the spars but not bound too tightly. Finish by cutting the ends neatly at each square knot but not so close the knots will loosen. Before moving the sail on board, fit the forward tabling with an appropriate number of 2" long threads for sizing the sail to the hoops. After the booms and gaffs have been fitted to the masts and the halyards and sheets rove off, the sail is then hoisted and the hoops secured to the sails with an "X" type sizing. Topsails, staysails and jibs are rigged in place.

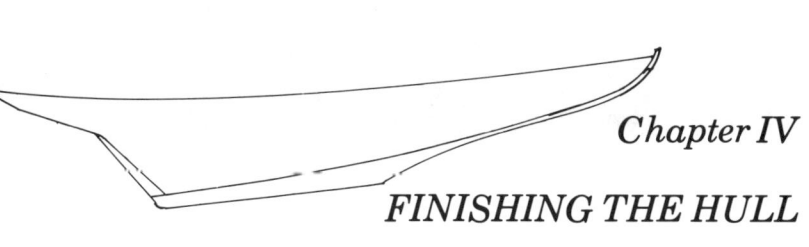

Chapter IV
FINISHING THE HULL

This is a continuation of Chapter I, covering all work to finish the wooden parts of each hull exclusive of deckhouses, gun carriages, and boats. Because some parts were used on only one or two of the vessels, each model is covered separately where necessary. Also, construction and design of some of the parts varied with the vessel's use, her building date and sometimes with the yard where built. Wherever possible, the order of presentation follows closely to the order of actual installation.

Builders must use some judgment in selecting materials for these parts. Woods traditionally used in ship construction do not necessarily scale-down properly and some commonly available lumber is not suitable. As examples, several varieties of oak were used for parts requiring strength and resistance to shattering. Their coarse grains do not permit making smooth scaled-down parts on models. Other lumbers do not take glue or paint readily. So suggested kinds of wood will be indicated throughout. These have been used by the author and were selected to meet the requirements of the part being made. Since some woods may not be available everywhere, various kinds are described in Chapter XX to help the modeler in selecting alternates for equally satisfactory results.

KNEES & BREASTHOOKS

Knees and breasthooks were not separate parts of the hull but they were used to tie parts together which met at angles. Since they were usually heavily stressed, they were made from natural crooks so the wood grain followed their shape to obtain maximum strength. They were cut from portions of trees where roots met the trunk and at the junction of large branches, as drawn in Fig. 58. Arms of knees form nearly right angles; those of breasthooks form acute angles.

Modelers who live in wooded areas can find branches with crotches and other appropriate shapes. Those who do not have this source can make these parts from laminated stock consisting of numbers of thin pieces glued together, so the grain in adjacent pieces is at right angles. Natural crooks can be taken from most any deciduous tree. Birch or maple is suitable for the laminated variety.

Knee ready to cut from root

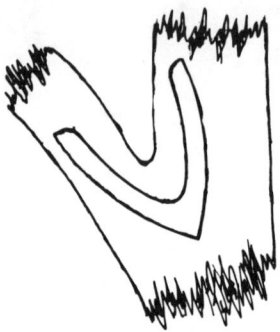
Breast hook ready to cut from branch

Fig. 58
Natural forms for obtaining knees and breast hooks

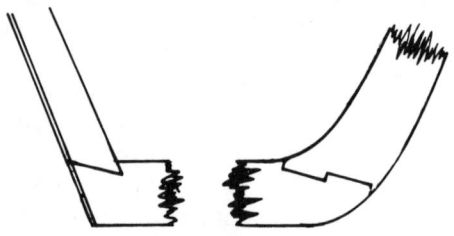

Fig. 59
Alternative method for joining the keel to stem and sternpost

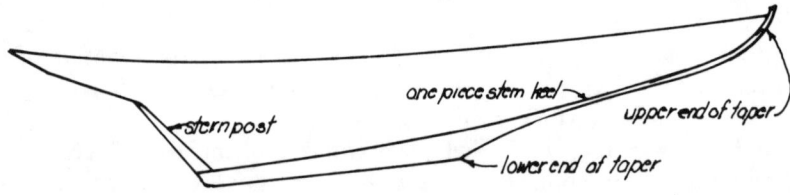

Fig. 60
Two part assembly for keel and sternpost

STEMS, KEELS, & STERNPOSTS

Sanding will inevitably be required at or near the rabbet to fair the hull into these members as revealed in Photo 19. Therefore, stems, keels, and sternposts should be made of a hard wood such as birch or maple so the difference in hardness allows the softer hull to be sanded away before the harder wood is damaged. Before the sternpost is set, lay out and cut the fan-shaped rudder port on *Lexington* and bore the rudder posthole in the others. These are described in the next section.

Stems, keels, and sternposts are fitted to the rabbet profile and shaped according to the sheer plan. They are installed with glue and fine brads. Before installing the stem, make certain that it fits the hull profile exactly and that its head fits snugly up under the bowsprit, as shown by the lighter colored wood in Photo 20. When shaping the stem for *Lexington* or *Wasp*, include cutting out the gammoning slot as shown in the sheer plan and round off the slot edges slightly. Also, the billethead and the forward extremities of the headrails must be carved on, as described later under the headings, "Cheek Knees, Headrails, & Trail Boards" and "Ornamentation."

After the stem has been glued and nailed in place, the keel is shaped and fitted. Shape its after end and install it in perfect alignment with the sternpost. Allow sufficient length to extend slightly beyond the stem. Before driving the brads fully, apply clamps crosswise over sheet plastic at the junctions between the keel and the stem and the keel and sternpost to assure perfect sidewise alignment. After the glue is dry, remove clamps and plastic, set all brads about 1/32" deep and fill the holes. Although it is not necessary, heels of both stem and sternpost can be joined to the keel like actual construction. Refer to Fig. 59.

The keel-stem assembly for *Helen B. Thomas* is made in one piece, as shown in Fig. 60. Before installing this assembly, shape the bevel by starting at the break in the keel and terminating at a point just above the eighth waterline. When beveling, leave the rabbet full-width and cut the faces perfectly flat and symmetrical so the forward or lower face is the width shown on both half-breadth and body plans. *Margaret Haskell*'s stem is beveled slightly on its forward end as drawn in half-breadth and body plans.

The keel on *Margaret Haskell* and on *Helen B. Thomas* projected aft to support the rudder. When beveling *Helen B. Thomas*' keel above the projection, be careful not to damage the lower surfaces. *Margaret Haskell*'s keel projects aft in its entirety, thus no bevel is required below the sternpost.

After the stem, keel, and sternpost have been installed and the hull faired into the rabbets, finish sanding the hull. Fill nicks or abrasions on

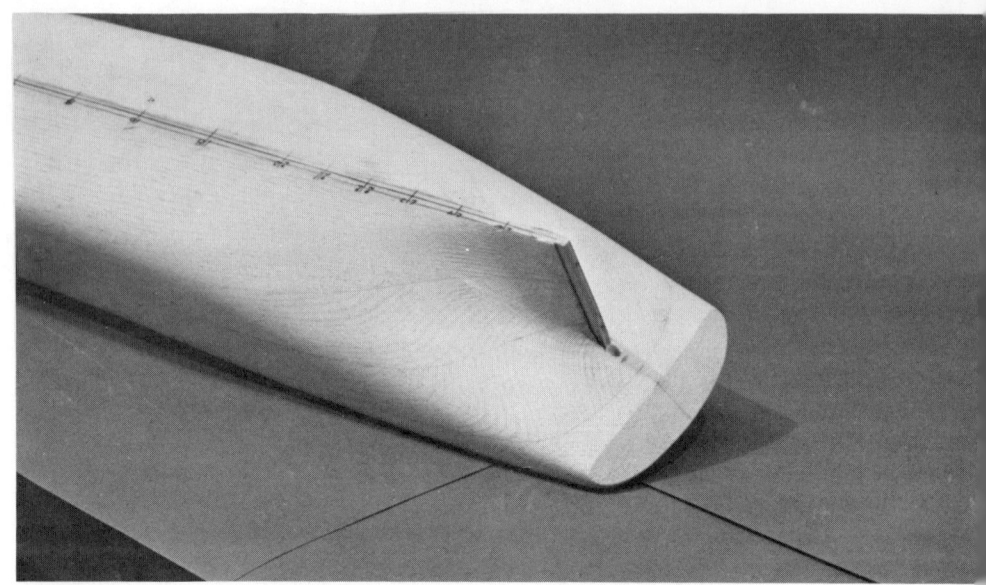

Photo 19—Sternpost fitted, showing material to be removed at the rabbet. Photo
Stern fitted, showing snug fit of bowsprit on the stern head.

FINISHING THE HULL 95

the outer surfaces. Sand the filler smooth, flush, and fair with surrounding surfaces.

The hull is now ready to set in its working cradle, as described in Chapter XIII.

RUDDERS

Two types of rudders were used on larger vessels. Each type was hinged to the sternpost and swung from side to side like a double-swing door. The older type used on *Lexington* was built so its stock (that part which extends into the hull) was an extension of the forward part, allowing the stock and rudder to swing as a unit. These were called rule-joint rudders after the joints in old-style folding rules. The newer type used on the other four models is called plug-stock rudder and was made with its stock offset forward, its axis aligned with the hinge pins below. Refer to Fig. 61 to note the difference between types.

Rudder shapes for these models are drawn in their sheer plans. They are the same thickness as the sternpost on their forward edges and taper to half-thickness at their trailing edges. Forward edges of the rudder and after edges of the sternpost were beveled as shown to permit a swing of about 45° each way.

The hinges referred to earlier in this section are described in Chapter IX under "Pintles & Gudgeons." The rudder can be hung after these are built and installed but not until the hull is completed and ready to rig.

Several kinds of mechanisms were used between the wheel and rudder-stock. Descriptions of this equipment, except the visible parts, will be omitted because it is very difficult to install and might be broken anyway by some admirer intrigued by the fact that it works.

WALES

Wales, as was mentioned before, were extra-thick belts of planking near the waterline. They were used on older square-riggers to obtain longitudinal strength and to provide a kind of armor belt on war vessels.

It is optional whether wales are fitted on models but, if done well, they add considerably to the hull's appearance. If they are fitted, they consist of narrow pieces of thin pine glued onto the hull to form a raised pad over the area between the two curved lines on the sheer plan. These curves are established by locating tick marks at close intervals using the same principle as shown in Fig. 27. Check for fairness by sighting along the hull and correct as necessary.

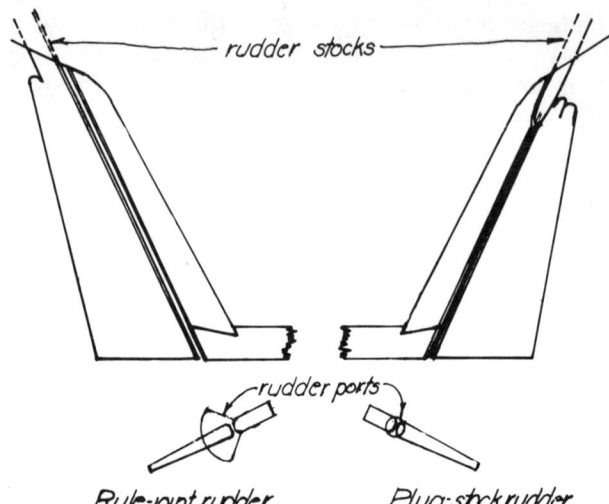

Fig. 61
Typical rudders

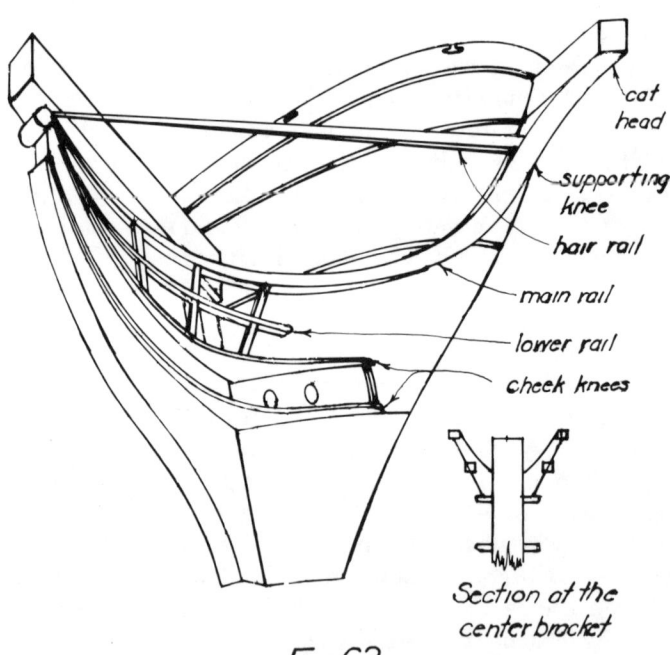

Fig. 62
Isaac Webb's port head rails

Glue 1/16" square pieces lengthwise of the hull to establish edges of the wales and fill between with successive strips. Because wales vary in width throughout their length, the last strips installed will have to be tapered. Fill all holes and imperfections after the strips have been glued on. When both glue and filler are dry, sand wales down to a uniform thickness of 1/32". Wales are feathered forward so they disappear at the rabbet.

At this point, wales on *Lexington* are completed. Around 1800, builders started cutting away the lower edge so it feathered into the lower planking. It is possible that the *Wasp* was also so built, but it is recommended to leave the lower edge as is, without feathering. At some later date the upper edge was feathered into the planking above. *Isaac Webb*'s lower wales were feathered and the upper edge coincided with the lowest rail; they did not show and do not have to be fitted.

CHEEK KNEES, HEADRAILS, & TRAIL BOARDS

The large, heavy projection on the upper fore part of a square-rigger stem was composed of several timbers on the vessel. This projection was known as the knee of head or, more commonly, the head knee. Because of their size and construction such stems had little strength against forces acting sidewise such as heavy seas smashing against them. Therefore, cheek knees on their lower part and headrails above were installed to provide necessary strength. The shape of these parts is shown in views in the hull plan. For more detail, refer to Fig. 62.

These head knees with their cheek knees and headrails were built on the vessels to also hide the bluff bow, plumb stem, and to lighten the appearance of the otherwise very heavy structure. Headrails had another more earthy function; refer to the body plan of *Isaac Webb* and visualize a crewman seated on the middle rail, his feet on the lowest and his back against the highest rail, as was done for a "comfort station." Naval language is heavily steeped in tradition and to this day comfort stations are known as heads aboard ship and at naval installations.

Cheek Knees

Cheek knees are made of pine cut in profile according to the shape shown in the model's sheer plan. Be careful to finish the profile with a thin section outboard and slowly increase the thickness toward the hull. Then try them in place, and cut the after ends so they fit snugly on the hull at the proper locations. If forward ends of the knees are to be formed as part of the billethead, make a clean tight joint where they meet. The outside shape is then roughly cut to shape and all four knees glued in place. Finish the shape of each pair with a fine, half-round file. Before proceeding to the headrails, the hawsepipe holes should be bored and the bolsters installed as described later under "Mooring & Hawsepipes." An integral part of this assembly to also be considered now is the ornamentation between the cheek knees and any finishing on the billethead, as described under "Ornamentation."

Headrails

Building and fitting headrails is one of the most difficult projects on these models. There are many variations shown in the hull drawings, but the general idea is to start with light members forward that increase both in size and distance apart as they curve backward to the bow. The middle, or main rail, which terminated in a curved knee supported the cathead. The upper, or hair rail, was quite straight and terminated aft against the main-rail knee. The lower, or foot rail, terminated where it abutted the hull. These rails were supported by athwartship members called brackets, bolted to the head knee and radiated outward in profile from a common point at about keel level.

Although this assembly can provoke strong language during its manufacture and fitting, it is not impossible to make a fine-looking head. Make and fit the brackets from maple, shape as taken off the sheer and body plans, including roughed-out notches for bedding each rail in every bracket. Saw and file or sand the profile of all rails to shape. It helps to maintain symmetry if these pieces are made wide enough to cut mating pairs from each. Try one lower rail in place after its interior shape has been roughed out. Make adjustments as necessary until it fits, and clean up the lower row of bracket notches. Then, by using the shape just obtained, form the interior of the other lower rail. When both rails fit, cut the exterior surfaces using the half-breadth plan as a guide. Repeat the same procedure for the rest of the rails. The main rail is a bit more difficult; its after end must be curved and shaped to allow the inner surface to fit snugly against the hull. It is easiest to make this rail by stopping just aft of the contact point and continuing on with another piece for the curved knee with a neat butt joint between the two which can be covered when painted. Install the rails in pairs, starting with the lowest, and work up.

The cheek knees and headrails are drawn on the plans to show the shape of these parts as accurately as possible but small errors in forming the bow tend to change the shape of these rails where they run along the planking; the modeler must adjust the shape to compensate.

Trail Boards

The trail boards on the head knee of *Margaret Haskell*'s bow were built similarly to square-rigger's cheek knees with the addition of a slightly recessed board between. Make the board from pine so it fits hull and stem and conforms to the shape shown in the half-breadth plan. Then cheek knees are added top and bottom so they extend outboard of the trail board about 1/32". Ornamentation and simple billethead can be shaped and added to the trail boards before fitting them to the hull. The end of the head knee can be shaped in profile after they are attached.

CHESSTREES & SKID BEAMS

Chesstrees were vertical members bolted to each side of *Wasp* as part of the equipment for securing the main tacks. They contain sheaves parallel to planking. Main tacks were rove from aft under the chesstree sheave and over a horizontal sheave set in the bulwarks so it could be belayed within the bulwarks. See Fig. 63.

Skid beams were a pair of heavy vertical timbers on *Lexington* and *Wasp*. They ran from below up to the rail for protection of planking while loading casks, etc.; see hull plans.

If the builder chooses to fit hammock nettings (for description of this equipment see middle of Chapter IX), skid beams must be extended up to the top rail of the netting. Each beam should be about 1/8" square and formed to fit snugly against the hull's side. If they terminate at the rail, pine is satisfactory, but if they extend above, a fine-grained hardwood should be used.

CHANNELS

Square-riggers were fitted with heavy timbers edge-bolted to their sides in the way of shrouds and backstays. They served two functions: The shrouds and backstays were spread farther apart for better leverage and they distributed the inward-acting forces that these shrouds and backstays exerted on the upper part of the hull. On *Lexington* and *Wasp*, the channels spread these forces horizontally over several timberheads. On *Isaac Webb*, upper and lower channels were provided to distribute the load vertically as well as horizontally.

These channels should be made of birch or maple. Their shape and depth is shown on hull drawings; they are full-depth at the hull and tapered to two-thirds full-thickness at their outboard edges. Their inboard edges

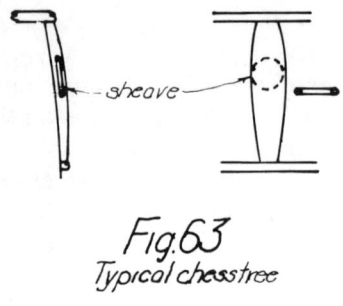

Fig. 63
Typical chesstree

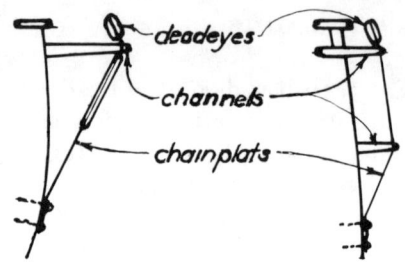

Fig. 64
Typical channels

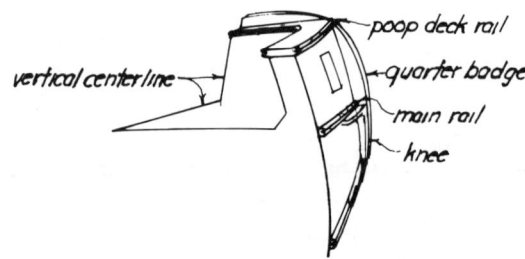

Fig. 65
LEXINGTON'S
port quarter badge

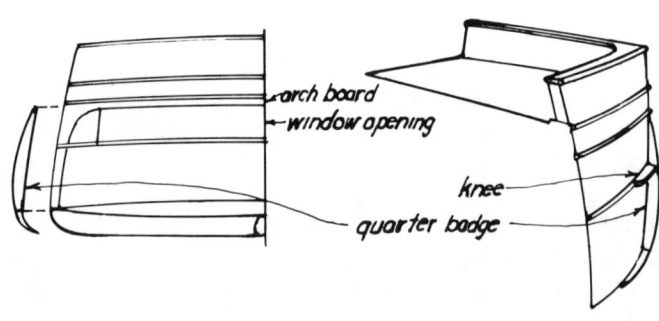

Fig. 66
ISAAC WEBB'S stern
and quarter badge

should be shaped to fit the hull and beveled as necessary so they stand off the hull horizontally. Outboard edges run parallel to those inboard and upper and lower channels are of equal width. Make deadeye straps on *Lexington* and *Wasp* so their lower part looks like the end of a chain's link. The outboard edges of their channels are notched to receive these straps and, after they are fitted in place, a molded board is fitted on the outside to hold them in place and to provide a finished appearance. *Isaac Webb*'s deadeye straps and chain plates may be made from one piece of copper wire so holes can be drilled through both channels near their outer edges and thus eliminate the separate molding pieces.

Where channels attach to the hull on the same level as a rail, install the rail first and then cut it away as necessary to install channels. Install with small wire brads and glue. It is recommended that *Isaac Webb*'s fore channels be installed with brads driven from inside. When driving the brads, hold a weight against the outboard edges of the channels to absorb the hammer shock and the fragile bulwarks will not be broken. Others can be nailed from the outside.

Channel arrangement of each type is shown in Fig. 64.

BUMPKINS

Bumpkins were spars that projected outward from the hull to provide better leads for fore tacks and main braces than could be obtained by securing them to the hull.

Foremasts on *Lexington* and *Wasp* were stepped close to the bow. When their yards were swung for beating to windward, the lower windward corners of the fore courses were too far outboard for the tacks to be effectively secured to the hull. Consequently, bumpkins were fitted in the bows on each side. Size, location, and length are indicated in plans. Note that corners are deeply chamfered over most of their length to lighten their appearance. The tremendous forces acting upward were partially relieved by a stay from each end to the stem near the load waterline. *Isaac Webb*'s tacks could be led to the ends of the catheads because her foremast was farther aft and tack bumpkins were unnecessary.

On large merchantmen with relatively narrow sterns like *Isaac Webb* the main yard braces were spread for better leverage by leading each to a bumpkin just forward of the transom as shown in her drawings. These bumpkins were slightly tapered over their length with a slight chamfer on each corner as shown. Outboard ends were fitted with a square ferrule. Eyes were fitted to each side for attaching rigging on top and forward with iron rods leading down and aft from the ferrule's other sides to counteract forces created by the braces and other attached rigging.

ARCH BOARDS, QUARTER BADGES, & QUARTER GALLERIES

These items are lumped together because they tend to lighten the appearance and dress up the square-riggers sterns which would otherwise look bald, heavy, and flat. Each is a carry-over from earlier craft with ornate galleries which extended across the stern and a short way forward on each side.

Plans of *Lexington* show quarter badges projecting outward on each side of the stern and fair into an arched board across the stern rail. For these pieces use 1/16" thick pine set so their after surfaces are flush with the transom and follow its curve. Shape the inside edges to fit the hull snugly and leave a slight excess outboard and above. After gluing these pieces in place, sand the profile to shape and the after surfaces flush with the stern. A knee-shaped chock just below the lower rail supports the quarter badges, as shown in Fig. 65, with a curved arm along the hull and the vertical arm shaped to match the outer contour.

Isaac Webb had a more elaborate form of quarter badge. Instead of having only separate pieces attached to each side and above, there was a half-thickness piece arched up over the stern windows and extended from the bottom of the lower transom to the main rail with extensions on each side. Make the arched piece first from 1/32" thick pine slightly longer than the width of the transom. Shape the arch on each side so enough height is available to cut the window openings. Also, its upper edge must be crowned to fit snugly under the main rail. Glue this piece in place and sand the outer ends fair with the sides of the hull. Make and fit quarter badges of 1/32" stock. Glue them on so their after surfaces match that of the piece just installed and finish the work by making and installing chocks on each side, as drawn in Fig. 66.

Wasp's stern was fitted with quarter galleries on each side and an arch board across the stern. Study the sheer and half-breadth plans in conjunction with Fig. 67 to make sure the quarter galleries' shape is understood.

Start work by making a temporary arch board from thin pliable wood to assist in shaping and locating parts of the quarter galleries. Make it fit exactly between the sheer and the transom knuckle, and shape its outer edges only according to that shown in the body plan. Locate it carefully, symmetrically with the hull's center line; fasten it with small brads for easy removal. If it tends to be too stiff to follow the transom's curvature, hold it for a few minutes in steam or boiling water to soften the wood's fiber. After completion of the galleries, this board should be replaced with a finished arch board.

Start work on the galleries by carefully marking the level of each floor on the hull. Then make the floors from 1/32" thick maple. Their outboard shape is drawn in the deck plan; it is recommended that the outboard surfaces of opposite floors be formed simultaneously to result in symmetry. Their inboard edges should be shaped so they fit the hull and beveled to stand off horizontally. When completed, each floor must fit so its outboard edge is 1/32" inboard of the temporary arch board's outer edge. After they are fitted, round off their outboard edges. Then make the sills and headers for the columns and windows. Shape as shown and size so their outboard edges are 1/32" inboard of the edges of the floors to which they are attached. Notches must be located exactly to obtain the desired radial effect and they must be cut accurately to obtain a perfect fit with the columns. Glue the second and third floors on the hull snugly in place against the temporary arch board. Then glue headers and sills in place.

Columns forward, aft, and between windows are made of 1/16" thick maple cut in widths shown in the sheer plan. Cut, fit, and glue each column in place so their outboard surfaces are flush with edges of headers and sills. Now compare the angle of each column for radial alignment with its neighbor. If noticeable errors exist, it is suggested the whole unit or units be removed and replaced from scratch since it is almost impossible to alter the configuration with replacement parts.

Pieces sandwiched between floors in the upper and lower parts of the galleries are solid, carved blocks of pine. Their inboard edges are cut to fit the hull and their outboard surfaces are shaved down to fit 1/32" inside the edges of the floors above and below. The lower pair have straight sides in cross-section; those above are slightly concave. After these pieces have been completed, glue them in place along with the highest and lowest floors. The pieces under the lowest floor are carved from blocks of pine. The inboard surface of each is shaped to set back 1/32" from the floor. The shape changes at mid-height so it is a segment of a circle and tapers to a shim below. This piece and the upper filler piece have carvings on the outboard surface and are described later under "Ornamentation." They should be completed before gluing to the hull.

After glue is dry on all of these pieces, remove temporary arch board. If it is partially glued to the galleries, a thin knife will break it clear. This will expose voids in the after end of each gallery; close with filler pieces glued in place. Then the whole transom is lightly sanded smooth along with filler pieces and the after end of the galleries.

Start work on windows by making quadrilateral-shaped blocks to fit window openings. Each block must fit its opening quite snugly and so it can be recessed at least 1/16". Shape their outboard surfaces to conform to that of the header, columns, and sill around openings. The outboard sur-

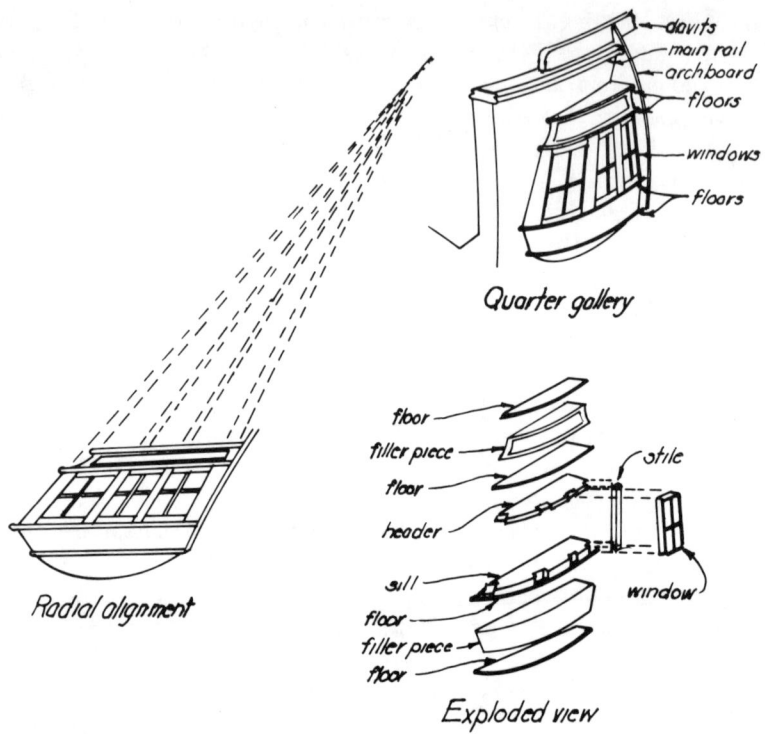

Fig. 67
WASP'S quarter gallery

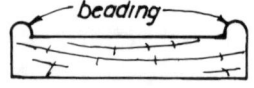

Fig. 68
Cross section of archboard

face of each block is then covered with black-and-white developed film glued on very sparingly around the edges. Window frames made of 1/32″ by 1/16″ maple are then glued, edge down around the edges over the film, and center stiles of the finest size possible glued in the middle. This requires careful gluing but makes a very realistic window installation. Finished window blocks are then installed in their opening; apply glue sparingly to opening surfaces only. Press into openings until frames project slightly outside the columns.

The same idea can be used when making *Isaac Webb*'s stern windows, but it is easier to cut the whole window panel out and make up a single insert containing six windows and five columns. This allows the modeler to make the whole panel on a bench rather than to attempt to fit pieces and windows individually.

Wasp's arch board is made from stout 1/16″ stock shaped as drawn in the body plan. If the temporary arch board was removed in one piece it makes a handy template for checking the outboard edges of the permanent one. It is better practice to glue this board up from at least three separate pieces so the grain nearly follows the board's shape. Note in the sheer plan that there is a slight angle between that part of the board and that below. This can be handled by sawing part way through from behind when installing the board. There should be a slight bead around both inboard and outboard edges as shown in a typical cross section in Fig. 68. When installing the board, glue it on so it is absolutely symmetrical.

ORNAMENTATION

Ornamentation on the vessels described in this book is lingering evidence of the practice for centuries of lavishly employing gilded and richly painted carvings and trim from bow to stern on larger war vessels and more costly merchant ships. Probably *Lexington* had no ornamentation except a carved billethead surmounting her head knee and a scroll on each side to apparently marry the two levels of the main rail together above the deck break. This assumption is consistent with the carvings on lesser merchantmen built around 1750. *Wasp* was a third rate war vessel in terms of size and armament. This is evidenced by the fact that, while she had some bow ornamentation, non-functional quarter galleries and an arch board, contemporary and later ships-of-the-line and frigates had elaborately finished and ornamented bows and sterns. *Isaac Webb* was modeled similar to frigates. In keeping with their design, the head knee with its cheek knees, headrails, and brackets were retained. The stern was scaled-down so only imitation gunports fitted with windows under a quasi-arch board and modest quarter badges were retained. The wide, bald space under the

Fig. 69
Typical billet head

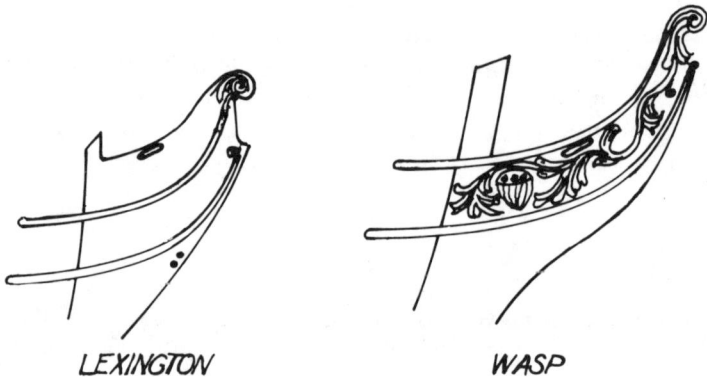

LEXINGTON

WASP

ISAAC WEBB

Fig. 70
Head carving

windows was fitted with a large, carved, gilded eagle. *Isaac Webb* and her sisters, designed by William Webb, had a carved, painted form shaped like an "S" inserted in a frame; this gave the illusion of supporting the forward ends of each poop deck bulwarks. By the time *Helen B. Thomas* and *Margaret Haskell* were built, hull forms had changed to such an extent that elaborate fittings and ornamentation were not appropriate and that whichever was used amounted to little more than shallow carved floral designs.

The upper forward ends of the head knee on *Lexington, Wasp,* and *Isaac Webb* were fitted with billetheads. Fig. 69 is a sketch of a typical billethead. The head was finished on its end with acanthus leaves in circular scrolls flowing astern, similar to the figures at the top of Ionic and Corinthian columns. A pocket in the bottom of the head fitted over a stub on the head knee so it fitted snugly against the headrails and upper cheek knee. The scroll and foliage were worked out so they blended into the forward end of the rails and the upper cheek knee. On *Wasp* and *Isaac Webb*, the carving continued down the head knee between the cheek knees. The central stem or trunk, from which the leaves apparently grew, wove in graceful curves between the cheek knees. *Wasp* probably had a national shield worked into the design down near the stem. These raised carvings were large and had very elaborate detail worked into them. Obviously, it is impossible to miniaturize these carvings on scale models without the skill of a money plate engraver, but suitable scale billetheads and carvings can be made by the modeler, as depicted in Fig. 70.

After the stem and its head knee have been carefully fitted to the hull and shaped in profile, pad out the upper end of the head on each side with fine-grained pine blocks glued in place. These blocks can then be carved to represent the scroll and to provide abutting surfaces for headrails and upper cheek knees. If available pine cannot be cut smoothly across the grain, basswood can be substituted. The location of cheek knees can also be drawn on and the floral carvings made before fastening the stem to the hull. Floral carvings are raised so they can be made and installed later. Make them of boxwood, pear, or white holly.

Stock thickness is a scant 1/32" for *Wasp* and as thin as possible for *Isaac Webb* and wide enough so the entire floral design can be made in one piece. Transfer the shape of the stem onto each block and fill in the shape of the leaves freehand. Saw out the shape with a used, fine-toothed jeweler's saw and finish the carving with needle files and edged tools. Discarded dentist's cleaning tools with sharp chisel-like edges make excellent instruments for this work. Stems should have a low height but acanthus leaves must be left quite thick in relation to their width. When fitting upper cheek knees, make the joint clean so paint will cover it. Multiple head rails terminate in a more-or-less common line which fairs into the upper part of

Fig. 71
Scroll to marry
LEXINGTON'S main rail

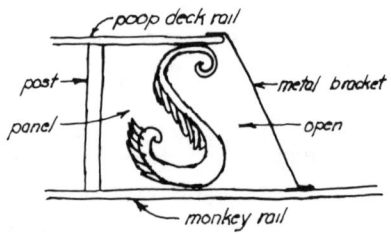

Fig. 72
ISAAC WEBB'S poop deck
bulwark ornamentation

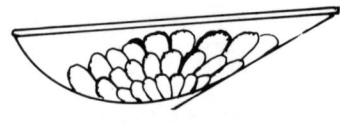

Fig. 73
WASP'S lower quarter
gallery ornamentation

the scroll. This area is usually very weak and it is very helpful to fit knees or a breasthook horizontally between the upper pair to stiffen the connection. This was done in actual practice for the same reason.

Trail boards on *Margaret Haskell* had recessed panels with either a raised grapevine decoration or one carved into the panels. The grapevine was skimpy when compared with the lavish scrolls on *Wasp* and *Isaac Webb*. Note that upper and lower cheek knees blend together on their forward ends, forming a simple scroll. Build the scroll into the upper knee and form the lower end with a shim end which is glued under the upper knee. The recesses in the trial boards can be carved before they are glued in place. The floral designs are very difficult to carve from wood, so it is better to saw them out of sheet brass and glue in place, especially if they are to be raised or just painted to simulate those carved in the panel. See detail sheet for design.

The main rail on *Lexington* had a scroll, as drawn in Fig. 71. The scroll shows both inside and out and can be carved from a piece of pine glued on each side.

Fig. 72 shows the piece inserted in *Isaac Webb*'s bulwarks. Make up very thin pine panels, one for each side, and carve the S-shaped forms from boxwood. Glue one to each side of each panel. Remember that the tails of each figure point aft so each of both pairs is opposite. Acanthus leaves hang below the upper part and under the tail of each figure. After the panels are completed along with their figures, set them in a border frame. The overall thickness of each assembly should not exceed 1/8''. These assemblies are then inserted in the poop deck bulwarks.

Wasp's quarter galleries were decorated on the upper filler pieces within the panel, shown in Fig. 73. The outside borders were plain and the center panel was a continuous carving probably consisting of overlapping leaves arranged in horizontal rows. This is almost impossible to miniaturize but a reasonable substitute is obtained by carving a shallow checkered pattern similar to that found on gunstocks. The piece below the lowest floor was carved with arch-shaped, adjacent sections projecting above the surface, as shown in Fig. 74.

It is quite unlikely that *Wasp* had any ornamentation on her arch board other than the raised beading around its edges. However, it is quite likely that she had something at the level of the gunport headers. Three raised stars 1/4'' in diameter would be appropriate, with one on the center line and the other two offset 1 5/8''.

Isaac Webb's stern was more ornate. It is quite possible that she had a relatively narrow vinelike carving along the section between the main and monkey rails which crossed the main rail in a fair curve and extended down nearly to the foot of the quasi-arch board. This is very difficult to carve and is best hand painted. The eagle below can be carved from pine.

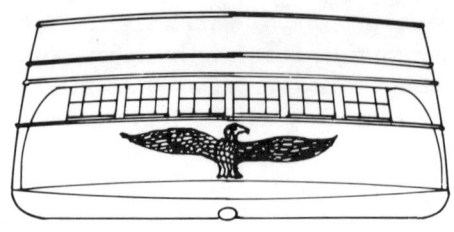

Fig. 74
ISAAC WEBB'S
stern ornamentation

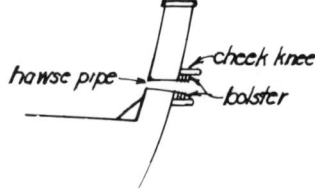

Fig. 75
Typical hawse pipe
showing bolsters

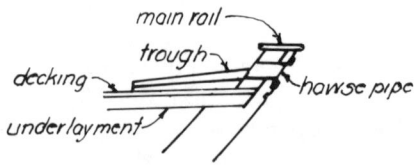

Fig. 76
Fore-and-aft cross
section of HELEN B
THOMAS' hawse pipe

Work the curve of the transom into a block 1 1/2" long, 3/8" wide, and 1/8" thick. The block should be left full thickness in the breast section and nearly full thickness at the arch of the wings. The tail and wings taper so that the end of the tail and the lower edges of the wings are about 1/32" thick. Hints of feathers can be obtained by shallow V-cuts. Carved, thin, columnlike pieces were set between and outside of the windows. This ornamentation is best painted on, as shown in Fig. 74.

Helen B. Thomas' ornamentation was restricted to a vinelike figure carved into the planking around her hawsepipes (shown in the sail plan) and a cove running lengthwise of the hull at nearly main deck level. The cove is described in the section on "Bulwarks." The figure around each hawsepipe can be painted on.

BILLBOARDS

Billboards are replaceable patches of sheathing aft of the catheads from the wales up to the main rail on the square-rigged models. Their purpose was to provide protection to the planking from the ends of anchor flukes while the anchors were being hoisted to the main rail for sea storage. Neither *Helen B. Thomas* nor *Margaret Haskell* needs this protection since fisherman's anchors were light enough to be handled without scoring planking and *Margaret Haskell*'s anchors were stowed by hauling their shanks into the hawsepipes.

Billboards were sheathed vertically and of the shape drawn in each sheer plan. They are made of very thin stock, a slack 1/32" for *Lexington* and *Wasp* and as thin as possible for *Isaac Webb*. It is recommended that a template be made of the billboard's profile so each side will be the same.

MOORING & HAWSEPIPES

These were passages through the hull so anchor cables or chains and mooring lines did not have to pass over the rail.

Hawsepipes on the three square-rigged models are all very similar. After the cheek knees have been installed, but before the headrails, lay out and bore the four hawsepipe holes. These holes must be horizontal and parallel to the center line. Do not force the bit when breaking through the inside to prevent splintering the wood. Because tremendous forces can be brought to bear on anchor cables, the lower surfaces of the pipes were cut away to form a radius so corners and edges were eliminated; this is done so the pipes are round on the inside and oval outside without noticeably widening the hole. Additional pieces, called bolsters, were added on the

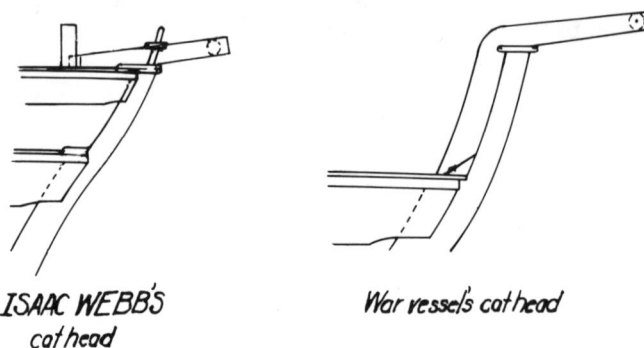

Fig. 77
Typical model cathead construction

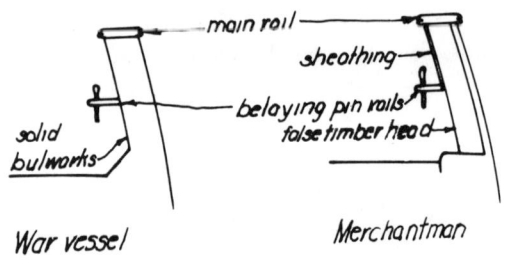

Fig. 78
Typical model bulwarks

planking in the way of the hawsepipes. A cross section through a typical hawsepipe is drawn in Fig. 75. Make bolsters from thin pine shaped as drawn in the hull plans and glue them in place. Drill a small hole through them from inside and ream to shape with a fine, round file. Note that *Lexington*'s hawsepipes were above the upper cheek knee and that half-height bolsters were used and false bolsters were fitted between cheek knees.

Helen B. Thomas had two hawsepipes. Bore these through tilted slightly upward and toward the foremast. Finish the outside with a purchased casting, called a hawsepipe lip, glued in place. A trough, called a hawse block, was bolted to the deck inside the bulwarks which directed the anchor chain or cable aft to the windlass barrel, as shown in the deck plan. A cross section through the hawsepipe and trough is drawn in Fig. 76.

The two hawsepipes on *Margaret Haskell* led upward and inward. Bore them toward the point where the forward end of the enginehouse crosses the center line on deck. Since stockless anchors will be fitted, bore the holes about 5/8'' deep so each anchor shank can be cut, pointed, and driven into the bottom of each hole.

Large vessels like *Isaac Webb* and *Margaret Haskell* floated high above wharves when partially loaded or light. Because of their tremendous size and weight, heavy stress could be exerted on the mooring lines which held the vessels at the wharf. Suitable holes were required in the vessel's sides to allow passage of these lines. *Isaac Webb* was fitted along the main deck with holes through the planking and blocking fitted between the timberheads. Glue solid blocking between the frames the same thickness as the adjacent frames which are then bored through and filed oval in shape with a distinct radius cut all around both in and out. Holes in the poop deck bulwarks are cut through and rounded off.

Since *Margaret Haskell* had an open rail she had iron chocks, which can be purchased, bolted between stanchions near each set of bitts and another pair on either side close to the bow. *Isaac Webb* and *Wasp* had chocklike openings cut into their buffalo rails.

CATHEADS

Catheads are the projecting timbers at main rail level on each side of the bow. They are cranes used to hoist the anchors by their rings to rail level. All catheads had sheaves in their outboard ends over which the fall of the heavy hoisting purchase was rove to a block below. These timbers were shaped and fitted to the hull in two ways. Refer to Fig. 77. Those for *Lexington* and *Wasp* were fashioned from the base of a huge oak tree with a large root included, similar to the description for knees. They were shaped

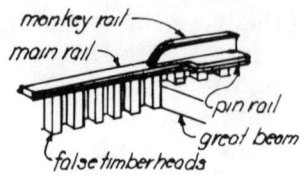

Construction at the break in HELEN B THOMAS' deck showing arrangement

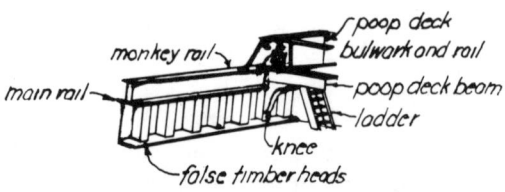

Similar construction – ISAAC WEBB

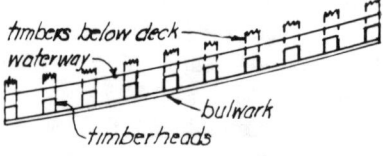

Construction at beveled frames

Fig. 79
Bulwark construction

Fig. 80
Cross section through HELEN B THOMAS' bulwarks

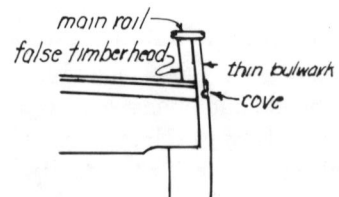

and fitted so the outboard part tilted slightly upward; frequently a shallow carving of a feline face adorned the outboard ends. Ring or eyebolts in their forward sides provided anchoring points for jibboom and flying jibboom backropes.

Refer to the section describing knees to cover making catheads for *Lexington* and *Wasp*. *Isaac Webb*'s catheads are simpler since they are straight and should be fitted with a short tenon in a shallow blind mortise in the bitts. The number and size of sheaves is shown in the plans. Purchased miniature sheaves can be fitted in slots cut for them or holes can be bored through to represent the ends of the slots with dummy sheaves carved in the intervening spaces.

BULWARKS

Bulwarks are those parts of vessels between the weather deck and the rail. Construction varied according to the type of vessel and her business. The craft described in this book require two types. Those on *Lexington* and *Wasp* were planked up on both in and outsides. *Isaac Webb* and *Helen B. Thomas* had bulwarks planked up on the outside only. *Margaret Haskell* had none. They provided some protection to the crew from heavy boarding seas and from falling overboard. In addition, those on war vessels provided a breastwork for the gun crews. Tops of frames, called timberheads, extended up to the main rail. War vessels' timberheads extended nearly full size with regular planking outboard and thinner, but substantial, planking inside. Timberheads in merchantmen and fishing schooners were reduced in size above deck with regular planking outside and none inside. *Isaac Webb* had a thin sheathing strip on the inside under the main rail but it was for appearance only. *Lexington* and *Isaac Webb* had high bulwarks around their after decks.

Because the models have no timberheads, bulwarks construction must deviate from actual practice, yet the end result must appear the same. Typical bulwarks construction of the two types is drawn in Fig. 78 and actual model construction is drawn in the detail sheets for each model. Bulwarks on *Lexington*'s main deck and throughout on *Wasp* are cut down full thickness. *Isaac Webb*'s and *Helen B. Thomas*' bulwarks are cut down to represent only the outside planking, 1/32" on *Isaac Webb* and 1/16" on *Helen B. Thomas*. A 1/32" thickness may be difficult to obtain unless the wood in the hull is extremely good. After carving is completed, sand these surfaces clean, smooth, and fair.

After sanding is completed, the bulwarks on the two models of war vessels are completed. Those on *Isaac Webb* and *Helen B. Thomas* must be fitted with false timberheads. Make the waterways and install them,

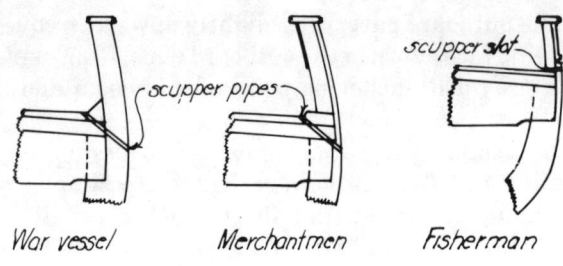

Fig. 81
Typical scuppers

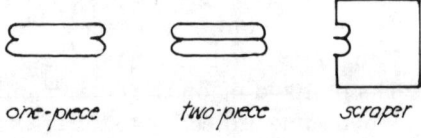

Fig. 82
Rail construction

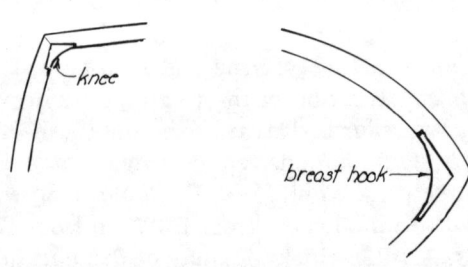

Fig. 83
Typical knees and
breast hooks in rails

followed by the timberheads as drawn in Fig. 79. Since timberheads are the upper end of the vessel's frames, which are set exactly athwartships and perpendicular to the design waterlines, they must be set plumb and square to the center line. Fig. 79 was drawn to show *Helen B. Thomas*' bulwarks at the break, *Isaac Webb*'s bulwarks without sheathing at the break, and *Helen B. Thomas*' timberheads which require severe beveling.

Bulwarks around *Lexington*'s and *Isaac Webb*'s afterdecks are described in the chapters on each model.

Helen B. Thomas had a belt of thin planking on the outside from bow to stern under her main rails as shown in her sheer and sail plans. On the model this is cut down so the planking thickness is reduced to 1/32", as drawn in Fig. 80. This cut can be made very easily by setting iron C-clamps on a short piece of broken file so the upper jaws are exactly 3/16" from one edge. Then, by placing the jaws on the top of the hull for a guide, work the file back and forth from a point near the bow to within a little more than an inch from the stern until a uniform 1/32" deep cut has been made. Feather out the cut at the rabbet and carve the upward sweeping curve at the stern. Refer to the figure and note the cove about 1/16" below the cut. This cut ran from about 1' astern of the hawsepipes to a point 3' forward of the stern. Make a jig from a block of wood about 2" long and 1" wide. Locate two holes so their edges are exactly 1/4" from one edge and insert short dowels in the holes. Then fasten a thin, round-edged file to the edge so the file protrudes exactly 1/32". By using this same described principle, set the block against the side of the hull with the dowels resting on the sheer, work the groove to a uniform depth between the two points.

Bulwarks tend to trap water on deck. Openings called scuppers carried this water overboard. Six or eight lead pipes about 3" in diameter spaced about 4' apart were installed in the low part of the sheer on vessels like the square-riggers. Installation of scuppers is shown in Fig. 81. Scuppers for *Lexington* and *Wasp* are 1/16" in diameter, on *Isaac Webb* 1/32". Scuppers for *Helen B. Thomas* were just slits cut through the planking at the main and poop deck levels. They were about 2" high by 6" long, spaced about 2' apart over an interval of about 15' on either side of the break. Bore very small holes on the model at each location and work them rectangular with a tapered, flat needle file.

Although *Margaret Haskell* did not have bulwarks, the construction at the rail trapped water. Scuppers to relieve this water are not mentioned in construction specifications for these schooners so one can only assume that their size and location was determined by the builder. Vertical, evenly spaced streaks on the sides of photographed vessels indicate that scuppers were set over the range of the after three masts spaced about 20' apart and were probably 3 or 4 inch pipe.

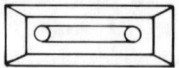
Trim on each side

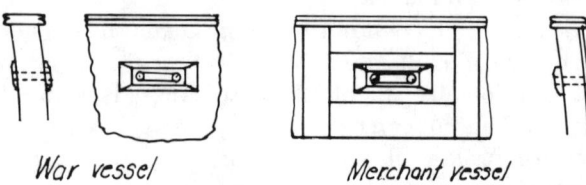

War vessel   Merchant vessel

Fig. 84
Bulwark sheaves

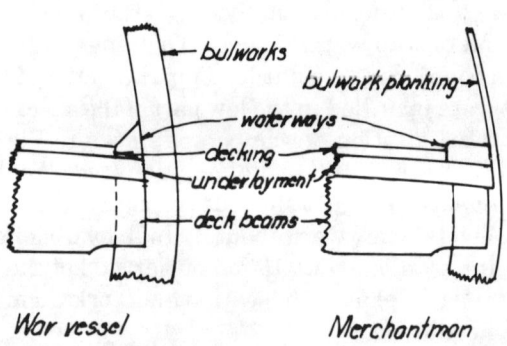

War vessel   Merchantman

Fig. 85
Typical model waterways

RAILS

Rails were heavy timbers installed horizontally around the upper works of the hull to strengthen it and provide a finished appearance. All vessels had one atop the timberheads called a main rail. Many vessels had other rails at various levels on the upper works. Those below the main rail were usually at or near the level of the next lower deck. Packets like *Isaac Webb* were built with their poop decks above the main rail. A timber edge-bolted on top of the main rail formed a continuous curve parallel to the sheer at poop deck level. A continuous rail around the hull at this level was called a monkey rail. *Lexington*'s poop deck was higher than the main rail but, instead of running two rails as on *Isaac Webb*, the rail at the poop deck level and the main rail were connected by a circular moulding. *Helen B. Thomas* had a monkey rail around her afterdeck. *Lexington* and *Isaac Webb* had raised poop deck bulwarks surmounted by a rail.

Although rails look small on a model, they were really heavy timbers. Builders molded their edges to produce a lighter appearance. See Fig. 82. In actual practice, the heavier part was above; for models it is quite satisfactory to make moldings equal in depth. There are two equally satisfactory ways to make model rails. The first is to make a forming tool, as drawn in Fig. 82. It can be made of any piece of reasonably hard sheet steel and shaped with a small, round file. This tool can be worked around the edges to round corners and cut the center bead. The other method consists of making identical, half-thickness pieces which are glued one on the other after the edges have been rounded off, as shown in the figure.

All rails are false below the main rail on these models. They must be either one continuous piece of wood or made up to be one continuous piece to avoid discontinuities in their fair curve. Their elevations are established as was described for locating the upper and lower edges of the wales. Inner surfaces of these false rails must be beveled so they stand off the hull level. At the portion around the bow this angle is quite large, so the stock must be wide enough to accommodate it. *Isaac Webb*'s main rail and monkey rails are waterways on the inside around the forecastle deck and poop deck, respectively. Over these portions the rails are only rounded on the upper inside corners.

Full-width rails on hulls with considerable curvature cannot be sprung into place; it is very difficult to join separate rail sections together without slight breaks in their fair curves. Consequently, it is better practice to make them from thin, wide pieces with the hull used for a template. If the rail is laminated, joints can be staggered and still retain fair curves.

All rails across the stern are crowned like the deck. Where rails across the stern set on the hull, as on *Wasp* and *Isaac Webb*, the hull must be fitted with a crowned piece because their hulls were carved flat across the top. Leftover deck-beam stock is ideal after the bottom has been cut away.

At corners in the rails, such as between side and stern rails on square-sterned vessels and between rails at the bow, knees, and breasthooks were worked into the inboard edges, shaped according to Fig. 83. Where laminated rails were used, laminated knees and breasthooks must also be used.

Selection of wood for rails is very important. It should be easily worked, quite pliable and very resistant to splitting. White pine is ideal for false rails and upper rails where there is little chance of them being nicked accidentally. Higher rails should be made of some harder wood such as maple or cherry.

BULWARKS SHEAVES

Sheaves are inserted at various places in the bulwarks of square-riggers. They appear in line with the lower part of the sheaves in chesstrees and in appropriate locations for the proper lead to lower sail sheets. Those in war vessel bulwarks were inserted in hardwood blocks which were in turn inserted through slots in the bulwarks between frames. The ends of these blocks were covered with a slotted, beveled trim piece to hold them in place. Sheaves in *Isaac Webb*'s poop deck bulwarks were made the same way. Those in her open main deck bulwarks were inserted through the planking and a heavy horizontal timber between timberheads. See Fig. 84.

If the model maker wishes, actual practice may be followed but it is far easier and just as effective to make only the trim pieces with a hint of the sheave carved in each trim piece. Care must be exercised to have mating trim pieces perfectly aligned.

WATERWAYS

After the bulwarks have been cut down and the underlayment installed, waterways can be installed. Waterways on war vessels with solid bulwarks need not be installed at this time but they must be installed before the false timberheads on *Isaac Webb* and *Helen B. Thomas*. Waterways are timbers along the inside of the bulwarks at deck level. On war vessels they were beveled on a 45° angle so carriage trucks could be rolled close to the bulwarks for firing. Typical cross sections of model waterways are drawn in Fig. 85.

Waterways on *Lexington* and *Wasp* can be sprung in from the catheads aft. From the catheads to the bow they must be carved to shape. It is helpful to fit the catheads first so the ends of the waterways can be butted against them. Since the angle between the deck and the bulwark changes, waterways have to be beveled for a snug fit yet full depth must be maintained throughout their entire length.

Waterways on the main deck of *Isaac Webb* and on both decks of *Helen B. Thomas* can be sprung in. Other waterways on *Isaac Webb* and those on *Margaret Haskell* are combination waterways and rails, made and installed as described in the section on rails.

DECK CONSTRUCTION

Decks consisted of relatively narrow planks which ran fore and aft and were fastened down to each deck beam. A curved plank, called a nibbing strake, provided a border within the waterways. After the deck was completed, each seam was wedged open slightly and tarred oakum driven deeply into the crevice. Then the seams were poured full of molten pitch to make them watertight. Ends of deck planks were notched into the nibbing strakes. However, as will be seen later, far more attention was given to this nicety of construction by builders of older square-riggers than on later schooners.

Timber sizes for decking varied considerably, according to both availability and current fashion. Since the British Navy was in the midst of a large shipbuilding program, timber for small merchantmen like *Lexington* was scarce; probably her decking was 6″ wide and did not exceed 24′ in length. *Wasp* was built in a navy yard under the supervision of her designer during a period of little shipbuilding activity when good heavy timber was available. Apparently no expense was spared and, as is described later, her decking was cut curving from wide planks. Maximum width was probably 9″ in lengths of 24′ or even 30′. Large native timber was still available when *Isaac Webb* was built so deck planks 9″ wide and 24′ long were probably used. Planking widths on fishing schooners were subject to fads. At the time *Helen B. Thomas* was built, planking 3″ wide was common and, since native pine was used, 20′ lengths were obtainable. Southern yellow pine was used extensively in large schooners like *Margaret Haskell*. This timber was still plentiful and widths of 6″ and lengths of 28′ to 32′ were reasonable.

Because none of these lengths spanned the entire deck length, end-to-end or butt joints were unavoidable. Shifting the butts of adjacent planks was necessary to obtain required strength and builders used the following rule:

> No butts shall be closer than 5′ from each other measured lengthwise, unless there be a plank between and then 4′ is allowable. Furthermore, no butts shall be on the same deck beam unless there be three planks between.

Deck beams in this context must not be confused with the beams under the underlayment. Beams can be assumed to exist at each station with another

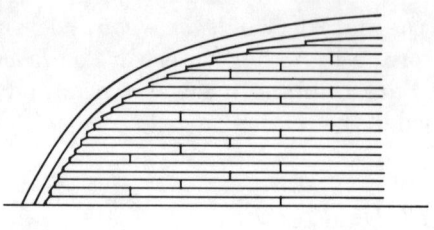

Fig. 86
LEXINGTON'S deck construction

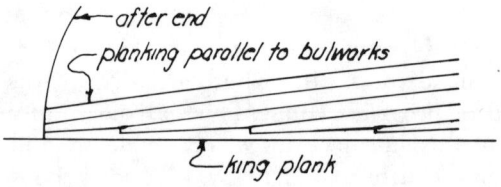

Fig. 87
Construction at king plank

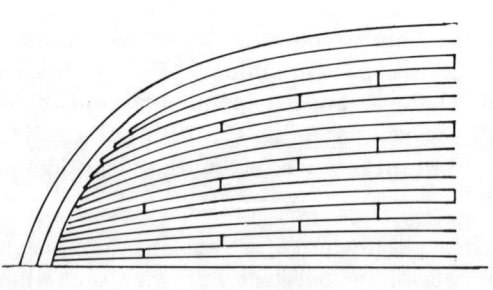

Fig. 88
WASP'S deck construction

midway between stations spaced at the larger intervals. If that spacing is too difficult to handle with the suggested lengths, the assumed spacing can be cut in half. Butts must land on a deck beam so that when viewing the deck from the side, butts form a perfect line regardless of the number of planks between.

Deck-planking stock for models is difficult to make and still obtain uniform pieces. Model supply houses carry precision-cut basswood strips in a variety of sizes suitable for decking and, although a bit expensive, the cost is worthwhile. Each model's deck is 1/16" thick. Planking width for *Lexington* is 1/8", for *Isaac Webb* 3/32", for *Helen B. Thomas* 1/16", and for *Margaret Haskell* 1/16". That for *Wasp* will be covered later.

The starboard side of *Lexington*'s main deck is drawn in Fig. 86 and is based on the foregoing description. Start work by fitting nibbing strakes from bow to break. These are joined forward by a fore-and-aft seam on the center line and are cut to fit snugly against the waterways. It is preferable to make each of them in two pieces with the butt joint an inch or so aft of the catheads so the grain runs nearly parallel to the edges. Locate all stations and intermediate beams; follow by drawing lines perpendicular to the center line across the underlayment at each. Then brad a straightedge down the center line on the port side, and the starboard deck is ready for laying.

Form the nib end on a piece of decking, with the end about 1/16" wide. Hold it over the nibbing strake and, with the point of a sharp knife, draw its outline and cut the notch away. Then, with the plank in place, lay out the location of Station D and saw it to length. From the same piece, cut the second piece which extends back to Station 4 and another piece to finish one complete plank. After this plank has been glued down, remove the straightedge. Repeat the process on the second plank with butts at Stations J, B, and 6. Butts on the third plank are at Stations H and ⌀. Those on the fourth are at Stations F and 2. On the fifth they fall at the same stations as on the first. Note that none of the planks have exceeded 24' in length, and shifting of butts is better than required by the rule.

At this point, five planks should be installed on the port side with the forward butt at Station F in the first plank, at Station H in the second, and so on. After five planks have been installed on each side, check if nib ends on the outside planks are exactly athwartships. If the bulwarks have been cut down exactly uniform and both waterways and nibbing strakes perfectly symmetrical, the nib ends will check out; if not, one side will be gaining on the other. When this situation exists, correction can be made by making the strakes slightly narrower on the gaining side.

Time can be saved and the modeler can still follow accepted practice by butting the forward ends of planks against the nibbing strake from the center line out until the ends must be cut to fit on an angle of less than 45°.

Outer planks are then nibbed into the nibbing strake. When cutting nibbing notches, make them wide enough so planks do not have to be forced in.

Lexington's afterdeck is installed in the same manner except very little nibbing has to be done because most of the planks butt against the relatively square stern.

Isaac Webb's main deck is very easy because her sides are almost parallel and, since the forecastle deck hides the forward end, planking need only be carried as far as Station E. Her afterdeck is installed the same as *Lexington*'s. Her forecastle deck was not nibbed until the planking approached the outboard side of the forecastle ladders.

Helen B. Thomas' foredeck and *Margaret Haskell*'s entire deck was installed without any nibbing whatsoever. Planking ends were just cut to butt closely to the waterways, caulked, and pitched without pretense to finer construction. *Helen B. Thomas*' afterdeck planks were sprung in parallel to the waterways. A king plank down the middle received the nib ends of the interior planks, as drawn in Fig. 87.

If *Wasp*'s deck is installed as designed it is quite a chore but, if done well, the results are worth the effort. An alternative is to nib in straight planks. According to her design, the first plank on either side was tapered. From there out to the edge the planks were sawed curved and tapering so that no nib end had to be cut aft of the cathead, as drawn in Fig. 88. To determine the number of planks required, divide the width of the unplanked space at Station ⏀ by 3/16". The quotient is approximately 16 planks. Then by dividing the unplanked space by 16 at each station, the width of the planks along their length is obtained. It is suggested that inboard edges be left straight from the first butt aft of the foremast to the stern and that pieces be tapered full-length. Each piece is then cut into appropriate lengths before laying. Pieces in the fore end must be cut to length individually and curved inside as well as out. It is suggested that the longer pieces be shaped from wide sticks and slit into 1/16" thick strips as was done for deck beams. After laying three or four planks on each side, recalculate widths and compensate as necessary. The outboard planks will have to be custom-fitted. Remember to shift butts and, when gluing pieces down, tack blocks at each butt so curves remain fair.

For unpainted decks to look right, the seams at nib ends, at butt joints, and between planks must be made black. If decking is a non-absorbent wood, all edges can be blackened with a felt-tipped pen. If absorbent wood is used, thin black paper can be glued to each edge all around. When decking is done and glue dry, sand deck lightly to smooth it up using strokes lengthwise of planking. Each model will have areas where decking is thicker, such as around masts, under riding bitts, under capstans, and under windlasses. These areas are built up with identical-width deck planking as was used below. Their locations and shapes are shown in deck plans.

GANGWAYS

Each of the three square-riggers was fitted with gangways consisting of steps on the hull, an entryway through or over the rail and a ladder down to the deck. Gangways were fitted forward of the main rigging on each side. Equipment at gangways is shown in Fig. 89.

Steps are shaped as shown and glued to the hull according to the sheer plans. Two vertically set planks, called gangway boards, are fixed to the main rail where shown. These boards were carved on the sides facing each other with a shallow appropriate figure such as an eagle clutching staffs of furled flags. The carving is obviously almost impossible to make, but properly made and shaped boards are very satisfactory. Those of *Lexington* and *Wasp* form the fastening points for the ends of the hammock nettings. Similar but lower units are the fastening points for the other ends of hammock nettings.

Ladders on the inside led from the rail to the main deck. If the model is rigged with sails, either omit the ladders entirely or show them on their sides lashed to ringbolts in the bulwarks under the gangways.

HATCHES

Hatches or hatchways were openings in the deck through which cargo, stores, ammunition and the like were transferred into or out of vessels. Deck openings for hatches were located so a deck beam was at each end. Heavy, fore-and-aft beams at each side were fitted between the end beams and received the inboard ends of any intervening beams. Raised timbers, called hatch coamings, formed a continuous watertight bulkhead around each opening. A cross section of a typical model's hatch coaming is drawn in Fig. 90. A rabbet cut in the coaming's inboard, upper edge received hatch covers. Covers were made up of several 3" thick, softwood planks in sizes two men could handle. Smaller hatches such as those on *Helen B. Thomas* had single covers with planks running fore and aft. Large hatches, as on *Margaret Haskell*, had heavy timbers called strongbacks down their fore-and-aft center lines with rabbets on each side to receive covers. The covers were set in two rows with the individual planks running athwartships. Instead of solid covers, the hatchways on war vessels were covered with wooden gratings to provide ventilation below in all but heavy weather.

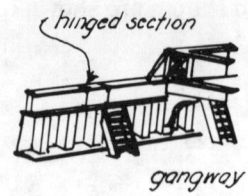

Fig. 89
ISAAC WEBB'S interior
starboard gangway ladder

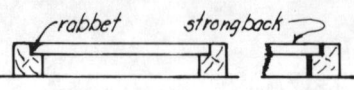

Fig. 90
Typical cross sections
of model's hatches

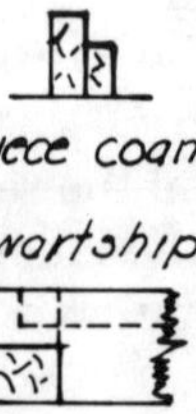

Fig. 91
Hatch construction

Fig. 92
Hatch with shot trough

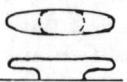

Fig. 93
Typical cleats

Modelers who have access to a power saw can rip out coaming stock including the rabbet; others can make coamings in two pieces, as shown in Fig. 91. Strongbacks are made by the same method as the coaming. Unless no other means of allowing minimal ventilation air to the hull's interior is available except through a hatch, it is preferable to leave the decking within the hatches so strongbacks can set on deck like the coaming. Corners of hatches should be halved together as drawn in the figure. They can be mitered but are hard to handle. When installing *Margaret Haskell*'s hatches, fasten a straightedge along one side and build them in place using the straightedge for a guide because they are all of an exact width. If they are not in exact alignment it will be obvious and look terrible. The same applies to strongbacks.

Gratings are very difficult to make so they look well; they also tend to warp. It is better to buy ready-made wood gratings and fit them with a border to fit in the coaming's rabbet. Hatch covers can be made by gluing excess decking stock to very thin material and sanding the whole so it fits flush with the coaming and strongback top surfaces.

Merchant ships normally installed custom-fitted tarpaulins over the hatches at sea. This entails making the tarpaulins, edge battens and straps, none of which can be made to look well, so it is better omitted. Note that *Isaac Webb*'s only hatch was covered with a temporary house, so it doesn't have to be fitted anyway. Also, it is probable that *Margaret Haskell* was sailed light in favorable weather without tarpaulins fitted; she would have had so much freeboard that normal seas would not break aboard.

War vessel hatches had a trough on all four sides, filled with shot for nearby guns. See a typical cross section with this feature added, in Fig. 92. Appropriately-sized shot can be obtained from dealers catering to sportsmen who load their own shotgun shells.

BITTS & CLEATS

Bitts were heavy, vertical oak timbers used to belay rigging, mooring lines, anchor rodes, etc., where stresses were heavy. Usually the lower ends of these timbers were mortised into deck beams or other structural members. They were set to be used singly or in pairs. Cleats were another form of a belaying device consisting of a deep center section from which arms projected.

Examples of single bitts are the posts on *Isaac Webb*'s forecastle which received the tenon on the inboard end of each cathead and *Helen B. Thomas*' mainsheet bitts. Paired bitts were used forward on the rails of *Lexington* and *Wasp* and just inside *Isaac Webb*'s bulwarks. Each of these pairs were used as a unit for belaying mooring lines in a figure eight

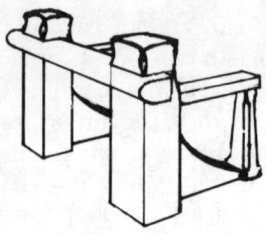

Fig. 94
Typical type of bitt
and fife rail assembly
for LEXINGTON and
ISAAC WEBB

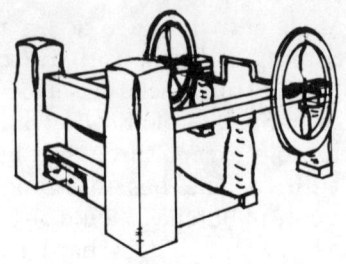

Fig. 95
Bitt and fife rail assembly
fitted with flywheel pump

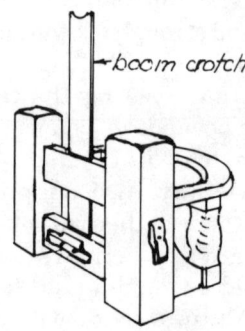

Fig. 96
HELEN B. THOMAS
main bitts and fife rail

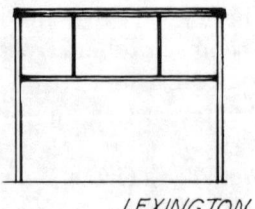 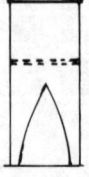

LEXINGTON   ISAAC WEBB

Fig. 97
Binnacles

fashion around each. Another type of paired bitts was used for riding bitts on *Lexington* and *Wasp* and at most masts on each of the five models. A heavy horizontal member slightly above mid-height was halved in the athwartship faces of the bitts in lap joint fashion. It can be noted in the plans that these pairs appear only on the center line with the horizontal member, or bolster, running athwartships. Usually the bitts were fitted with knees running fore and aft. This bitt arrangement was used because the ropes attached thereto were under heavy stress, but each bitt of the pair was a separate entity in terms of belaying. The assembly consisted of a pair simply because a bitt was needed on each side and the bolster with knees strengthened each bitt sufficiently to withstand the stress.

Bitts for models are made of hardwood with a square shoulder below with an integral peg which is glued into a snug-fitting hole. Where ropes cross corners they are chamfered so the rope fibers will not be abraded or broken. Tops of bitts are chamfered or rounded so they appear finished. Bolsters on riding bitts are rounded on their after edges only, while those on bitts at the masts are rounded both fore and aft. Exact sizes and configuration of bitts and their parts are shown in each set of drawings. Bitts at most masts had extensions running aft and some encircled the after side of the masts. These are called fife rails and contain belaying pins for lighter running rigging and are described in the next section.

Beech is one of the better woods for these parts because its grain looks like scaled-down oak and takes on a natural hue when finished with oil. It also takes paint well for bitts which are so finished. A suitable substitute is heartwood of birch.

Cleats were used to belay some of the rigging such as *Wasp*'s spanker sheet, some of *Margaret Haskell*'s lower and staysail sheets, and some of the lower square sail sheets and tacks. A belaying plan is provided for each model. Where cleats are used instead of belaying pins suitable notation is made.

Cleats were made of oak with a relatively deep center section from which horns projected on each end. Lines were wound figure eight fashion around the horns for belaying. There was another type made like the others except it had only one horn. This one-horned type was not designed for belaying but was used to pass rigging under to redirect it for belaying elsewhere, as described later. Fig. 93 shows how cleats were made.

Make cleats of beech, birch, or maple, as shown. Each horn must be high enough to allow the line to pass under it freely. Sizes have to be judged according to location and use. Where possible, cleats should be fastened with beads or lill pins in conjunction with glue.

FIFE & PINRAILS

Fife and pinrails contained belaying pins, usually for lines from above, but some pins in forward pinrails were used for headsail downhauls and sheets. As was stated previously, fife rails were extensions of the mast bitts. Pinrails were fastened to the bulwarks, rails, or in the rigging where needed to belay lines from above. Between fife and pinrails at each mast there were at least four separate areas for securing rigging. Since there were so many lines from above, particularly on a square-rigger, this separated the sailors when working sails and gave each more work space.

There is no way bitts and fife rails can be separated in this description since they are usually connected both mechanically and by function. The bitts were used on square-riggers for belaying topsail sheets, hence the name topsail sheet bitts. This name, slightly foreshortened, has been carried over into schooners as topsail bitts even though there was no relationship. Fig. 94 shows bitts and fife rails for *Lexington* and *Isaac Webb*. The only difference between the two is in the stanchions; *Lexington*'s were square and slightly tapered with chamfered corners while on *Isaac Webb* they were turned. Bitt and fife rail assemblies in Fig. 95 for *Margaret Haskell* did not have a real bolster. Instead, a heavy timber was fitted at fife rail level between the bitts. Another timber was also fitted below the quasi-bolster with a cleat on its forward face for belaying the sheet of the next forward lower sail. The assembly drawn in the figure has extra long fife rails with a second set of stanchions. This extended section was added to provide support for the bilge pump crankshaft bearings. Topsail bitt and fife rail assemblies on *Helen B. Thomas* were similar to those on *Margaret Haskell*, except the fife rails were horseshoe-shaped with a third stanchion on the center line. Also, a mortise in the mainmast bitt bolster and a blind mortise in the member below was cut to receive a vertical board which served as a crotch for the foreboom when the foresail was lowered. This assembly is drawn in Fig. 96.

Unlike all others, *Wasp*'s were not physically connected and bolsters were fitted through topsail sheet bitts with both edges rounded. Fife rails at her fore- and mainmasts were more or less crescent-shaped on three square, tapered, and chamfered stanchions. The mizzen fife rail was circular with athwartship extensions. Stanchions were fitted one each side of the mast on the center line and under outboard ends of extensions. These units are drawn in the plans.

Fife rails can be made with rounded corners but they should be molded like rails. Where forward ends land on squared-off knee arms, glue them in place. Fife-rail stanchions have an integral peg end in the deck and into the fife rail which are glued while assembling. Turned stanchions can be made on a lathe but, with slightly more effort, nice looking ones can be made by hand. Where shown in the figures, a cleat (not to be confused with a belaying cleat) was spiked into the lower outboard side of the bitts. Rigging under heavy stress was led under these cleats and up to a belaying pin. This brought a downward-acting force on the fife rail to partially counteract the upward-acting forces from lines on other pins.

Pinrails are shown in deck plans. The number of pins in each rail is shown in the belaying pin plans. Pinrails connected to the inside of rails were really an integral part of these rails with a fillet at each end where they joined. Make these pinrails from the same material as rails and, if part of the rails, form them simultaneously with the same edge finish.

BINNACLES

A binnacle is the housing in which a vessel's steering compass is mounted. It must be located so the compass is in plain view of the helmsman and artifically illuminated at night with a soft light which does not seriously effect night vision. Before electric lights were used, it was quite a trick to build a light source structure and enclose the oil lamps well enough, from an illumination standpoint, to shield them against high winds and yet allow sufficient air through for the flame and ventilation. It is doubtful if these needs were ever wholly realized. Consequently, many vessels with deck structures close to the wheel mounted the compass on the interior after end with a window between the compass and the helmsman.

Fishing schooners had theirs mounted centrally in the afterhouse with a sliding panel for the window similar to the windows on *Isaac Webb*'s houses. Without doubt, *Wasp*'s was mounted similarly in her after companionway. *Margaret Haskell* had a house over her wheel and binnacle. So, of these models, only *Lexington* and *Isaac Webb* had binnacles mounted on deck. Fig. 97 is a drawing of them. Actual sizes can be taken from the sheer plan.

Lexington's stood on four legs with three compartments on top. The center compartment contained the compass with an open panel on its after side to allow an unobstructed view. Those on the end contained lamps. A very good miniature binnacle can be made from thin cherry with an oil finish. When mounting the binnacle make sure the legs have been cut so it stands plumb.

Isaac Webb's binnacle was a turned column with a squat, spherical brass cover for the compass. The cover was cut on a slant with a window for viewing the compass. If the builder has a lathe it is a simple matter to turn up this binnacle. If not, it can be carved nearly to shape and smoothed up with sandpaper. The flat glass surface can be formed with a flat file and sanded smooth. Make the binnacle from some dark wood, such as black

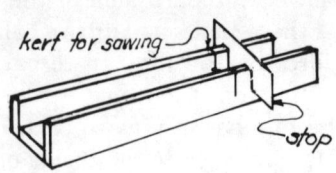

Fig. 98
Set up for cutting tread slots

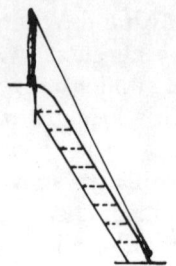

Fig. 99
Ladder with handrails

Fig. 100
Steering wheel stand

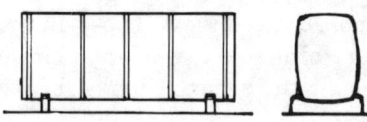

Fig. 101
Water cask and cradle

walnut, and oil the base. The flat portion can be painted black to simulate glass and the cover gilded with gold paint. Do not use bronze paint because it tends to oxidize with age and no self-respecting seaman allows corroded brass on the binnacle.

LADDERS

Ladders were made similar to house stairs without risers. Risers were omitted so there were no pockets to collect water, ice, or snow. Each ladder was fitted with a railing on each side for user's support.

They were made of stock less than 2" thick. Even on the scale of *Lexington*, these members are only slightly more than 1/32" thick. Members that thin are difficult to handle and must be made from wood with close, hard grain such as boxwood and maple. They can be made by shaping sides, sawing slots for treads, tapering ends of treads to fit slots, and gluing the whole together. Slots must be parallel with each other and with base cut. The best way to assure parallelism is by using a miter box. Saw two parallel slots at the proper angle and space as shown in Fig. 98. Make a stop of 1/32", or thinner, sheet metal and slide it into one slot. Slide first side against the stop and, by using second slot for a guide, saw one-third the way through for the first tread. Then move the side until stop fits into tread slot and saw the slot for second tread, and so on for all tread slots. The opposite side must be sawed from a second set of slots on a reverse angle. Sawing tread slots from two sets of kerfs causes difficulty if they are not spaced exactly alike, so lay out and saw each set of kerfs precisely. When gluing this assembly together apply a small amount of glue to each slot and insert treads on one side. Finish work by pressing the other side in place. Before glue is dry, wrack the assembly until treads are perpendicular to the sides. When fitting ladders in place, sand the bottom of one side to allow for the deck crown so ladders stand plumb when viewed from forward.

The four ladders on *Isaac Webb* are too small and delicate to be made by the method just described. Although purchased ladders may not have the correct number of risers and do not look as well as desired, they are recommended for this small scale.

A stanchion 3' high was placed on each side close in to the ladder's sides. These can be some hardwood scaled-down from 4" square, either turned or square and beveled and fitted with a peg end for gluing into the deck. Thread white cotton through holes in stanchions and through ringbolts in the lower deck for handrails, as shown in Fig. 99.

STEERING WHEELS & GEAR

All of the vessels described in this book were steered by a wheel. Various mechanisms were used to connect the steering wheel shaft to rudderpost so turning the wheel turned the rudder. As was discussed earlier in this chapter, at least part of this connecting mechanism should be omitted, therefore it will not be described.

Wheel shafts on square-riggers are mounted in brackets or stanchions, as drawn in Fig. 100. Brackets on war vessels are let into athwartship strips which are in turn fastened to the deck. A spool with raised lips on each end is fitted between brackets on the shaft. On these vessels, an endless tackle fall was wound with three turns around the spool. Ends led through a slot in the deck with rollers on either side. One end was led to port and the other to starboard where they rove off to tackles which hooked to the sides of the vessel and to the tiller which was connected to the rudder. By turning the wheel, the spool hauled on one tackle while slacking off on the other and, thus, the tiller was swung from side to side.

On these models it is sufficient to wind the three turns around the barrel and glue the ends into holes in the deck underneath. Leave just enough slack so the spool will turn readily (so those industrious hands mentioned earlier will not pull the rope out of the deck while playing with the wheel). Spools can be readily turned on a lathe or cut a dowel to length and fit slightly oversized, thin discs on each end. Wheels come with a short stub shaft so the forward end of the spool can be bored to receive this after it passes through the bracket. A short piece of wire or small dowel will suffice on the after end. There is just one caution required, the after bracket should be sufficiently shorter than the other one so the spool will be parallel to the waterline. *Isaac Webb*'s steering gear is easy to make because the spool, shaft bearings and ropes are hidden in the steering-gear box, as drawn in the detail sheet, and the wheel stub is glued into a hole in the forward end.

Helen B. Thomas' steering gear was enclosed in a slanted-roof box as shown in the detail sheet. The gear was a patented, compact arrangement, which because of its design required that the forward end of the wheel shaft be allowed slight horizontal movement. Therefore, a slight elongation of the hole in the box with the wheel stud glued in its center adds realism, along with a thin paper strip painted black to represent an athwartship strap to hold on the top.

Margaret Haskell's wheel was mounted inside the wheelhouse, so it need not be shown.

Steering wheels are almost impossible to make and, although an exact miniature of a fishing schooner's wheel cannot be purchased, it is better to purchase boxwood wheels which were stained dark brown on square-riggers and painted black on *Helen B. Thomas*.

A touch of realism can be added to square-riggers by gluing a grating down on deck just forward of the wheel. It should be long enough fore and aft to represent three feet and wide enough to extend slightly beyond the wheel spokes on each side athwartships. Their purpose was to keep helmsman's feet above the water sloshing on deck. Apparently, fishing schooners were not so fitted probably because fishermen's habitual footwear was rubber boots. Construction of gratings should follow that described earlier under "Hatches."

WATER CASKS

Water storage on oceangoing vessels was a serious matter. Obviously the containers had to be tight and accessible. Although fresh water was only used for drinking and cooking, a relatively small supply was carried; it was rationed to allow making the next port with allowance for head winds and stormy weather. An idea of the quantity carried is had from the fact that the U.S. Frigate *Constitution* had a capacity of approximately two quarts per man per day when provisioned for a six-month cruise.

Primary water storage tanks were built to fit parts of the hull where other storage was not practical on war vessels, *Helen B. Thomas* and *Margaret Haskell*, so they had no casks on deck. Since *Isaac Webb* carried passengers, a relatively large supply of water was carried. Part of her primary water supply was carried in large oak casks lashed to the deck on each side of the forward house. This location made access easy from the galley where water was used and doled out yet to prevent theft could be continuously watched by mates on the poop deck. See Fig. 101 for size and construction of these casks. Beech or heartwood of birch is suitable and can be either stained brown or left natural. Their color would depend on their age. A new one would be light and would turn darker with age. Belts of narrow paper should be glued on where shown and painted black to represent iron hoops.

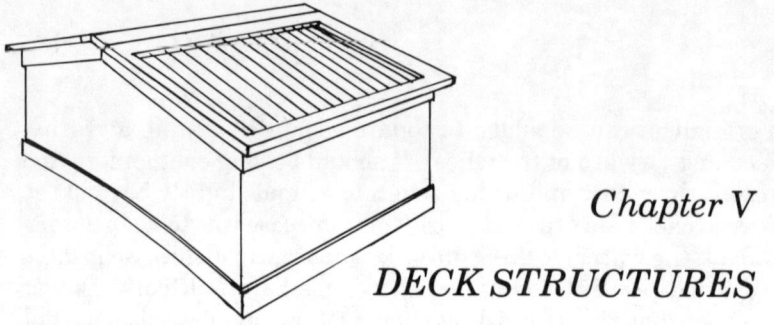

Chapter V
DECK STRUCTURES

Structures described here are deckhouses, deck companionways, and deck skylights; the construction of each is similar and therefore they are grouped together.

Arrangement of deck structures on any vessel was characteristic of the vessel's period and use. War vessels were almost devoid of these structures because they would have been a source of flying splinters when hit by gunshot and a hindrance when in action trying to simultaneously man the guns and handle sails. *Lexington*'s plans show two low companionways for access below. *Wasp*'s plans show a companionway aft of the mizzenmast and a skylight forward of it, probably to provide natural light and ventilation for the wardroom.

Large North Atlantic packets had cluttered decks, as drawn in *Isaac Webb*'s plans. There was a companionway under the forecastle deck for access to crew's quarters; next to it a large house just aft of the foremast contained the galley, maintenance shop and second class passengers' quarters. The house over the hatch just forward of the mainmast was moveable. In port, this structure was lifted off so stores, passenger baggage and mail could be loaded or discharged. Preparation to sail included fitting an inclined ladder in the hatch, used for access to steerage passenger quarters, and lashing the house in place. Her afterdeck was fitted with one skylight and two companionways which provided natural light, ventilation and access below to officer and first class passenger areas.

All later fishing schooners had deck layouts similar to that drawn for *Helen B. Thomas*. There was a companionway forward leading to the galley and quarters for part of the crew. A large house aft with half of its depth below deck provided quarters for captain, cook, and balance of crew. All bulk cargo schooners with four or more masts had houses as shown in *Margaret Haskell*'s plans. The house under the foremast was built on deck and housed the steam boiler with a hoisting engine and maintenance shops. Houses under the mainmast and aft were sunken part way into the deck. The forward one provided space for the galley and crew's quarters, the after one for officers' quarters. The practice of lowering houses into the deck allowed booms to be set lower which made sails larger and improved the vessel's appearance.

GENERAL CONSTRUCTION

Wood for model house construction must not be too close-grained or else the painted surfaces will appear metallic. Woods like cherry or black walnut do not take the metallic sheen but are hard enough to be suitable for the houses. *Wasp*'s deck structures were definitely varnished, so cherry should be used.

Each structure on a model is built with corner posts. Builders who have power saws can make corner post stock with slots to receive side and end pieces. Those who make these parts by hand can make corner posts from two pieces. This construction is drawn in Fig. 102. Under either method, the end grain of the side and end pieces is buried in the construction and the excess at each corner is sanded away.

Side views of deckhouses and other structures are drawn in the hull plans. End views of houses, etc., are drawn in detail sheets. Where pertinent, partial or whole profile views are also included. When determining length of side and end pieces, do not neglect to account for thickness of each end piece. After exact length of each piece has been determined and marked on the stock, score the surface at each mark with a sharp knife pressed against a square or bevel. Then saw along the score with a very fine-toothed saw.

Before assembly, shape the upper and lower edges of the end pieces to conform with the deck's crown. Also, shape the lower edges of side pieces to match the curve of the deck's sheer. Cut the corner pieces about 1/16" too long and simultaneously assemble ends and sides with corner pieces. Structures with right-angle corners can be squared up before glue sets. Those with curved sides are glued together so angles at opposite corners are equal and, after glue is dry, a full-depth brace is forced in and glued crosswise at the structure's mid-length to bend the side pieces into the desired shape. Since corner pieces must be sanded to remove excess stock on the outboard edges and both top and bottom, it is helpful to glue wide horizontal braces in for rigidity.

Isaac Webb's forward house and the house under *Margaret Haskell*'s mainmast were fitted with a galley chimney, known to seamen as a Charley Noble. Also, *Margaret Haskell*'s forward house was fitted with a boiler chimney. The construction of these metal parts is described in Chapter IX, but provision must be made to hold them in place. Glue a piece of side or end stock across the houses below the windows or portholes. Bore snug-fitting holes through the roof but only partway through this member. This provides both vertical and horizontal support. If one of these braces is in the way of a mast, bore a snug-fitting hole through the roof and a clearance hole in the brace.

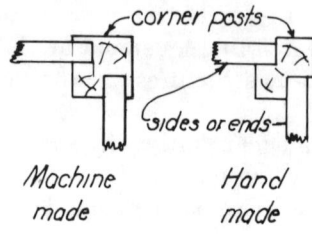

Fig. 102
Corner posts for
model houses

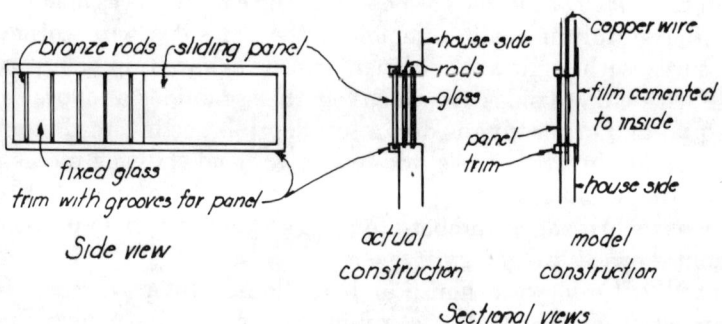

Fig. 103
Model deck house
window construction

While making houses and companionways, keep in mind that no outside doors had sills at deck level. Instead, the sills were at least 6" above deck to keep water from running inside.

Most structures had thicker planks around the bottoms and moldings under the roof overhangs. This feature can be simulated by fitting pieces made of 1/32" thick stock where shown in detail sheets. Glue these pieces in place and sand them down to a thickness of 1/64" with slightly rounded corners on the lower belts.

WINDOWS

Windows were fitted into *Wasp*'s companionway and into all structures on *Isaac Webb* except the companionway under the forecastle deck. Although these windows appear to have been two panes of glass side-by-side, they had only one pane surrounded by a double-length trim in which a protective panel was mounted and could be moved over the windows in heavy weather or slid to the other end during favorable conditions. Bronze rods set vertically in the window frame between the trim and glass provided additional protection against being hit by a crewman working on deck. Side and sectional views of this construction are drawn in Fig. 103.

For model structures, thin narrow trim is glued in place and sanded to a thickness of 1/32" on *Wasp* and 1/64" on *Isaac Webb*. Shim thickness panels may be glued into frames on the opposite end from the window or they can be omitted without seriously detracting from the realism. Because there did not seem to be a consistent pattern for locating windows in the frames, it is suggested that openings be cut in after ends of trim on side walls and inboard on the ends. This follows one scheme which was used. The protective rods are fitted in holes drilled from the top of the side pieces down through the opening and about 1/8" into the sill. Make sure they are evenly spaced. Before the roofs are fitted, copper wire is fed through these holes. After the structure is completed, developed film is cemented on the inside.

By the time *Helen B. Thomas* and *Margaret Haskell* were built, the rectangular windows had been replaced with round portholes. Although these can be turned from brass rod on a lathe, excellent ones in many sizes are available at model supply houses. These portholes are inserted in tight-fitting, accurately-located holes after the sides and ends have been painted. *Helen B. Thomas* had a glazed, oval window in the after end of her house on the center line at mid-height. The compass was mounted directly behind the glass. This window was protected by a panel which slid to starboard and should be made with trim, as described for rectangular windows. It can be left with just the trim as though the panel were closed, or an oval opening can be cut out with developed film cemented on the inside.

HOUSES

Houses on *Isaac Webb* and the two schooners will be very prominent features of these models and must look right so they are not eyesores. The built-up construction described here requires more craftsmanship than for those found on many models made from solid blocks. Somehow, no matter how well they are constructed and finished, they always look like wooden blocks rather than miniature houses.

Sizes of houses must be carefully scaled off the plans or detail sheets. This is particularly true on *Margaret Haskell*, where slightly oversized houses would seriously decrease space for some of the sheets and because the after end of the boiler house is the same width as the house for the crew. All houses were sized by the designer who had beauty in mind, and deviations are usually unsightly. When assembling houses, make sure all parts fit correctly or the finished house will be twisted and difficult to glue onto the deck. When ends and sides have been glued together, fair up both sides and ends of corner posts. Try the house in its location on deck and fair its lower surface, if necessary, to fit snugly without rocking. Then fit, glue, and sand the belt around the base and, if it's visible, around the top of the house.

Margaret Haskell's wheelhouse was built in the same style as her other houses except there was a high continuous row of windows across the front with one window on each side to aid the helmsman's vision. Corner pieces extend full height in the after corners and those forward from deck up to the sill of the windows. Make the fore end piece wide enough to reach up to the sill and cut the sides back for the side windows. Glue a filler piece across the top front before adding the belts around the top and bottom. Glue vertical pieces in each corner and the three across the front to make four equally-sized windows. Then make frames without muntins to fit each opening. They should be made of 1/32" stock with outboard edges slightly rounded and sized to be a sliding fit. Cement film on the inner surface and glue the frames in place so they are recessed about 1/64" from surrounding surfaces.

Paneled doors were located where shown. It is impossible to include panels, but raised stiles, as shown in the detail sheets, are glued on and sanded down so they are as thin as possible. Trim should be glued on so there is a hint of seam between it and the door and sanded down to the same thickness as the belts around base and top. Doors in the after end of *Margaret Haskell*'s forward house were made to slide their own width to inboard direction exposing door openings, as shown in detail sheet. However, it is suggested that both doors be located in the outboard position to avoid cutting door openings and fitting film behind. Unfinished houses for this model are shown in Photos 21 and 22.

Roundhouses were fitted in the after corners of *Wasp*'s deck. They were built to exactly fit against the bulwarks at the side and against the stern. Their roofs were just under the main rail. Probably there was a belt of thicker plank at deck level but it is doubtful if there was trim under the roof. Start work by gluing pieces up the bulwarks, up the stern, and on deck to prepare to glue the inboard edges. Then make the forward ends and sides to fit perfectly. Miter the corners of the ends and sides where they join along with the belt around the base. Fit a door on each side, as described before. After these pieces are glued in place, make pieces with the same crown as the forward ends and glue them to the stern for a guide to land the after ends of the roof planks.

Deckhouse roofs were made of planks laid fore and aft with a narrow border around the upper surface. Make the planks from stock about 3/4" wide. Those for *Helen B. Thomas* and *Lexington* are a strong 1/32" thick and for *Isaac Webb* and *Margaret Haskell* a slack 1/32". The borders, where shown, are the same thickness as roof planks. Roof planks are cut to extend outboard of upper trim on all four sides, by an amount equal to their own thickness, and are finished with rounded edges. Make the border pieces with rounded outboard edges, square inboard edges and mitered corners.

Isaac Webb's forward house was fitted with skid beams for the boats. These beams were made of wide plank, edge-bolted to the roof and shaped as drawn in the detail sheet. They were mounted in pairs and spaced about two-thirds of the boat's length apart. Their lower edges were cut away at intervals to allow passage of water lengthwise on the roof. Note that a small hatch was located between the after ends of the boats. Possibly the cover was removed or swung up on one end to act as a wind scoop to provide ventilation in the second-class passengers' quarters.

Make the coaming about 1/16" deep with the cover of 1/32" stock slightly larger than the coaming. An attached structure was located on the fore end with a sloping hinged cover for storage of sundry gear. Make the sides and end from 1/16" stock and 1/32" for the cover. Before final attachment, cut snug-fitting, carefully-located slots in the fore end to receive the after end of each for fife rail. Attach this structure after the house has been glued in place.

The belt of plank around and above the roof on deckhouses tended to trap water similar to waterways on deck. Since fresh water promotes rot, scuppers were fitted at the lower corner to lead the water to the deck where it could run off through deck scuppers.

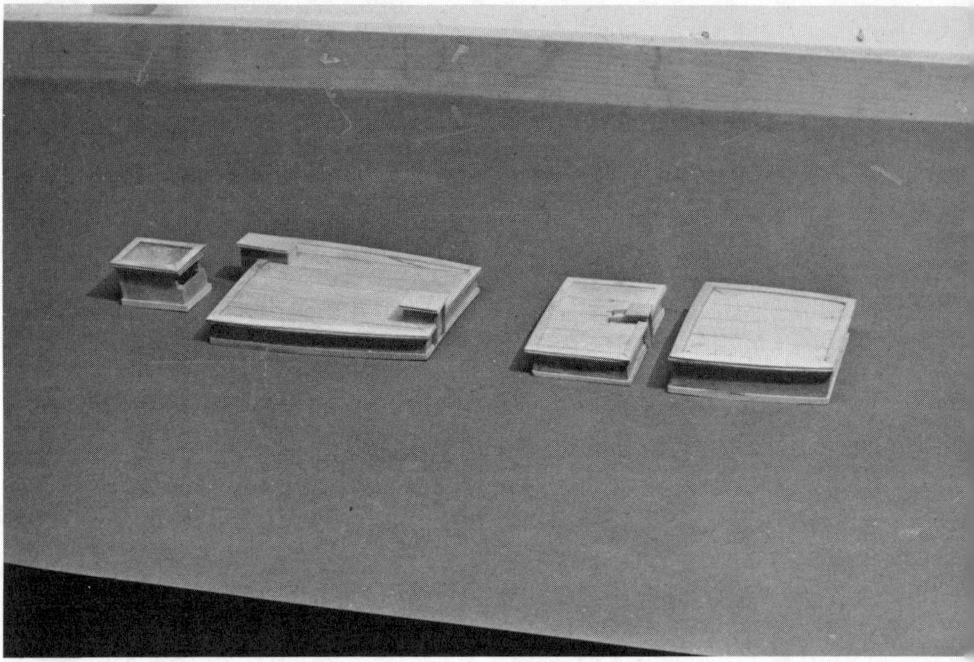

Photo 21—Partially finished houses for *Margaret Haskell*. **Photo 22**—*Margaret Haskell* houses upside down, showing internal bracing.

SKYLIGHTS

Skylights were of two types. The more elaborate type had plain sides and ends with sloped glass roofs, as on *Wasp*. The other type had flat roofs with windows in the sides, as on *Isaac Webb*'s deck and on *Helen B. Thomas*' afterhouse. Construction of a sloped top skylight is shown in Fig. 104. Cherry is suitable for this skylight since it will be finished with oil or varnish. Construct sides and ends as described for houses. Make frames for the sloped glass roof as shown in the detail sheet. Note that the upper stile is double width. Bore holes through for protective rods before beveling the mating edges. Then insert the rods, cement film in place, and glue the roof in place. Construction of *Isaac Webb*'s skylight, including the windows, is as described for houses. The roof is single thickness with rounded edges. *Helen B. Thomas*' skylight is built without trim at either top or bottom, with a round edged, single thickness roof. Its side windows are double without trim at either, but with protective rods.

Since these skylights are relatively small they can be made without corner posts. The corners can be mitered and glued together. After the roofs are glued on, the structures are strong enough to withstand any necessary sanding on their lower edges to make them fit the deck or house roof. This type of construction is also applicable to companionways.

COMPANIONWAYS

Companionways are small structures with an opening in their after ends continued forward into the roof. Because these structures were quite low, the roof opening permitted sufficient headroom for the user to stand erect. The roof opening was closed by a sliding cover on side rails, as drawn in Fig. 105. *Wasp*'s companionway and those on the poop deck of *Isaac Webb* were fitted with paneled doors. The forward companionways on *Isaac Webb* and on *Helen B. Thomas* had solid panels which slid down from the top in rails on each side of the door openings. Note that the sides of *Helen B. Thomas*' companionway extended forward on an upward slant and the roof overhang was curved on its forward end. Companionway-type slides and paneled doors were fitted in the after end of *Margaret Haskell*'s house under her mainmast. *Helen B. Thomas* had a companionway slide and solid sliding panels in her afterhouse.

Rails and crossmember are made from 1/32" thick stock. They are slightly tapered as shown, formed by sanding after being glued in place. Then make and glue the sliding cover in the closed position. Paneled doors and door trim are made as described for those on houses. Doors composed of panels which slide in from the top are made from thin pieces of wood with

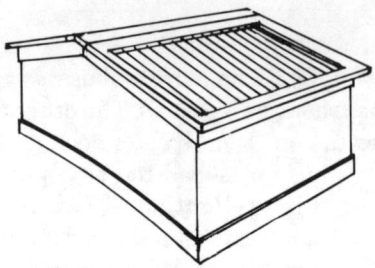

Typical skylights

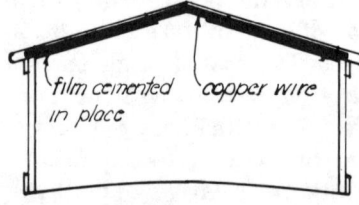

Cross section

Fig. 104
Construction of model's sloped roof skylight

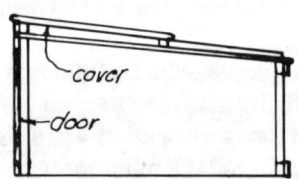

Cross section thru fore-and-aft centerline

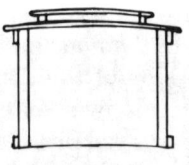

Cross-section of fore end of cover

Fig. 105
Typical model companionways

grain running horizontally and are lightly scored to represent three panels. Glue these imitation doors in place with a very narrow, raised trim piece on each side. Trim for doors must be in exact alignment with cover rails.

GALLEY HATCH

Helen B. Thomas had another low structure forward of her windlass. It was round with a circular piece of glazed glass in a metal frame centered on its top surface. The structure was built up of square-edged timber and turned inside and out on a large lathe. The cover was turned like the base and could be removed. This hatch is easy to make if one has a lathe. Turn the outside diameter, smooth off the top, and bore the top surface to receive a 1/8" porthole so its flange is flush. Then switch ends and bore a shallow relief in its base with a wall thickness of about 1/16". This permits shaping the base to fit the deck crown easier. Builders without a lathe can make the hatch from 5/8" dowel; saw off square to proper length. Lay out the exact center on one end. Select a drill with same diameter as porthole flange and bore until its full diameter has cut to the depth of flange thickness. Follow through with a drill the same size as the porthole. Gouge out the lower end slightly, sand the top smooth, and fit the base to the deck.

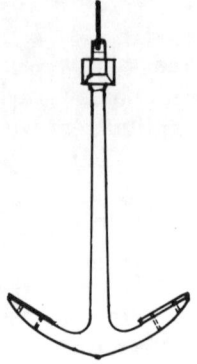

Chapter VI
GROUND TACKLE

Ground tackle is the general term used when referring to anchors, anchor hoisting equipment, and/or anchor rodes or chain. This equipment, used to secure a vessel at anchor, is a very important part of every vessel's gear and should be modeled and arranged properly to look right according to the vessel's occupation. Plate II shows individual pieces of equipment, their sizes, and shapes.

ANCHORS

There were four types of anchors used on these historic ships. The war vessels and *Isaac Webb* used old style, wooden stock anchors. *Helen B. Thomas* used two types; one was a relatively light, but large, wooden stock unit used on the fishing banks and the second was an all-metal unit with a folding stock especially useful in harbors. *Margaret Haskell* carried stockless, modern-type anchors.

    Shanks and arms for the old style and fisherman's anchor are sawed and filed to shape from brass of appropriate thickness. Refer to Plate II for sizes, proportions, and shapes. Particular attention must be given to their weights. If too heavy, they look clumsy; if too light, they appear weak. After their profiles have been filed to size, shanks and arms are chamfered or rounded, as shown. Flukes are made of sheet brass or copper and soldered on. Pins in snug-fitting holes through both arms and flukes are helpful to maintain alignment while soldering and can be filed flush afterwards.

    Stocks on old-fashioned anchors were held in place by a raised section on the shank. This can be made by forming a square ring from wire and soldering it in position. Then the solder above is filed away and that below filed to a neat fillet all around. Stocks for the fisherman's bank anchors were held in place through a diamond-shaped section forged into the shank. This section is bent to shape from 1/32″ thick sheet brass, 1/8″

wide; hard solder at one corner. The shank is cut away in this area with studs filed on the ends which fit into bored holes top and bottom of the diamond. Then assemble the three pieces, soft solder together, and follow by filing fillets on the outside and cleaning the solder out on the inside. Fisherman's harbor anchors were made with iron-folding stocks, shown folded in Plate II. A circular swelling in the anchor's profile was bored just large enough to allow the bent part of the stock to be worked through. Another, but smaller, circular swelling on the upper end was bored to receive the anchor ring.

Stocks for old-fashioned anchors were made in two halves with a vertical, longitudinal seam. Assembled stocks were square and parallel-sided for the middle quarter of their length. Outboard ends were tapered on the sides and bottom so the ends were two-thirds as large as the center part. Then heavy iron bands were driven over the tapers, as shown, to hold the stock together. Model stocks should be made in one piece, tapered properly, and have snug-fitting holes on the shank. Bands are not necessary, but four made of shim brass add to the anchor's appearance. Stocks for fisherman's bank anchors were small for their length. Their cross sectional shape was that of a diamond to fit the shank. Top edges were straight with lower sides cut on a curved taper so outer ends were about half as large as the center. Stocks are made of maple and stained dark brown.

Folding stocks for harbor anchors are bent to shape from hard brass wire slightly less than 1/16″ in diameter. Two scraps of copper are drilled with a snug-fitting hole to fit over the stock. These are slid over the stock, one near the center and the other on the straight end, and soldered in place. The one in the center is filed up round; the one on the end is filed hexagonal to look like a nut. The ball on the bent end is made after fitting the stock in its shank by winding clean, fine copper wire to a spherical shape and coating the whole with solder, followed by filing it to shape. If a lathe is available, a ball can be turned and bored, followed by soldering it in place.

Anchor rings are made from copper wire and of the diameters indicated in Plate II. They are sprung into holes in the shanks, reshaped, and the joint soldered shut. Remember that holes in the shanks must be parallel with stocks. If chains are going to be used, the end link should be threaded on the ring before soldering the joint.

Modelers who do not wish to make anchors can purchase reasonable miniatures of old style, wooden stock anchors from model supply houses. The two types used on fishing schooners are not available, but wooden stock and folding types, as purchased, look fairly well since stocks are unshipped and lashed to the shanks when stowed. Stockless anchors, as fitted on *Margaret Haskell*, cannot be made without casting equipment; purchased ones look so well it is not worthwhile attempting to make them.

ANCHOR RODES

Rodes were heavy rope which, when in use, were secured around windlasses or riding bitts, rove through the hawsepipes, and seized to the anchor rings. After outward-bound merchant and war vessels were clear of land, the rodes were disconnected from the anchors and stowed below. Then plugs were hauled into the hawsepipes from outside to prevent seas from pouring through. Fishing schooners of *Helen B. Thomas*' time were fitted on the starboard side with a heavy hawser about 3" in diameter and eighteen hundred to twenty-four hundred feet long for anchoring on the banks. At all other times it was coiled just aft of the foremast, starboard side. Rodes on *Lexington* and *Helen B. Thomas* should be about 1/16" in diameter, on *Wasp*, 3/32".

ANCHOR CHAIN

By the time *Isaac Webb* was built, larger merchantmen had been using chain for a couple of decades. So, without doubt, she was fitted with chain on both sides. *Helen B. Thomas* was fitted with chain on the port side. *Margaret Haskell* had chain on both sides but this is of no consequence in terms of her model because they are hidden. Chain for both *Isaac Webb* and *Helen B. Thomas* should have about eight links per inch.

ANCHOR STOWAGE

Although most vessels carried more, only two anchors are shown on each model and their stowage is as important as their shape. All but *Margaret Haskell* have anchors stowed on deck or at the rail. Hers were stowed by hauling the shanks into the hawsepipes until the flukes were jammed solidly on the lips.

Anchors were stowed for sea so they could not shift. *Lexington*'s were swung up aft of the cathead with one fluke hooked over the rail and around a conveniently located bitt in the rail so the shank was outboard with the stock standing upright. The arm was lashed to the bitt and the anchor ring to the cathead. *Wasp*'s anchors were stowed with arms hauled through the forward gunports and lashed to the deck with the stocks against the rail. If the port had to be used for firing or weather became so bad that the ports had to be closed, stocks were disassembled and anchors stowed below. *Isaac Webb*'s anchors were secured with shanks laying alongside the after sides of the catheads. Stocks stood more or less vertically and hard against the rail with arms lashed to the cathead bitts and rings to the catheads. While running to and from the banks, fishing schooners stowed their anchors with arms hooked over windlass winches and their ring ends forward. Bank anchors were on the starboard side and folding-stock type to port with arms lashed to the windlass bitts and the rings to appropriately located ringbolts in the deck. If models are displayed with sails set, the methods just described are proper. The stowage scheme described for *Helen B. Thomas* is proper whether sails are set or not.

It is also proper to have one anchor rigged out on the catfall whether sails are set or not, as shown in Fig. 106. Anchors were frequently left rigged this way at dockside and on the way out of port until clear of land or after landfall. Catfalls are rove off with one less sheave in the block than in the cathead. This block is stropped with the standing end of the fall spliced into its tail and an oversized hook in the other end. The fall is rove off from one side to the other (so there are no riding turns) and adjusted so the block hangs about 1″ below the cathead. If rodes are used, rig one through the hawsepipe and tie an anchor bend, see Plate II, to the anchor ring. Hang the anchor on the hook and belay the catfall to a cleat on the upper side of the cathead. The rode should be left slack outside so the anchor hangs just above the waterline. Rodes are secured to riding bitts by reeving the part from the hawsepipe outside the bitt up and over the after side of the bolster, forward and around the bitthead, and aft again over the bolster. They then lead aft to the nearest hatch where they disappear below through the hatch grating.

If chain is used, as on *Isaac Webb*, the end is hooked into the ring, as described before. Since her windlass is not visible, it is not fitted; the inboard end of the chain is hooked to a small loop in the middle of a piece of wire about 1″ long. The chain is snaked out through the hawsepipe and pulled through until the wire is crosswise the hawsepipe and inside against the bulwarks before it is secured to anchor. Rigging for *Helen B. Thomas'* harbor anchor when ready to "let go" is messy and not recommended.

CAPSTANS

War vessels were fitted with a mechanism called a capstan to hoist anchors and to provide power for other heavy hoisting jobs. The rope was wound around a large vertical barrel surmounted by a disc with a series of horizontal, radial holes equally spaced around the perimeter. These holes received the ends of heavy oak bars. Crewman lined up on each bar and, by pushing on them, the barrel was turned and the rope hauled upon. As the rope was hauled in, other crewmen took the slack away while keeping some force on the last turn, providing necessary friction between rope and barrel. This probably sounds like a dubious method of hoisting a *Wasp* anchor with its rode, weighing upward of two tons. However, friction between barrel and rope was tremendous and, if the crew was strong enough, a sufficient strain in turns around the barrel could be exerted to force the natural oils out of new Manila rope when trying such work as breaking out an anchor stubbornly caught on the bottom.

The heart of a capstan consisted of an eight-sided oak spindle. A disc was fitted at its upper end with square capstan-bar holes. Another disc near the spindle's lower end was fitted. Oak pieces were fitted vertically between the discs and edge-bolted to each face of the spindle to form the barrel. These pieces were called whelps. Capstan bases were heavy, circular iron castings with four equally spaced lugs on the perimeter through which they were bolted to extra thick deck padding. Top surfaces of bases had circular troughs with inside diameters equal to that of lower discs. Gravity-operated lugs on loose fitting bolts in the lower disc trailed in the trough which had a continuous series of radial webs to prevent reverse rotation. This safety feature was very important in situations like that described previously because, if the force overpowered the crew on the bars, the capstan would spin rapidly ejecting the bars through centrifugal force with disastrous results.

Construction details of a model's capstan appear in Plate II. If a lathe is available, it is a small job to turn a spindle with discs and base as an integral unit from a piece of birch or maple. Then the whelps and base bolting lugs can be shaped and glued in place. Eight capstan bar holes are then bored in alignment with the whelps and are squared up with a jeweler's graver or a square needle file. This completes the capstan with all necessary detail unless the trough was cut and it is desired to fit the four pawls and about sixteen webs. If a lathe is not available, each disc and the base must be fashioned around central holes which fit snugly on a round spindle. It is a bit of a chore to make each piece exactly round but worthwhile even if some have to be discarded. After these have been assembled and glued on the spindle, whelps are installed as described before. It requires some patience to get them spaced evenly but, if those at 6 and 12 o'clock are glued in first, followed by those at 3 and 9 o'clock, allowed to dry, then the four remaining ones can be glued in so they bisect the 90° angles. It could be helpful to leave the top disc off for alignment purposes until all whelps are glued in. Pawls and the trough are impossible to fit well on these built-up units and should be omitted.

Regardless of their diameters, capstans must be made with bar holes scaled 54" above deck so average-height sailors could apply maximum force on the bars. Appropriate diameters are given for each model in the table in Plate II.

The table includes dimensions for capstans on *Isaac Webb*. At about the time of her construction iron capstans were coming into vogue and possibly she was fitted with them, although it is not certain. If the iron type is fitted they must look like the one drawn freehand in Fig. 107. It is best to purchase this style, but avoid poorly shaped ones because they look unattractive. It should be noted that *Isaac Webb*'s capstans were not part of ground tackle so they were somewhat lighter than a unit on a war vessel of comparable size.

Bars for iron capstans were round throughout, with largest diameter at the capstan's surface. Inner ends were tapered to about two-thirds diameter; outboard ends to a little more than half. This type for *Isaac Webb* is 1" long with a maximum diameter of 1/16". Those for wooden capstans were made square with equivalent tapers and chamfered on each outboard edge. Bars for both *Lexington* and *Wasp* are 3/32" square at the head and 2" long. If wooden capstans are used on *Isaac Webb*, the bars are square and of the same dimensions as already given.

Although they were unshipped when not in use, capstan bars were not stowed below so they must be properly stowed if gear is to look complete. Racks for stowing capstan bars consisted of wide planks with appropriately sized holes to receive the bars. They were arranged for either vertical or horizontal stowage near the capstan. Typical racks are shown in Fig. 108. Rack members are spaced so one eighth of the bars protrude and are made of 1/16" stock on the war vessels and 1/32" stock on *Isaac Webb*. Holes should be a snug-slide fit using a drop of glue or cement on each bar to hold them in place. The rack on *Lexington* is mounted on the athwartship bulkhead above the hatch. There is no readily available space on *Wasp*, so fit a deep rack allowing bars to lay fore and aft above the nearest hatch. Bar length may have to be increased to 2 1/4" to stow properly. Stow *Isaac Webb*'s forecastle capstan bars horizontally on each side of the bulwarks just aft of the forecastle deck. Her poop deck capstan bars are stowed on poop deck bulwarks just forward of the boat davits.

WINDLASS

A windlass is a mechanism similar to a capstan except that it has two barrels and its axis is horizontal. Its primary use is anchor hoisting. It is interesting to note that war vessels were generally fitted with capstans and merchantmen with windlasses. Although both are sophisticated pieces of equipment and driven by electric motors on modern vessels, this tradition has been carried through to today.

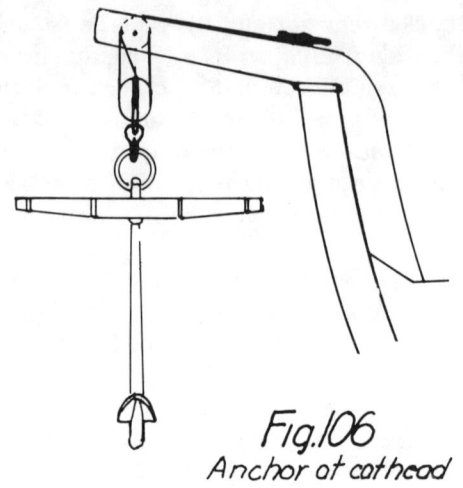

Fig. 106
Anchor at cathead

Fig. 107
Typical iron capstan

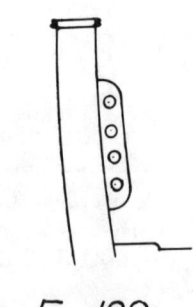

Fig. 108
Capstan bar rack

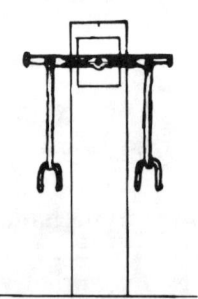

Fig. 109
Front view of windlass rocker arm and linkages

Since windlasses are very difficult to make, the modeler is fortunate in that only *Helen B. Thomas* has to be fitted with one. As has been stated before, *Isaac Webb*'s capstan was so far under her forecastle that it doesn't have to be fitted and *Margaret Haskell*'s steam driven windlass was below deck.

Construction is shown in Plate II. Note that barrels are turned, exclusive of the whelps on the starboard barrel. Smaller diameters are turned between the barrels and winch heads on each end to fit in a hole shown in the bitts in Section C-C. The heavy post forward of the capstan's center line was called a pawl post and was fitted with a pawl that trailed in a toothed, iron gear to prevent reverse rotation. The pawl can be made of sheet copper with its forward edge looped around a staple driven into the after side of the pawl post. Section A-A can be a bit confusing because the pawl as labeled is the one just described and is behind the section.

The parts labeled "ratchet gear" and "ratchet housing" are in Section A-A and are directly connected. The ratchet gears had rings cast on their sides which fitted within circular grooves in the housings so they remain attached and can be moved along the gear. A pawl within the housing engaged the gear in such a way that when the housing was lifted it engaged and when lowered it disengaged. This ratchet housing and its mate on the other side were connected to the rocker arm by linkages, as shown in both the plate and Fig. 109. The capstan was turned by inserting heaver bars into the rocker arm and working them in a seesaw motion. One pawl housing was being lifted while the other was dropping, until the motion of the heavers was reversed and each housing changed function. By this action the windlass barrel was rotated counterclockwise, as viewed from starboard.

When shaping the barrels, turn the one to port in the curved shape shown and the one to starboard in a straight taper, according to dotted lines. One set of whelps on the starboard side is made of small, square stock with mating surfaces curved to match the barrel diameter. They are full-length and are set 90° apart. The short, high whelps are shaped as shown and mounted between the others on the inboard end of the barrel. Whelps on the port barrel were iron strapping let into the barrel so their surfaces were nearly flush. These can be simulated by gluing narrow strips of paper at 45° intervals around the barrel. This windlass is too small to attempt cutting teeth on the gear for the center pawl or on the pawl gears, but they look very realistic just painted black.

Pawl housings are shaped from 1/16" thick maple and glued to surfaces which represent the pawl gears. The linkage is made of 1/32" or smaller diameter wire. The rocker arm is made as Chapter IX describes for pumps. It was pivoted on an iron casting which can be simulated with a wood block of appropriate thickness having an escutcheon pin for the pivot bolt.

Heavers are made as shown and should be just long enough to allow standing room between their bars and the bulwarks, with a bend in their ends so the bars are parallel to the rails when viewed from above. Stow the heavers alongside of and lashed to the anchor shanks. Sufficient dimensions are given in Plate II to establish proportions of parts.

Modelers who do not have access to a lathe must purchase this windlass. Select one from model supply houses which sell quarter-inch-scale kits of fishing schooners. Be careful not to purchase a more modern type or one driven by steam or electric motor.

Isaac Webb's windlass was operated by heavers in a rocker arm on the forecastle with long linkages through the deck to pawl castings below. The rocker arm and upper linkage is like that used on *Helen B. Thomas*, scaled to half-size. Do not bother with heavers because they were stowed under the forecastle deck.

Finish homemade windlasses with dark brown stain and paint the metal whelps, gears, and pawl castings with flat black. Purchased windlasses have to be treated so they look the same but the material from which they are made will govern what is used.

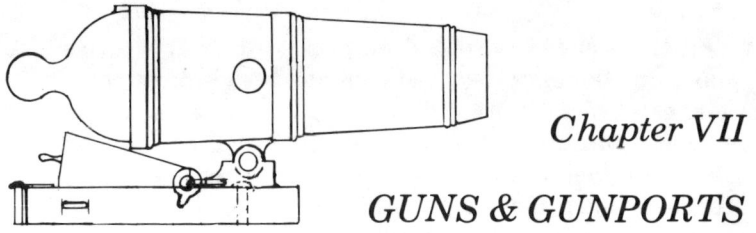

Chapter VII
GUNS & GUNPORTS

The only reason for the existence of sailing men-of-war such as *Lexington* and *Wasp* was to serve as floating batteries regardless of whether they were actively engaged in warfare, showing the flag in some foreign port, or just part of the nation's naval strength in peacetime. Because the battery was an important part of the vessel's equipment, guns were mounted and fitted with care. Consequently, armament on models must also be made with care.

As the Revolutionary War approached, colonists had difficulty obtaining guns suitable for arming vessels. Embargoes which included guns before the war and an effective blockade once hostilities commenced made it almost impossible for the Continental Navy to procure desired armament. Therefore, early American war vessels were armed with whatever was available. *Lexington* was probably armed with whatever 4-pounder guns could be found. Even as late as 1797, some of the large guns for the *Constellation* and *Constitution* class of frigates were purchased in England. By the time *Wasp* was built, suitable guns were available either from American foundries or from abroad but, regardless of where the armament was manufactured, the U.S. Navy was following British practice. Therefore, the drawings of guns, their carriages, and mounts are typical of English armament at the end of the eighteenth century.

Guns for *Lexington* and *Wasp* were of two types. The first, the carriage gun, was manufactured in two lengths for a given bore. Those in the battery along the sides were shorter with less range. Longer guns, if installed, were mounted farthest forward and had more range. These were called chase guns and were so mounted that they could be fired at fleeing craft. In desperate circumstances aboard the fleeing vessel these guns were hauled aft and fired at the pursuer through stern ports. The second type was called a carronade, a heavy, short bore gun with very limited range. It was easier to handle and, for equal barrel weights, fired a heavier shot than the carriage gun. Guns, regardless of whether they were carriage or carronade type, were designated by weight of a round shot fired.

In battle, long range was not necessarily critical because guns were not accurate and aiming was done without aid of sights. Therefore, vessels fired at each other at close range. Frequently one vessel sailed alongside the other and the issue was settled on deck with pistol, cutlass, and boarding pike after the aggressor had poured a broadside at point-blank into the other vessel. Vessels preparing for battle in two-ship engagements maneuvered for advantage. One very advantageous position was had while crossing the other vessel's path where the favored vessel could rake or fire a broadside down the length of the other with little danger from return fire. The other position was to windward of the other vessel which gave the favored craft two advantages. Firstly, the favored vessel showed far less hull to the other. Secondly, her guns recoiled "uphill" as opposed to those on the leeward vessel that recoiled "downhill" and had to be hauled or pushed back to fire.

Plate III shows these two types of guns, their mounts, hardware around the ports, and accessories.

Carriage gun mounts were wagon-like assemblies that moved in a straight line on trucks. The guns tilted on the trunnions to obtain proper elevation. Elevation was maintained and controlled by a wedge-shaped quoin under the breech. Recoil was arrested and controlled by a heavy rope called a breeching. A turn in the middle of the breeching was slid over the cascabel. Each end was led through one breeching ringbolt and thence to one of the pair of ringbolts on each side of the port at sill level. The second ringbolt of each pair was used in the event that the other broke or pulled out. Breechings were of sufficient length to allow guns to roll back so their muzzles were at least a foot inside the bulwarks for loading.

Carriages were slewed sidewise to a limited angle for changes in azimuth. The slewing was done by side tackles with one end hooked into the side tackle eyebolts and the other to ringbolts spaced some distance from the ports. In the heat of battle when slewing had to be done in a hurry, a heavy, oak-handled, iron shod implement, shaped and used like a crowbar, was employed in conjunction with the side tackles. There were two eyebolts located centrally and slightly above the pair of breeching ringbolts. Temporary tackles were hooked to these eyebolts and to the carriages of heavier guns to haul them forward into battery. These eyebolts were probably not fitted on *Lexington* because her guns could be rolled around by hand. *Wasp* was fitted with these eyebolts but tackles should not be rigged.

In heavy weather carriage guns had to be secured from breaking loose and running uncontrolled on deck. Guns were run-in, the quoin removed and carriages hauled forward, muzzles forced against the bulwarks over the port. Then each muzzle was lashed to two eyebolts. There were two eyebolts on the carriage, not shown, one in the fore and the other in the after axletree. The forward one, for hauling the guns around deck, was called a transporting bolt. The one in the after axletree was called a train bolt, which in action was connected by a tackle to the ringbolt behind each gunport, as shown in the deck plans. This tackle was used to haul guns inboard and hold them there while loading.

Carronades were mounted on a two-part, semi-fixed assembly. The lower piece, called a skid, rested on the port sill where it was swung in azimuth about the pivot bolt. Trucks set crosswise supported the after end and permitted easy and rapid aiming. Recoil was provided by the slide which was guided in its motion by bolts in a skid slot. Trunnions varied, but it is quite certain those on *Wasp*'s carronades were part of a lug beneath the barrel. However, carronades during that period were built with trunnions one-third or halfway up the barrel's diameter and the slide was fitted with small brackets like those for carriage guns. Breechings were fitted as described for carriage guns. Side tackles were hooked to the skid. Sill tackles were hooked to the slide, but can be omitted if the builder chooses. Rings and eyebolts in the bulwarks for working carronades were placed on identical locations as those for carriage guns except for those over the ports which were not necessary because their mounts did not travel. Train tackles also were not required, but it is likely ringbolts were fitted in the deck so carriage guns could be worked at the ports in an emergency.

GUNS

Batteries consisted of sixteen 4-pounder guns on *Lexington* and sixteen 32-pounder carronades with two 12-pounder chase guns on *Wasp*. Barrels were cast in one piece of iron including cascabel, trunnions, and bore. Model barrels can be cast in sand, turned on a lathe, or purchased from a model supply house. Brass is preferable to other materials because it turns or casts well and changes to a dark color with age which resembles weathered black paint. Barrels made of any other material must be painted dull black. Barrels shown in Plate III are typical of those used but it is almost impossible to include all of the detail. Those drawn in detail sheets show sufficient detail to look realistic.

Patterns for casting barrels are made of close-grained wood such as boxwood. It is suggested that trunnions be included on the patterns. Only one pattern should be made for each size of barrel so duplicate castings will be identical. To prevent warping, patterns should be well oiled before use. Casting sand must be fine and clean and sufficiently moistened with glycerine or water to guarantee close and even packing. Parts of the casting flask must align perfectly and only clean molten brass should be poured.

Turned barrels must be made on a lathe with a reasonably accurate graduated compound. Saw a sufficient number of pieces from brass round stock about 3/4" longer than the barrel. Turn a square-shouldered stud on one end about 1/4" long and center-drill the other. If a collet is available, make the stud to fit it; if not, mark the stock and one chuck jaw so the piece can be returned to the same exact location each time it is replaced. When placing pieces in the lathe make sure the shoulder is hard up against the nose of the collet or chuck jaws and that the tailstock center is properly set. So all guns in the run will be alike, it is recommended that turning with each tool be completed on each piece in succession using the graduations both crosswise and lengthwise on the compound. A trick used by machinists, which is frequently unknown to amateurs, consists of marking the dials and non-mating surfaces of compound slides for reference when making several different cuts on each piece.

Make the gun with its cascabel on the tailstock end. Rough down the outside diameter with a standard roundnosed tool. Turn cylindrical and tapered sections with a bit similar to a cutoff tool modified with suitable rake for turning. Raised trim around the barrels is left square until all are turned and then a radius is filed on each corner while the lathe is running. The bell muzzle radius can be turned with a roundnosed graver on a steady rest. A properly ground form tool can be used to shape the breech end and half of the cascabel. At this point the ends are cut off to length and the rest of the cascabel filed round. All model gun barrels tend to be muzzle-heavy, so they are bored back to the trunnions. This is done by chucking each barrel, lightly center drilling and boring. Bore sizes are 1/16" for 4-pounders, 3/32" for 12-pounders and 1/8" for 32-pounders.

Barrels can be purchased from model supply houses by modelers who do not wish to make them. Purchased barrels are usually shaped slightly different than shown and exact lengths may not be obtainable but barrels within 1/8" to proper length are satisfactory. Founders did not necessarily adhere strictly to specifications anyway and this difference on the model represents only 6" on the vessel.

Modelers without suitable machinery have to drill by hand for the bores and trunnions. Make sure the bore is centrally located in the muzzle and that the trunnion holes closely follow the barrel's diameter. Also, trunnion holes in *Wasp*'s carronades for the alternate mounting position must be bored, shown in Plate III. Modelers with lathes can turn rings, as shown in Fig. 110, from which lugs can be sawed and filed to shape. Lug trunnions are 1/16" in diameter. Hard solder lugs to the barrel. Except for barrels with trunnions included, trunnions are made of copper or brass wire soft soldered in place using a minimum of solder. Each trunnion should extend about twice its diameter outside the barrel so it can be filed square and flush with the outer sides of the brackets.

CARRIAGES

Carriage parts must be made from a reasonably hard, close-grained wood such as birch or maple. The exact shape of brackets, trucks, etc., is given in detail sheets. Widths of carriages shown are for barrels with the shapes drawn. If barrels differ in diameter or taper, make width at the trunnions just slightly larger than barrel's diameter and the lengthwise taper equal to that of barrel's from breech to trunnions. Aprons, brackets, and transoms are made of material the same thickness as bore's diameter. Axletrees are made of square stock with same dimensions as the bore. Blocking and quoins are sized as shown.

For guns and their carriages to look well, there must be no noticeable variation between carriage assemblies. To assure that all parts are alike, saw them in a miter box; then these identical parts are glued together on a jig.

A typical miniature miter box is shown in Fig. 98. The bottom is pine with maple sides. Surfaces of each piece must be flat and parallel. Glue the sides to the bottom without permanent metal fastenings. Use a very fine-toothed backsaw with a blade 6" long by 3/4" wide. The kerfs are made with this saw after carefully drawing guidelines. It is worthwhile to make several boxes of varying widths and depths to suit the work at hand. They can be invaluable in producing several identical parts, and if used carefully, their useful life is almost unlimited. Kerfs can be made to cut pieces perfectly square, beveled vertically, beveled horizontally or any combination. By clamping a piece of wood to the bottom or one side of the box with its end a measured distance from the kerf, an endless number of identical pieces of perfect length can be sawed off simply by sliding the stock firmly against the stop before sawing.

A typical gluing jig is shown in Fig. 111. The locating pieces are arranged and fastened on a smooth board so the finished assembly is exactly symmetrical about the center line. The configuration, as drawn, allows the brackets, transoms, and axletrees to be glued together as one unit and yet be removed from the jig after the glue has dried. This assembly has all the rigidity necessary to allow the breast pieces, trucks, quoins, and ironwork with rigging to be installed and fitted without distortion.

Start work on the carriages by making brackets. Set the stop to exact length of brackets and saw off a complete complement plus a couple of extras to allow for mishaps. Then reset the stop for cutting the first step. Depth of cut can be gauged by sawing down to the surface of a piece of hardwood, equal in thickness to height of the step above the bottom of bracket. Each step is consecutively sawed down. After sawing is completed, score top surface of each step on each side using a marking gauge and cut away excess with a knife. Pair brackets at this point. There is a

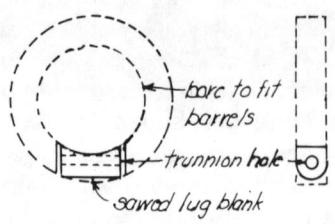

Fig. 110
Rings for making carronade lugs

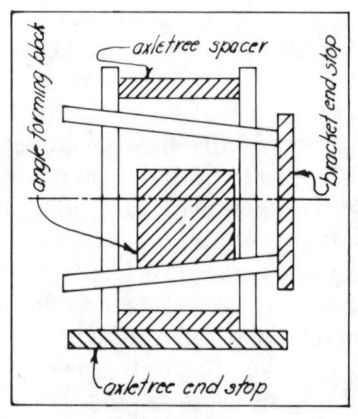

Fig. 111
Carriage gluing jig

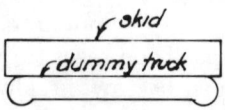

Fig. 112
Dummy trucks for carronades

slight curved portion in the lower edge of each bracket between axletrees. Set each pair in a vise and file this curve on both to finish the brackets.

Transoms are beveled slightly on each end to establish the carriage's vertical taper. Their length determines side clearance between barrels and brackets described before. They must be deep enough to reach within 3/32" of the top of brackets. After gluing, their upper edges are worked down with a round file to provide clearance for the barrel. Transoms tilt slightly, so their lower edges should be beveled. The exact angle is fixed by the jig.

Forward axletrees are square and of the same dimensions as the gun's bore, with ends rounded to receive the trucks. Rear axletrees are double the bore in width and equal to it in depth between brackets, with square horns on each end rounded off to receive the trucks. The extra width of these axletrees is a deviation from actual practice to provide a "bed" for the quoin. In actual practice, quoins set on a bed and stool inside the carriages, but this arrangement is not necessary on models.

Trucks can be turned and bored on a lathe or made by cutting off lengths of previously bored dowels of appropriate diameter. Bores in trucks made by the latter method will not be exactly centered and must be rotated slightly so all set firmly on deck. Only a slight touch of glue is required to hold them on.

It is optional whether breast pieces are fitted because they are nearly hidden by the barrel and breeching. However, they can be custom fitted and glued in place.

Make and install the eye- and ringbolts for both carriages and bulwarks. Stock for breeching ringbolts should be about one-fifth the bore's diameter; that for all others should be one-sixth. Inside diameter of breeching ringbolt rings should be at least half the bore. Drill snug-fitting holes for all eye- and ringbolts in the bulwarks and install all except the breeching ringbolts closest to the gunports. Make the shanks short enough so they will not break through. Grip the eye of each in needle-nosed pliers, apply a drop of airplane cement and push them in until the eyes are snug to the surface. Eye- and ringbolts in carriages must be secured reasonably well to hold while installing rigging. Bore holes slightly undersized and flatten or score shanks slightly before setting them in cement.

Score brackets with a fine round file to receive the lower half of the trunnion. Then drill snug-fitting holes on one side of the scores about 1/4" into each bracket. These holes are fitted with the shank of a curved, flattened section which encircles the top of each trunnion. Make the quoin and fit it under the breech so barrel is level. Glue it in place and recheck barrel level. Set a small belaying pin in its large end to simulate a handle. Finish the carriage by setting the shanks of the curved metal clamps in cement to hold trunnions in the brackets. Rigging of breechings and tackles is described later in this chapter.

CARRONADE MOUNTS

Skids are made to dimensions and shape shown in detail sheets. The slot for the fighting bolt can be omitted. However, with a little effort, neat, straight slots can be made as shown in Plate III. Ends are rounded with a small, round file. Then surfaces are sanded flat and outside cut to shape.

Although trucks are nearly hidden, dummies must be made to support the rear end of the skid. An easily made appropriate shape is shown in Fig. 112. Their heights are cut so skids are level when forward ends rest on the step under the port sill.

Slides are shaped as shown. If the alternate method is used, the slide must be tapered to parallel the sides of the barrel from the trunnion to the breech with allowance for clearance, as described for carriages. Brackets for alternate mounts are sawed and cut like those for carriages. If trunnion lugs are used, the trunnion bosses are made of maple, shaped and bored through in pairs. Then one boss is glued to the slide, the carronade trunnion pushed through, and the other boss glued down after pushing it into the other trunnion. Setting of quoins, eyebolts and ringbolts, etc., follows the description for carriage guns regardless of which type slide is used.

Before gluing slides in place, holes must be bored for the pivot bolts. These holes are bored down from the sheer, through port and into the step below the sill. An escutcheon pin makes an excellent pivot bolt and can be pushed all the way down with pliers. Then the slide can be glued to the skid.

Wooden parts of gun carriages were usually painted red on *Lexington* and *Wasp* when they were in commission. However, since carronade barrels weighed a ton and the gun and its slide had to be hauled forward after each discharge, it is reasonable to assume that mating surfaces of slides and skids were bare with cooking grease liberally applied and dark brown in color.

ACCESSORIES

Accessories were the implements used while working the guns. These can be made by those who have patience to miniaturize parts. It is helpful to those who wish to make these parts to understand their function; each is drawn in Plate III.

Handspikes were crowbar-like implements, referred to earlier in this chapter. They were 5' long, made from 2 1/2" square oak. The handle end was 1 1/2" in diameter and tapered for 3'; then it became octagonal for 6". The rest was square with one face rounded off. A metal shoe started at the end of the octagonal section, down over the radius and back up the other side. In addition to slewing, carriage gun handspikes were used to lever up the breech so the quoin could be moved.

Rammers were used to load the piece. First, powder in bags were inserted in the bore, followed by a canvas wad, called a selvagee. The rammer was used to drive both into the breech. Then the ball, followed by another selvagee, was driven against the first selvagee and the gun was ready to run out for firing. Rammer heads were slightly smaller than the bore in diameter and the same length. Head faces were hollowed with the same radius as that of the shot. Rammer staffs were slightly longer than the bore and had grooves cut circumferentially at appropriate intervals to show the size of the powder charge.

Sponges were used to swab out the bore after each firing and to extinguish any sparks in remaining pieces of powder bags or selvagees. The heads were 8'' long and an inch smaller than the bore and their staff ends had a slight taper. Heads were covered with sheepskin sheered to fit tightly in the bore. Sponge staffs were long enough to extend slightly beyond the muzzle when the heads were driven full-depth in the bore.

Ladles were used to remove unfired charges from the guns. Their heads were shaped as part of a truncated cone, three times the bore in length and 1/16'' less in diameter than the bore on its larger end. Heads were cut back two-thirds their length so that one-third of the circumference on the larger end remained. The inside was hollowed out to produce a shell thickness of 5/16'' with a long internal chamfer at the head end so the edge left was 1/16'' measured radially. Staffs were long enough to extend 4'' beyond the muzzle when the heads were driven as far into the bore as possible.

Sponge tubs were used to soak sponge heads during action. The tubs were somewhat oval in shape with tapering sides held together by brass hoops. Each top was made of heavy timber rabbeted around its lower edge so it fitted snugly with only a thin lip above to cover the tub's upper edge.

In time of war, implements were stowed in leather slings nailed to bulwarks on each side of the port at about chest height. The ladle and handspike were slung on the right with rammer and sponge to the left. Sponge tubs were located between guns about 2' from bulwarks. In peace time this equipment was normally stowed below.

Because this paraphernalia was not necessarily stowed above deck, it is perfectly acceptable to omit these parts but, if any are fitted, the whole compliment must be rigged. Rammer, sponge, and ladle heads can be turned from boxwood on a small lathe at high speed. Each head is drilled through the center for a fine wire staff. Ladle heads are cut as shown and hollowed slightly. Handspikes are made of boxwood stock, a strong 1/32'' square. Sponge tubs are fashioned from an appropriately-sized, oval, wood rod. File an appropriate taper on the end and saw off to length equal to 18''. Repeat for each tub. Make covers of very thin wood shaped to fit the sponge tub tops, and round the edges slightly. Implements and tubs are stained medium brown. Sponge heads are dark gray to represent sheep's wool soiled with burned gunpowder. Handspikes are painted a dull black at the shoe. Brass bands near the top and bottom of sponge tubs are simulated with gold paint covered with varnish.

Model's implements are stowed in short lengths of rigging twine with ends glued into holes in bulwarks just below the rails. Since these holes have to be quite large, it helps to drive a small, round tapered plug after the ends; cut flush. Sponge tubs are nailed to the deck with fine brads before tops are glued on.

RIGGING FOR CARRIAGES & MOUNTS

Carriage guns are rigged with side tackles and breechings. Breechings are the most difficult to rig. They must be quite large twine adequately long to have a turn around the cascabel with each end long enough to reach the bulwarks with the muzzle 1/4" inside the bulwarks. To make this neat, the ends should be spliced into their ringbolts. Cut enough pieces somewhat too long and splice a ringbolt into one end of each. Then, with a gun set on deck, rig breeching temporarily to establish where the other splice goes. Reeve unspliced ends through breeching ringbolts and splice in other ringbolts so all breechings for one type of gun are of equal length. Set guns in place and drill small holes through two trucks on opposite corners. Nail them down lightly but firmly with lill pins to prevent shifting. Now the ringbolts can be pushed with pliers into the unused holes close to the sills. Then take one turn in the center of the breeching with ends rove off the top, with a drop of cement to hold the turn in place. These will appear awkward at first because the line is stiff, but in a short while it will take on a natural sag. Side tackles are gun tackles with hooks stropped in the blocks and the becket block is hooked to the carriage. Rather than using separate ringbolts for each tackle between guns at bulwarks, one can be used with a triangular ring for hooking both tackles. Ends of side tackle falls should be left about 6" too long, coiled and tied to the block at the carriage.

Breeching and side tackles for carronades are fitted similar to those for carriage guns. If sill tackles are fitted they are hooked up similar to side tackles.

Side tackle blocks on both models are 5/32". Sill tackle blocks for *Wasp*'s carronades are 3/16" if fitted.

GUNPORTS & SHUTTERS

Gunports were located in the space between frames to form their sides. Heavy blocking between frames parallel to the deck formed the sills and headers. Planking was stopped a couple of inches away from the opening to form a rabbet all the way around. Shutters fitted into these rabbets when ports were closed. There was more than one way to rig port shutters but those on *Lexington* and *Wasp* were split horizontally. Each lower half was hinged to the hull so when they were open they stood horizontally and were held up with a small chain on each side. The upper halves were hooked to the sides when in place and were removed altogether when ports were open. Normally, ports above the weather deck were left open unless guns were run in because of heavy weather.

Locations of ports are shown in the sheer plans. Their sides are laid out carefully. Locate one side of each with a knife point and step off the width of each port with dividers so they will be exactly the same width. Sills and headers are located temporarily since ultimately the height of each sill will have to be set a measured distance above deck. Remember that sides are perpendicular to the waterline. Score sides at mid-height and cut ports through to make a narrow slot without splitting the inside surfaces. Note that the sides of ports forward of *Wasp*'s catheads were not perpendicular to the center line as were others. They were more or less perpendicular to planking because frames close to the bow were canted to eliminate excessive bevels. Now cut a square piece of stock 2" long, exactly the same height as sills are above deck. Place this gauge on deck and cut down the ports until the sills match. Then make a piece of wood the same depth as the ports to use as a gauge when cutting up to the headers.

Sills for *Wasp*'s carronade ports are below the planking line, as shown in detail sheet. Cut ports through to the sills and fit a dutchman which overlaps each side of the ports by about 1/8" and 1/32" deep to simulate planking. After the glue is dry, lightly sand the outside until surfaces are smooth and flush with those adjacent on the hull.

A very simple means of attaching lower shutters is to make them of 1/32" thick stock and glue them on flush with the lower part of the opening. Hinges can be made or purchased but they are hidden anyway and are very difficult to fasten to the thin section of *Wasp*'s carronade ports.

It is also advisable to omit cutting the rabbet around outside of the ports because it in only about 1/32" wide and deep. There is a potential risk of splitting the outside surface, it is very difficult to obtain smooth bottom surfaces, and paint tends to fill it in.

Reference was made in Chapter VI to stowage of *Wasp*'s anchors in the forward gunports. Obviously, because of their weight and size, considerable juggling had to be done to work the arms through the port. It is equally obvious that a hinged lower lid could be severely damaged during the operation. Therefore, without better information, it would seem that the lid was made in one piece and fitted with hooks to hold it in place during heavy weather when all other ports were closed. Otherwise, it would have been stowed below and need not be shown on the model.

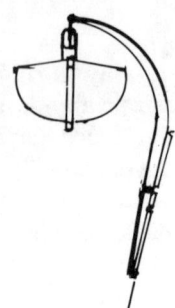

Chapter VIII
BOATS & DAVITS

Carefully made, properly stowed boats add immeasurably to the appearance of models. The type of boat, its cost and method of stowage varied considerably with date of building and use of the mother ship.

Genuine war vessels were fitted with several boats of various types, ranging in quantity from five on a brig to twelve on a ship of the line. These boats were designed to row easily and were very well constructed. Launches and cutters were workboats. Launches were the largest and cutters the next smaller. Both were square-sterned. Whaleboats were light rowing and sailing boats of lighter displacement than cutters. Gigs were long, narrow, fast rowing boats for the captain's use. Barges were usually ornate whaleboat-type craft for a flag officer's transportation in port. Whaleboats were double-enders; i.e., pointed on each end. All others had square sterns.

While the vessels were in port, their boats were either suspended over the side from davits or were moored at boat booms alongside. There was always work for these boats, such as making hull repairs, carrying stores, liberty boat duty, dispatch boat duty, and transporting officers. At sea, large war vessels stowed boats below the weather deck. Smaller vessels like *Wasp* stowed all boats on the weather deck except for one in the stern davits. Where more than two boats were stowed on deck, they were nested. Nests consisted of the largest boats set in cradles on deck with the thwarts, or seats, removed and successively smaller boats cradled therein. Where only two boats were stowed on deck they were either cradled side by side or in a two-boat nest. Before battle, boats stowed on deck were frequently put overboard and cast adrift to be picked up by the victor after the fray. This was done to clear the decks and to eliminate a source of flying splinters when hit by gunshot.

Launches, cutters, and whaleboats were usually painted white throughout, with top strake and gunwales black. Sometimes a square-sterned boat's transom was also painted black. Normally these otherwise painted black areas made of a dark wood were varnished. Gigs and barges were of a bright finish or otherwise according to the officer's whim.

Large merchantmen like *Isaac Webb* carried two heavy square-sterned boats upside down on skid beams over the forward house roof and carried two lighter whaleboats in davits on either side between main and mizzen rigging. These lighter boats could be lowered at sea for a "man overboard" and could be used in port for transportation ashore and back if water taxis were not available. All boats were used if the vessel had to be abandoned. Usually these were painted throughout. A common color scheme was white with dark upper works, as described for those on war vessels.

Fishing schooners, like *Helen B. Thomas*, while engaged in groundfishing on the banks, nested an equal number of dories on each side of the deck between masts. They were swung over the side and hoisted back with special tackles hooked to each crosstree. Davits were not required to handle the light dories. In general, dories remained nested on board except when fishing. They were painted such colors as brown, buff, green, or gray.

Large colliers, like *Margaret Haskell*, had little use for boats except for abandoning ship. Even under this extreme condition, a small boat was adequate to carry the entire crew. Usually these vessels anchored in busy ports where water taxis or agents' boats were available so a boat was not required to go ashore. These boats were heavily constructed and square-sterned, customarily slung in stern davits. Usually they were fitted with a slow-turning, inboard engine connected to a three-bladed propeller and were painted like those on *Isaac Webb*.

Research has revealed nothing concerning *Lexington*'s boats, but books describing contemporary craft indicate their shape. Because she was outfitted under trying circumstances, it is likely few were fitted. The frontispiece of *Lexington* shows a reasonable scheme of two square-sterned boats stowed upright on either side just forward of the deck break. A full complement was provided on all other models. *Wasp* was not fitted with a gig because her commander was probably a senior lieutenant and did not rate one. Hence, his boat was probably a light whaleboat slung in permanent stern davits. The other boats were nested between the fore- and mainmasts. Boat stowage on other models is similar to that already described. Boats slung in davits along the side were hoisted with bows forward and on the stern with bows to starboard. Plans for each boat or nest of boats are drawn in detail sheets. Typical construction methods and steps are shown in Plate IV.

SINGLE BOAT CONSTRUCTION

The boats on *Isaac Webb*'s forward house are the easiest type to make since they are mounted bottom up and only the outside needs to be shaped. The description under Method 1, Chapter I, is applicable; i.e., from a suitably-sized block carve the side profile, gunwale shape and sides; follow by fitting stem, rudderpost, and keel. After painting, they are ready to fasten on skid beams.

There are two ways to make open, upright, unnested boats. The first consists of hollowing out the hull after shaping, as already described, followed by fitting risers, floorboards, thwarts, and gunwales. The second consists of building a stem, keel, rudderpost, and counter assembly and gluing very thin shells to it, representing planking on each half of the hull. Then ribs, risers, floorboards, thwarts, etc., are fitted to make a realistic approximation of a built-up rowboat. Obviously, the latter is more difficult to build.

When making hollowed out hulls, carve out the interior before fitting stem, keel, and sternpost. The hull is hollowed out so the skin is as thin as possible. It is preferable to cut the transom away to allow better access for carving the interior. A reasonable thickness is 1/16" in the bottom tapered to 1/32" at the gunwales. While working on interior, hold the hull up to a strong light to find thicker areas, and make sides as uniform as possible in thickness. When sanding is completed, make a transom from 1/32" thick birch to fit in the stern with grain running horizontally.

It is impossible to keep a wooden boat totally free of water, so a platform composed of thin boards set 1/4" apart supported on crosswise pieces, called floors, was installed a few inches off the bottom to raise passenger feet above the wet bilge. Unless indicated otherwise, the lowest waterlines for each open boat drawn in detail sheets are at floorboard level. Boards should be a scant 1/32" thick, glued to floors of same thickness. Make the assembly slightly larger than that shown in top views and fit in place by cutting and sanding the outside to shape, then bevel floors so it fits in place snugly without forcing. Glue floors down to prevent warping.

Seats, or thwarts, are spaced along the hull in locations and elevations shown in the boat's sheer plan. A relatively small strip, called a riser, runs from bow to stern to support these members. Risers in miniature boats should not be over 1/32" square. After they are sprung in and glued in place at the proper elevation, make seats of 1/32" thick birch or maple and glue them to the risers. Then glue a 1/32" square strip on the inside at sheer level, with knees in the quarters and a breasthook in the bow.

Plans for each single upright boat drawn in detail sheets include drawings of stem, keel, rudderpost, and counter assemblies for modelers who wish to build the more exotic type. Stems and keels will protrude inside like actual construction does. Shells should be glued to the stem, keel, and edges of the counter. The most critical operations consist of making shells so they are exact mirror images of each other and fitting them to the backbone in exact symmetry. Templates for profile and top view shapes are made of sheet metal with locating pinholes so they will fit each block, from which the shells are made exactly the same. See Plate IV. Also, aligning holes near each end of the profile template allows drilling holes in each shell and backbone so that snug-fitting brads (through all three parts) will assure perfect alignment when gluing them together. After glue is dry, brads are removed and holes filled with wood filler.

Start work on shells by marking the profile shape on both sides of each one. Then drill shallow holes for the locating pins on the inside surfaces and screw template in place. Shape profile to the marks and to the profile template. Continue by locating the top template and screwing it in place. Cut down the outside and, with both templates still screwed in place, shape the outside of each shell in turn. Leaving the templates in place tends to increase accuracy and helps prevent turning the edges while shaping or applying station templates and during final sanding.

After the outside of each shell is finished, bore aligning holes from the profile template and remove both templates. By careful work the inside can be carved out to leave a very thin skin. Thicknesses between 1/64" and 1/32" are not extraordinary. The trick mentioned earlier of holding hulls up to a strong light can be applied equally well to the shells for checking uniformity of thickness. Be careful not to turn the edges while sanding the insides because gluing will be difficult.

Stem, keel, and rudderpost assemblies are made of birch or maple and shaped as drawn. The keel should be extended up just enough so its upper surface is flush with the inside of the shell. Deadwoods on each end receive the lower end of the ribs; all other ribs run continuously from gunwale to gunwale. Counters are cut to shape minus the thickness of the shells and are fitted before shells are glued in place.

After shells are glued to the backbone and aligning brads withdrawn, the hull is ready to frame out. Purchased basswood strips 1/32" square make ideal framing and represent stock about 1 1/2" square at a 1/4" scale. Drawings show frame locations and spacing which is transferred to the inside of the hull. Each frame can be worked close to shape by bending with the hands. After each fits the hull reasonably well, force it into place by pushing down on each end at the top. When a perfect fit is achieved, apply a light coat of glue and replace it in the hull. Wooden clothespins make ideal clamps to hold frames in while glue is drying. When successive frames are fitted, check for parallelism and spacing against those already installed. After all frames are installed, cut off the excess above the rail and sand flush with the sheer.

Risers should be about twice as wide and somewhat thinner than frames which, in these boats, can be made of 1/16" wide stock sanded to a strong 1/64" thick. Bend these in and glue in place. Before going on, make and fit floors and floorboards. Then seats and thwarts can be fitted, followed by the rail, etc. Knees are fitted in the quarters and a breasthook in the bow. Knees on each side of each thwart on their ends, made of 1/32" thick stock, add to hull appearance but are not absolutely essential.

NESTED ROUND-BOTTOMED BOATS

Each of the nests on *Wasp* consists of two boats. The lower is a launch with a cutter inside. Launches are made as described for the boats on *Isaac Webb*'s forward house. Only those parts of the cutters above the launches' sheer are made and glued on. Plans of the nests are drawn in *Wasp*'s detail sheet. Construction methods are shown in Plate IV.

Each cutter's profile is cut to shape with particular attention paid to mating surfaces. Shapes at top and bottom are drawn on the blocks and the sides carved by eye; then glue them down. Follow by carving out the inside according to templates cut from the plan. When the inside is done and sanded, fit the floors, floorboards, risers, seats, etc., as described for open, upright boats.

DORIES

Although dories were not stowed singly, it is helpful to understand a single dory's construction and to visualize what its interior looked like and how they were nested. Refer to Plate IV. The bottom consisted of two or three wide boards running lengthwise, held together with a few boards nailed crosswise midway between the locations of future frames. The bottom was sawed to shape and buckled down in the middle so it was about 3" below the ends.

A slender stem was erected forward and narrow, tapered stern board affixed aft. These boards were called tombstones and had a semicircular cut in the center of their tops so the boat could be steadied or directed with an oar in the cut. Frames consisted of long-armed knees which extended from one side of the bottom to the opposite gunwale. Each set consisted of two knees set side by side to form a complete continuous frame. The size of dory used for trawling had five sets of these frames. After these parts were installed on the bottom, sides were planked up with three or four boards to each. A rub rail of oak about 3" wide and 1/2" thick was fastened on the outside at sheer level and a similar but narrower piece was set into the upper ends of the frames inside. A cap rail covered the upper edge of both pieces to form a solid gunwale. Thwart risers ran between the forward and after frames. Each thwart was cut to fit snugly between sides, with a notch in each end to receive the frame. When the thwart was slid over the frames and down onto the riser, it stayed in place without fastenings. There were variations of this design but they were all made so when nested there was about 6" vertically between gunwales, as shown in the detail sheet.

A very easy method for building nests consists of carving the lowest dory to shape by using a profile template and a template for both top and bottom surfaces. Since sides are perfectly straight, except for a slight rounding at the bow, station templates are not necessary. After the lowest dories are shaped, cut the profile to match the exposed portion of each nested dory and make a template for the lower surface. Using the cut profile template and top and bottom templates, shape all of the nested dories. After the highest dory is glued in place, carve out the upper part of the nest to represent the interior. Then fit frames, false stem, and rails to complete nest.

ON-BOARD STOWAGE

Isaac Webb's boats on the forward house set upside down on skid beams, shaped as drawn in the detail sheet. Lashings over each boat rove off through ringbolts in the deckhouse roof near the end of each boat.

Dory nests are lashed to the deck right side up on each side of the main deck just forward of the break. There are four ringbolts on deck at each nest. Lashings between hooks over the rail to these ringbolts hold the nests in place.

Nested boats were set in cradlelike pieces fixed to the deck close to hatches. Each piece is shaped to fit the lowest boat about one quarter of the boat's length from each end. They are made of 1/16″ thick stock and built so the keels are about 1/8″ above deck and extend up the hull about 1/4″ above the rabbet.

DAVITS

Davits were made of both iron and wood. The shift from wood to iron started about 1820 although whalers used the clumsy, awkward wooden ones to the very end—one of their trademarks. The only wooden davits on these models are on the stern of *Wasp*. *Isaac Webb* had iron davits for her whaleboats on each side between the main and mizzen rigging. *Margaret Haskell* had iron davits on her stern.

Wooden stern davits are deepest at the stern. They taper slightly on the upper surfaces toward their forward ends. Lower inboard surfaces are shaped to fit the rail so that davits appear to be an extension of the sheer. Both upper and lower outboard surfaces are tapered, as shown in the sheer plan. When completed and attached, they must align perfectly with each other when viewed from the side. Each davit's outboard end is fitted with two dummy sheaves like those in the catheads. Imitation sheave pins are fitted with an eye in each end. Outboard eyes take the splices in the standing ends of the boat falls and inboard eyes are used to secure a line between davits. Sheaves were also fitted in the inboard ends for main

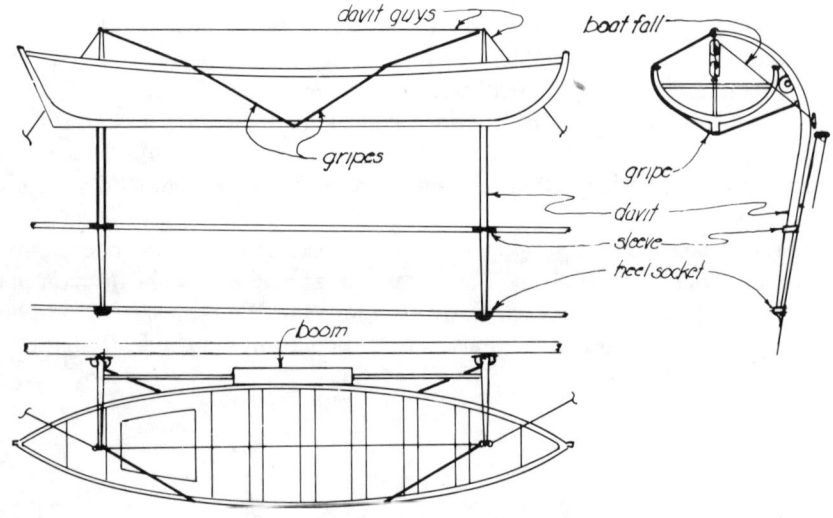

Fig. 113
Boat stowed in davits

braces, as shown in sheer plan. These should be dummies and carved out before davits are fitted. Boat falls are secured to small cleats located on upper surfaces near the inboard ends.

Iron davits were round and were made so their lower ends set in a socket with a sleeve above to allow rotation. See Plate IV. Sockets on *Isaac Webb* are at lower rail level and sleeves are at poop deck rail level. Those on *Margaret Haskell* are set in the main rail and monkey rail, respectively. Each davit's largest diameter is at the sleeve and tapers slightly to the socket. Upper ends have a long curving taper from the sleeve to the end where it is about one-third its largest diameter and terminates with an eye.

Modelers with lathes can shape these davits with a file from brass or copper rod. Turn balls on the outboard ends which are filed on each side and bore through. Modelers without lathes can file davits to shape and bend the eyes into the ends; follow by soldering, as described for eyebolts in the next chapter. After shaping, they are bent to form in pairs as drawn in Plate IV. Note that the upper end of *Isaac Webb*'s davits form a perfect quarter circle and that a tangent to the uppermost part of the davit should be level. Sleeves and sockets for *Isaac Webb* are made up of sheet brass or copper, as shown, with holes for fastening with cut lill pins. *Margaret Haskell*'s davits are inserted into holes in her after rails.

DAVIT RIGGING

Iron davits could rotate in their sleeves and sockets. This was done deliberately to allow suspended boats to be swung inboard, one end at a time, by manipulating davits. At all other times davits were secured in a position perpendicular to the hull. This was done by securing heads together, with guys from each davit to the hull. Guys on *Isaac Webb* were tarred rope with eye splices in each end, seized to the eyes in the davit ends and to eyes in the main and mizzen channels. The span between heads was also tarred rope with its eyes seized to davit heads. *Margaret Haskell* had eyes on the davit and in the upper rail. An iron rod with hooks forged into each end was fitted between each pair of eyes. In addition, a 2" by 8" plank was lashed across the top of the davits close to their eyes. *Wasp*'s davits had a span between the inboard eyes in the sheave pins, rigged as described for those on *Isaac Webb*. Rope or plank spans steadied davits and provided a handhold for the two or three crewmen in the boat while preparing to lower it into the water. Davit rigging on models is identical.

Boats on these models were handled with a double purchase, i.e., double blocks or the equivalent in each boat fall. On *Wasp*, the standing end is spliced into the outboard eyes in the sheave pins and rove off like her catfalls. The hanging blocks are stropped with hooks. Boat falls on *Isaac Webb* and *Margaret Haskell* have hooks stropped into both blocks of each tackle with the standing end of the falls spliced into the tail of each higher block. Each fall should be long enough to allow lower blocks to hang just below the waterline and still be belayed to the cleats. When hoisted, excess is coiled and hung on the cleats.

Lower boat-fall-block hooks were hooked into heavy ringbolts in the bow and stern, spaced the same distance apart as the heads of the davits. The rings were mounted just above the seats, or thwarts, to keep boat's center of gravity below rings to prevent capsizing while being hoisted. After the boats are hoisted and falls secured gripes were rigged to prevent their swinging in the seaway. On these historic vessels, gripes were heavy canvas straps with a ring in each end. One ring of each was lashed to the upper end of the davits. They were then hauled under the boat from outboard and securely lashed to the opposite davit. These straps are too small to miniaturize; rigging lines with an eye splice in each end are used as substitutes. See Fig. 113. On *Wasp* and *Margaret Haskell* the gripes are arranged to haul the boat's inboard gunwale up to and jammed against the underside of the davit in order to prevent chafe. On *Isaac Webb*, a boom with heavy padding in the middle is lashed horizontally to the davits just below the gunwale, and gripes force the boat against the padding. The booms are 1/16" in diameter with padding 1" long and 1/8" in diameter. They are made by rolling 1/8" wide paper saturated with glue onto the boom shaft until the required diameter is obtained.

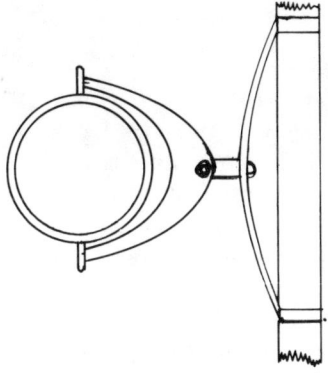

Chapter IX

IRONWORK

Ironwork in varying degrees was used on the vessels of the era covered in this book. Most iron parts used on *Lexington* and *Wasp* were on the hull and about the deck. During the next half century rigging was being refined and perfected at an accelerated pace. *Isaac Webb* had many iron rigging parts where rope and rawhide had been used traditionally. By the beginning of the twentieth century relatively sophisticated cast- and wrought-iron parts and fittings were used extensively, as will be seen on *Helen B. Thomas* and *Margaret Haskell*.

Cast-iron and some of the other more sophisticated parts were made in foundries and machine shops. All other metal parts were made by blacksmiths. For most of the period, while vessels used ironwork extensively, blacksmiths were usually specialists. Those who worked on parts for vessels were called ship's smiths. Their tools were anvils, forges, hammers, tongs, and a limited variety of unique tools. Their trade was learned through serving an apprenticeship. They were designers as well as manufacturers of their products. Their knowledge regarding size and design of parts and assemblies was based on experience, time-honored practices, and common sense.

Blacksmith's raw material was primarily wrought-iron bar, flat and round stock. This material was heated in a forge and hammered to shape on an anvil. It is resistant to rusting from contact with salt water and can be joined by fusion. The finished parts and assemblies were painted with a solution of lampblack in linseed oil and driers or with oil-base paint.

Modeler's raw material is brass and copper bar, rod, sheet, and tubing. It is bent to shape with pliers or bent over homemade forms and joined with hard or soft solder. Although brass and copper can be painted, it is unnecessary because both take on a weathered patina which does not hide craftsmanship.

The order of presentation follows the order of installation as nearly as possible which, incidentally, closely follows the order of complexity. This permits modelers to gain experience with simpler parts before tackling those of more difficult construction. Plate V, in two parts, is included to assist the reader in visualizing shapes and construction of these parts.

EYEBOLTS, RINGBOLTS, & HOOKS

Without doubt one of the most tedious chores for modelers is making the seemingly endless quota of eye- and ringbolts. This is work for a stormy winter evening with little else to do. It is wise to be well stocked with supplies before starting a model so some interesting work does not have to be interrupted while replenishing inventory.

Eyebolts are made from copper or soft brass wire. An eye is turned on the end with small roundnosed pliers. Then the shank is bent with flat-nosed pliers so it aligns with the center of the eye. It takes practice to obtain round eyes, but the knack is easily learned. The eye's inside diameter must be no more than three times the wire's diameter. After the eyebolt is formed, apply soldering flux to the eye and touch it to a puddle of hot solder on a soldering iron; coat the entire eye and joint. If the eye is closed, tap it to remove excess while the solder is still molten.

A ringbolt is an eyebolt with a ring in the eye. Rings can be mass formed by winding several turns of wire around a finishing nail and sawing the coil through with a fine jewelers' saw worked along the nail's axis. The end result is several split rings ready to be sprung into the eyes, straightened and soldered closed. A ring's inside diameter should be about five times wire size.

Hooks are made by starting with eyebolts and bending the hook part on their shanks. The diameter of hooks varied from eye to end which is impossible to simulate, but eyes must align with the center. The hook is bent to shape with roundnosed pliers and the eye bent into alignment. Dory hooks were very long versions of regular hooks used to hoist dories over the side and back aboard.

Before these or any other soft soldered parts can be considered complete, they should be cleaned with soap and water or acid to remove all traces of flux. Otherwise this greasy substance will attract dust and lint.

DEADEYE STROPS & CHAIN PLATES

Deadeyes, their strops and chain plates were assembled as units to provide anchors for standing rigging on the square-riggers and on *Helen B. Thomas*. On *Margaret Haskell*, deadeyes and strops were replaced by rigging screws.

There are three types of iron strops used on deadeyes. Each type is made of copper wire. Those for war vessels are made by forming elongated rings, hard soldering them closed, and bending them to shape around the deadeyes. Exact size of rings must be found by trial and error, and must be large enough so the lower loop extends below the channel to permit fitting the chain plate. Strops and chain plates for *Isaac Webb* are made from one piece of wire. The wire's end is wound tightly around the deadeye and around itself with two turns; follow by tightening it all and cutting off waste. *Helen B. Thomas'* deadeye strops are doubled and run side by side in the groove, with loops in each end that are turned downward so they are parallel and fit snugly over the upper end of the chain plate. An alternate method consists of a single wire with a loop on each end. A second alternate consists of purchased, stamped-out strops made so the lower part fits into a loop formed on the upper end of the chain plate. This type may be available from model supply houses along with a strap chain plate.

Before fitting strops, clean out the grooves. When fitting deadeyes, the odd hole must be exactly centered in the bottom. Rings for deadeye strops can be formed around an appropriately sized round stick or dowel. Those for *Helen B. Thomas* can be made around two brads driven into scrap wood. Wire for all single part strops should be about 1/32" in diameter. For doubled-up ones it should be two-thirds that. These sizes are on the large size, but smaller wire would be too weak.

Before starting to make chain plates, study rigging plans. Note that lower shrouds fan out as they leave the mast and that all chain plates attach on a line parallel to the sheer. Because of this, chain plates abreast the masts are shortest and those for other shrouds increase in length according to their displacement from athwart masts. Chain plates for war vessels are two elongated links. Each link is formed over a thin hardwood stick of appropriate thickness and width with rounded corners. Forms are slightly tapered in width so links can be gradually elongated by making each set of successive chain plates closer to the wide end. Refer to Fig. 114. Use only hard solder because the continuous pull of the shrouds will ultimately break soft solder. Wire size is 1/32".

After the chain plates and strops have been assembled and soldered, cut shallow notches in channel edges, where shown in sail plans, to receive deadeye strops. Lightly pencil a line parallel to the rail at the lower extremity of the chain plates under each channel. The attaching points along this line are located by using a string tied to the head of the mast, set in place with proper rake. Then by holding string in the center of each strop slot in turn, the exact alignment on the hull can be established and marked so each shroud and its chain plate will be in a perfect line when viewed from the side. Alignment of backstay chain plates is established the same way except that the string is moved up the spar to the appropriate head.

After attachment points have been established, try assembled units in place. Deviation from established points should not exceed 1/32" vertically. It takes some practice to make sets so that all assemblies fall on the marks perfectly, but the knack is easily acquired. After all fit, brad on the channel molding to hold them in place. Before attaching the lower links to the hull, make the backing links. These are 3/8" long, made double, and soldered together with an eye in each end. They are then bent to fit, and the whole is nailed in place with escutcheon pins.

Chain plates on *Isaac Webb* are pushed through holes bored about 1/16" inboard from edges. Alignment is done as described before. After each chain plate has been fitted in the channels, its lower end is finished by making one turn around a partially driven escutcheon pin at the mark. After the pin is withdrawn, the turn is worked into a neat eye. Backing links are made single with an eye in each end and fitted as on war vessels.

Helen B. Thomas' chain plates were iron straps with a loop in their upper ends for the deadeye strops and a series of holes below for bolting to the hull. They are made from sheet brass, 1/64" thick, and cut 3/32" wide. The curl and twist resulting from cutting can be straightened on a small anvil or other smooth, metal surface. Then drill three holes, one at the lower end and two at 1/4" intervals; they should make a snug fit for lill pins or fine nails. File away all burrs from the cutting and drilling. Locate point where each chain plate pierces the highest rail and, by using techniques described before, draw lines down the hull at the center line of each chain plate. Each chain plate passes through all rails and is partially let into the planking. To cut slots in each rail to receive chain plates, drill small holes at each end and remove the wood inbetween, using a sharp knife. Carefully score the hull on each side of the chain plate slots and remove wood between to a depth of 1/64".

Instead of slotting the rails, a less satisfactory method consists of cutting notches in the rails to receive the chain plates. Fit each chain plate temporarily to determine where the loop is to be turned into its upper end for connection to the deadeye strop. Loops are formed around a 1/64" diameter nail so the loop in the strop is snug to the upper rail. Then the deadeye strops are fitted, as shown on Sheet 1 of Plate V. When soldering the pins in place, apply it to one side only so the deadeye strop can turn in the chain plate loop. Finish chain plates by inserting them in their slots and fastening them in with three lills or fine nails.

Chain plates for *Margaret Haskell* are made and fitted in a similar manner to those on *Helen B. Thomas* except that they are not recessed into the hull and the lower ends of rigging screws should be fitted into a slot in the loop. See the same Sheet 1 in Plate V for this arrangement and an alternate.

PINTLES & GUDGEONS

Pintles and gudgeons, as mentioned in Chapter IV, were the hinges for the rudder. Generally the forgings for both parts were identical, consisting of continuous straps with a hole in their centers. Ends of straps embrace

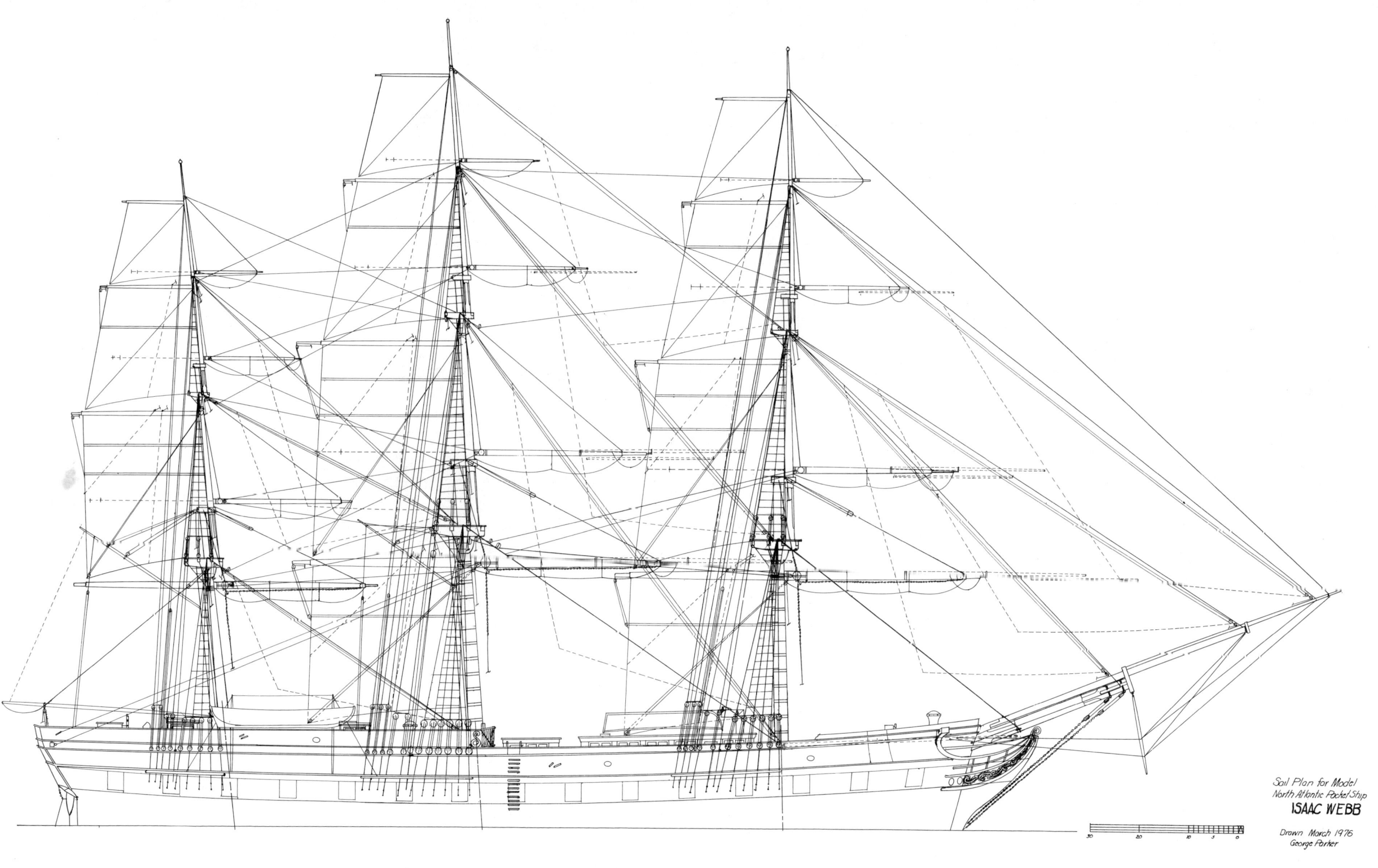

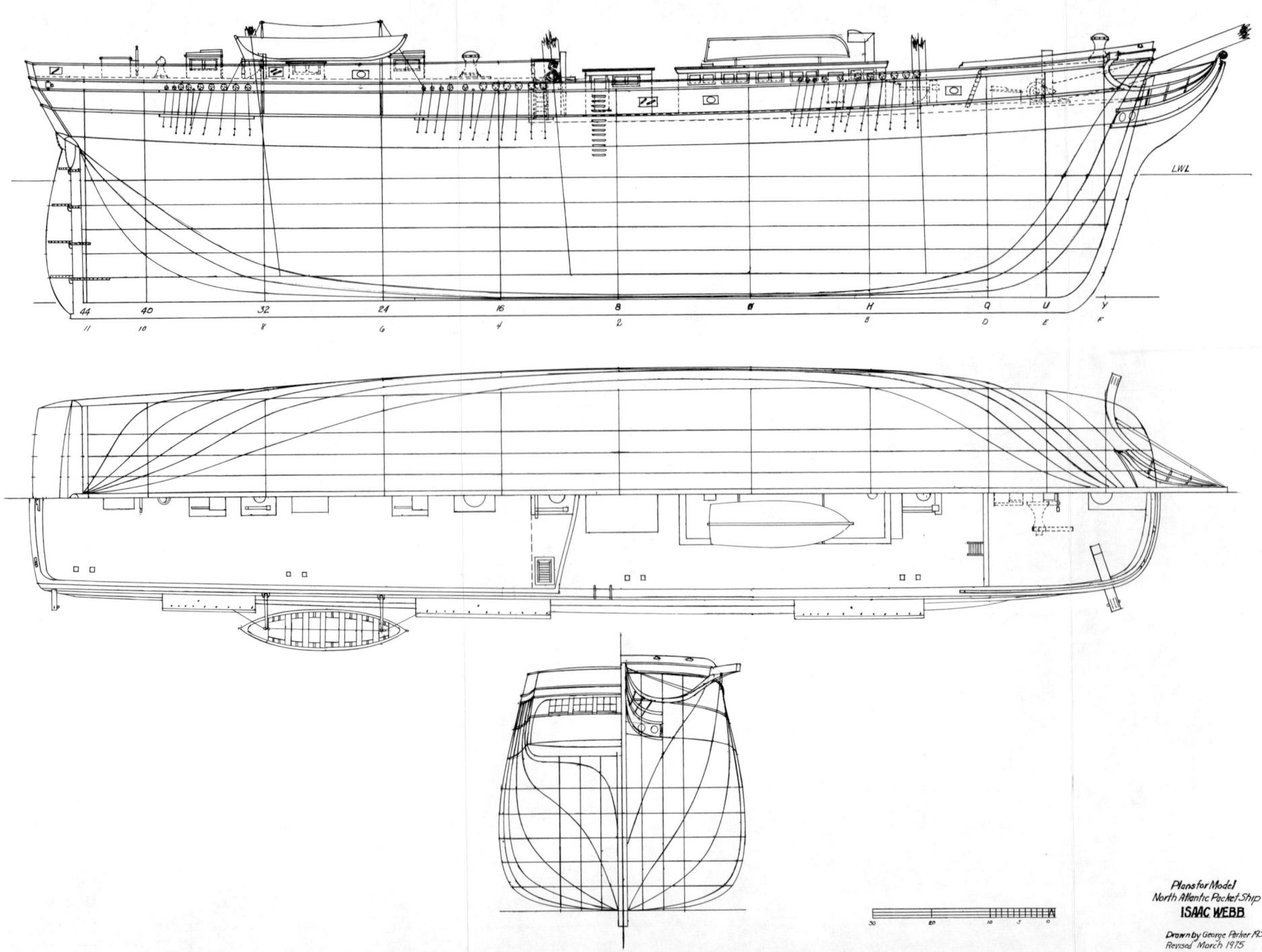

rudder or sternpost with through bolts to hold them in place. The difference consists of a pin in the hole of one, which makes a pintle. Pintles are fitted on the rudder with pins pointed downward and slide into and turn in the gudgeon holes.

These can be miniaturized on 1/4" scale models. Refer to Plate V. Pintles and gudgeons are bent up from sheet brass or copper, as shown. Sizes are as drawn in sheer plans. They must be made and fitted so distance between rudder and sternpost is negligible. Holes in each set of gudgeons are exactly in line and centered with the stock of plug stock rudders. This can be achieved by threading pintle pin stock up through gudgeons and into rudder stock hole before fastening them in place with shortened and re-sharpened lill pins. Pintles must also be in exact alignment under stock. This can be achieved by eye. Any slight error can be corrected with pliers. Pintle pins are cut so the exposed part is half again longer than the width of the gudgeons. A cutout below each pintle allows gudgeons to fit underneath and rudder to be hung and removed. Fit gudgeons so they are evenly spaced and pintles bear on the gudgeons.

An alternate method consists of eyes driven into the sternpost so they are flush. Pins in the rudder are bent to engage the eyes. Straps are simulated with strips of paper glued to sternpost and rudder with shortened and resharpened lills driven to simulate driftbolt heads. This alternate method is mandatory on small-scale models like *Isaac Webb* and *Margaret Haskell*. It is also quite effective on the other models. Refer to Plate V.

RUDDER CHAINS

Rudder chains were fitted on each of the square-riggers. They were permanently rigged to use when unshipping the rudder or for jury steering if the regular steering gear failed. Two chains were fastened to a ringbolt in the upper after part of the rudder. They ran upward to the knuckle on the center line where they were lashed to a ringbolt, allowing enough slack so the rudder could be swung 45° each way. Chains were then led outboard, one to port and the other to starboard along the knuckle. They were held up by lashings to ringbolts spaced 10' or so apart. Actual practice is followed on the models; use wire about a 1/32" in diameter, chain with twenty-nine links per inch, and fine black thread for lashings.

BOBSTAY PLATES

Plates were through-bolted to the stems of *Isaac Webb* and *Margaret Haskell* for attaching rigging. Bobstays on both vessels were attached to

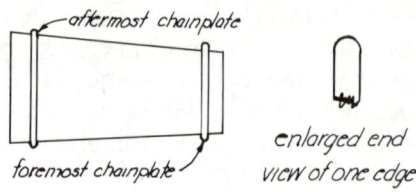

Fig. 114
Form for making
chainplate links

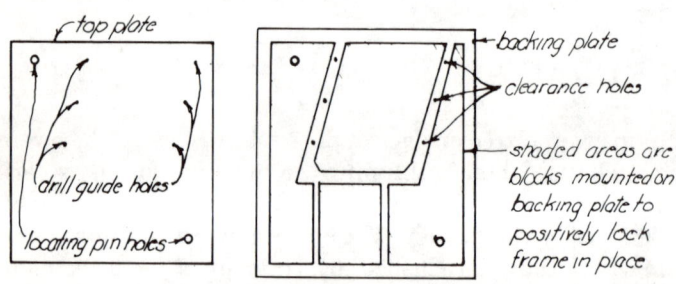

Fig. 115
Drilling jig for
hammock netting frames

them, and on *Margaret Haskell* two additional plates were installed for attaching lower ends of jibstays. In actual practice, separate plates were fitted on each side of the stem in alignment with the stay. These plates extended slightly forward of the stem with a bolt through, over which the stays were shackled.

Plates and bolts scaled-down would be too thin and delicate to use on models. One substitute consists of a heavy eyebolt driven into the stem, with imitation straps made of strips of paper. Another consists of a piece of wire shaped in the form of a deep U, with integral horns on each end to fit in a hole through the stem. Widths and lengths are shown in sail plans. That portion on each side of the stem is flattened by hammering and horns are left round. See Plate V.

BOWSPRIT SHROUD PLATES

Margaret Haskell's bowsprit shrouds and rigging for the jibboom were fastened to iron plates, with eyes in their forward ends. Several bolts through the planking held the plates in place. There are two ways to make these plates for models. The first consists of hammering the middle of a length of copper wire flat. One end is turned down at right angles to form a horn and the other is turned into an eye and soldered closed. The horn is driven into a predrilled hole in the hull, and two or more lills are driven along its length. The other way consists of a thin strap with an eye soldered on one end and a short length of wire soldered into a hole on the other. It is attached as described for the first type.

HEAD STAY IRONWORK

The forestay for *Helen B. Thomas* was secured to a shoulder eyebolt. This can be made by soldering a small, snug-fitting washer to the shank of an eyebolt close to the eye, but a very good one can be purchased under the name of pad eye. It has a shoulder, and its shank is threaded to provide holding-power in the deck.

The jibstay was secured to a two-plate assembly on the stem, similar to bobstay plates, except that each plate had a shoulder bent into it so the protruding parts were about 6″ high and 2″ apart. They were made from 1″ by 3″ or 4″ iron, therefore they can be miniaturized, but it is easier and just as effective to use a pad eye like the one described with paper straps glued to each side of the stem. Lill pins cut short and resharpened can be driven through the paper bands to simulate driftbolt heads.

The fore-topmast stay iron was made of 1/2″ by 2″ iron about 2′ long and let into the face of the stem with an off-center eye in its upper end. Since it was let into the stem it was concealed with paint so an eyebolt with an off-center eye can be driven into a snug-fitting hole in the forward part of the stemhead for this fitting. Refer to Plate V.

PUMPS

Pumps for *Lexington* and *Wasp* were of the piston type and set in pairs, operated by heavers similar to those used on windlasses. From *Isaac Webb*'s time onward the diaphragm pump with the tremendous capacity on a short stroke was used. They were, also, set in pairs. Those on *Isaac Webb* were operated through connecting rods on a crankshaft which ran horizontally athwartships and was supported by bearings on top of raised rails, usually extensions to fife rails. Long demountable cranks on each end were used to operate pumps. Momentum was maintained by two flywheels mounted just outside the supporting rails. Two separate pumps on *Helen B. Thomas* were installed with hand levers pivoted on the lip of the pump castings.

Pump cylinders on *Lexington* and *Wasp* are set in pairs in a raised platform through the deck. Loose-fitting pistons were fitted in the bores and connected through linkages to rocker arms. The rocker arm on *Lexington* pivoted in a slot in the upper end of a heavy stanchion. A pair of rocker arms secured to a common shaft between stanchions on *Wasp* operated four pumps simultaneously.

Pump cylinders are made of 1/4", thin-walled, brass tubing cut about 2" long and driven into snug-fitting holes so their lips protrude about 1/8". Pistons are made of 3/16" tubing about 1/4" long, eased on the outside for a free fit in the bores. Bails similar to those on pails are soldered to their upper ends and connected to the rocker arms through linkages. Rocker arms are made from 1/16" thick copper or brass and are about 3/32" deep at their pivots. They are cut and filed to shape, shown in Plate V. Sockets for the end of heaver bars are made of sheet brass or copper bent up into a rectangular shape to fit snugly over the end of the rocker arm for about 1/16" and soldered in place. Each socket is finished by bending a piece of copper wire to fit over the end where it is soldered. Heavers are shown in Plate V, but they need not be fitted because they were stowed below except when in use.

Flywheel pumps for *Isaac Webb* also need not be shown because they were behind the mainmast on the main deck and would be hidden by both mast and coach house.

The diaphragm pump shown in Plate V is typical of those used on fishing schooners and, without handles, of those used in flywheel pumps. Plate V is taken from a drawing by the author made years ago of a discarded excavating contractor's pump. Miniaturized pumps cast in white metal are available at model supply houses where 1/4"-scale fishing schooner kits are made. Since *Margaret Haskell*'s pumps had to be larger, the same size pumps are suitable for her model. These castings come without handles which is proper for *Helen B. Thomas*, as handles were stowed below. For *Margaret Haskell* the diaphragms were operated by the crankshaft through connecting linkage.

Flywheels are difficult to make because of the S-shaped spokes with four, six, or eight per wheel. Refer to Fig. 95. These can also be purchased from model supply houses with crankshafts, but usually the shaft has to be discarded and a new one bent from brass wire to fit over the fife rails substituted. Connecting linkages consist of copper wire inserted in a hole bored in the pump casting's center with the upper end flattened and formed into the shape of an eye to fit the crankshaft. These assemblies should be painted flat black with flywheel rims and pump interiors painted vermilion.

SHEET HORSES

A heavy iron rod with its ends bent at 90° angles was fitted on deck for securing sheet-blocks on *Margaret Haskell*'s lower gaffsails, her two inner staysails, and *Helen B. Thomas*' foresail. The turned ends were threaded for a washer and nut below with a flange at deck level. These can be miniaturized by simply bending copper wire about 1/32" in diameter to shape and pushing the ends into snug-fitting, predrilled holes in the deck until the crosspiece is about 1/8" above the deck. A more elegant approach consists of adding small copper washers 1/16" or 3/32" in diameter for flanges, using soft solder to hold them in place. Refer to Plate V for construction, and see the schooners' deck plans for lengths and locations. A close-fitting ring on each horse provides an attaching mechanism for the sheet-block.

BOLLARDS

By the time *Margaret Haskell* was built, the heavy rounded-off square bitts along the vessel's sides for mooring had been superceded by cast-iron bollards, as shown in Plate V. See her deck plan for location and length. Their height can be scaled off the sheer plan. They were bolted to a heavy, wooden, oval pad on deck, shaped as shown in deck plan and should be about 1/32" thick on the model.

These bollards are difficult to make to look proper, so it is recommended they be purchased. There are several varieties made, some of which are for steamships of a later era and are totally unacceptable. Be careful to obtain those of proper shape.

WINCH HEADS & HOISTING ENGINES

Helen B. Thomas had two winch heads mounted on a common shaft in bearings on the forward faces of her main-topmast bitts. They were operated with demountable cranks and had pawls to prevent reverse rotation. They were used to hoist the gaff for the last few feet when the full weight of the sail and boom was on the halyard. On the model it is sufficient to fit turned or purchased winch heads of 1/8″ diameter on a brass rod in holes bored through the bitts close to their forward faces. Refer to deck and sail plans for location.

Margaret Haskell's sails were hoisted by at least two engines. One was in the forward house with winch heads on drive shaft extensions through the sides of the house, as shown in detail sheet. All the modeler need do is mount two 1/8″ diameter winches. The other engine was mounted between the jiggermast fife rails and the after hatch. There may have been others and it seems probable that halyards were led through blocks at their fife rails and to the winch heads of the nearer engine. Actual construction of the engines is not available, but the drawing in Plate V is based on contemporary engines.

By searching through model supply catalogs, modelers may find a reasonable likeness of suitable proportions, but do not install cargo winches, windlass engines, or any engines driven by electric motors.

To better understand these engines while reading the following description, refer to Plate V. Winches were mounted on a cast-iron base about 6″ high and 4′ fore and aft by 6′ athwartships. On the after end (right side in the drawing) the crankshaft was mounted on two bearing supports. The shaft had an integral disc on each end with crankpins near their circumference for the connecting rods. A small, wide-faced gear was mounted in its center and drove a large gear on a longer shaft with winch heads on either end and a sprocket which aligned with the starboard flywheel of the pumps. The sprocket is shown just inboard of the starboard winch head, but it can be shifted anywhere along the shaft to align with the starboard pump flywheel, as long as the chain clears the other parts of the engine. This may require shifting the pump flywheels to the inboard side of the fife rails. The gear reduction arrangement was used to reduce the drive shaft speed so winches would turn quite slowly. The rectangular boxes on the forward end of the base were steam cylinders mounted so their center lines were level with the crankshaft. It is not worthwhile to attempt the small-scale miniaturizing of steam supply piping, operating levers, crossheads, separate piston, and connecting rods or valve assemblies.

Although engines were mostly of cast-iron and forged steel, painted wood will suffice on the model with metal winches, shafts, and connecting rods.

Start construction by making the base 1/2" by 3/4" of 1/16" stock. Make the assembly to represent the two gears as they would appear with a heavy iron guard bolted to the base and formed on top like the circumference of the gears. The smaller gear is 1/8" in diameter, 1/8" above the base. The larger one is 1/4" in diameter, mounted 3/16" above the base. Crankpin discs are 3/16" in diameter on a 3/64" diameter shaft. Cylinders are 1/8" in diameter by 1/4" long, mounted on pads underneath so their centers are 1/8" above the base with their piston ends a strong 3/16" forward of the discs. The six bearing supports are made of 3/32" stock, a scant 1/32" thick, and long enough so the shaft holes can be bored through. Winch heads are 1/8" in diameter and the sprocket 3/16" in diameter. Crankpins and connecting rods are of 1/32" copper wire. The chain for driving the pump would be too small to purchase, so it is omitted.

Paint all wooden parts with flat black and leave metal bare.

HAMMOCK NETTINGS

On war vessels the hammock nettings were canvas troughs within metal frames surmounting the highest rail. Gangway boards formed one end and a similarly shaped board aft of the cathead was the other. On *Wasp* the nettings were also carried aft from the gangways to another board on each side just forward of the davits. During the day and during battle the hammocks and bedding were rolled up and placed in these troughs so the top of the hammocks paralleled the rail. Then a canvas flap was laced over the top to keep out water and provide a neat appearance. These nettings served the dual functions of being convenient storage for hammocks during the day and providing additional protection to men on deck during action.

The height and extent of hammock nettings are shown by the endboards and gangways of both *Lexington* and *Wasp* in their sheer plans. The frames were spaced about 4' apart (1" on these models) and are shaped as shown in Plate V. These are very difficult to miniaturize; they must all be alike and are made of very small wire with equally small holes for rope.

To assure that all frames are alike, they must be bent and assembled to fit a jig and drilled while in the jig. Fig. 115 is a drawing of a suitable jig made from sheet brass about 1/16" thick and soft soldered together. The aligning pieces in the jig can be "tinned" and clamped on the outside plate. Then, by heating the whole, the tinned surfaces adhere to joining surfaces for a permanent bond. The outside plate is drilled with a #76 drill at the location of each rope hole and, after the frame is set in the jig, these holes are used as guides when drilling for the rope holes in the frames. Since the holes' locations are critical, they must be located very carefully and center-punched lightly before drilling the jig. When drilling frames, turn the jig upside down on a block of wood.

Stock for frames is brass wire 1/32" or slightly larger in diameter. Cut pieces for studs in the rail and hard solder them in place. Then bend the frame to fit the jig. Each leg must be straight with short radii at the corners. If the wire tends to crystallize and break at the corners, anneal the wire by heating. After frames fit the jig, remove them and hammer the upright arms until the fore and aft dimensions are about 1/50", while allowing the athwartship dimension to increase as it will. When the hammering is completed, the upright arms should fit very snugly. Rebend as necessary so frames fit the jig without forcing. Then drill holes with the #76 drill, using the plate as a guide. After frames are all drilled, cut excess from upper end of the uprights, file them in a neat radius around the upper holes and remove any burrs.

Install frames with studs pushed into the rail's snug-fitting drilled holes equally spaced at approximately 1" between gangway and endboards. After installation, each of the uprights is bent so it follows the curve of the vessel's side and forms continuous fair curves when viewed from either end. Bending uprights to form continuous fair curves is the hardest part of building these nettings. Before installing frames on each end, make a frame without studs to use for a jig when drilling the six holes in the gangway and endboards. Bend uprights to conform with each board's shape and to continue the curve. When all frames are set and boards drilled, reeve thread through the boards and each frame to form continuous curves parallel to the rail. Cement the thread in the boards while holding it taut until cement dries, and then cut excess off, flush with board.

Simulating hammocks stowed in the nettings is done by rollng a piece of white percale into a tight roll just long enough to reach from board to board with raw edges tucked under. Rolls should be sufficiently large to fit snugly in the trough with top surfaces slightly above upper ropes. Before installing the rolls tie white thread around them at intervals of 1/2" to pucker them slightly with knots all in line close to the lengthwise edge of the cloth. When putting the rolls in, place edge and knots on the bottom. Remember that if nettings are installed, skid beams must extend up slightly above them.

NAVIGATION LIGHT BOXES

Prior to the 1860s the light on a vessel running at night was simply a white lantern hung ahead of the headsails with perhaps another one aft, at the ready to warn nearby vessels. Later, American navigation laws required side lights to be carried during the hours of darkness; a green light to starboard and a red light to port; each had to be visible over a prescribed angle with the starting point dead ahead so neither could be visible across the bow. This permitted, within limits, the other vessel to judge the vessel's general course. Without doubt none of the square-riggers carried these lights when built. Since neither of the schooners had generators, their lights were kerosene lanterns, removed and refueled each morning in readiness for operation that night.

To comply with the law, a schooner's light boards were seized to the fore shrouds about 8' above the rail. Boards were 4' to 6' long and 1' wide, seized outside the shrouds with wedge-shaped chocks behind, so they stood vertically and parallel to the hull's center line. Before 1890, lights were simply hung on the after, outboard face of these boards. By the time these schooners were built, boards were added on the after end and along the bottom to form a boxlike arrangement with three open sides.

Stock thickness for these boxes is a stout 1/64" on *Helen B. Thomas* and half that on *Margaret Haskell*. So they will be reasonably sturdy, it is suggested that each be cut, bent and soldered together from a single piece of sheet brass or copper. Because wire rigging will be used, the wedge-shaped chocks can be made of 1/32" thick stock and soldered for permanent connection to both the back of the boards and the shrouds.

FORESTAY FITTING

By virtue of its being secured directly to the hull and being the shortest stay with the least slack, the forestay for *Margaret Haskell* had to withstand a large share of the forces in the head stays. Also, the scheme used for pivoting the staysail boom brought heavy radial forces on the lower part of the stay. A heavy steel forging was used to provide the staysail boom pivot and anchoring for the stay. Refer to Plate V, Sheet 2 of 2, for its shape above deck. It consisted of a plate in the form of an isosceles triangle elevated above deck and perpendicular to the stay, with the long dimension along the center line. A leg at each corner supported it. Forward legs were spread so the part below deck passed on each side of the bowsprit and their ends were through-bolted at the stem. The after leg was bolted through a deck beam. A heavy strap parallel to the stay extended up from the fore end of the triangular plate. Its upper end was turned toward the stern, perpendicular to the stay. In both the lug and the plate, a hole bored close to the strap received the stay which was secured below the plate. Another pair of holes slightly aft received an iron rod on which the staysail boom pivoted.

On the model, the triangular plate and legs can be cut from sheet metal and bent to shape with either integral tapered horns or horns soldered on and tapered. Spread the forward legs so horns clear the bowsprit. The after leg horn is shorter so it will not penetrate the lower surface of the underlayment. This arrangement will allow removal of the stump in the event of a broken bowsprit. All horns must be parallel to drive into the deck. A strap with a bent upper end and rounded off is fitted as described. Unlike actual practice, only one hole is bored through for a piece of copper wire with a tight eye in its upper end. The wire is soldered in the plate and lug. The eye provides a simple attaching point for the stay. For the staysail boom it is better to slip the eyebolt onto the wire rather than trying to form it later.

FUTTOCKS

Futtocks provided the same function for topmast and topgallant shrouds that chain plates did for lower shrouds and backstays. Before 1820 they were rope and were led as shown in Fig. 38. These are described in Chapter XI. *Isaac Webb*'s futtocks were iron rods fastened to deadeye strops above and to eyes in an iron band about the mast. On her model, futtocks and deadeye strops are one piece of copper, as described for chain plates. They pass through holes in the tops or crosstrees and secure to the mast-band eyes with a simple eye turned in their lower ends. *Helen B. Thomas* was not fitted with topmast shrouds and, hence, no futtocks. *Margaret Haskell*'s topmast shrouds were set up at the crosstrees by rigging screws. On her model the futtocks are twisted around eyes in the lower shank of the rigging screws led through holes in the crosstrees and secured below to the mast bands, as described for *Isaac Webb*. See Plate V, Sheets 1 and 2. Futtock stock size for *Isaac Webb* is .020" and .025" for *Margaret Haskell*.

CRANCE IRONS OR TRUSSES

Crance irons were used to constrain lower yards to their masts on *Isaac Webb*. They consisted of a heavy band around the mast and a yoke between two bands on the yard, with a connecting mechanism between yoke and mast band. The connecting mechanism contained two pivots at right angles to each other so the yard could rotate in both vertical and horizontal planes. Again refer to Plate V.

Make a band about 1/8" wide for each lower mast, to fit locations, as shown in sail plan. Lugs with holes are soldered diametrically opposite each other. The after yoke is sawed out of 3/32" thick sheet brass and filed to shape with all corners rounded off. Work shoulders into the arms with round studs to fit into the lug holes where they are soldered and where the ends of the studs are then to be filed away. If the modeler wishes working trusses, a horizontal slot is sawed and filed into the forward end of the yoke with a vertical pivot hole bored through the ears. Then the short pivoting piece is filed to shape so its after end fits in the yoke slot and the forward end is fitted with a shoulder and stud to provide the vertical pivot bolt.

Bands about 3/32" wide are made to fit the yard with lugs underneath for the clew garnet blocks (none are fitted on the crossjack yard). The forward yoke is sawed, filed to shape, and soldered to the yard bands so they are 1/2" apart on the fore and main yards; 7/16" on the crossjack. A hole in its center receives the pivot stud which is cut and riveted over slightly in the forward side. The assembly is finished by drilling for and inserting the horizontal pivot bolt which can be made from a small cut escutcheon pin riveted lightly on the cut end. If the modeler wants a rigid truss, pivots can be omitted and the whole assembly soldered together.

SPAR BANDS

Spar bands were iron bar stock forged into rings and any lugs, eyes, eyes and rings, ears, etc., welded to their circumferences.

There are three techniques from which the modeler may choose. The first consists of bending a strip of sheet brass or copper into a ring with integral folded parts which are soldered together and filed to form ears and eyes. The second consists of bending up a plain ring and afterward soldering on separate ears or eyes. The third optional technique consists of turning the bands on a lathe and soldering ears or eyes with shanks in drilled holes into their circumference. Refer to Plate V.

Bands must fit spars snugly without forcing. This fit sets up perpetual forces in the band with resultant tensile stresses in the solder joints which will ultimately break unless hard solder is used.

It is difficult to form bands to exact size regardless of how carefully they are measured, cut, and joined. However, there are many bands of varying size required, so a band which is a little too small or large for the particular application can probably be used elsewhere. Modelers can use a jeweler's ring mandrel to advantage. It is a tapered, hardened steel rod. By driving the band up the taper, slightly undersized bands can be expanded. Also pounding bands around their circumferences, when placed on the horn of a miniature anvil, will result in increasing their diameters. Both of these methods tend to improve the band's shape, sometimes being all that is needed. Oversized bands cannot be shrunk without cutting and rejoining.

Some of these bands and other parts will have several solder joints. Novices may have difficulty with melting the solder in previously made joints until acquiring the knack of controlling the heat. This problem can be partially overcome by using silver solders of differing melting points and using the highest temperature solder for the first joint, and so on.

Modelers will have to use considered judgment concerning band stock thickness. Recall that these bands were hand-forged and welded by fusion. Probably 1" thick metal is the thickest that could be handled. It is only .020" thick on the 1/4" scale model and half that on the 1/8" scale model. Therefore very thin stock must be used.

These bands take on many configurations according to their applications, covered in Chapters XI and XII.

SMOKESTACKS

Galley stacks have various shapes, as shown in detail sheets. They are made from hard brass tube, cut to shape (as shown), and soldered together. Each part is also cut to shape (as shown). The tapered bottom on *Helen B. Thomas*' stack can be turned from brass by those who have a lathe or it can be fashioned from a piece of wood and the whole assembly painted flat black.

Margaret Haskell's boiler stack on the forward end of the house of the foremast is easily shaped and assembled from brass tubing, but do not make it so high it will interfere with the forestaysail boom.

Helen B. Thomas' afterhouse had a stove with a vertical stack on the center line between the companionway slide and the skylight. To smother sparks and provide sufficient draft, a hood with open ends was fitted athwartships. It was semicircular in cross section, 36" long, and 12" wide. It is simulated by taking a 3/4" length of 1/4" brass tubing and cutting it down the middle and cementing one piece to the roof.

MAINSHEET BUFFER

This fitting was called both a *jiber* and *buffer* and was made so a considerable amount of the shock imparted to the hull when changing tacks was absorbed. It was used instead of a horse and, on *Helen B. Thomas*, was mounted on the transom under an extension of the rail. *Buffers* were made under patent by the Edson Corporation of South Boston, Mass. They consisted of heavy cylindrical rubbers on an iron shaft with triangular linkage connected to both iron collars (between the rubbers below) and to the mainsheet ring which protruded slightly above a slot in the rail. Modelers need only make two links connected to eyebolts in the transom with a single ring above, as drawn in detail sheet.

STERN LANTERN

As with everything else concerning specifics for this vessel, the shape of and perhaps the existence of *Lexington*'s stern lantern is guesswork. However, similar lights were carried on British vessels well into the 1700s. It would be an almost impossible undertaking to model this light, but similar ones are sold at model supply houses offering the mounting shank attached, so it can be set in a snug-fitting hole in the rail and cemented in place.

Fitting this light is optional, but it makes a fine ornament for *Lexington*'s otherwise unadorned stern.

FOREBOOM GOOSENECK

Sometime before 1890, fishing schooners were fitted with goosenecks instead of jaws on their main booms. On the model of *Helen B. Thomas*, bands are fitted to the mast with ears on their after sides. A pin in these ears provides the horizontal pivot for the boom. The boom has two long straps let into the sides and through riveted. They are bent at the boom with a reverse bend near the end. The ends are parallel and just far enough apart to receive a short connecting piece. The connecting piece has two holes perpendicular to each other. The after hole takes a bolt through the boom straps to provide a vertical pivot, and the forward hole fits the pin in the band ears. A ferrule over the end of the boom prevents it from splitting. Refer to detail sheet.

Modelers may use this construction or simplify it by inserting an eyebolt in the fore end of the boom to fit over the pin in the bands with a ferrule on the boom. If sails are to be rigged, some method must be devised to secure the clew of the sail. Actual practice is shown in detail sheet. This can be simplified by soldering an eye on the connecting piece or eyebolt.

SHEET BANDS

Sheet bands on the schooner's booms, including booms on headsails, were fitted with bails to which sheet-blocks were secured by a ring. Refer to detail sheets. The bails acted as a kind of horse which allowed blocks to move around the lower half of the booms, thus minimizing any twisting action on spars, jaws, or goosenecks.

The bands are made to fit snugly with an ear on each side. Bails are bent to shape and ends inserted in the holes; then solder them in place. Except for *Helen B. Thomas'* foreboom band and those on *Margaret Haskell*'s headsails, small eyes are turned into the bails above the ears. Main boom footropes are seized to the eyes on *Helen B. Thomas* and double topping lifts are connected to them on *Margaret Haskell*.

MASTHEAD CAPS

Both schooners have metal caps. They are made from two bands with a connecting piece between to establish spacing and a strap on each side to provide necessary strength to support topmasts.

Make a tight-fitting band for the masthead and a second ring sized to slide on the topmast. Then cut and solder in place the short spacer to establish the distance between spars. The trestle and crosstree assembly must be fitted previously so this assembly can be checked with the topmast in place and adjustments made in the spacing before proceeding. After the spacing is correct, the side straps can be soldered on and the ends filed to blend with the rings. Studs are soldered into holes bored where shown in sail plans. Leave these studs about 1/8" long, until bails are fitted. Then they can be cut off and filed flush with the bails. Both studs and bails should be made of hard brass wire because it will resist stresses better than annealed copper. After studs are soldered in, make and solder on the eyes and ears required, as shown in sail plans. Caps are finished by bending tight-fitting eyes on the stay bails and slipping them over their studs. Bails should be bent so they have to be sprung onto the cap studs.

STUDDING SAIL BOOM IRONS & SADDLES

Studding sail boom irons are appropriate on *Wasp*'s and *Isaac Webb*'s lower, topsail, and topgallant yards. They are fitted to fore- and mainmast yards only. Since *Wasp* had very light royal rigging and *Isaac Webb* was built for service where heavy winds prevailed for most of the year, it is doubtful if either vessel carried royal studding sails. Fitting the yards with their booms and saddles does not commit the builder to fitting sails because they are a permanent part of yard ironwork. Refer to Plate IX, Sheet 1 of 2, for their construction.

Irons had a round shank outboard of the yard with a 90° bend. Inboard ends of the shank fitted into a round end plate or ferrule with two integral straps which were let into the yardarms where they were spiked or through bolted. A band was shrunk on at their mid-length for further support. Outboard ends were fitted with a band, sized for a sliding fit over the studding sail boom. These can be miniaturized but it is probably better to bend a 90° angle in pieces of brass wire with bands soldered on. Then the shanks can be driven part way into the hole drilled in the end of the yardarm.

Saddles on *Wasp* were similar to that used for *Lexington*'s jibboom and, when fitted, the boom was lashed in place around itself and the yard. Those on *Isaac Webb* consisted of two bands: one a shrunk-fit on the yard and the other was hinged so the boom could be slid through. When the boom had been run out, the hinged section was closed to clamp the boom in place. A connecting piece held the bands together. This fitting can be miniaturized by making the bands and soldering the connecting piece to each. There are only two qualifications: one, the boom and yard must be parallel to each other and, two, the boom must be offset 45° forward to allow for rigging yard lifts and sheets.

Chapter X

BLOCKS, BULL'S-EYES, DEADEYES, HEARTS, & RIGGING SCREWS

These items are lumped together because they are somewhat related in function. Blocks are generally known to landsmen as pulleys. They were used by seamen to gain mechanical advantage and to redirect the lead of ropes for easier handling. Deadeyes were used to set up standing rigging and remained as part of the rigging system. Bull's-eyes were substituted for deadeyes and blocks in light duty service. Hearts were used instead of deadeyes on older vessels in fore- and mainstays, bobstays, and bowsprit shrouds. These four rigging items were made primarily of wood. Blocks had moveable sheaves over which ropes were rove, all others had no moving parts. Rigging screws were built on the same principle as American turnbuckles and were used on *Margaret Haskell* instead of deadeyes.

There are purists who make many of these parts, but it is an exacting tedious chore. It is difficult to make the large number of different sized blocks and deadeyes so they all look alike. Therefore, it is suggested that those parts be purchased; they are machine-made and have a better and consistent shape not possible to achieve by hand. Each of the square-riggers was fitted with a few specially-shaped blocks which cannot be purchased. Methods for making or suitably modifying standard blocks are explained next. Bull's-eyes and deadeyes have been the same for the last two or three centuries, and purchased ones can be used without modification for all applications. Hearts were custom-made and must, likewise, be made by the builder to fit each particular application. The rigging screws required are of a very small size; jeweler's equipment would be needed to even closely miniaturize these parts. Purchased ones are almost exact miniaturizations of originals and therefore are highly recommended to the builder.

Plate VI shows the shapes and typical applications of this equipment.

BLOCKS

Blocks are referred to according to the number of sheaves in them. Single, double, and treble are terms used to designate those with one, two, and three sheaves, respectively. Blocks with four or more sheaves have been made, but none with more than three will be used on these models.

Before 1875 or so, blocks had been made the same for centuries. Shells were carved from solid blocks of a hard, durable wood such as oak with the grain running lengthwise. Corners in profile were rounded off and sheave slot or slots were cut through to provide just enough clearance for sheaves to turn freely. Sheaves in the better blocks were made of lignum vitae and had a score made in their perimeters to receive the rope. They turned on oak sheave pins in snug-fitting holes through the shell. Scores in the upper and lower corners of the shell admitted an endless rope loop, called a strop.

After 1875, block makers started improving their product and finally developed the wooden-shelled, iron-stropped block known today. The sheaves are iron with roller bearings turning on iron pins. The shells are made of many pieces and the iron strops fit into grooves on the inside surface of the shells, thus, the blocks on the two schooners were smooth on the exterior surfaces.

The blocks available from model supply houses are miniatures of the old style, rope stropped variety as used on square-riggers. The same style block is available with wire strops and hooks. Although these are not exactly right, nevertheless when they are painted, they look quite realistic and, for use on the schooners, the external strop is hidden.

Uses

In the first of two ways blocks were used, two blocks were assembled on a rope, called a fall. This assemblage of blocks and fall was called a tackle and was used in such applications as moving guns, hoisting stores aboard, moving equipment about the deck, and as separate parts of the rigging. A tackle usually consisted of two single blocks, such as the gun tackle, or of one single and one double block, as for the luff tackle. Note in Plate VI that each block has a hook worked into the strop and that the standing end of the fall is attached to the strop of one block.

In the second way, blocks were used as an integral part of the vessel's rigging. Strops on these blocks were arranged in several ways, and simplified arrangements are recommended for models, so the finished part is not oversized and clumsy. An example is the halyard tackle, drawn in Fig. 43. In actual practice these blocks were stropped with hooks. Upper blocks were hooked into a cringle in the tyes and the lowers into eyebolts in the deck. On the model, tyes are eye spliced to form a tight-fitting strop for the upper block. Lower blocks are stropped directly to the eyebolts. In other applications actual practice must be followed, such as brace and lift blocks at yardarms where strops include both block and yardarm.

Types & Characteristics

The specially-shaped blocks referred to earlier are shown in Plate VI and must be made by hand from boxwood or hard maple. Fiddle blocks were the most picturesque and so named because the shell resembles a fiddle's sound box. Sheaves of differing sizes were fitted in line instead of side-by-side as in a double block. Shoulder blocks were used for sheet-blocks at the yardarms. Normally-shaped blocks would tend to jam the sheets between themselves and the spars, so the shoulder was incorporated to make them stand off the spar. Topsail yard tye blocks (their use is described in Chapter XVI) were circular and conspicuously large when viewed from their sides. They were thin, double stropped, and fitted with large sheaves. When making these blocks, plane up stock equal to their width and thickness. Form their profile shapes with a knife and fine file. Cut half-round scores with a small, fine round file to simulate the sheaves, and bore holes through at the upper end of each sheave score. Finish blocks by filing deep scores at the upper and lower corners of the shells for the strops and curve the sides of the shells slightly, like the larger sizes of purchased blocks. There was one more type of odd block called a bullet block. These were used until the use of carved shell blocks was discontinued. They were used for jib and staysail sheets. During each tack, as the sail swung across the next inboard stay, these blocks were dragged over the stay. Normally-shaped blocks with square edges would tend to foul on the stay, so the blocks were made without any square corners. These do not have to be made from scratch because purchased single blocks can be reshaped to suit.

Rope strops were lengths of rope worked into endless loops. For models, endless loops are made by splicing the ends of short lengths of rigging twine together. The splice is fitted under the lower end of the block. The upper end is seized together close to the block so the strop is snug. Strops were of different lengths according to where they were attached. To be capable of judging the length of strops for the various sizes of block and applications comes with practice, but the knack is easily learned. For many applications the falls of tackles must be attached to the lower ends of blocks. In actual practice, a cringle was seized into the strop. On models, it is better to thread the fall between block and strop, and follow by splicing in a very small eye.

BULL'S-EYES

Bull's-eyes were deadeyes with one hole. The holes were flared and rounded on each end to allow free passage of rope where they were used in place of blocks or in lieu of deadeyes. Their perimeters were scored to receive rope or iron strops. Choice of strop material was governed by the particular bull's-eye's use. If the deadeye it replaced would have been stropped with rope, so would the bull's-eye, etc. Bull's-eyes are the exception to perfection in machine-made model parts. Usually they are quite roughly made and must be reworked to make them look right (Plate VI).

DEADEYES

Deadeyes were rigged in pairs with a rope (lanyard) between. One in each pair mounted on chain plates, iron futtocks, and bowsprit bands is described in Chapter X. Descriptions here cover installation of deadeyes in rope futtocks (as on war vessels), turning in other deadeyes of each pair, and setting up lanyards.

Deadeyes in rope futtocks had strops like those in the channels, with lower loops which penetrated the lower mast tops or topmast crosstrees. Futtocks had a hook spliced into one end which was hooked into the deadeye strops below the tops and crosstrees; lower ends of futtocks were secured to futtock staffs. These were oak poles equal in diameter to the lower shrouds and were lashed horizontally on the inboard side of the lower and topmast shrouds just above the level of the hoisted yards. The futtocks were wound with two turns around the staff and secured on their own ends with two or three seizings. This method can be followed, but an equally satisfactory scheme consists of substituting a tight eye splice in the futtocks for strops and hooks with each futtock fed down through holes in the tops and crosstrees. A drop of cement on each splice fixes them in the holes, and a little cement applied between the eyes and deadeyes helps to prevent turning when lanyards are being set up. Lower ends are secured to the staffs as described.

Deadeyes are seized into rope shrouds and backstays, as shown in Plate VI. Those in wire rigging are spliced in. After splicing the wire, apply soldering flux to splice and flood it with soft solder to be assured of a permanent connection. If twine is used in lieu of stranded wire, splice the deadeyes into the shrouds and backstays.

When completed, each set of shroud or backstay deadeyes must be in a line parallel to the rail. This is the most difficult part of rigging deadeyes. If perfect parallelism is not maintained, the result is not consistent with all that goes above, and it looks abominable. Spacing is as shown in sail plans. It is recommended that deadeyes be turned or spliced in and lanyards rigged temporarily. After each whole set is rigged, allow it to stand for a few days to stretch out all kinks and slack. Then adjustments can be made as required so all upper deadeyes form a straight line.

Lanyards are rigged with the standing end in the left-hand hole of the upper deadeye, as viewed from inboard regardless of side. An overhand or figure eight knot is tied in the lanyard. Then the lanyard is rove through from inside until the knot is jammed against the hole. The lanyard is then rove from left to right with the crossovers on the inside. Each loop is tightened in turn until the whole is set up and the hauling end hitched around the shroud or backstay and seized to itself. This deadeye rigging is drawn in Plate VI.

HEARTS

Hearts were common equipment for setting up forestays, bobstays, and bowsprit shrouds until after the War of 1812. They are peculiarly shaped deadeyes, and suitable miniatures cannot be purchased. They also vary considerably in shape and their only common feature is an open center with three or four scores to receive side by side turns of the lanyards. Those in rigging lines had heart-shaped or round profiles with scores in their perimeters like deadeyes. Those attached to the bowsprit for the forestays were custom-made, as drawn in Plate VI.

Hearts in stays and bowsprit shrouds are fitted with eye splice strops. Bobstay hearts at the bowsprit are stropped with single collars. Each collar is long enough to almost girdle the spar, and the splices are lashed together. Cleats on the bowsprit prevent the collars from slipping inboard. Bowsprit shroud hearts were seized into a common collar. These collars are somewhat difficult to make because the hearts must be diametrically opposite each other and the eyes some distance apart. Collars on forestay hearts are long enough to provide two or three turns around the collar and bowsprit.

RIGGING SCREWS

Instead of deadeyes and lanyards or similar equipment, *Margaret Haskell*'s standing rigging was set up with rigging screws. These were extra heavy versions of the common turnbuckle and were designed to withstand tremendous stress. The bodies were heavy forgings and end screws were about 2" in diameter with coarse, square threads. Miniatures should be brass with eyes on each end. Lower ends are fastened to the chain plates, as described in Chapter IX. The upper ends are spliced and soldered into the shrouds or backstays if stranded wire is used or just spliced if twine is used. Either way it is almost impossible to make splices in exactly the right location, which has no provision for adjustment. Small working miniatures do provide this adjustment, but they cost six or eight times as much as dummies. If dummies are used, minor adjustments in the connections to chain plates, etc., will help. Also, chain plates can be lowered or elevated slightly to provide necessary adjustment before fastening them in place permanently.

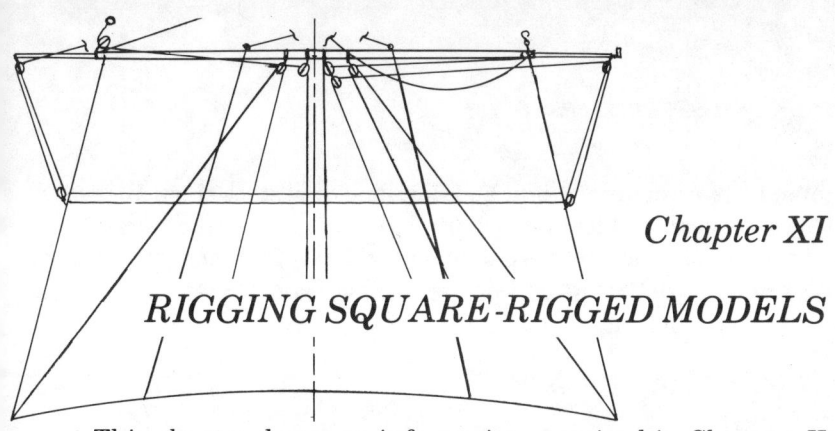

Chapter XI
RIGGING SQUARE-RIGGED MODELS

This chapter draws on information contained in Chapters II, IX, and X and, when coupled with that contained herein, completes the general information needed to rig the three square-rigged models. Specifications for the exact leads of rigging will be provided in the chapters covering each model. Although there is no set order the model rigger should follow when applying rigging, the sequence of described work in this chapter and in Chapters XIV through XVI can be followed. This arrangement is intended to help the modeler prevent omissions and minimize the possibility of neglecting items before it is too late to make proper installations. While studying this chapter refer to the sail plans to better understand functions of the parts.

SPARS

Spars must be made of clear, straight-grained, soft wood such as white pine, white cedar, and Port Orford cedar. Dowels are sold for spar stock but they are totally unsuited; they are made of birch with little regard to parallelism with the grain and, consequently, they twist and warp. The rigging of a finished model must be finely adjusted to appear taut. This fine adjustment cannot be maintained on unstable spars; spars made from recommended woods will remain straight and true indefinitely under most climatic conditions. Regardless of the kind of wood used, it must be thoroughly dry. It is recommended that spar stock be purchased along with that for the hull and be stored in a dry space until needed. Plate VII supplements descriptions in this section.

Choosing Stock

White pine and cedar can be purchased from lumberyards. Inspect the stock before buying. Make sure the grain is straight and parallel to the sawed surfaces. Standard 3/4" stock is satisfactory. However, heavier stock is preferable because it can be split on perpendicular planes to assure that a spar axis will be parallel with the grain. Refer to Fig. 116. The split surfaces must be reasonably straight and flat, if not, the stock should be set aside for less critical applications. After splitting, plane the surfaces straight and smooth so they are perpendicular to each other, and use these surfaces for reference planes when sawing stock for spars.

Construction & Characteristics

Start work on spars by planing the stock down to size with the proper tapers in the square, leaving excess of about 1/32" throughout their lengths. The squared and tapered spars are then planed eight-sided so all sides are of uniform and equal width. Refer to Fig. 117 for a typical jig to hold the spar while planing. A stop at its far end prevents slippage and the slot holds the spar in proper position. Spars with diameters of 3/16" or more are planed again with the iron set for very fine cuts to make the spars sixteen-sided. Round parts of spars are rounded and cut to size by wrapping medium grit sandpaper around the spar with the paper grasped with one hand while with the other the spar is worked in a combined twisting and reciprocating motion. Spars are finished by a reciprocating motion with fine sandpaper, removing scratches made from the coarse paper.

Lower masts were octagonal from just above the deck to their heels. Decks were cut with oversized octagonal openings to allow wedges to be driven about the masts. The wedges were covered with mast coats. The coats were made of waterproof canvas cut to fit the mast and were circular on deck. Refer to Plate VII, Sheet 1 of 2. Omission of mast coats on models is of little consequence, and round masts are fitted in round holes, but modelers who have a lathe can turn up simulated coats from hardwood and fit them in place first, before the masts.

Fore- and mainmasts on *Lexington* and *Wasp* and all lower masts on *Isaac Webb* were built-up from four or more trees because logs large enough to make them from one stick were usually impossible to obtain. Interior surfaces were trued and a series of mortises with tenons and interlocking grooves were worked in to lock these pieces together. Then the outside surfaces were hewed to shape and the whole was held together with iron mast bands driven in place, in a way similar to hoops on a barrel. Obviously, model's masts are made from one piece, but hoops can be simulated by winding fine thread in glue about the spars or using at least two layers of paper in glue. Locations and widths are shown in sail plans. When bands are painted flat black, they look like the authentic metal bands.

Wasp's fore- and mainmasts were padded out forward and on each side with long strips called fishes. They not only strengthened the spars but provided protection for them and for those above when higher masts and yards were being hoisted or lowered.

Though not necessary, inclusion of side and front fishes add realism to the model. First, the masts are made and finished. Then the fishes are made of strips glued on side-by-side to obtain the desired length and width, followed by sanding to a scant 1/16" thick with edges feathered to a scant 1/32" before applying the simulated bands.

Upper ends of lower masts are finished square and will be oriented so one pair of surfaces is parallel with the hull's center line. After sanding the spar round, locate the lower edge of the trestletrees and cut a fine score around the spar's circumference and follow by cutting four shallow notches above the score, approximately 90° apart. These notches are elongated and made deeper until four equal width flats have been obtained which are exactly at right angles to each other and extend the full length of the head. Final shaping should be done with a fine, flat file to obtain true surfaces which must be sufficiently deep but not deeper than to just remove all traces of the rounded surface. Each lower mast is fitted with cheeks to support the trestletrees. Locate their lower extremities on opposite sides of the mast and cut flats to receive them. Refer to Plate VII, Sheet 2 of 2 construction drawing, and note the taper with the center line of the cheek flats.

Topmasts had square heels, an eight-sided section for most of the balance of the doubling, and were round from there to the head which was square without cheeks. To achieve this, the modeler will plane the stock to size, as described before. Leave the heels square for about one and one-half diameters. Then cut chamfers to start the eight-sided section, which must be sufficiently deep so each side is of equal width. The spars are planed over the balance of the length, sanded as described for round spars, and followed by cutting the head square. *Wasp*'s topmasts had an additional feature consisting of a tapered eight-sided section just below the heads. This requires a little ingenuity on the builder's part but the eight-sided sections and the adjoining heads can be accurately layed out and carved. While working on any topmast remember that heads must align with heels, or higher masts will be offset to one side.

Fids are one-fourth as wide as the spar's heel dimensions and twice as deep. Their length is just sufficient to rest across both trestletrees when inserted in slots in the spars. Slots for fids are made by drilling through on each end and cutting away the material between.

Each topmast had a sheave on the lower part of the eight-sided sections. Slots for these sheaves ran lengthwise of the spar and were oriented 45° to the hull's center line so as to appear on the port side when viewed from forward. They were part of a temporary block and fall system used to hoist or lower the spar. The fall was secured to one side of the cap. It then rove under the sheave and through a block on the opposite side of the cap. It led from the block to deck where it was hauled upon or slacked away.

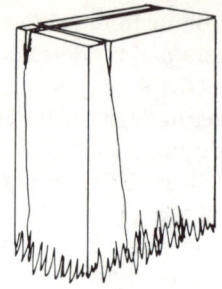

Fig. 116
Timber split for spars

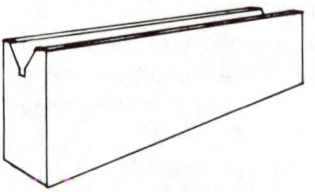

Fig. 117
Spar planeing jig

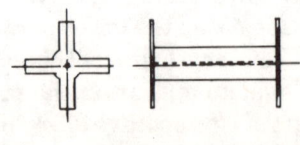

Fig. 118
Halyard reel

Like many other features, these sheaves can be omitted, but carved dummies or real sheaves add to the model's realism. Topmasts on *Wasp* and *Isaac Webb* had a vertical sheave in a fore and aft slot just below the heads for hoisting or lowering topsail yards. These are necessary parts of the vessel's rigging and can be either dummies or real sheaves.

Wasp and *Isaac Webb* carried both topgallant and royal masts as one stick. Heels of these combined masts were the same as those for topmasts including the square section, the fid slot, the eight-sided section, the spar handling sheave, and a round section above. When shaping these spars use the heel, diameter of the topgallant head, and diameter at the royal masthead to determine taper. Shape the heel, the eight-sided section, and round off the balance. Score the spar at the topgallant head and cut a shallow notch above it, follow by sanding the royal mast to size. The shoulder at the royal masthead is formed in the same manner, follow by carving the pole and truck. An alternate method of forming the poles and trucks consists of turning them on a lathe with reduced-diameter shanks below the tapers which are glued into a snug-fitting hole bored down the axis of the mast. Sheaves in both topgallant and royal masts were fitted to handle the yards. *Wasp*'s topgallant mastheads had an eight-sided section similar to that below the heads on each topmast. *Lexington*'s highest masts were topgallant masts shaped as described before but with their upper ends terminated with a pole and truck.

Yards are largest in their centers and taper toward each end. *Lexington*'s are eight-sided for the middle third of their length and then become round with a short square section within the yardarms. Yardarms are round and tapered, similar to mast poles. *Wasp*'s yards are round throughout but, instead of reduced-diameter yardarms, shoulder cleats are fitted to hold the rigging in place. A sheave in a vertical slot is fitted just within the cleats for sheets of the sail above. *Isaac Webb*'s yards are round throughout with reduced-diameter yardarms and sheet sheaves similar to those on *Wasp*.

Bowsprit shapes differ widely. *Lexington*'s is round throughout its length with the inboard end beveled to match the deck, so it appears to penetrate the decking. *Wasp*'s bowsprit is square at its heel. Its shape changes to eight-sided before becoming round where it leaves the hull and changes back to square on its outer end. Note that its upper side is straight with all tapering done on the other sides. *Isaac Webb*'s bowsprit has a decided angle just within the hull. The heel is square and fits between bitts. The shape remains square to a point forward of the hull where it becomes eight-sided for a short distance, then round, and finishes square at its outer end.

Jibbooms, flying jibbooms, booms, gaffs, studding-sail booms, and studding-sail yards were all shaped nearly the same. At some point along their length they were constrained by caps, studding-sail boom irons, halyards, or sheets. They are made round throughout with the largest diameter at the point of constraint and taper toward each end.

Lexington's lateen yard (the fore-and-aft spar alongside her mainmast) is round throughout with its largest diameter at the mast and tapers toward each end without reduced-diameter arms. Instead, shoulder cleats similar to those on *Wasp*'s yards prevent the rigging from sliding toward its center.

As described later in this chapter, booms and gaffs had jaws on their forward ends which embraced the mast to allow radial movement. Because lower masts were very large when compared to their booms and gaffs, the jaws had to be very large and cumbersome to obtain sufficient jaw width. By 1820, designers and builders started using a smaller mast just aft of the regular one, named spencer mast after its inventor; it allowed much smaller jaws. Spencer masts are about one-third the diameter of the mast to which they are attached, with a spacing with one-half their own diameter.

Before final stepping of *Isaac Webb*'s main- and mizzenmast assemblies, fit these spars in place. Cut the spencer masts so they fit between the tops and the deck. Lightly notch each side in the way of the trestletrees and install blocking so they fit snugly between where they are glued. Then make assemblies, as shown in Plate VIII, to contain their lower ends to the mast. The assembly on the mizzen is made of wood and serves also as a saddle for the spanker boom; that on the main is formed from two metal rings with a connecting piece and serves only to constrain the spar, since a boom is not fitted.

ASSEMBLING & FITTING MASTS

Model mast assemblies, bowsprit assemblies, and yards must be fitted with all metal and wooden parts before they are placed in the hull. Spars, made as discussed in the two previous sections, are ready for this work. Refer to Plate VII for drawings keyed to the descriptions.

Parts at doublings must be made and fitted so the axes of connected spars are parallel and aligned when viewed from the side and either end, respectively. Spacing between spars must only be sufficient to allow free passage of the shrouds. Before installing any parts, fit the futtock bands or hoops and crance irons on *Isaac Webb*'s lower masts because they must be slid on from the top.

Cheeks on lower masts are made and fitted first according to the size and shape shown in the sail plans. Note that trestletrees are level, so use a bevel. Set according to the rake of the mast when fitting the cheeks. It is helpful to bore snug-fitting holes through both cheeks and the mast for two small dowels in order to maintain the angle while gluing. Recall that the faces for the cheeks on the mast are tapered, therefore the outboard sides of cheeks must be sanded down to make them parallel with the masts.

Trestletrees and crosstrees must withstand some stress so they should be made of hardwood, such as maple. Their dimensions are given in the table in detail sheet for each model. Make each set of trestletrees in pairs so they will be identical. Notches for crosstrees and the piece across their forward ends are cut full depth for a snug, but not force, fit. Crosstrees are full depth for the middle half of their length and taper outboard to half-full depth on their ends. After parts are made, glue the trestletrees in place being careful to have the forward crosstree notch snug to forward side of the masthead and their upper surfaces in exact alignment. Then fit the crosstrees with a drop of glue in each notch.

Lower masts were fitted with tops, wooden platforms made of plank 2″ or 3″ thick. They served as working platforms for sail handlers and, on war vessels, stations for marines with rifles. Tops extended 3″ beyond the ends of trestle- and crosstrees with rounded edges. Differences in their shape between merchantmen and war vessels are shown in Plate VII.

A rectangular hole, called a lubber's hole, on each side of the masthead, allowed passage of the shrouds and other rigging leading to the fife rails. Holes also must be provided for passage of stays, slings, and the like which must pass through the top to run fair. It is best to bore these holes as the rigging is being done so they can be properly located. Tops of war vessels, as well, had narrow, thin cleats running radially outward on the upper surface. These may be omitted on *Wasp*'s model without impairing its appearance. A rail about 3′ high on three or four turned stanchions was fitted across the after end of war vessel tops with a netting hung vertically. These also may be omitted, but they do add a realistic touch. The netting can be made by threading fine black thread through a series of small holes bored in the top, the rail, and in the stanchions, as shown in Plate VIII. Make tops out of thin maple and glue them in place. Holes for futtocks are bored after tops are fitted. This assembly is completed by fitting quarter-round stock, called a bolster, to cover the trestletrees on each side of the mastheads, thus easing the bend on the lower shrouds as they leave the head.

Caps were heavy, thick members which embraced both lower and upper spars at the top of each doubling. They can be either built-up from several pieces or made from one solid piece with a round hole for the upper spar and a square one for the lower. Each of these holes must be angled slightly so when the cap is fitted it is parallel to the trestletrees below. When making and fitting these parts on lower masts, remember to slide the caps on the topmast before fitting its trestletrees and crosstrees.

Topmast trestletrees, crosstrees, bolsters, and caps are fitted in a similar fashion, but tops and cheeks are omitted and futtocks pass through the outboard ends of crosstrees. Corners of mast and topmast heads should be slightly beveled from just above the bolsters to just below the caps.

All bowsprits had caps similar but thinner in construction to those on mastheads. They were usually positioned square, or nearly so, to the spar's axis or as shown in the sail plans. Two chocks, called bees, were fastened inboard of the cap. They not only provided support for the cap but contained the holes for reeving the topmast stays through. Inboard ends of bowsprits must be securely fastened in place. *Lexington*'s can be nailed directly to her deck. *Wasp*'s and *Isaac Webb*'s fit between bitts which have heavy crosspieces both above and below the heels to hold them firmly in place. Lower crosspieces can be set slightly high to necessitate notching the lower part of heel. The shoulder thus formed prevents the bowsprits from working inboard.

Bowsprits on *Lexington* and *Wasp* were fitted with wooden saddles under the inner end of their jibbooms. Lashings, consisting of half a dozen turns around both jibboom and bowsprit with two or three turns around the lashing between spars, held them firmly together. *Isaac Webb*'s jibboom fitted against a chock, shaped like an extension of the spar on its inboard end. A metal strap around the jibboom's heel bolted to the bowsprit and held the heel in place. On the model, a brad through the heel and into the bowsprit covered with a paper strip strap is sufficient.

Jibboom caps on *Wasp* and *Isaac Webb* are offset 45° to port so the flying jibboom runs alongside the jibboom instead of directly above it. This arrangement permits head stays to pass without interference over sheaves on the center lines of jibbooms. Heels of flying jibbooms are secured to the bowsprit cap by a strap. A staple made of copper wire flattened over the curve with a little glue between wooden parts will suffice on the model. Caps on jibbooms are made similar to the others and are set square to the spar. Locate heels of flying jibbooms far enough to one side on the bowsprit caps so their forward ends are on the center line of the bowsprit and jibboom.

Stays for jibbooms and flying jibbooms are led over a spar at the bowsprit cap called a dolphin striker or martingale. *Lexington*'s martingale is a single member spiked to the face of the bowsprit cap with holes in its lower end for the martingale stay. *Wasp*'s is double with holes in each lower end for her martingales and head stays. *Isaac Webb*'s is round and hinged to the lower surface of the bowsprit cap. It is round and tapers toward each end with a ferrule on its upper end. Martingales and head stays reeve under hooks which are made on the ends of wire through the spar.

YARDS

This section discusses fittings and rigging on yards; they can be completed before they are rigged. Yardarms were discussed under the spars section and may be studied in Plate VII, Sheet 1 of 2.

All lower yards on *Lexington* and *Wasp* are fitted on their forward sides with thumb cleats about 1/4" off their centers. Topsail and higher yards on all these square-riggers had saddles on their after sides to embrace their masts. Their shapes are shown in Plate VIII. Their thicknesses are about one-quarter the diameter of the yards where they are attached. Each saddle has cutouts on its forward edge to allow bands or ropes to be fitted under them. Saddles, also, have holes close to their after edges for attaching their parrels. Cleats and saddles are made of birch or maple and glued in place. *Lexington*'s lateen yard had thumb cleats on the lower quarters near the middle to prevent the derrick block strop from sliding up the yard.

Isaac Webb's yards are fitted with iron bands which must be installed before any other part. In the center of every yard there is a band. On lower yards the band has an eye slightly off plumb to the rear above and two eyes on the center below. Bands in the center on other yards have a single eye in the center above. Each yard except the royals has two bands slightly off center with single eyes below. Those on the lower yards have the connections for the crance iron yokes on the after sides. All yards have bands on the yardarms against the shoulder, with two eyes, one on top and the other aft.

GAFFS & BOOMS

Gaffs and booms were fitted on the mizzenmasts of both *Wasp* and *Isaac Webb*. *Isaac Webb* had another gaff on her mainmast and both main- and mizzenmasts had spencers. Each gaff and boom is fitted with jaws on their forward ends, sized to fit loosely around their masts or spencers. The thickness of jaw stock is about one-third the diameter of the gaff or boom and should be made of maple or birch. Sides of the spars in the way of jaws are flattened slightly and the jaw stock glued in place. Refer to Plate VII for the drawing of a typical spar with rough stock on one side and a finished jaw on the other. A staple driven into the gaffs between the jaws receives the strop of throat halyard blocks.

If sails are to be fitted, a wire can be fed through, vertically, with an eye turned on each end, the upper for the strop of the throat halyard block and the lower for the sail's clew. Peak halyard and sheet-blocks on *Wasp* were fitted with long strops that encircled the spars. A small batten on each side close to the sail had a hole through which these strops were rove to prevent them from sliding lengthwise. On the model, small staples driven in the spar can be used in place of battens. On *Isaac Webb*, tight-fitting bands with eyes are used instead of long strops. If sails are to be fitted, a staple between the boom jaws provides a securing point for the clew. Eyes on the outboard ends of both gaffs and booms provide securing points for the outboard clews.

STANDING RIGGING

The leads of standing rigging are shown in sail plans and discussed in the chapters on each model. All rigging line should be dyed black except for tackle falls. The following is a general discussion of how this rigging is applied.

Gammoning

It consists of nine or eleven turns through the gammoning slot and over the bowsprit. A small eye is worked in one end. The other is passed through this eye to form a loop around the bowsprit which is slid back against the cleats and drawn tight. Then the line is passed through the forward end of the gammoning slot, followed by the required number of turns, rove figure eight fashion, working aft in the slot and forward on the bowsprit without riding turns. Pull each turn taut and finish the last over the bowsprit. The end is then fed from forward aft through the gammoning in the lower loop. Then an equal number of turns are tightly wrapped around the gammoning, working upward without riding turns. These frapping turns are finished by working the end under the last two turns and cutting it off flush with a drop of cement applied to prevent it from unreeving. This applies to the two war vessels. *Isaac Webb* had an iron gammoning strap over the bowsprit; its ends through-bolted to the stem. It was hidden behind the hull construction so need not be fitted.

Bobstays & Bowsprit Shrouds

Inboard ends of bobstays are connected to the stem where shown. Those on *Lexington* and *Wasp* are rove through holes in the stem and set up on their own ends. Outboard ends have hearts in tight-fitting eye splices. *Isaac Webb*'s bobstays are chain with the end link in each fastened to a bobstay plate. Inboard ends of bowsprit shrouds are set up on their own ends to bull's-eyes stropped to eyebolts in the planking. *Isaac Webb*'s were chain with the end link fastened to the eyebolt. These eyebolts must be just inboard of the catheads and in line with or just below the axis of the bowsprit when viewed from the side. If the shrouds were too far outboard the anchor would carry them away while being hoisted to the cathead. Yet, if too far inboard, they would not be adequate to stay the bowsprit. Hearts on *Lexington*'s and *Wasp*'s bowsprits are seized into collars, as shown in Plate VIII. *Isaac Webb*'s bowsprit is fitted with eyes in iron bands to receive her bobstay and shroud heart strops.

Lower Shrouds

Normally the order of installation of rigging at mastheads is shrouds first, followed by stays leading forward unless stays leading aft have collars under the shrouds, in which case their collars are rigged first. Jam the collar down tightly on the bolsters with the bull's-eye exactly centered abaft the head.

Shrouds are rigged in pairs, the forward starboard pair first, the port forward pair next, followed by the second starboard pair, and so on until each pair has been rigged. To rig each pair, pass the rope around the head and seize the two parts together, snug up to the head. Then feed both parts down through the lubber's hole and work the loop down tightly on the bolster. Forward gangs should leave slightly ahead of center with each gang slightly behind that below, so no seizings in successive gangs ride on top of the one below. If there was an odd number of shrouds, the single ones were fitted last. The correct way to fit them is to make them from one piece with a cut splice around the head. Alternate methods consist of seizing a piece of line to the shroud in lieu of the splice or using separate shrouds on each side with tight eye splices around the head. Bending deadeyes into lower ends of shrouds and rigging lanyards is described in Chapter X. After shrouds are all set up on both sides, fit a blackened copper rod, called a sheer pole, just above the deadeyes and sieze each shroud to it to prevent shrouds from turning.

Lower Mast Stays

Upper ends of stays had a small eye splice in the end. The lower end was fed up through the lubber's hole, around the masthead, and through the other lubber's hole. Then it was rove through the eye splice which jammed against a raised lump, called a mouse, on the stay. The mouse was located so it was about four feet ahead of the top rim. Model builders can miniaturize the mouse by winding thread around the stay until its diameter is about three times the stay's diameter and shaped like a ball. It can be held in place by reeving several turns through itself and the stay. This whole arrangement can be simulated by substituting a large eye splice that girdles the head. Customarily, the fore- and mainstays are double with a single mizzen stay. Methods for setting them up below are described in the chapter on each model. By the time *Isaac Webb* was built, fore- and mainstays were still double but made of one piece of rope passed around the head and seized together forward of the tops.

Futtock Shrouds

These connected the lower topmast and topgallant shroud deadeyes to their anchoring points below. On the war vessels, the deadeyes are turned into tight eye splices in the rope futtocks which reeve through the tops (crosstrees on the topmast head) and lead to the shrouds below on an angle of about 45° and secured below, as described in Chapter X. *Isaac Webb*'s futtocks are wire stropped to the topmast shroud deadeyes like those on the channels. They secure by turning eyes in them through ears on the futtock bands below the crance iron bands.

After the lower shrouds and futtocks are rigged, ratlines can be applied, as described in the next section.

Topmast Rigging

Shrouds and topgallant shroud futtocks are set up as described for the lower masts, followed by ratlines. Backstays are rigged next, which are put on like lower shrouds and set up to deadeyes in the channels. They have sheer poles which may or may not be extended to include backstays from higher masts. Stays are rigged on the mastheads as on lower masts. Usually two are fitted on the fore- and main-topmasts with one on the mizzen.

Topgallant Mast Rigging

Shrouds and backstays are about the same as those for topmasts. Higher masts did not have shrouds, so futtocks were not required at the topgallant masthead. Stays on all masts were usually single and had a tight eye splice slid over the higher mast and rested on the backstays.

Royal Mast Rigging

No shrouds were fitted, but backstays and stays were fitted as on topgallant masts.

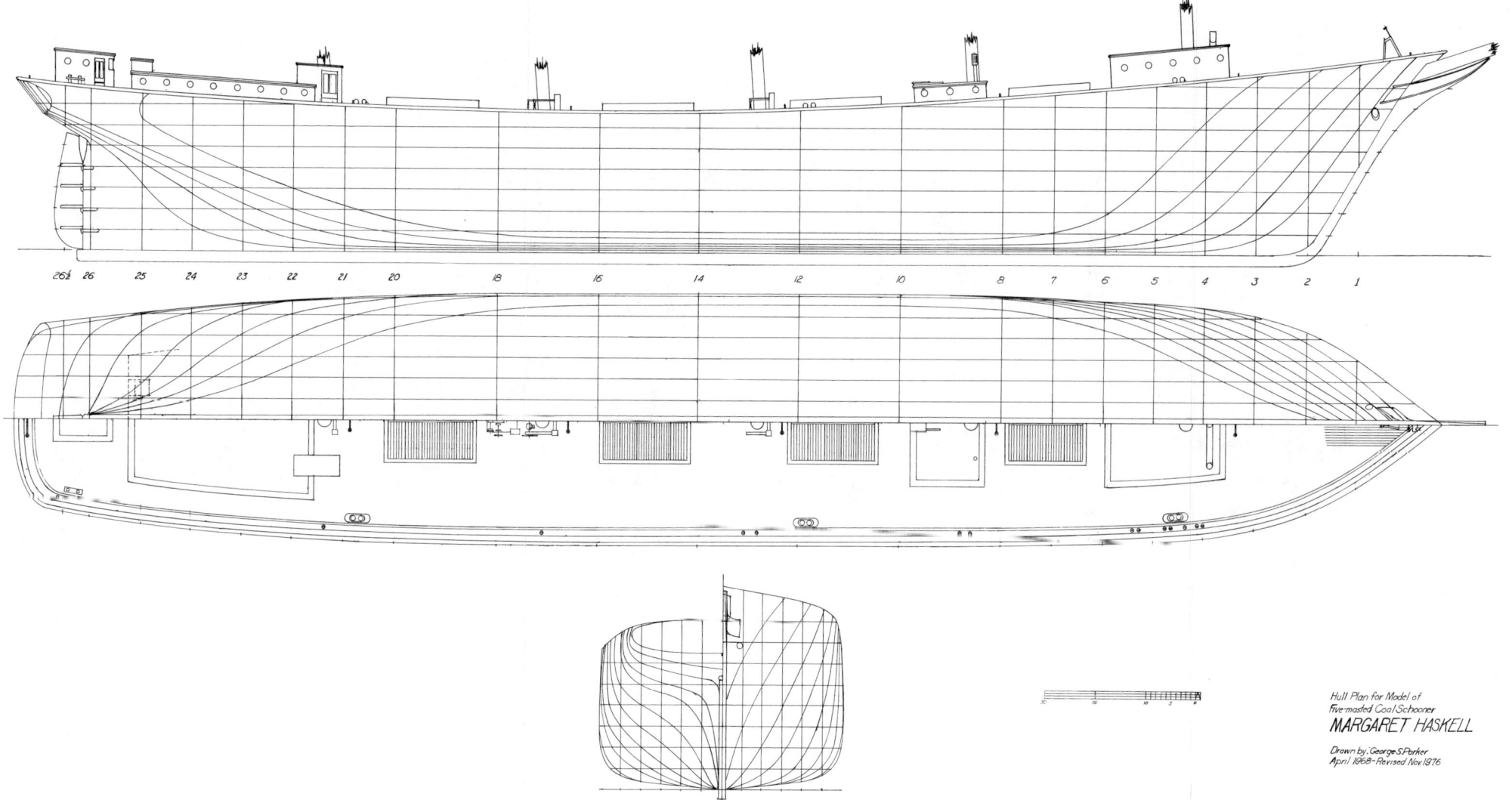

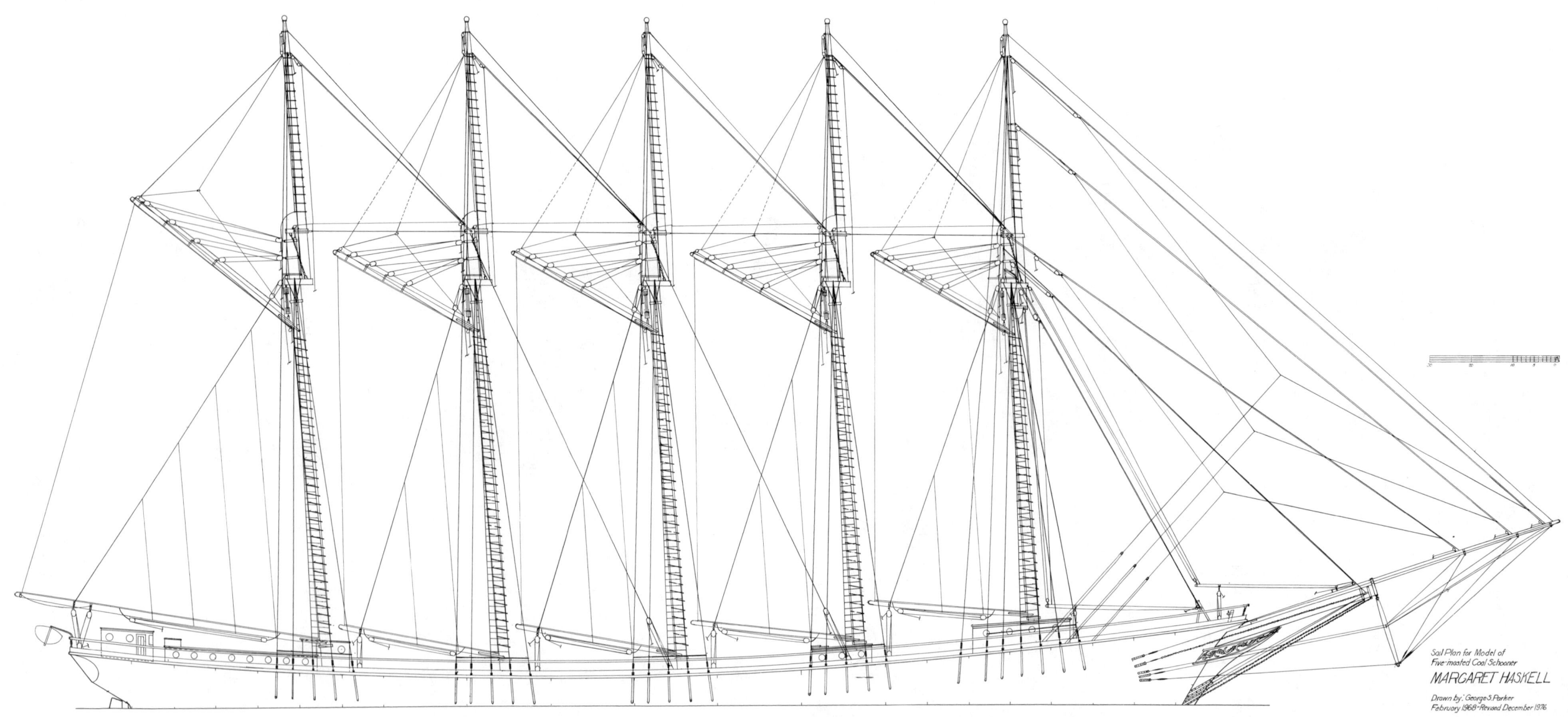

General

Normally the order of fitting rigging over heads is shrouds first, followed by backstays and stays. If stay deadeye collars are to be fitted above the trestletrees, they go on before the shrouds. The distances between deadeyes and hearts are shown in sail plans and should be followed. When setting up shrouds and backstays make sure that the rake of each mast has been set and that no spar is pulled out of alignment when viewed from either end. Never set up any rigging "humming taut," rather, when they have enough stress to look taut, they are sufficiently tight without further straining. It is good practice to set up all standing rigging temporarily and adjust as necessary, so all lines are stressed nearly equally, while maintaining proper rake and alignment. Because of slight changes in length due to changes in relative humidity, final setting up should be done in one sitting.

Descriptions of standing rigging on jibbooms and flying jibbooms has been omitted here; generally it is best held in abeyance until all other work associated with the head stays is complete. It varied considerably on these three square-riggers and is covered in the chapter on each model.

RATLINES

Ratlines are a series of lateral ropes attached to shrouds and futtocks to form ladders aloft. Those on war vessels crossed all shrouds and futtocks on all masts. Those on the lower shrouds of merchant vessels did not normally cross all shrouds and stopped on the next to end shrouds, except every sixth ratline which was all the way across. Vertical spacing was about 14".

Ratlines were clove hitched to each intermediate shroud with eye splices in each end which were lashed to the shrouds. Clove hitches are very easily handled on models, but it is impossible to turn eye splices on the ends without having too little or too much slack. Some slack must be allowed in every ratline between each shroud so they do not tend to pull them together. Ends are clove hitched, turned back on themselves, and the end woven through.

The easiest way to avoid tightness is to rig each ratline about half a space nearer the wider end. Then the ratline is slid into place and each hitch is held to its shroud with a drop of cement.

JACKSTAYS

Jackstays were the mechanisms by which the heads of square sails were attached to yards. They ran along the top of each yard. Sails were stretched taut across their heads by lashing the yard earings to the inner end of the yardarms. Sails were lashed to jackstays by rovings, short lengths of small tarred rope, with about six turns around the jackstays and through a grommet in the sail, spaced at 2' intervals.

Lexington's jackstays were made of tarred rope. They had an eye splice in each end. Outboard ends fitted snugly over the yardarm and were slid up against the shoulders. Inboard ends had an eye splice around a cringle which layed about one foot from the center of the yards. Cringles were lashed together with several turns of tarred lanyard. They were held in place by being rove through eyebolts driven into the top of yards at 2' intervals.

Jackstays on *Wasp* and *Isaac Webb* were continuous pieces of iron rod threaded through eyebolts and stopped 1' or so short of the sheet sheaves.

Jackstays for *Lexington* are made with an eye splice which fits the yardarms and a small eye splice on the other. Make them exactly equal in length for each yard so the small eye splices are 1/2" apart. Eyebolts are sized to just allow the eye splices to be drawn through and are driven into the yard at 1/2" spacing. Thread the splices through and lash the eyes together with six or eight turns of fine thread. Stock for eyes and thread for jackstays should not be any more than .025" in diameter on lower yards and should decrease by .005" for topsail yards and an equal amount for topgallant yards.

Jackstays for *Wasp* and *Isaac Webb* have eyebolts driven into the yards at 1/2" and 1/4" intervals, respectively. Eyebolts and jackstays are made of the same size copper wire. Sizes of eyes are just sufficient to allow rods to be slid through. Rods are one piece from sheet sheave to sheet sheave. If sails are not going to be fitted, jackstays on *Isaac Webb*'s upper yards can be fitted without eyebolts and consist of a fine wire with ends turned at right angles and pressed into holes in the ends of the yards. Wire diameter for *Wasp* is the same as specified for *Lexington*. For *Isaac Webb* it should be about two-thirds as that for *Wasp*, but it may be necessary to use slightly larger wire.

When fitting jackstays, drive the eyebolts so thread or rod is just above the yard. If jackstays stand too high or are too large they will be too prominent.

FOOTROPES

Footropes hung below yards, jibbooms, etc., for use by the crew who lined up on them to reef or furl sails on the spars to which they were attached. They were made of tarred Manila, so they appeared black. All rigging for footropes was arranged so they hung on the after side of the yards. Outboard ends of footropes had an eye splice just large enough to be snug-fit over the yardarms. Inboard ends had small eye splices which were lashed to a jackstay eyebolt on the opposite side of the mast. They were sufficiently long to hang about 3' below the yard's upper surface while crewmen were standing on them. On long yards one or more evenly-spaced short ropes, called stirrups, supported the footropes. Stirrups were eye spliced around the footropes below with an eye splice above which was lashed to jackstay eyebolts. Stirrups and footropes for models are fitted in the same manner except that it is easier to drop the eye splices at the yards over the eyebolts before the jackstays are threaded through than to try to lash them on afterwards.

Yards with reef points were fitted with another rope, called Flemish horse, on each yardarm. They were eye spliced to an eye in the extreme end of the yardarm or were lashed to the studding-sail boom iron. Inboard ends had an eye splice which was lashed to a jackstay eyebolt near the yard's end. While reefing, a seaman straddled the yardarm facing inboard with both feet braced on the horse. From this position he could lash the reef band earing to the yardarm. Horses hung about 30" below the yardarm on the after side of the yard.

Footropes on jibbooms and flying jibbooms were spliced to eyebolts on the inner spar cap and outboard ends were lashed to the spar backropes. One was fitted on each side so men could work from both sides while furling staysails and hung about 3' below the spar. Those on vessels such as *Lexington*, with excessive steeve, had knots worked into the footropes at 3' intervals to prevent crewmen's feet from slipping aft.

Footropes and horses must hang in natural curves, including those sections between stirrups. Those for large-scale models can be made from blackened rigging, liberally treated with beeswax, after fitting to obtain proper shape. On *Isaac Webb*, proper shape may be impossible to obtain with rigging. If shaping becomes a problem, make them from blackened soft copper wire with a couple of tight twists of the free end around the standing part in place of each splice. The wire can be smoothed out and formed in shallow curves in the shape of shallow catenaries.

Rope sizes are scaled down from 1 1/2" diameter on the lower yards, from 3/4" on the highest yards, and from evenly graduated sizes for yards between.

RUNNING RIGGING

Running rigging is, in general, that rigging used to adjust sails whether attached to the moveable spars or directly to the sails. Except for pendants, slings, trusses, tyes, and other black lines stropped to blocks, the running rigging is the color of Manila rope.

Plate IX demonstrates the arrangement of this rigging, including that associated with the rigging of sails. Actual leads of rigging for the models rigged without sails are described in a list in each of Chapters XIV, XV, and XVI. This approach is used because most models are rigged without sails. The list would be excessively long, for a model rigged with sails, and it would be difficult to differentiate which is to be omitted, if sails are not rigged, and still retain the proper order of presentation.

Most rigging on sails is identical between lower sails or topsails, etc. It just decreases in quantity on higher square sails. The rigging for staysails, if triangular, is the same regardless of where the sail is located and that for quadrilateral staysails is the same except for a controlling line, called a tack, on the forward lower corner.

Plate IX shows rigging of lower sails and topsails. Each figure is divided in the middle; that on the right for *Isaac Webb*, that on the left for the older war vessels. But there is some difference between *Lexington* and *Wasp*, covered in the chapters on each model.

Lower Yards

Lower yards are different from those above because they remain at one height regardless of whether sails are set or not. Also, the lower yard (called crossjack) on mizzenmasts is not fitted with sails and, therefore, does not require jackstays nor Flemish horses. Footropes should be fitted, however, to allow access to the yardarm for service and repair work. The sail plan for *Lexington* shows the main yard without rigging for sails because the lateen yard would interfere with the operation of this sail, particularly before the wind.

Lower yards were held up in their centers with slings from the masthead. They were held to the mast with trusses which allowed a large degree of motion in the horizontal plane and limited motion in the vertical plane. The ends were supported with tackles, called lifts. Their sails hung over the forward side and were seized to the jackstays between each jackstay eyebolt and with a lashing to the inner ends of the yardarms. Lower corners of the sails are fitted with clews. On the war vessels blocks were used at the clew for both sheets and tacks. Loops in their strops were fed through the clew and a toggle inserted through both loops to secure them in place. On *Isaac Webb* the sheet-block was hooked to the clew. The tack was a single large rope hooked to the clew. All other lines shown in Plate IX were used while *handling* sails, as opposed to *controlling* them.

Clew garnets are rove aft of the sail. The lower block on the war vessels has a loop on its strop which fitted on the toggle between the sheet and tack-block strop loops. The lower block on *Isaac Webb* is hooked to the clew ring. Buntlines and leech lines are rigged forward of the sail. They are hitched to earings in the boltropes and reeve through bull's-eyes lashed to the jackstay, through small blocks on the forward rim of the top and belay below, as shown in the belaying pin plans. When furling sail these three lines were hauled upon until their ends were up to the yard, so the sail could be dragged up over the yard and rolled up by crewmen standing on the footropes. Reef tackles are stropped to an eye in the end of the yardarm or to the studding-sail boom iron, if fitted, and to an earing in the boltrope just below the lowest reef band. When reefing, these were used to haul the sail up so the reef points could be passed around the upper part of the sail and the jackstay. Also, the earings being used at the reef band were lashed to the yardarm.

Topsail & Higher Yards

These were hoisted when their sails were set and lowered to a point just above the next lower masthead when their sails were not in use. Ropes rigged through blocks or over sheaves in their mastheads, called tyes, were used to hoist them. Tyes for topsails were led down to port at the foremast, to starboard at the main, and to port on the mizzen. They also alternated for higher yards: fore-topgallant tyes to starboard, fore-royal tyes to port, etc. Saddles, as shown in Plate VIII, steadied upper yards on the mast, and parrels held them in place. Lifts on topsail and higher yards on the war vessels were adjustable. Lifts on *Isaac Webb*'s topsail and higher yards were fixed; they were called standing lifts and were just long enough to allow the yards to be lowered to their sails-furled position. Upper sails were secured to their yards in the same fashion as the lowers. Since their lower clews were controlled by the yard below, only sheets were necessary. Sheets rove through blocks or over sheaves on the ends of the yards and led in to blocks near the yard's center, called quarter blocks, and led below on the after side of each yard underneath.

Higher Sails

Because higher sails were smaller, the need for purchases in the clews (note that the term "garnet" was dropped and is not to be confused with that part of the same name) and in both leech and buntlines diminished, so leech lines were omitted first; both buntlines and leech lines were omitted on the royals, and the clews were reduced to single parts, all as shown in the sail plans and indicated by their absence in the belaying pin plans.

Likewise, higher sails were not fitted for reefing, as shown. Leads of reef tackle falls varied considerably between war vessels and *Isaac Webb*. Lower sail reef tackles on the war vessels led through the upper sheave of a sister block lashed into the upper end of the topmast shrouds and to the deck. Those for higher yards along with the buntlines and leech lines, if so fitted, were rove through one in a cluster of bull's-eyes stropped to the mastheads. Reef tackles on *Isaac Webb* led along the underside of the yards to a block stropped to the strop on the quarter blocks and below. Leech lines and buntlines for higher sails were rove as described for war vessels.

Studding Sails

Those who wish to rig studding sails should refer to Fig. 48 for their spar and rigging configuration. There seems to be no indication of permanently designated belaying pins for their rigging. It appears from all literature consulted that this rigging was temporarily rigged and belayed each time the studding sails were set and removed when the sails were taken down. Small wonder that self-respecting merchant seamen steered clear of vessels sporting studding-sail boom irons on their yards.

Braces

Braces have not been covered here because their leads are covered in the chapter on each model.

Staysails

Staysails on head stays and on stays between the masts had halyards which ran alongside their stays. Unless the stay terminated on deck, each was fitted with a downhaul which consisted of a rope rove through a small block at the foot of the stay and secured to the lower halyard block or to the end of the halyard if it was a single part. The pins to which these were belayed are shown in the belaying pin plans. It has been an impossibility to find belaying points for sheets or tacks for staysails except for those on head stays of larger vessels like *Wasp* and *Isaac Webb*. Apparently they were considered temporary rigging and were belayed wherever convenient.

DOS & DON'TS

If the model is going to be rigged without sails, it is quite proper to omit halyards and downhauls for staysails between masts. When in port these were removed along with buntlines, clew lines, and leech lines. Probably rope sheets for square sails were also unrove. However, experience has proved that clew lines attached to sheets on the yards tend to steady them when tuning up the rigging. Where rigging appears to be sparse (as on head stays) on each model and between masts on *Isaac Webb*, staysail halyards and downhauls tend to fill the void.

Sheets must be included on models rigged with sails. Where stays exist, either below or inboard, these sheets must be double; one for each side so when the vessel tacks the windward one can be slacked off while the leeward one controls the sail. Otherwise, men would have to go aloft or out on the bowsprit to haul a single sheet over or around the stay.

Staysails on *Lexington* and *Wasp* were attached to their stays with short ropes through earings. Toggles in one end were inserted on loops in the other to form rings around the stay. By *Isaac Webb*'s time these had been replaced with hooks. Neither is recommended to those who rig sails. Simple small rings on the stay and seized to the sail are much better.

Belaying pin plans are included for each model. It will be noted that there are unlabeled extras which should be included, as are all of the others whether they are used or not.

In general, rigging on square sails and their yards, if off the center line, is symmetrical. Sail plans are arranged to show as much rigging as possible without presenting an impossible maze. Because there are so many lines, some explanation is necessary. Yards on the right side of the masts are in their lowered position. Dotted line extensions on the left side show the actual length of the spars and the yardarms. Rigging on these yards is pretty much confined to that which was used for handling the spars or that which is rigged on models without sails. Yards drawn on the left are in their hoisted position with the port half of the sails drawn, including port sail handling rigging. Circles centered on the yards to the right of the masts represent end views of the squared yards, to allow a reasonable representation of the lifts and starboard braces. Staysail outlines are drawn in dotted lines. Likewise, studding-sail booms and yards are drawn dotted on the lowered yards.

BOWLINES RIGGING

There is one more category of rigging associated with the sails, called bowlines and fitted to the leeches of square sails with bridles, as shown in Plate IX. These lines ran forward. Only the weather bowlines were set up when beating to windward to prevent the weather leech from slatting. Although they are needed to complete rigging on a model with sails, bowlines tend to distort leeches unless rigged very loosely. References clearly define leads and belaying points. However, since no evidence can be found on separate belaying pins for bowlines, it would appear they were treated as secondary rigging, probably because they could be belayed over other rigging and had to be cast off before primary rigging was removed from belaying points.

Leads & Belaying Points

Leads and belaying points are as follows:

foresail—
  Reeves through blocks lashed to collar of the forestay, and belays to fore-topsail sheet bitts on war vessels and to pinrail in bow on *Isaac Webb*
mainsail—
  Reeves through blocks lashed to foremast about 5" above deck and belays at fore fife rail
fore-topsail—
  Reeves through blocks lashed to eyes on bowsprit cap and belays as for foresail
main topsail—
  Reeves through blocks lashed to eyes just below fore cap and belays as for mainsail
mizzen-topsail—
  Reeves through blocks lashed to opposite after main shroud just below futtock staff or band and belays to main fife rail
fore-topgallant sail—
  Reeves through bull's-eyes lashed to end of jibbooms and belays as for foresail
main-topgallant sail—
  Reeves through bull's-eyes lashed to fore-topmast shrouds close to futtocks and belays to fore fife rails
mizzen-topgallant sail—
  Reeves through bull's-eyes lashed to main-topmast shrouds close to futtocks and belays as for mizzen-topsail

It is unlikely that bowlines were rigged on the royals of either *Wasp* or *Isaac Webb*.

NOTES ON RIGGING

There is a knack to successful splicing. Open the line for three or more inches and spread the three strands so they are equally spaced in a plane perpendicular to the line's axis. Apply a drop of cement to hold them that way and to prevent further unlaying of the line. Thread each strand through a short needle with the point slightly blunted on an oilstone. The needles are then used to weave the strands under those in the line. The idea is to weave each strand alternately, under and over strands in the line in the opposite direction to the lay. Each strand is woven under separate strands on the line so they enter and leave one at 120° from its neighbor. After one tuck has been taken with each strand, draw each up so the cemented section is tight against the line. Then make one more tuck with each strand, draw each tight, and so on until there are three or four tucks in each. When completed, cut each strand close to the line and apply a drop of cement.

When making and setting up rigging, it must be symmetrical. As examples, lift and topping lift pendants must be exactly the same length on each side. When arranging clews and sheets on war vessels, keep their blocks or toggles the same distance above the yardarms on each side. While rigging each yard, set up rigging on each side simultaneously so symmetry or lack of it can be noticed and observed.

Size of rigging is almost as important as its location. Although stays were slightly larger than shrouds on the same spar, the rigging sizes available do not usually allow differentiation this small. Normally, sizing them the same will be adequate. Sizes are decreased in order for topmasts, topgallant masts, and royal masts. Within the range of sizes available, rigging on foremasts and mainmasts are equal and that on mizzenmasts is one size smaller. The same idea applies to other rigging. Sizes of major rigging components and line are tabulated in the chapters on each model. The line sizes are scaled down from actual sizes. Builders will have to select the nearest size available.

Most running rigging is belayed to belaying pins, bitts, or cleats. In each case the line is wound around the belaying member in a figure eight fashion usually consisting of one or one and one-half full turns with the end tucked under the last loop. After the rigging has had time to settle and final adjustments have been made, the rigging can be permanently belayed. It is recommended that a drop of cement be applied to the tuck and cut off.

Many lines are belayed some distance from their ends. As an example, when yards are braced square, extra lines must be available at each pin to allow the yard to be braced for beating to windward. Conversely, tye halyards on yards in their lowered position are belayed on their ends. Where extra line existed, the excess was coiled up and hung to the belaying pin with its own end or, in the case of cleats or bitts, the coils layed on deck nearby. Model rigging will not coil up by itself. It must be stretched while damp on a suitable form which allows the coil to be removed after the line is dry. Then one end of the coil can be attached to the belaying member so the coil looks natural, to be part of the belayed line.

The terms lashing and seizing are used frequently. Seizing implies that two parts of a line are bound together. It is done by winding several turns of thread without riding turns around both parts with two or three turns lengthwise between the parts and the end worked into the seizing with a needle. Lashing implies that two different lines are bound together, such as lashing the loop of a block strop to a stay. This is done by winding several turns of thread around both parts and neatly knotting the ends.

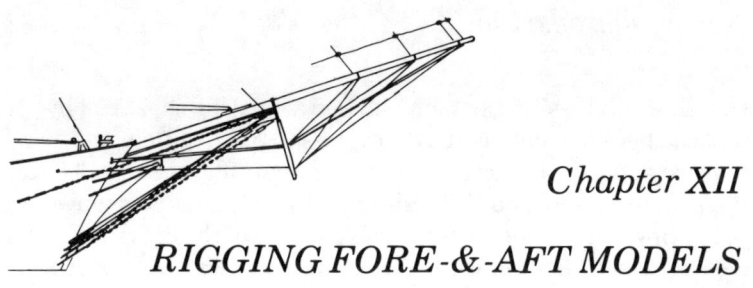

Chapter XII
RIGGING FORE-&-AFT MODELS

Together with the information contained in Chapters III, IX, and X, this chapter completes the general information needed to rig the two schooner models. Specific leads of rigging are covered in Chapters XVII and XVIII.

Although there were major differences in appearance and hardware, the rigs of fishing schooners and big colliers were basically the same.

SPARS

It will be recalled that spar stock for square-riggers was in short supply, particularily for lower masts, so they were made of several sticks. Lower masts and bowsprits on vessels like these two schooners were long and relatively large but a new source of spar stock had been found in the pine and fir forests of Oregon. Single sticks sufficiently long and thick could be readily found, therefore making spars was unnecessary.

Spars for these models are made the same way as those for square-riggers except that the sides of all spars adjacent to sails are straight. Therefore, full tapers are cut on the opposite sides and half tapers on the athwartship side. This was done so sailmakers had straightedges to work with and better fitting sails could be made.

Unlike those for square-riggers, mastheads on these schooners were round in the doublings. Square heads went out of style in the 1890s and even the few square-riggers built at that time had round heads. The schooners' lower masts tapered very little from deck to trestletrees and can be neglected. Mastheads were tapered with reduced diameter heads and had shoulders for the trestletrees to set on. On *Margaret Haskell* a mast band was fitted just under the trestletrees for added support. *Helen B. Thomas* had cheeks similar to those on square-riggers. When fitting trestletrees, recall that they are parallel to the waterline.

Margaret Haskell's bowsprit was square and of constant size throughout. Her jibboom was similar to the flying jibbooms on *Wasp* and *Isaac Webb* except slight shoulders were formed at each band for martingales and backropes. Its end was rounded off and vertical sheaves were fitted for each of the four head stays. Topmasts on *Helen B. Thomas* were square at the heels with a short eight-sided section and had a hoisting sheave above. The after part of the heel was cut, as shown in the sail plan, to clear the forward crosstree with a fid in the center of the remaining section. Those on *Margaret Haskell* were round throughout with sufficient clearance in the doublings to allow full diameter topmasts forward of the crosstrees. Hoisting sheaves were set about one-third the doubling length above the trestletrees. Note in the sail plan that *Margaret Haskell* had an auxiliary set of trestletrees below the futtock hoop or band on her foremast, with cheeks below. The forward ends were open so did not constrain the topmast from kicking out forward. Rather, it provided a second fid to assist the other against downward acting forces. This scheme was not universally used on big schooners but was used by some designers to overcome failure of the spar due to the crushing forces created by three head stays and four backstays. When making topmasts, remember that there is a slight shoulder at each band with a reduced diameter section above.

Staysail booms, lower sail booms, and gaffs are shaped so their largest diameter is about two-thirds the distance from their forward ends and taper each way. Bands on these spars must be a snug fit because there are no shoulders.

TRESTLE- & CROSSTREES

Trestletrees were not two separate members, as used on square-riggers, except the lower set on *Margaret Haskell's* foremast. Instead, they were made with blocking between a round hole to fit the masthead and a rectangular or square hole on the forward end to receive the topmast heel. The heel was prevented from working forward by a metal piece called a gate. Gates on *Helen B. Thomas* were rectangular links hinged on one side and clasped on the other. Those on *Margaret Haskell* were similar except they were solid plate. See their detail sheets. Sides of the trestletree assembly were fitted with bolsters alongside the mast as on square-riggers. The wooden parts of the assemblies can be made from a single piece of boxwood or maple or can be glued up from four single pieces. The holes must be a tight fit on the masts, and topmasts should be a snug fit. Gates are made of sheet copper and hard brass wire. Rather than make hinges and clasps, horns can be soldered on each end and cemented into tight-fitting holes.

Crosstrees were bolted onto the top of the trestletrees. Those on *Helen B. Thomas* consisted of one long member with a slight curve aft which fitted between spars. It curved aft slightly so the topmast backstay led in a straight line when viewed from the side. Refer to detail sheet. The exact amount of curvature will have to be determined on the model. The after crosstrees were shorter, with an angling iron brace nailed to the top of each. On the model, the brace can be made of wire inserted in holes and straightened afterward. Each long crosstree had two eyes in both sides, as shown for securing on end of solid rod lifts which hooked to a link on each side of the cap. These lifts were necessary to support the weight of crewmen working aloft and of dories when hoisted in and out from an eyebolt near the crosstree's end.

The shorter crosstrees also had one lift fitted in the same manner. *Margaret Haskell*'s crosstrees were of equal length and served to spread topmast shrouds. Iron rod futtocks to bands below were connected to rigging screws which set up the shrouds. Another member called a spreader was bolted to the top of the crosstrees on an angle, as shown in the detail sheet. A hole in the outboard ends provided passage for the backstays. Spreaders on the foremast accommodated two backstays. Because spreaders did not swing aft far enough to land on the after crosstree, a member was fitted fore and aft between ends of the crosstrees to support them.

MAST ASSEMBLIES

After spars are made, assemble the masts. Fit any bands just below the trestletrees. Then make and fit crosstrees and trestletrees followed by bands on the mast in the doublings. Bands for blocks have holes drilled on their after sides through which ringbolts are driven for connecting peak halyard blocks. On *Helen B. Thomas* the upper shank of the throat halyard crane is driven into a band and its lower shank is driven into the mast below the trestletrees. Fishing schooners' throat halyard blocks were rigged so their sheaves were fore and aft; hence the need for cranes to keep them away from the mast. Throat halyard blocks on coasters were rigged so their sheaves were athwartships and they were hooked to a staple bolt with the bail below the after part of the trestletrees.

After the bands on doublings are fitted up, install the caps including bails for stays, etc. When assembling *Margaret Haskell*'s foremast do not neglect to fit the lower trestletrees and the raised shoulder for the forestay. Also, ringbolts must be inserted on each side of the upper peak halyard block bands for attaching the shifting forestays on her mizzenmast and jigger mast. Customarily, large coal schooners carried heel chains from an ear on each side of the cap to a heavy eyebolt in the forward end of each trestletree, with rigging screws to make them tight. They may be omitted but can be fitted quite easily by soldering an eye, including the end of the chain to the cap. The lower end of the chain is cut to length and rigged through a long-shanked staple made of copper wire. The staple shanks are inserted through the end link and holes drilled in the trestletrees with the ends twisted together below until the chain is taut. The twisted portion is then cut short and forced into a groove previously cut between the holes (hidden by paint).

Before fitting topmasts to their masts, fit all of their mast bands. The bands were used only for providing ringbolts for the blocks. Except where noted, all shrouds and permanent stays went around the spar and used the upper edge of the bands for a shoulder, so do not provide eyes or ears on the bands for them. After topmasts have been housed, set the masts in their holes and tie them plumb. Then sight from each end to make sure all topmasts are in a perfect line. If any are out, shift them to proper alignment before proceeding. Usually a slight twist of the cap will suffice.

Before fitting the gooseneck and boom saddles, mast hoops must be slid on the mast. These are represented in the sail plans by a series of heavy lines slightly cocked on the masts. They were the means by which the forward edges, or luffs, were connected to their masts and allowed to turn with the booms and gaffs. Since these plans were made, it has been learned that the number shown on both masts and topmasts should be reduced by one-third.

Actual hoops were made of ash bent into rings and joined at a long tapered overlap with rivets. When scaled-down for models the stock for hoops on lower masts is a slack 1/32" and on topmasts about half that. Since they are so slender it is suggested that they be simulated with endless brass wire rings made and joined, as described for rings in ringbolts. Their diameters should be about one-quarter larger than the spar.

Boom saddles were made in two halves with an iron circumferential band to bind them on the masts. They were held up with four chocks below, as shown in sail plans and detail sheets. Model saddles are made from one piece of maple and glued directly in place. The chocks can be pine or other softwood. There is another wooden ring about *Helen B. Thomas'* foremast below the gooseneck bands which can be made the same way. Before fitting it to the mast, drill for the belaying pins. This ring is fitted with inverted thumb cleats on the sides of the mast for fore throat and peak halyards which are led under the cleats and up to belaying pins in the ring.

Blocks attached directly to the mast should be installed before the masts are stepped. Study sail plans and detail sheets carefully so none are missed. In general, the hooks on the wire strops are just fed through the eyes, ears, or rings. The only exceptions to this on *Helen B. Thomas* are the jumbo halyard blocks and throat halyard blocks on both the fore- and mainmasts. Eyebolts (pad eyes with threaded shanks shortened) are screwed into lower faces of the forward ends of the fore-trestletrees, so a single block can be hooked to each for a double-ended halyard. Fore-throat halyard blocks hooked to a shackle in the crane; main-throat halyard cranes had a heart-shaped shackle so two double blocks could be hooked on; note detail sheet. Throat halyard blocks on *Margaret Haskell* are hooked into inverted staples with long shanks in holes drilled through the trestletree blocking and after-crosstrees. A nail can be inserted in the staples while shanks are twisted together so staple will not be drawn up too tightly. The twisted section is cut and forced into a slot between holes, as described for the heel chain staples. Topping lift blocks were hooked into straps with an eye hanging aft of the crosstrees and bolted down through the trestletrees. It is suggested that pad eyes be screwed into the after ends of each trestletree for this connection.

It is also easier to fit the crosstree lifts on *Helen B. Thomas* and the futtocks on *Margaret Haskell* before stepping masts.

BOWSPRIT RIGGING

Margaret Haskell's bowsprit was square throughout with a cap on its end. The cap consists of a square band to fit the bowsprit's end with a band for the jibboom soldered to its top surface. Eyes are soldered to each side for attaching whisker booms on the center line of the jibboom, and one eye is attached below for the dolphin striker. Two bands are fitted aft of the cap for attaching bobstays and bowsprit shrouds. A piece of shaped copper or brass is soldered mid-height on each side with vertical holes in the middle for reeving the jibstays through. Bobstays are attached to an eye in the underside of each band and shrouds to an eye on each side of the after band. The jibboom is made and fitted similarly to the description for *Isaac Webb*'s jibboom, with three slight shoulders to prevent slippage. Chain bobstays and shrouds are rigged, as shown in sail plan. Martingale rigging is taken directly from designer's plan but, since the plan was drawn for demonstration purposes, it is not certain that this vessel or any other vessel was so rigged. It seems more likely that the martingales were chain and rigged, as shown in Fig. 50, Chapter III. This opinion is based upon the fact that other schooners by the same designer were rigged as drawn in the figure. The descriptions in Chapter XVIII follow the plan. If the alternate and more likely scheme is chosen, leads of head stays and martingales are altered. Instead of the head stays securing to plates below the shroud plates they are set up on their own ends abreast and close to the bowsprit on bull's-eyes strapped to pad eyes. Chain martingales follow the lead, described in Chapter XVIII, outboard of the dolphin striker. The two leading from the dolphin striker back to the bow run just inside of the bowsprit shrouds and set up to plates just under the rail.

BOOMS & GAFFS

Booms and gaffs on quadrilateral sails were customarily connected to their masts with jaws which allowed pivoting both horizontally and vertically.

After these spars are made, each side is slightly flattened on their forward ends in the way of the jaws. Jaws are made from maple. It is best to glue rectangular pieces on the sides and shape the jaws in place, as shown in detail sheets. When cutting these spars to length, cut them short by the length required for the rubbing block which is pivoted on a piece of copper wire through the jaws. If modeler chooses, the rubbing blocks can be omitted and spars run forward to the mast with only slight detraction from the model's appearance or authenticity. Parrels held the jaws to the mast. Parrels on *Helen B. Thomas* are small wooden beads threaded on a fine wire with eyes in each end connected to small eyes on the upper side of the jaw ends. Apparently coasters were not fitted with beads so they are omitted on *Margaret Haskell. Helen B. Thomas'* fore boom was connected to the mast by a gooseneck, as described in Chapter IX.

Gaffs are rigged for connecting their halyards and for their topsail sheets. Throat halyard blocks hook to a link assembly which is connected to an eye in each jaw. Peak halyards hook to eyes or ears in snug-fitting bands. Topsail sheet-blocks hook to similar bands on the end of each gaff or to staples soldered to the inside of a ferrule.

A staple on the underside on the fore end of the gaff provided a lashing point for the clews on the sail. An eye on a band outboard provided the same function for the peak clew.

The topsail sheet-blocks hook to similar bands on the end of each gaff or to staples soldered to the inside of a ferrule. Lead blocks for sheets were hooked to an eyebolt in the gaff jaws.

Both boom jaws have belaying pins set in them for belaying rigging, as shown in detail sheets. All booms were fitted with a heavy band and bail for securing sheet-blocks. This allowed the sheets to draw on a line through the center of the boom and thus reduced the twisting and wringing action on the jaws. All booms, except the fore boom on *Helen B. Thomas*, had boom tackles which hooked to the eye in a tight band forward of the sheet band and to an eyebolt driven into the underside of the boom aft of the jaws.

Boom tackles could very well be considered as useless rigging by a tyro modeler anxious to finish and omit them. However, they should be rigged because they served two very important functions. First, they prevented the booms from slatting against their sheets in calm weather with a sea running when the forward block was rigged to a convenient place and the tackle hauled taut against the sheet. Second, they prevented an unintentional jibe. Refer to the middle drawing in Fig. 52, Chapter III.

Consider *Margaret Haskell* as she sailed before the wind with the spanker boom almost on the backstay in moderate or heavy wind. Through a slight error in steering or a fluke in the wind, the wind strikes the forward side of the sail. Almost instantaneously the boom lifts, crosses the center line nearly vertical, and slams down on the other side while dragging upwards to two tons of sail, a 50′ gaff, and its gear with it. Unless one has witnessed this cataclysmic event it is almost impossible to comprehend the bone-jarring blast which occurs when the sail fills on the other side if, of course, everything stood throughout the jibe. To prevent this the boom tackle was led forward outside of the standing rigging and hove taut.

Booms are finished similar to gaffs, in terms of attaching points for the sail clews. Any other equipment or rigging required is covered in Chapters XVII and XVIII.

Margaret Haskell's fore-staysail and jibbooms are equipped as shown in sail plans.

RIGGING

Shrouds were wire rope. Each pair was one piece passed around the masthead and seized together to form a loop. Upper deadeyes were inserted in eye splices. Odd numbered shrouds were rigged first as forward shrouds with cut splices over the masthead. Splices on models can be made by unlaying 1/2″ of the end, laying it back about the standing part, and coating the whole with solder. Shroud loops are seized together with thread or fine wire. The first shroud, if an odd number, can be spliced around the head and soldered with a soldering gun. Before soldering at the deadeyes or rigging screws, work all kinks out of the wire.

Remember that dummy rigging screws allow no adjustment, so rig all shrouds on the foremast. Reeve each through its rigging screw hole and partially bend it back. Adjust each so the tension is equal in all with the mast at its proper rake and plumb athwartships, follow by cutting and soldering. As shrouds are rigged on each aftermast make sure the mast is in proper alignment with the rigged foremast before cutting and soldering. Topmast shrouds and backstays are rigged in the same manner.

All stays are rigged as shown in sail plans. Stays between lower mastheads are cut and soldered so heads are slightly farther apart at the head than on deck. On these models, 1/16″ is adequate to prevent the optical illusion of the masts being closer together at the heads. Where stays are difficult to solder in place, a small link can be bent on between the splice and its connection. Usually the link can be soldered shut with a soldering gun. Where chain is used, a link must be worked in to make the connections on each end. *Margaret Haskell* had four preventer stays, one on each side of the mizzenmast and jigger mast, to relieve the head stays of some of the tremendous forces created by the quadrilateral sails and their sheets when beating to windward. Upper ends are connected to the higher peak halyard bands. Lower ends connect to luff tackles with the double block hooked to the stay and the single block hooked to eyes in the waterways.

Windward preventers hook to eyes abreast the next forward mast. Otherwise, they hook to eyes abreast the forward shrouds of their own masts.

Deadeyes on *Helen B. Thomas* are rigged with lanyards the same as described for square-riggers. In addition, belaying-pin racks fitted between the lower shroud lanyards and lashed to them with an X-shaped lashing provide additional belaying points for running rigging.

Each of the schooners had sheer poles across each of their lower shrouds. These are made from copper or brass wire and seized to each shroud just above the deadeyes or rigging screws. Rigging cord ratlines on *Helen B. Thomas* are set 5/16" apart and fitted as described for square-riggers. Those on *Margaret Haskell* cross only two shrouds, as shown in the sail plan. They are set 5/32" apart. They were made of iron rod or wood lashed to the shrouds but, if carefully done, they can be made of copper wire soft soldered with a gun on the outboard side of the shrouds. The hull can be turned on its side as each mast is rigged so adequate space from the after end is available. The only problem with this method is the greasy residue from the flux which must be thoroughly cleaned off afterward. If the modeler does not wish to go to this trouble, they can be made of rigging line.

Leads of running rigging are covered in Chapters XVII and XVIII and shown in sail plans. A few general statements should be made.

Margaret Haskell's rails were open and her monkey rail did not have attached pinrails as did *Helen B. Thomas*. Rather, her pins were set in the middle of the monkey rail. Since the halyards were composed of many parts, the hauling ends were hundreds of feet long when the sails were hoisted and no feasible attaching scheme for these coils was available on deck. But unless some means of containing them was devised the leeward ones would be washed overboard and trail astern. A very unsightly but effective reel, as shown in Fig. 118, was set about 8' above the monkey rail between either the forward or after pair of shrouds on each side of each mast. The barrels were 6" to 8" in diameter and just long enough to fit between shrouds with slight clearance for the battens nailed at right angles to each other on each end. The battens were about 24" long. Modelers may omit these unsightly contraptions but, if they are fitted, drill a hole lengthwise of the barrels and mount them on copper wire rods lashed horizontally between the two shrouds.

Most blocks on these schooners hook to eyes, etc., and those for the models can be purchased with wire straps which include hooks, as mentioned in Chapter X. After hooks are slid over their eyes, etc., close them slightly with tweezers or pliers so they do not fall off while reeving the rigging. Where tackle falls connect to the tails of blocks, the straps can be lifted slightly with a needle so the rigging line can be worked through before splicing.

Where pairs of identical parts are rigged, such as the double topping lifts on *Margaret Haskell*, make them identical or they look bad.

There may be occasions where it is almost impossible to work a splice into a line because of other rigging being too close (usually due to an oversight during preliminary planning). If this happens, the hedge mentioned earlier consisting of a small copper wire link for the final connection is usually a solution.

RIGGING SAILS

Some existing sail plans of these schooners do not clearly indicate location of reef bands, apparently because sailmakers used time-honored rules. Reasonable locations for those on *Helen B. Thomas* are one-quarter the way up from the boom for the single reef in her foresail, and another approximately one-half the way up on her mainsail. Because *Margaret Haskell* had so many sails, some could be lowered to reduce sail area until the canvas in the remaining sails was overstressed. Therefore, only single reef bands were used, located about one-quarter of the way up.

Head staysails on both schooners and topmast staysails on *Margaret Haskell* were hanked to their stays. Hanks were either solid rings, horseshoe-shaped with eyes in each end, or were heavy snap hooks. It is suggested that small rings be used and, if sails are hoisted, downhauls should be threaded through two or three equally-spaced rings.

Fisherman's staysails were not hanked to the main-topmast stay. Instead, they were fitted with a steel wire boltrope and allowed to billow out to leeward.

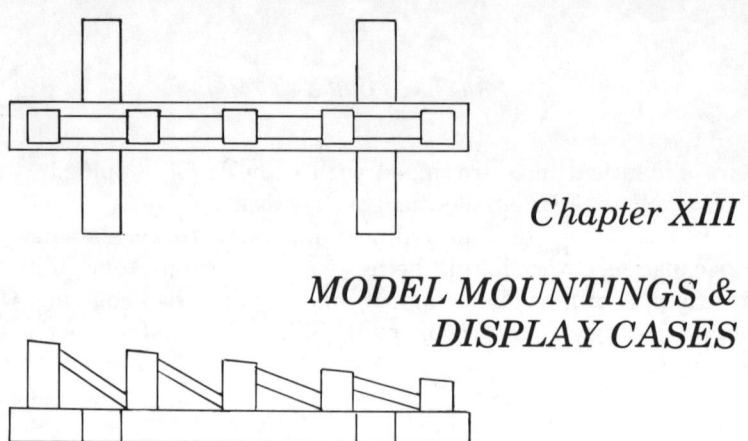

Chapter XIII
MODEL MOUNTINGS & DISPLAY CASES

Each model must have a mounting during its construction. It is used to support the model from the time the stem, keel, and sternpost are fitted and final outside sanding is done until the model is rigged and ready to set in its *permanent* mounting. *Working* mountings need not be fancy but they must fulfill certain vital functions: hulls must be held so their load waterlines are level both fore and aft and athwartships; they must not scar the hull, and they must hold the hulls in place while being worked upon. Because each model requires a specialized working mounting, description of the required design for each model is now needed as well as pertinent data on permanent mountings and related accessories.

Permanent mountings are a different matter. Their structural strength need be only adequate to support a relatively light weight but they must retain their shape. Their design must be such that they hide as little of the hull as possible and do not detract attention from the model. There are many, many designs for these mountings, some better than others. Several styles are suggested in this chapter.

Every model deserves a case to provide protection from dust and unauthorized, busy hands. It must be made so it detracts as little as possible from the model both in its appearance and in obstructing view. Since the mounting and the case are both extensions of their model, they should be made well and finished like a piece of fine furniture.

Location for displaying a model should be well chosen. It is of paramount importance that a model be out of the way from physical harm. A broken spar or rigging line may be almost, if not, impossible to replace. Repair work is usually obvious because color hues are difficult to match and the fine adjustment of rigging is awry. No model should be located where it will receive direct sunlight. Sun's rays obviously tend to generate excessive heat and, more subtly, accelerate the rate of deterioration of rigging lines. Damage of this kind is further accelerated if the case is made from clear plastic sheets with cemented seams because no ventilation is possible. Rapid changes in humidity also have a very deleterious effect on the hull and rigging. In model making, recall that the hulls were not sealed tightly and likewise well designed cases admit small amounts of fresh air. Both of these ventilation schemes smooth out the effects of ups and downs

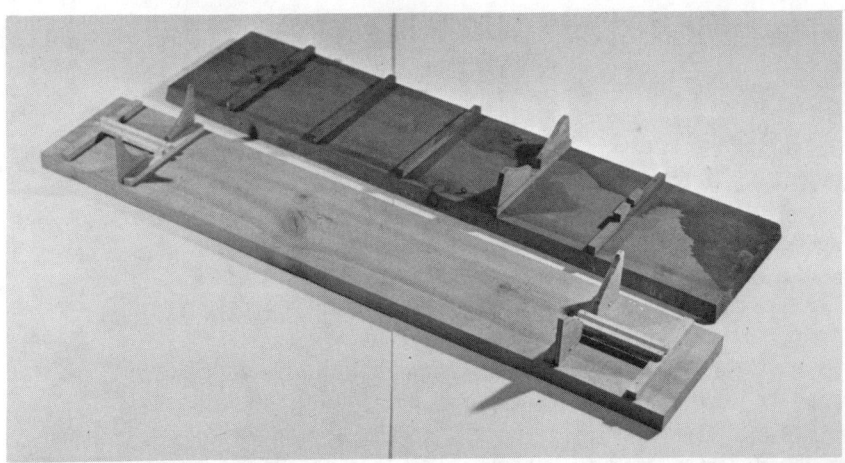

Photo 23—Working mountings used while building *Wasp* and *Margaret Haskell*. **Photo 24**—Suitable working mounting for *Helen B. Thomas*. **Photo 25**—Permanent mounting for *Lexington*.

Photo 26—View of stern before fitting boat showing house and rail construction along with rigging details. Note chock on log rail. Photo 27—View of bow showing rail construction and rigging detail on bowsprit and jibboom. Photos by Mark Convertito.

of humidity in ambient air. Humidification during the heating season prevents continuous drying out, and air conditioning or dehumidification on excessively humid days reduces water absorption by both hull and rigging.

WORKING MOUNTINGS

Working mountings for the three square-riggers and *Margaret Haskell* are very easy to make. For a baseboard, select a straight board slightly longer and wider than the hull. Secure a keelblock about 1" wide down the center of the baseboard with short pieces of square stock running lengthwise on each end to fit the keel between. Keelblocks for the war vessels must be tapered since their keels were deeper aft. The taper is equal to the angle between design and load waterlines, as shown in the sheer plan. Then thin boards shaped with the aid of station templates to embrace the hull at one or two locations along the hull are fastened to the baseboard to hold the hull upright. Variations of this scheme are shown in Photo 23. They have been successfully used while building *Wasp* and *Margaret Haskell*.

The similar type just described cannot be used for the canoe-shaped hull of *Helen B. Thomas*. Indeed, no type is wholly satisfactory because the hull is very difficult to hold from sliding lengthwise. A reasonably satisfactory type is shown in Photo 24. It consists of sawing the hull shape below the waterline including the keel slot in pieces of thin stock at Stations 5 and 10. The mating surfaces are smoothed and beveled. Then 3/8" holes are bored through the lower corners. Dowels are fed through these holes and the supports separated on the dowels until the hull fits. Nails through the supports and dowels hold the assembly together and, when the excess dowel stock is sawed off, the mounting is ready for use.

PERMANENT MOUNTINGS

Baseboards for permanent mountings should be made of dark stock, either dark colored lumber or lighter wood stained. Suitable darker woods are cherry, mahogany, or teak. Lighter woods which take stain very well are birch, beech, or maple. It is suggested that this stock be purchased along with hull stock so it will be dry and stable by the time it is needed. These boards should be finished with shellac, varnish, or other durable material and hand rubbed to obtain a mat finish. All parts above the baseboard can be just sanded and oiled so they have a semi-finished, older look.

Photo 25 shows mounting for *Lexington* which is not unlike those described for working mounts. An alternative consists of using the same

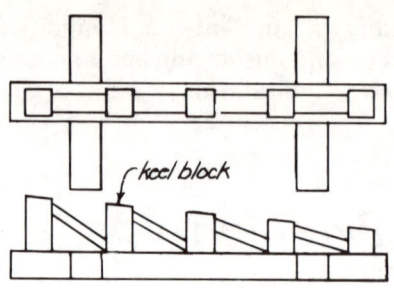

Fig.119
Permanent mounting arranged for HELEN B. THOMAS

keel block

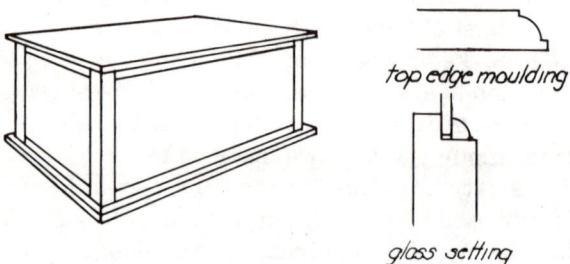

top edge moulding

glass setting

Fig.120
Suggested construction of model display case

hinged glass door with narrow wood frame

shelving to suit

Fig.121
Model case built into shelving

scheme but brass rods with tight eyes bent up on each end and screwed to the hull and baseboard on each side amidships to steady the model athwartships. This type shows off the hull to the best possible advantage, but there will be small screw holes in the hull which some modelers may find objectionable.

Another effective mounting consists of brass pedestals slotted on the top to embrace the keel and secured on a screw up through the baseboard. Purchased pedestals come in pairs and can only be used on models with load waterlines parallel to the keel. Modelers who have lathes can turn appropriately shaped pedestals of differing lengths from either brass or hardwood for hulls which have drag to their keels. Judgment must be used when considering pedestal mounts with regard to the model's weight and rig. Heavy wide rigs on tall masts can cause quite large torques while being moved which may wring off or damage the keel, so rods from the hull to the baseboard may be advisable.

Mountings for models with hulls and keels like *Helen B. Thomas*' are difficult to design. One effective but not too attractive type is a well-finished, dressed-up version of the working cradle. Another more nautical mounting is shown in Fig. 119. For this version, however, rods are needed to both hold the model upright and to prevent it from sliding aft.

Modelers may devise other styles and types, keeping in mind that a permanent mounting must support the model under normal circumstances and should not detract from it in any unnecessary way.

Models have even been mounted on miniature launching ways with launching cradles. Although this type of mounting is quite impressive, it seems that it should only be used for unrigged built-up models which appear to be nearing completion since some planking is omitted. Normally, only coasting schooners were launched with rigging on, so a rigged model of any other type is not appropriately shown on launching ways. Also, the cradle hides the lower part of the hull and the inclination of the ways gives the masts an unnatural rake, spoiling the model's appearance.

CASES

Cases for models are more or less standard in design, as drawn in Fig. 120. The wood must be of cabinet grade lumber. The base must be flat on its top surface so the mounting baseboard does not rock. The outside dimensions of the base must be large enough to receive the framed glass top. The top is fitted with glass on all four sides. Whether glass is fitted in the upper surface depends upon the height of the case above the floor. It is recommended that the case be mounted high enough so viewing from above is unnecessary and, hence, glass need not be fitted. The frame for the top should be made of 3/4" stock with the glass set from the outside. The glass rabbet should be 7/16" deep with a quarter round to firmly hold the glass in place.

A totally different concept can be effective; build the case as part of a shelf arrangement, as drawn in Fig. 121. This unorthodox case lends itself to office, study, or other situations where space may be at a premium or another table is unwanted. Since only one side is glass, some artifical light may be needed to "show off" the model for brief periods, but the type and size of lighting must be carefully selected so the heat that is generated is as little as possible.

Regardless of the type, each case should be provided with some natural ventilation. The openings must admit air in the bottom and let it out at the top. Since holes are unsightly and are not part of the design, openings must be disguised or hidden as much as possible. A total area of less than a square inch is required so narrow slots in the base just within the side of the top and directly under the overhanging cover provide sufficient area.

Chapter XIV

LEXINGTON

Lexington was one of a fleet of merchantmen converted to war vessels for use in the Continental Navy. The major portion of this work consisted of planking up the inside of the bulwarks and piercing them for sixteen guns. She had formerly been a British merchant brig named *Wild Duck* and was probably built ten to fifteen years earlier. It is doubtful that many other modifications were made because time was at a premium and money scarce for the work.

She sailed on several cruises under the Continental flag with varying degrees of success. Her last cruise around the British Isles was very successful and she captured fourteen ships in one five-day period. On her way home she was engaged by the British cutter *Alert* and was surrendered after expending her ammunition.

Now, two centuries later, there is little information available about this vessel. As a consequence, plans for her hull and rig must of necessity be pieced-together, from scanty information. Sources for this are the applicable books cited in the Bibliography. Her hull drawing is a composite of this information and is a suitable form representational of the time. The masting and rigging plan was made from data in the contemporary books listed. Some alterations were made in spar lengths to produce a rig of apparent symmetry and balance. The deck plan is a total reconstruction based upon those of similar vessels of her period.

Charles G. Davis in his excellent 1930s work, *The Built-Up Ship Model*, drew *Lexington* as a single-decked vessel. Based upon research, it seems that she was not so built. In which case, Mr. Davis may have preferred to present just a very simple hull for his work.

It follows that the plans, as drawn, are reasonably representative of this vessel and show a nicely modeled hull capable of carrying her armament and a snug, readily manageable rig which would drive her well in all but light breezes.

Lexington. **Lithograph by George C. Wales, depicting two Revolutionary War period war vessels, with** *Lexington* **in the foreground. This was one of the author's sources for hull details and rig. Courtesy of Goodspeed's Book Store, Boston.**

HULL

Methods described in Chapter I must be modified for this hull. Construction is easiest by building the hull up to the sheer forward and to the poop deck level aft. Poop deck bulwarks are a separate piece, formed with the hull and glued on after the poop deck has been installed. Side views of these blocks with their profiles drawn are shown in Fig. 122.

Lumber for the hull consists of pieces 7" wide and 1/2" deep. Ten pieces 23" long are needed for the hull while three pieces 9" long are required for the poop bulwarks. Shape bow and sheer profiles on the hull block. Cut the lower surface of the poop deck bulwarks so it fits the hull sheer and screw the bulwarks block in place in holes counterbored below the sheer of the poop bulwarks. Draw this upper sheer line and cut it to shape. Lay out the upper transom and the rabbet at the sternpost. Note the curved lower transom which is dead flat athwartships. Draw a straight line from the cross seam, through the knuckle, and to the rear of the block. Saw down this line to the cross seam. Then saw down the upper transom and up the sternpost rabbet. Finish the stern's profile by shaping the curve of the lower transom with a half-round rasp while using the stern template for a guide. When cutting is done, replace center lines and station lines, and draw rabbet offsets.

Before proceeding, study deck plan as viewed from above. Over the length of poop deck bulwarks there are two sheer plans, one for the rail at the top of the lower block and the other for the top of the poop deck bulwarks. There is a considerable amount of bulging of the sides between these levels and it continues below poop deck level. Because of this bulging a large angle must be allowed when cutting down the sides. In view of this large angle and bulging, it is advisable to make two top view templates. One for the shape of the hull at the sheer forward and on the poop deck level, the other on the level of the poop deck bulwarks sheer. Remove the poop deck bulwarks block, draw on these shapes, and cut down the sides of each block. After cutting sides down, replace upper block carefully so it is in perfect alignment with the lower block.

The outside of the hull can be shaped now according to its templates. It is not a difficult hull to shape except over the short portion forward of Station I where the shape is somewhat across the grain and changes rapidly. If there is any lack of understanding concerning the hull's shape and construction at the cross seam review the descriptive materials associated with Figs. 4 & 5 in Chapter I. While shaping the hull aft of the last station, check the transom's shape by eye against that shown in the body plan and be careful not to "turn the edge" at or close to the edges around the transoms. Because opposite sides require slightly different operations due

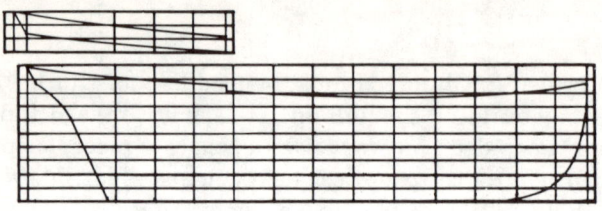

Fig. 122
Hull blocks for LEXINGTON
under Method 1

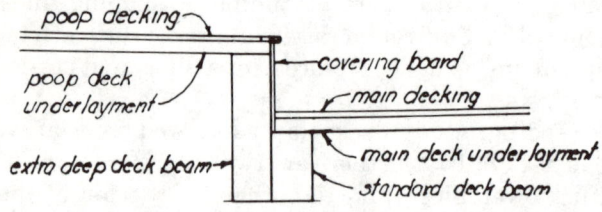

Fig. 123
Construction at deck break

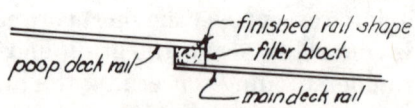

Fig. 124
Construction of rail
at break before carving

to their orientation with the builder, the second side must be checked against the first for symmetry. Upon completing the sides, shape the upper transom's curvature, as described in Chapter I, and remove the upper block.

While hollowing out the hull block leave about 1 1/2" in the bottom and 3/8" to 1/2" around the sides. The work described in Chapter I for cutting down bulwarks, making deck beams, and laying the underlayment must be modified because the deck breaks just forward of the mainmast. This is an example of two weather decks. The finished level of the main deck along the side coincides with the top edge of the lower outside rail; that for the poop deck is the lower edge of the main rail.

Bulwarks around the forward or main deck are 3/16" thick. Scribe this line the whole length of each side of the hull block and allow 1/4" across the stern. When cutting down allow 1/8" thickness for the underlayment and 1/16" for the decking. Perhaps the builder should set the ends of the poop deck underlayment more than 1/4" forward of the transom to avoid breaking through the lower transom or weakening the stern.

Deck beams are made of 5/8" stock crowned 1/8" and slit into pieces 3/8" wide. They are located on the main deck under the riding bitts, under the galley chimney hatch, at Station B and between Stations 2 & 4. Those on the poop deck are between the pumps and hatch at Stations 11 & 13. The deck beam at the break follows construction in Fig. 123. Set the extra-deep deck beam so its forward surface is plumb and its ends exactly match the surface of each underlayment undercut. Do not neglect to crown its top surface. Its ends must be carefully located so it is exactly perpendicular to the hull's center line and set 1/16" aft of the break surface shown in drawings. After its glue is dry, set a regular beam in place on its lower forward surface. When all deck beams are in place and glue is dry, set poop deck underlayment with its forward end flush with the forward side of the extra deep beam followed by installation of the covering board made of 1/16" thick stock. Fit covering board so its ends match the main deck bulwarks neatly and snugly without forcing, and roughly cut its lower surface to reasonably match the regular deck beam's crown. After glue has dried, sand its upper edge to match the surface of the underlayment without "turning its edge" and set the main deck underlayment. Cross sections of the bulwarks construction at Stations G & 8 are drawn in the detail sheet.

At this point the hull is in the same state of construction as that of the "Merchant Vessel of 1800" and the *Margaret Haskell* at the close of Chapter I except for the poop deck bulwarks which were set aside before hollowing out the hull. Further work on this block and fitting it to the hull is held until other work is completed.

FINISHING THE HULL

Make and install stem, keel, and sternpost. Remember to cut the gammoning slot and to carve the billethead with the very forward ends of the headrails carved into the upper part so the forward part of each rail fairs neatly into the billet's scroll. Cut out the fan-shaped rudder port, bevel the trailing edge of the sternpost, and make the rudder. Inspect hull for perfect fairing at the rabbets and sand away excess hull material as necessary. Now the hull is ready to set in its working cradle. If wales are to be fitted, install them now followed by fitting the false rails along their top edges. Make and install cheek knees and false bolsters on the hull between each pair of knees. It is recommended that work on the exterior be discontinued at this point and started on the inside.

Square off the forward end of the scroll and undercut for the main rail, as drawn in Fig. 124. Make bowsprit and cut the bow to receive it so it rests snugly on the top of the stem. Then make and fit main rails from the bowsprit to the undercut in scrolls at the break. Unless the builder can do fine carving it is suggested that this rail have plain rounded-off edges so no center groove has to be carried into the scroll. Make and fit both catheads. Recall that the lower arm rests firmly on the underlayment and shape the upper arm so it rests fairly on the rail. Notch rails on the inside in the way of the catheads to avoid shaping the catheads to accommodate the rail's inner curve.

Start work on main deck by making the waterways from stock 3/16" square. Bevel inside surface and leave 1/16" surface on the lower edge for abutting the nibbing strake. Remember that one continuous piece can be installed from the catheads to the break and that the forward pieces must be carved to shape. The outboard edges must be beveled around the bow for the waterways to fit flush with the bulwarks. After they fit perfectly, glue them in place. Make nibbing strakes 1/8" wide and cut to shape so they will fit with a minimum of forcing. Hold them in place with partially driven lill pins until glue is dry. Then lay deck with the double thick layers for pads where shown in deck plan.

At this stage of construction the poop deck must be finished. Carve out inside of the block for poop deck bulwarks. Finish sides to a thickness of 3/16" and 1/4" across the stern. It is recommended that sides be done first while material in the stern is yet quite thick, because this end-grain section becomes very fragile while it is worked down. However, if the piece breaks it can be glued back together. After it is completed, glue it onto the hull followed by waterways, nibbing strake, and decking. After nibbing strakes are installed, fit a piece of 3/16" stock across the break as shown in Fig. 123, and a similar but curved piece across the stern for butting the decking against. Then lay decking and double thick sections. Butt water-

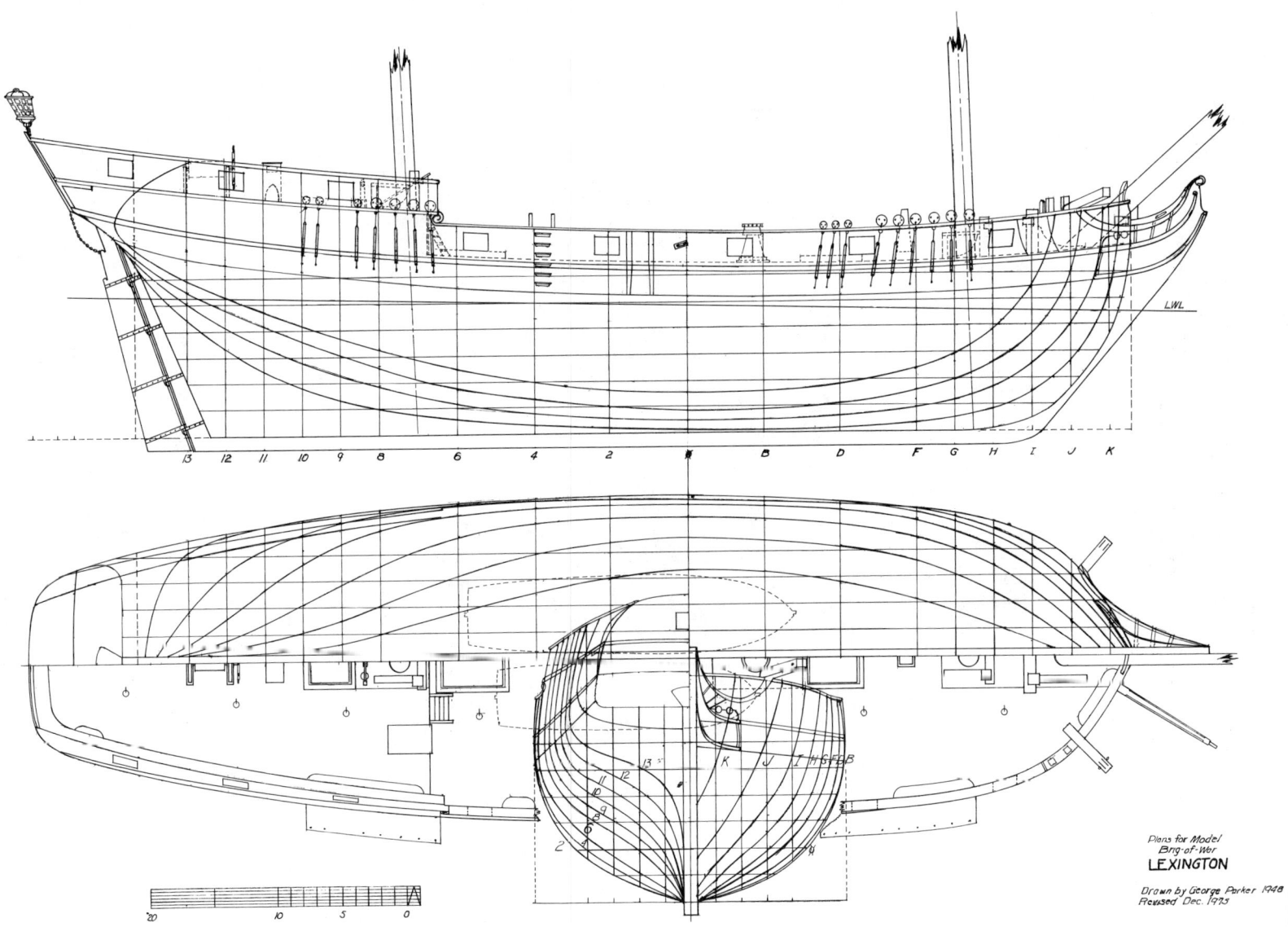

Plans for Model
Brig-of-War
LEXINGTON

Drawn by George Parker 1948
Revised Dec. 1973

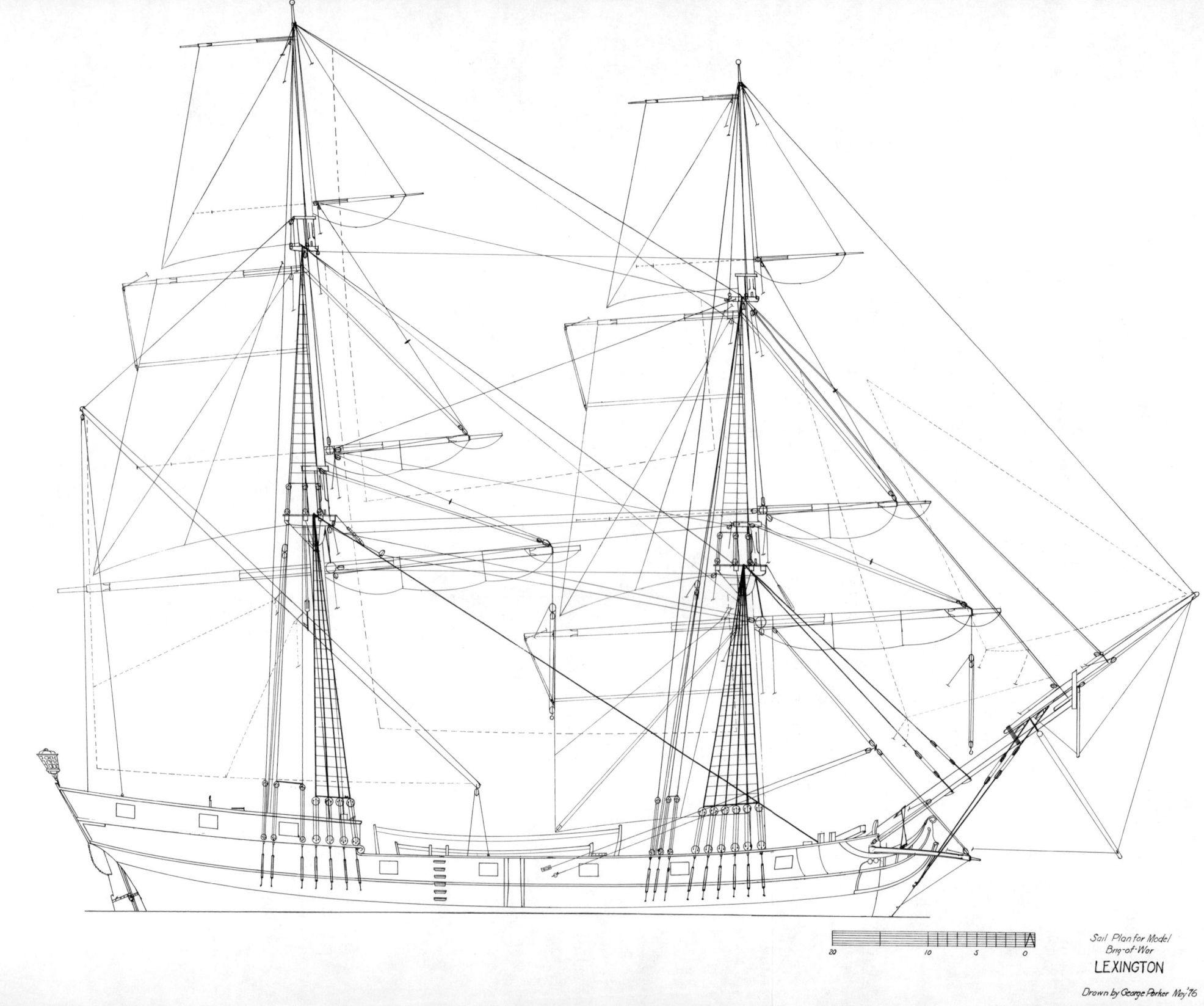

ways against the stern and stop just aft of the break by rounding off their ends.

After poop deck bulwarks are in place fit the quarter badges and the curved piece across the stern. Fit main rail at poop deck level on each side with the after ends against the quarter badges and the forward ends projecting to the extremity of the rails. Then glue a short piece of thin pine between the upper and lower rails, both inside and out from which connecting scrolls are carved. Make and fit the knee, shown in Fig. 65, for quarter badge support followed by the poop deck rail along each side and across the stern. Round forward corners slightly and fit knees on each side aft to form a graceful curve at the quarters.

With this done the balance of the outside work can be completed and the gunport openings cut out. Before fitting brackets and headrails, bore the four hawsepipe holes and fit bolsters. Then make and fit the fore tack bumpkins but do not install them until the rest of the hull work is completed. Now is a good time to fit up the rudder with its pintles and gudgeons or with alternate equipment, as previously described. Fit bulwarks sheaves and main tack chesstrees followed by skid beams whose length is governed by whether hammock nettings wil be fitted or not. If wales were fitted, make and fit billboards. Installation of channels finishes up the hull's exterior unless gunport lids are to be glued on. Bore the two mast holes exactly on the hull's center line. Then make and fit riding bitts and topsail sheet bitts with fife rails and stanchions for pumps. Bore snug-fitting holes for the pumps. Make and fit hatches, hatch gratings, and gunshot troughs. Make and fit cradles for the two boats. Finish deck work by making and fitting the steering wheel with its gear, binnacle, poop deck ladders, and companionways.

Pinrails are made and fitted where shown in deck plan and belaying pin layout. Cleats are fitted on the bulwarks close to the sheaves and on the stern bulwark for lateen sail sheets. Make and fit bitts on the main rail just aft of the catheads and, if hammock nettings are to be fitted, the boards for their forward end. Finish hull work by making and fitting the short, heavy curved piece over the bowsprit. At this point the hull is completed through Chapter IV.

DECK STRUCTURES

This vessel carried two slanted roof companionways for entry below from the main deck with doors facing forward as shown in detail sheet. Cut sides to the shape shown with corner posts at the forward corners only. The decking which projects forward of the break is cut away over the width of the companionways to simplify construction. Single doors in the forward

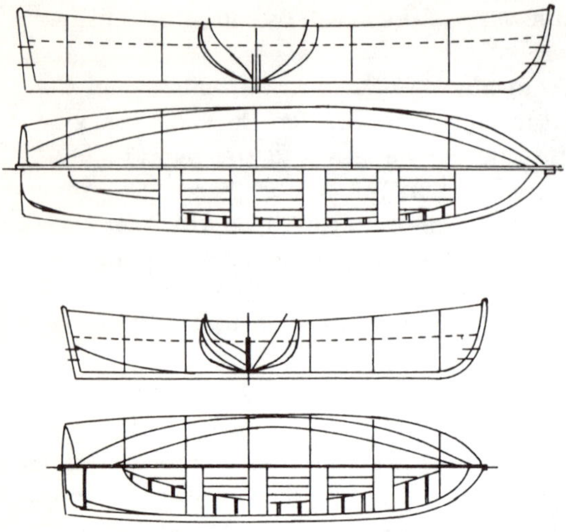

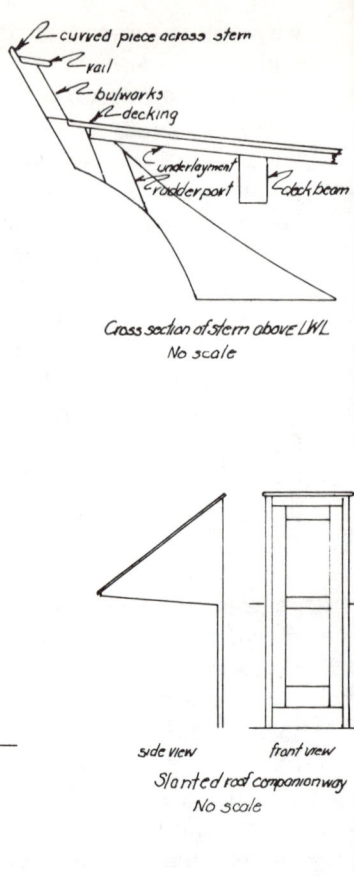

Cross section of stern above LWL
No scale

Scale for boats

Slanted roof companionway
No scale

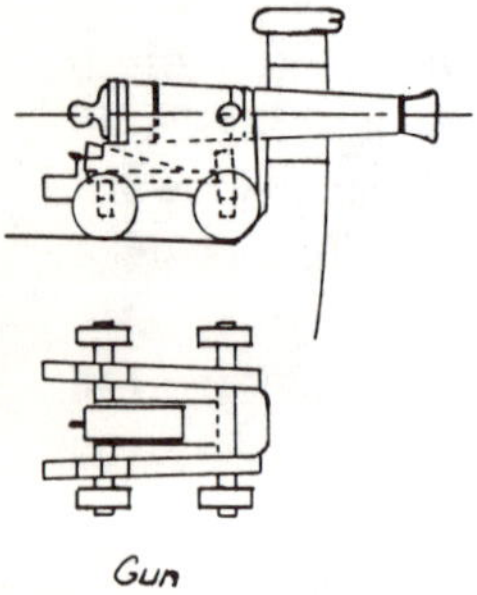

Gun

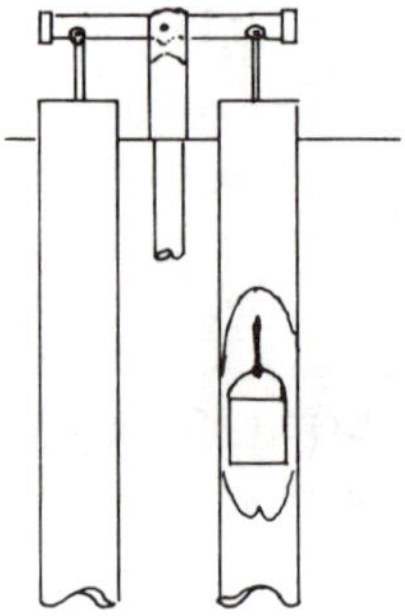

Pumps

Scale for gun and pump

White: Below the waterline, bowsprit, lower masts, doublings, yardarms, poles and trucks
Black: Topsides
Yellow: Moldings, ornamentation and rails
Vermillion: Inside of bulwarks, carriages, and companion ways
Lead color: Stern
Light brown: Decks
Dark brown stain: Fife rails, bitts, hatches, binnacle and balance of spars

Paint scheme

LEXINGTON
Detail Sheet
Scale as noted

sides are sufficient because they could have been hinged on their inboard edges and hooked to the ladders during good weather to ventilate below. Since deck plan is a reconstruction, these companionways are not necessarily fact and may be omitted entirely.

Mention of the galley chimney has not been made. At the time this vessel was refitted some cast-iron stoves were being used to supplant the traditional masonry fireplace with masonry flue. The *Wild Duck* may have had the fireplace which would not have been replaced during refitting for the Continental Navy. Consequently, a small hatchway is drawn just aft of the foremast with a tapered flue in it. Probably this flue was originally brick but repairs would have consisted of rough pargeting. Therefore, it would have been dirty concrete. This flue is made of pine with a blackened square hole in its top. Builders can use their own ingenuity in painting its outside to obtain a realistic result.

GROUND TACKLE

Refer to Chapter VI and Plate II for a description of this equipment. Fit up two old-fashioned type anchors, a wooden capstan, and capstan bars.

GUNS

Refer to Chapter VII and Plate III for a description of this equipment. Install ringbolts behind each gunport for the train tackles and each ring or eyebolt at the ports except those for the breeching which are installed *with* the breechings. Make carriages and rig guns to them completely before mounting on deck and installing breechings and side tackles. The amount of accessory equipment installed is up to the builder.

BOATS

Refer to Chapter VIII for a description of methods for building upright, unnested boats and refer to detail sheet for design. They are mounted in cradles on deck and lashed down.

IRONWORK

Lexington's ironwork consists of chain plates, backing links, deadeye strops, pumps, pintles and gudgeons, rudder chains, hammock nettings,

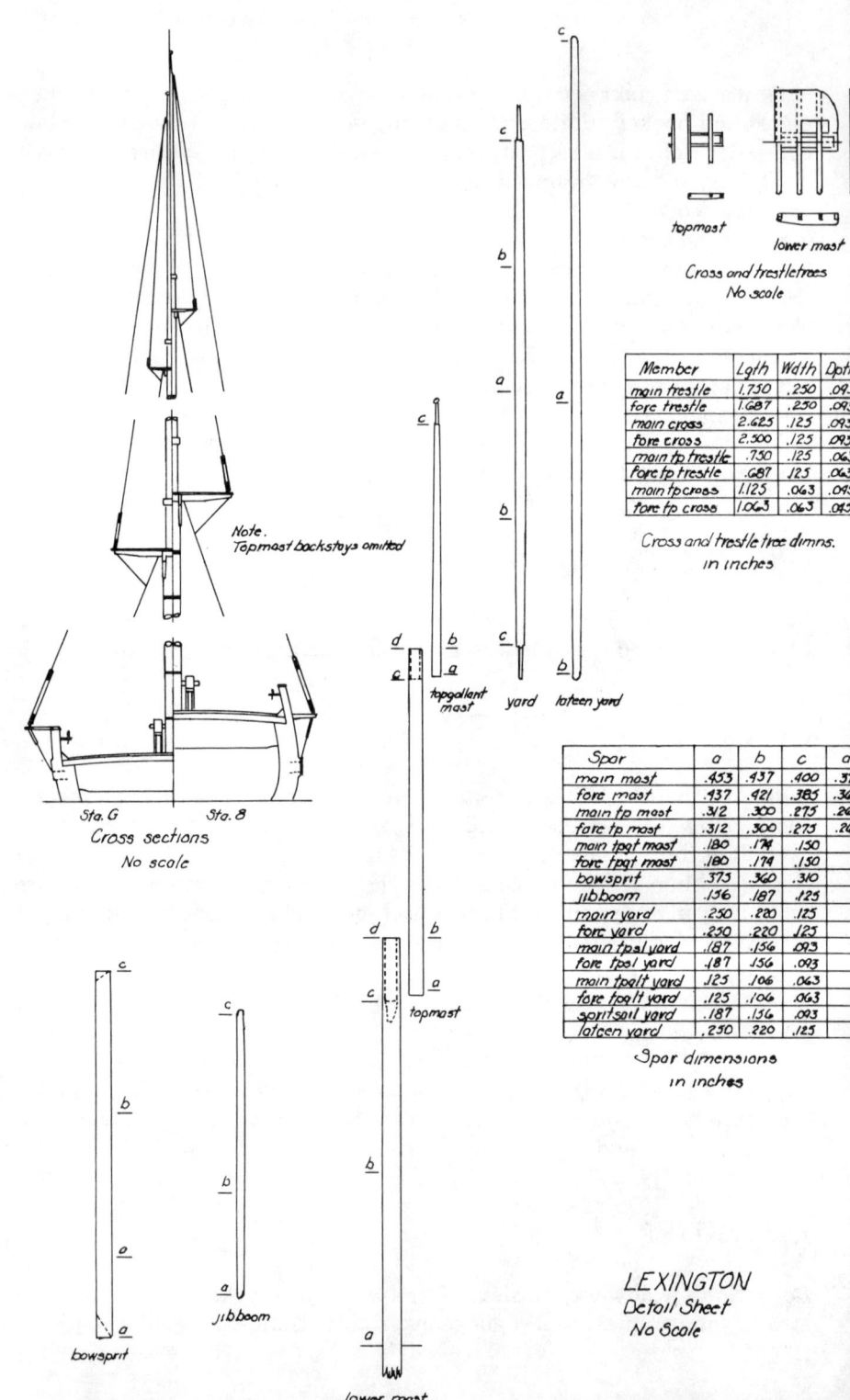

and eye- and ringbolts for guns and rigging. These parts are discussed in detail in Chapters VII and IX. Pintles and gudgeons are already installed. All other hull and deck ironwork should be made and installed now except hammock nettings which should be installed just before rigging is commenced.

SPARS

Directions for making spars and the general scheme for rigging them are given in Chapter XI. Since ironwork aloft is limited to eyebolts in the trestletrees and caps and jackstays eyebolts, no special directions are necessary for their installation.

Spar lengths can be measured directly from the sail plan. Diameters of spars along with their measuring points and dimensions of cross- and trestletrees are tabulated and shown in the detail sheet. Spar diameters are given "in the round" before squaring up, if squaring is done from round sections, such as mastheads. If rounding is done after squaring, such as heels of topmasts or ends of yards, the dimensions are for finished size.

Complete mast assemblies first from lower mast heels to trucks, including cheeks, trestletrees, crosstrees, tops, caps, and fids. Recall that spacing in the doublings should not be exaggerated and that all spars in each assembly must be parallel to each other when viewed side to and be in exact alignment when viewed from the end. Note that the rake of the mainmast is greater than that of the foremast so the trestletrees and caps must be adjusted accordingly.

The bowsprit assembly is easy to make but when fitting it to the hull cut its heel for a perfect fit on deck, and when nailing it down check its alignment with the masts and its steeve before driving the brad home.

Fitting out yards before rigging them to their masts is covered in general terms in Chapter XI. More specifically, they can be fitted with their slings or tye blocks, quarter blocks, clew blocks, lift and brace blocks or lines, yard tackles, jackstays, footropes, and Flemish horses as each item applies to the specific yard as listed later in this chapter under "Running Rigging." With this work done, the lower yards can be adjusted to height with slings and trusses rigged. Tyes can be rove off and secured below on topsail and topgallant yards followed by attaching parrels. Each yard is then held aloft to its mast and the lifts, braces, etc., rigged easily.

The lateen yard is fitted with the vang blocks on each end, the lower derrick block, and the brail blocks. It can then be hoisted up, the parrel fitted and angled with its topping lift which allows easy rigging of the vangs, brails, and sheets.

The spritsail yard is fitted with backrope staples and its lift blocks. Once the collar is passed, this yard is ready to have its rigging rove.

248 FIVE HISTORIC SHIPS

Before stepping the masts, read through the next sections. Make note of each eyebolt and any blocks attached to them. After the list is complete, set all ringbolts and attach all blocks which do not have falls spliced into their strops.

With this work done, the model is ready to rig. Table II gives sizes of major rigging components.

TABLE II
—Lexington—
Major Rigging Component Sizes
(dimensions in inches)

Rigging	Blocks (etc.)	Rigging Dia.
Gammoning		.030 black
Bobstays		.030 "
	3/16 hearts	.015 "
Bowsprit shrouds		.030 "
	3/16 "	.015 "
Lower shrouds		.035 "
	3/16 deadeyes	.015 "
Lower mast stays		.050 "
	7/32 hearts	.020 "
Topmast shrouds and backstays		.025 "
	1/8 deadeyes	.010 "
Topmast stays		.030 "
	1/4 blocks	
	5/32 blocks	.020 natural
Topgallant shrouds and backstays	bull's-eyes	.020 black
Topgallant stays	3/16 blocks	.020 "
	1/8 "	.015 natural
Yard tackles		.030 black
	1/4 "	.020 natural
Slings		.045 black
Lower yard lifts	5/32 "	.020 natural
Lower yard braces	5/32 "	.020 "
Clew garnets	5/32 "	.015 "
Lower sheets and tacks	5/32 "	.030 "
Topsail tyes	1/4 "	.030 black
	3/16 "	.020 natural
Topsail lifts	1/8 "	.020 "
Topsail sheets	3/16 "	.030 "
Topsail clews	1/8 "	.015 "
Topsail braces	1/8 "	.025 "
Topgallant tyes		.020 "
Topgallant lifts	bull's-eyes	.015 "
Topgallant braces	3/32 blocks	.015 "
Lateen derrick	1/4 "	.030 "

STANDING RIGGING

Bowsprit

Gammoning—Nine turns of rigging with nine turns of frapping.

Bobstays—Two stays set up on their own ends through holes in the stem with hearts in their outboard ends connected by lanyards to hearts in collars about the bowsprit.

Shrouds—One on each side spliced to an eyebolt in the bow with hearts outboard. Hearts on the bowsprit are seized into a common collar.

Horses—One on each side with an eye splice in each end. Outboard eyes are lashed to eyebolts on each side of the upper part of the bowsprit cap. Inboard ends to eyebolts in the curved piece over the bowsprit.

Lower Masts

Stay Collars—A bull's-eye is turned in one which is set on the foreshroud bolsters. A large single block is turned in the other and lashed about foremast below cheeks.

Shrouds—Six shrouds on foremast and four on mainmast with sheer poles across all.

Stays—Double on both fore- and mainmasts. Forestays set up to hearts at about mid-length of bowsprit. Mainstays pass on each side of foremast and set up to hearts stropped to pad eyes in the bulwarks close to the bowsprit. Euphroes and crow's-feet are rigged on both stays.

Topmast Shroud Futtocks—Three on each side of each mast with shroud deadeyes turned into tight eye splices and lower ends attached to a wooden rod lashed under the lower shrouds.

Ratlines—Cross all lower shrouds and topmast shroud futtocks.

Topmasts

Stay Collar—One on the fore-topmast bolsters with a bull's-eye turned in.

Shrouds—Three on each side with a sheer pole and ratlines across all.

Backstays—Two on each side of each mast with a sheer pole.

Stays—Two on the fore and one on the main. Lower ends of fore-topmast stays reeve through bee holes and lead aft with gun tackles connected to pad eyes in the bow close to bowsprit. The falls reeve through holes in curved piece over the bowsprit and belay to pins in the pinrails. The mainstay sets up on its own end to the bull's-eye at fore-bolsters.

Preventer Stay—On main-topmast only. Single and rigged before the stay. It reeves through a large single block in a collar around the foremast and down abaft the mast. A fiddle block is turned in its lower end which connects to a single block stropped to a pad eye in the deck. The fall belays to a pin in the fife rail.

Jibstay—A hoisting stay. It reeves through a single block stropped to the fore-topmast head so it hangs just under the starboard trestletree forward of the shrouds. The stay leads down through the starboard lubber's hole and sets up to a tackle, as described for the main-preventer stay on the after-starboard side inside of the fife rails. The other end is spliced to upper ring of a traveler on the jibboom. The traveler consists of two rings, one sized for a sliding fit on the spar and a small one soldered above for connecting the stay, the outhauler, the downhaul block and the jib clew. The traveler allowed the jibstay to be hauled in to the cap for furling on the jibboom and to be hauled out on the bowsprit when sail was set. The outhaul is a line spliced to the traveler ring and reeves over a sheave in the jibboom just aft of the fore-topgallant stay. It leads aft to a gun tackle connected to a pad eye in the starboard forward face of the bowsprit cap. Its fall leads aft and belays as described for fore-topmast stays.

Topgallant Futtocks—Two on each side of each mast with a bull's-eye turned in one end. The futtocks reeve through holes in the crosstrees and secure to topmast shrouds as described for topmast futtocks.

Sister Blocks—Before rigging the futtocks seize two single blocks, one above the other, into the forward gang of shrouds as far up as possible without jamming upper one into the trestletrees.

Topgallant Masts

Shrouds—One pair on each side of each mast set up on their own ends in the bull's-eyes on each crosstree. A bull's-eye is set between each pair close to the seizing at the head. Ratlines are optional since there was no regular work done above topmast heads.

Backstays—One on each side of each mast set up as those below.

Stays—Single on each mast. The fore-topgallant stay reeves through the outer sheave in the jibboom and connects to a gun tackle rigged and belayed, as described for jib outhaul, except it is to port. The main-topgallant stay sets up on its own end on a bull's-eye at the fore-topmast bolsters.

Preventer Stay—On main-topgallant only. Single and rigged before the stay. It reeves through a single block in a collar around the fore-topmast and down through the port lubber's hole and sets up below, as described for the main-topmast preventer.

Jibboom

Martingale—Single with a large eye splice to fit snugly to shoulder on the end of the jibboom and reeves through a hole in lower end of the martingale. Then a small eye splice is turned in the inboard end through which the stay is lashed to the bowsprit.

Backropes—Single on each side with eyes outboard which slide against shoulder in the jibboom and reeve through eyebolts on the upper surface of the jibboom. They are set up with gun tackles connected to pad eyes just forward of catheads.

RUNNING RIGGING

Spritsail Yard

Collar—Secures yard to underside of the bowsprit. Refer to Chapter XI.

Lift—A single block is stropped to an eye in the bowsprit cap and another to the yardarm. The fall is eye spliced to strop of the block on the cap, and reeves through both blocks and belays, as described for fore-topmast stay.

Foreyard

Slings—Refer to Chapter XI for rope slings.

Truss—Refer to Chapter XI for rope trusses.

Jackstay—Refer to Chapter XI for rope jackstays.

Footrope—Refer to Chapter XI and sail plan.

Brace—An eye splice is lashed to mainstay at the splice. It reeves through a block stropped to the yardarm, to a block lashed to the stay, to a block stropped to an eye on the main trestletrees, and to the fore fife rails.

Lift—A single block is stropped to an eyebolt on each side of the cap abreast the topmast. The fall is spliced to its strop and reeves through the small sheave of a fiddle block stropped to the yardarm, through the block at the cap. It belays to the fore fife rail.

Topsail Sheet—An eye splice in the end is toggled to the topsail clew. It reeves through the larger fiddle block sheave, abaft the yard under footrope and stirrups, through quarter block, and belays to the topsail sheet bitt.

Yard Tackle—Rove as shown in sail plan. It hooks to an eyebolt in the fore channel and belays to the fore pinrail.

Clew Garnet—An eye splice is lashed to the yard close outboard of the clew garnet block. It reeves through a block toggled to the tack and sheetblocks, through the clew garnet block and belays to the fore fife rail.

Tack—An eye splice slides against the shoulder on the fore tack bumpkin. It reeves through a block toggled to the clew garnet block, through the block on the bumpkin, and belays to the pinrail in the bow.

Sheet—An eye splice is lashed to a ringbolt in planking. It reeves through sheet-block on the same toggle as the tack block, under the chesstree sheave, over the sheave in the bulwarks, and belays to a cleat on bulwarks nearby.

Flemish Horse—Refer to Chapter XI and sail plan.

Main Yard

Sling, Truss, Jackstay, Footrope, Lift, Topsail Sheet, Yard Tackle—Same as for foreyard.

Clew Garnet, Tack, Sheet, Flemish Horse—Omitted.

Brace—An eye splice is lashed to an eyebolt in the fore cap. It reeves through a block stropped to the yardarm, through a block stropped to an eye in the after end of the fore trestletree, and belays to the fore fife rail.

Lateen Yard

Parrel—A two row ball and truck assembly around the mast and lashed to the spar.

Derrick—Two double blocks, one stropped to the yard and the other to an eyebolt in port main-trestletree. The fall belays to the main fife rail.

Topping Lift—An eye splice in one end is slipped over upper end against the shoulder. It reeves through a block stropped to an eye in main-topmast cap and belays to main fife rail.

Upper Vang—Blocks are stropped to upper end of spar. The vang has an eye splice lashed to a pad eye in the poop deck rail, reeves through one of the blocks, and belays to after pinrail.

Lower Vang—Same for upper vang except fall secures to a pad eye in the waterway and belays to pin in rail on after end of main deck.

Brails—Each has a block stropped to the spar. When sail is set, a line is led through the block, through an earing on the leech or foot of the sail and back to the spar on the other side where it is hooked into the block strop. When furling sail these are hauled in, gathering the sail to the spar in folds. If model is rigged without sails, hook ends into the stropo of the sheet-blocks. Brails belay to main fife rails.

Sheet—A luff tackle with single block stropped to a pad eye in the deck off center line. Its fall belays in the after pinrail.

Note: Mention has been made of tuning up the rigging. The lateen topping lift and vangs can be used to adjust stress in topmast and topgallant stays.

Fore-Topsail Yard

Parrel—Single with one row of balls.

Tye—The end has an eye splice lashed to head above the stay and leads down starboard side, through a block stropped to middle of the yard, and through a block stropped below the port trestletrees. The hauling end has a luff or long tackle stropped to an eyebolt in the port channel and belays in the pinrail.

Jackstay, Flemish Horse, Footrope—Same as lower yard.

Lift—An eye splice is lashed to forward shroud. It reeves through smaller sheave in the fiddle block stropped to the yardarm, through lower sister block, and belays to fore fife rail.

Brace—An eye splice is lashed to mainstay at the splice. It reeves through a block stropped to the yardarm, through a block stropped to an eyebolt in the main trestletrees, and belays to main pinrail.

Topgallant Sheet—An eye splice is toggled to topgallant clew. It reeves through larger sheave in fiddle block at the yardarm, abaft the yard, as on lower yard, through the quarter block, abaft lower yard and belays to fore bolster.

Clew—An eye in its end is toggled to topsail sheet. It reeves through the clew block and belays at the fore pinrail.

Main-Topsail Yard

Parrel, Jackstay, Footrope, Lift, Topgallant Sheet, Clew, Flemish Horse—Same as on fore-topsail yard.

Brace—An eye splice is lashed to an eyebolt in the fore-topmast trestletrees. It reeves through a block stropped to the yardarm, to another stropped to an eyebolt in the fore cap, and belays at fore pinrail.

Tye—Same as fore-topsail tye except hauling end tackle is rigged on starboard side.

Fore-Topgallant Yard

Parrel—Single row of balls.

Tye—The single end reeves through a slot in the saddle and around yard in the middle. It loops behind yard from above, back around, and up through the slot where it seizes to itself. It reeves through a block stropped to masthead (or over a sheave in masthead) and sets up to a gun tackle in starboard channel. The fall belays to the fore pinrail.

Lift—An eye splice is slid over the yardarm. It reeves through the bull's-eye in the shrouds and belays to fore pinrail.

Clew—As on topsail yard.

Jackstay, Footrope—As on lower yards.

Brace—An eye splice is slid over the yardarm. It reeves to a block stropped to an eyebolt in the main-topmast trestletree and belays at main pinrail.

Main-Topgallant Yard

Parrel, Clew, Jackstay, Footrope—Same as fore-topgallant yard.

Tye—Same as fore-topgallant yard except it sets up to port.

Brace—Same as fore-topgallant yard except it reeves through a block stropped to an eyebolt in the fore-topmast trestletree and belays at the fore pinrail.

FINISHING THE MODEL

If sails are to be fitted, follow instructions in Chapter XI. At this point clean the model of all rigging debris and check for loose or unsecured lines, etc. When this is done the model is ready for its permanent mounting and case.

Wasp. Woodcut "The Wasp Boarding the Frolic," with *Wasp* on the right. Courtesy of the Anne S. K. Brown Military Collection, Brown University.

Chapter XV

WASP

Wasp was built during a period when official national policy was directed away from marine and naval affairs. Most craft built for national defense were relatively small, single-masted, rowing gunboat types. No frigates or ships-of-the-line were planned nor built from 1800 to the beginning of the War of 1812. During this era a squadron of naval vessels broke the power of pirates along the North African Coast. Otherwise, existing larger vessels were in ordinary and inconsequential duty. It is difficult to conceive today, during an era when such a large portion of national resources is spent to provide weaponry and military force as a war deterrent, that without preparing for it a fledgling nation in uncertain times would race headlong into a war with the most powerful nation on earth.

Although both congress and the administration were not inclined to invest in large war vessels, money was appropriated in 1804 to build two 16-gun vessels. One design for them was prepared by Josiah Fox, a former British shipyard apprentice, who immigrated to this country and worked for awhile as constructor in the Washington Navy Yard. His original design called for brigs. *Wasp* was built under Fox's supervision in the Washington Navy Yard but during construction her rig was changed to that of a ship-sloop. Her sister, *Hornet*, was built privately in Baltimore and was commissioned as a brig; but her rig proved to be too large for her hull and she was later changed to a ship.

These ships were never true sisters however because they were not built exactly alike, and when *Hornet* was rigged the mast locations differed from those on *Wasp*. Some external fittings also differed. When launched, both vessels carried sixteen 32-pounder carronades and two long 12-pounders. By 1812 each vessel was armed with two additional carronades.

Wasp was considered to be a fast and superior war vessel. Although never repeated, the design influenced that of larger sloops built during the War of 1812. She joined the US Navy in routine duty functions until war was declared. Late in 1812 she fought her only action in the Navy. She defeated HMS *Frolic*, an 18-gun brig, on October 18, 1812, about five days at sea, off the Virginia Coast. Shortly after this action, but before battle damage could be repaired, the 74-gun ship-of-the-line, HMS *Poictiers*, appeared on the scene and captured both *Wasp* and her prize. She was thus assigned to the Royal Navy, and renamed *Peacock*. She returned to these shores but was lost off the Virginia Capes shortly afterward.

HULL

The description in Chapter I covers the work to be accomplished on this hull; the block is to be one piece from keel to sheer.

Lumber for the hull should consist of pieces 29 1/2" long by 8 1/2" wide. To exactly conform with the drawing, nine pieces 5/8" and one piece 11/16" thick are needed. However, the odd-sized piece can be disregarded and the block made from ten pieces a full 5/8" thick. These lifts plus the nine glue joints are sufficient to obtain the required depth and to maintain reasonably close elevation of glue joints with waterlines.

Transoms are similar to those on *Lexington* and are fashioned in the same manner. When cutting down the sides remember that the hull bulges outward below the sheer from just aft of the foremast to the stern. Carving the outside is quite simple because lines are easy curves except the forward 3" or 4" and the undersides just forward of the cross seam. Finish shaping the hull by forming the upper transom curve.

When hollowing out the hull, leave about 2" in the bottom and 1/2" along the sides. Bulwarks are 1/4" thick along the sides and 5/16" across the stern. Allow 1/8" for underlayment and 1/16" for decking. Stop underlayment 1/4" forward of the bulwarks across the stern to prevent breaking through the lower transom.

Deck beams have a crown of 1/8" at Station ⌽. They are made of stock 5/8" thick stripped into pieces 1/2" wide. Set them under the bowsprit's heel, under the riding bitts, midway between the fore and main hatches, under the main-topsail sheet bitts, just aft of the after hatch and under the mizzen-topsail sheet bitts. Underlayment should run the full length of the hull. Finish work on this portion of hull building by setting a piece across the top of the stern bulwarks as described under "Rails" in Chapter IV. The curve of its upper surface is 3/32" and follows that of the deck beams.

At this point the hull is in the same state of construction as that for the "Merchant Vessel of 1800," as at the close of Chapter I.

Finishing the Hull

Make and install stem, keel, and sternpost. Cut the gammoning slot and carve billethead so it will receive the forward end of the curved headrails, upper cheek knee, and ornamentation. Bore rudder port before fitting the sternpost, bevel the trailing edge of the sternpost, and make the rudder.

Sand hull as necessary at the rabbets. If wales are to be fitted, install them now. Bore hawsepipes and install the cheek kness, bolsters, and ornamentation. Now pick up work on the inside.

Make bowsprit and cut the bow to receive it. Before the main rail is fitted make and install the arch board and quarter galleries. Then install the main rail followed by the catheads. Install waterways, nibbing strakes, and decking with pads. Great pains are not necessary with decking in the quarters and across the stern since this area will be covered with roundhouses, etc., at the after end.

With this done, finish work on the outside. Cut gunports, including bridle ports in the bow, and stern ports in the transom. Ports along the sides must be located perfectly so chain plates will not be located in front of them. There are eight small ports with their sills on the same curve as those for gunports on equal spacing from abreast the foremast to the mizzenmast. These were row ports through which long oars (sweeps) could be fitted to move the vessel in calm weather. It is optional whether these are cut out but, if they are, now is the time to do it. Then fit chesstrees, bulwarks sheaves, and skid beams. If wales were installed, fit the billboards. Make and fit but do not install the fore tack bumpkins followed by installing headrails and cathead knees. After the main rail has been installed, make and install stern davits, the bitts just aft of the catheads, and knightheads on either side of the bowsprit. Knightheads are the upper ends of the forward frames which are set parallel to the stem. Buffalo rails with a chock for mooring lines cut in their top edges are fitted between the knightheads and catheads. Make and install gangway steps and gangway boards along with the boards for the forward and after ends of the hammock nettings if they are going to be fitted. Make channels and hang the rudder; this finishes work on the outside except for the gunport lids. If the lower halves of the lids are going to be shown in their open position they should be glued in place before chain plates are fitted.

Make and install hatches, including the hatch-like box with a flush top just aft of the main fife rail and the small hatch forward for the galley stack. Drill four holes through the flush top and decking for the pump cylinders and holes for all masts. Then make and install skylight and companionway. This companionway is installed with the opening forward and a window for the compass aft. Make the roundhouses, rudderpost cover, and crosspieces at sternport sill level followed by the steering gear. Make the riding bitts, topsail-sheet bitts, and fife rails along with stanchions for the bilge pump shaft. If it is decided to fit a manger forward, install it before the bowsprit heel bitts. The manger was a frame shaped as shown in the deck plan and under the bowsprit with a roller on its top. It collected mud as the anchor rode was hauled in, and the roller kept the rode above deck so seamen could attach the messenger stoppers. Mangers on

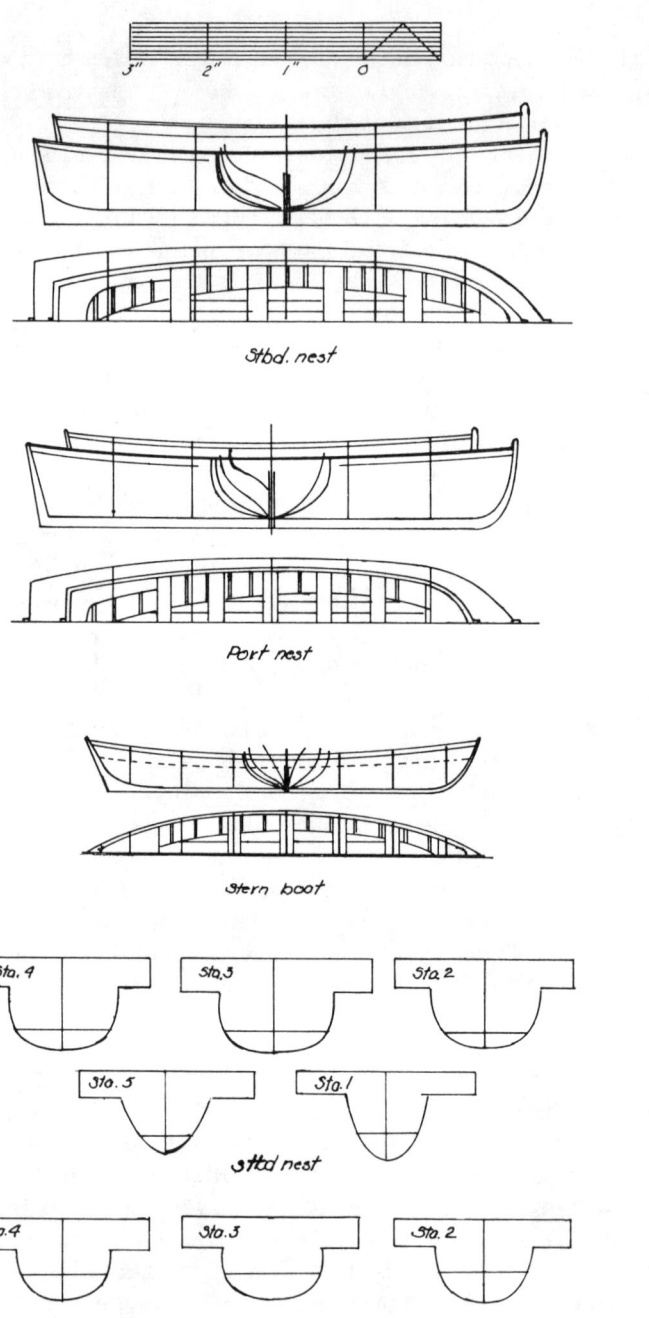

the model are made of thin stock 1/4" wide with a round piece 1/8" in diameter glued to the top. Make and install pinrails, where shown in deck plan and belaying pin layout, along with cleats for the fore and main sheets, main tack, and spanker sheet. Finish bowsprit assembly and fit its heel to the heel bitt and knighthead chocks. Make and fit cradles for boats, where shown in deck plan. The hull is now completed, as covered in Chapters IV and V.

GROUND TACKLE

Refer to Chapter VI and Plate II for a description of this equipment. Fit up two old-fashioned type anchors, a wooden capstan, and capstan bars.

GUNS

Refer to Chapter VII and Plate III for description of this equipment. Install ringbolts behind each gun and carronade port for train tackles and each ring or eyebolt at the ports except those for breechings which are installed with the breechings. Remember that only two long guns are to be rigged and all the rest are carronades, so ring and eyebolts are fitted accordingly. Make the carriages and carronade mounts and rig the guns and carronades to them completely before installing them on deck followed by rigging side tackles and breechings. The amount of accessory equipment is up to the builder.

BOATS

Refer to Chapter VIII for description of methods for building upright boats and how to stow them both on deck and in davits. The design of each boat is drawn in detail sheet. Those stowed on deck can be installed just prior to rigging, but the boat in stern davits should be set aside until rigging is complete.

IRONWORK

Wasp's ironwork was no more sophisticated than that on *Lexington* and consisted primarily of chain plates, backing links, deadeye strops, pumps, pintles and gudgeons, rudder chains, hammock nettings, and eye- and ringbolts for guns and rigging. Pintles and gudgeons should be fitted and

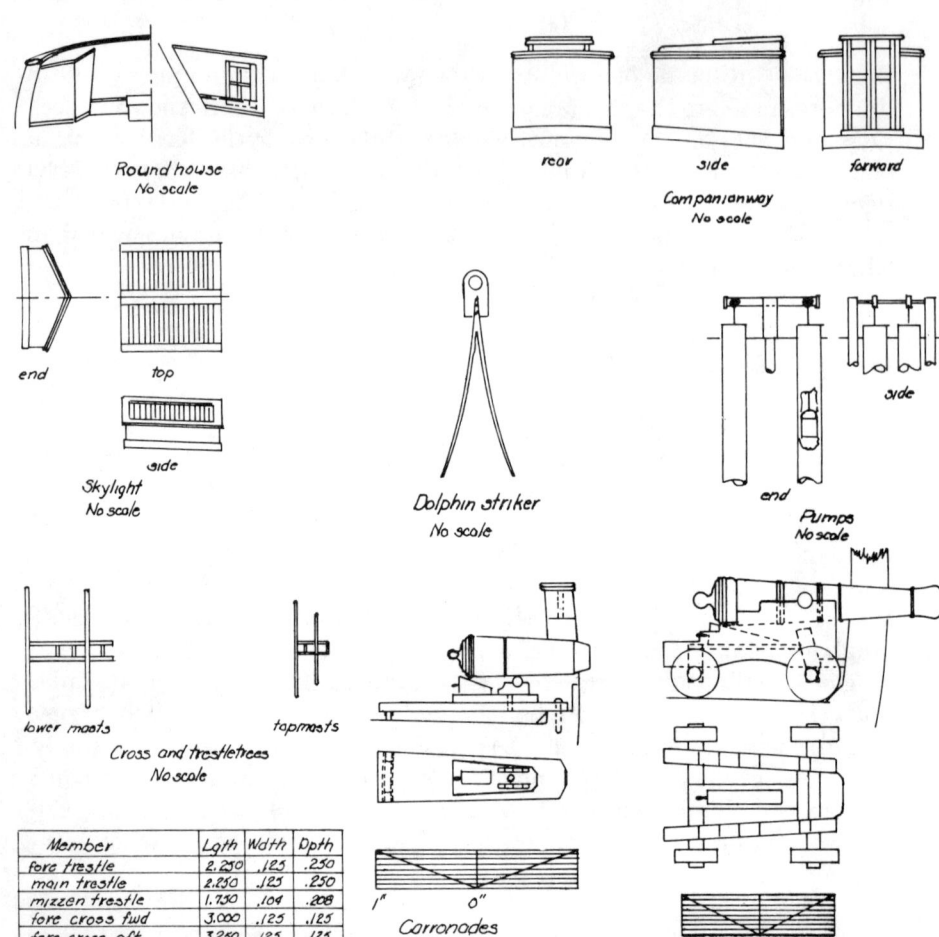

Member	Lgth	Wdth	Dpth
fore trestle	2.250	.125	.250
main trestle	2.250	.125	.250
mizzen trestle	1.750	.104	.208
fore cross fwd	3.000	.125	.125
fore cross aft	3.250	.125	.125
main cross fwd	3.000	.125	.125
main cross aft	3.250	.125	.125
mizzen cross fwd	2.250	.104	.104
mizzen cross aft	2.500	.104	.104
fore top trestle	.960	.083	.166
main top trestle	.960	.083	.166
mizzen top trestle	.810	.063	.125
fore top cross fwd	1.750	.083	.083
fore top cross aft	2.250	.083	.083
main top cross fwd	1.750	.083	.083
main top cross aft	2.250	.083	.083
mizzen top cross fwd	1.250	.063	.063
mizzen top cross aft	1.620	.063	.063

Cross and trestletree dimns.
in inches

White: Below waterline (possibly copper), bowsprit, lower masts,
  doublings, mastheads, yardarms, poles, and trucks
Black: Topsides and outboard surfaces of gun port lids
Yellow: Belt along sides at gun ports, moldings, and ornamentation
Yellow and red: Billet head
Vermillion: Inside of bulwarks and port lids, hawse pipes,
  carriages, carronade mounts, and round houses
Dark brown stain: Fife rails, bitts, hatches, skylight,
  companionway, and balance of spars
Light brown: decks

Paint scheme

WASP
Detail Sheet
Scale as shown

the rudder hung now, if it has not already been done, along with deck ironwork.

No mention has been made of the galley stack. It pierces the deck through the small hatch abaft the foremast. Unlike *Lexington*, probably a cast-iron range was used set in a sheet metal housing with one open side. The stack or chimney was an integral part of this housing, shaped as drawn in the hull plans. Without doubt the entire assembly was galvanized to prevent rust. It therefore should be finished in a metallic grey.

If hammock nettings are going to be installed do not set them until the hull is completely ready to rig.

SPARS

The discussion in Chapter XIV under this heading should be reviewed. In addition, the builder should decide before starting to rig the yards whether studding-sail boom irons and saddles since Flemish horses are connected to the irons if fitted. Spar lengths can be measured directly from the sail plan. Diameters of spars along with their measuring points and dimensions of cross- and trestletrees are tabulated and shown in the detail sheet. The hull is now ready to rig. Table III covers the size of major rigging components.

STANDING RIGGING

This section is divided into two parts. The first part covers shrouds, backstays, headstays, and those stays between masts which support spars. The second part covers those stays between masts rigged only for setting staysails.

PART 1

Bowsprit

Gammoning—Eleven turns of rigging and eleven turns of frapping.

Bobstays—Two stays set up on their own ends through holes in the stem with hearts in their outboard ends connected by lanyards to hearts on collars about the bowsprit.

Cross sections

Note:
Topmast and tpglt mast backstays omitted

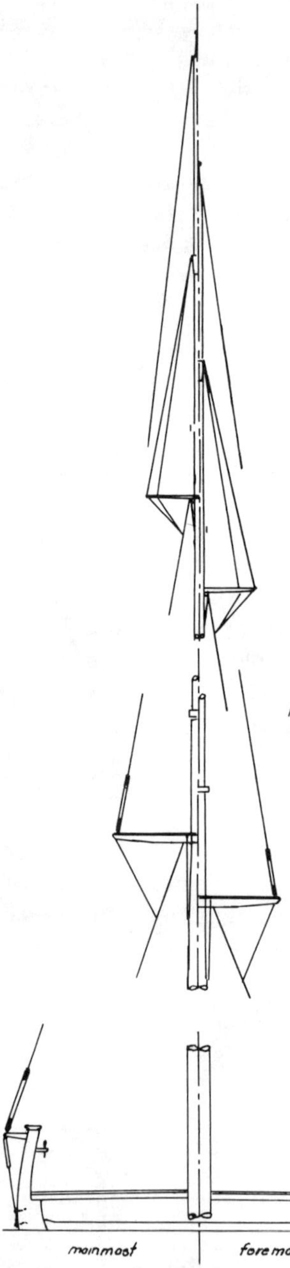

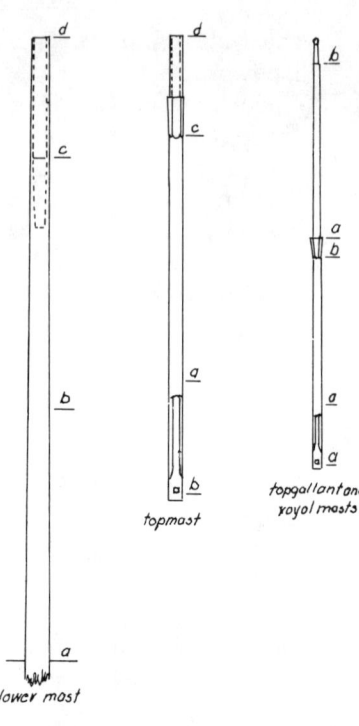

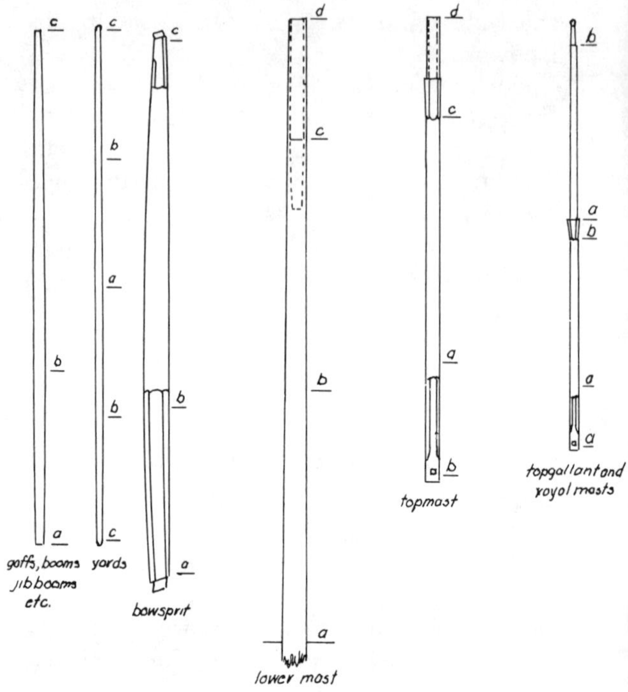

Spar	a	b	c	d
fore mast	.479	.452	.396	.373
main mast	.500	.482	.416	.387
mizzen mast	.375	.363	.312	.291
fore-tp mast	.265	.255	.240	.230
main-tp mast	.276	.265	.250	.240
mizzen-tp mast	.210	.204	.195	.187
fore-tpglt mast	.163	.145		
main-tpglt mast	.170	.150		
mizzen-tpglt mast	.125	.110		
fore-royal mast	.135	.110		
main-royal mast	.140	.115		
mizzen-royal mast	.100	.090		
bowsprit	.412	.500	.312	
jibboom	.229	.270	.166	
flying jibboom	.125	.146	.104	
fore yard	.333	.291	.229	
main yard	.354	.309	.240	
cross jack	.229	.205	.146	
fore-tp yard	.208	.182	.135	
main-tp yard	.229	.205	.146	
mizzen tp yard	.166	.146	.104	
fore-tpglt yard	.156	.137	.100	
main-tpglt yard	.166	.146	.104	
mizzen-tpglt yard	.114	.100	.071	
fore-royal yard	.104	.092	.057	
main-royal yard	.115	.100	.073	
mizzen-royal yard	.083	.073	.055	
spritsail yard	.187	.160	.100	
spanker boom	.167	.229	.125	
spanker gaff	.125	.167	.083	

Spar diameters
in inches

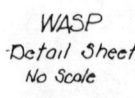

WASP
Detail Sheet
No Scale

Shrouds—One on each side eye spliced to an eyebolt in the bow with hearts outboard. Hearts on bowsprit are in a common collar about the bowsprit.

Horses—One on each side with an eye splice on each end. Outboard eyes are lashed to eyebolts in the cap and inboard ones to eyebolts in forward faces of knightheads.

Lower Masts

Stay Collars—Collars with bull's-eyes are fitted to both fore- and mainmast heads under the shrouds.

Shrouds—Six shrouds on the fore- and mainmasts and four on the mizzen with sheer poles across all.

Stays—Double on fore- and mainmasts and single on the mizzen. Forestays set up to hearts on the bowsprit. Mainstays pass on each side of the foremast and set up to hearts stropped to pad eyes in bulwarks close to the bowsprit. The mizzen stay sets up to a bull's-eye in a collar around the mainmast just high enough to clear the fife rails and pump stanchions. An ephroe and crowfoot is fitted on fore- and mainstays. The ephroe for the mizzen is set up on the mizzen-staysail-stay.

Topmast Shroud Futtocks—Three on each side of all masts. The deadeyes are turned into tight eye splices. Lower ends attach to rod lashed under the shrouds.

Ratlines—Cross all lower shrouds and futtocks.

Topmasts

Stay Collars—Collars with bull's-eyes are fitted to fore- and maintopmast heads.

Shrouds—Three on each mast with sheer poles and ratlines across all. Sister blocks are seized into the forward pair close to the seizing for topsail yard lifts and reef tackles.

Backstays—Two on each side of all masts with separate sheer poles.

Stays—Double on foremast and single on main- and mizzenmasts. Forestays reeve through bee holes and set up in the bow alongside bowsprit

TABLE III
—Wasp—
Main Rigging Component Sizes
(dimensions in inches)

Rigging	Blocks (etc.)	Rigging Dia.
Gammoning		.040 black
Bobstays		.040 "
	1/4 hearts	.020 "
Bowsprit shrouds		.040 "
	1/4 "	.020 "
Lower mast shrouds		.050 "
	1/4 deadeyes	.020 "
Lower mast stays		.060 "
	9/32 hearts	.020 "
Topmast shrouds and backstays		.035 "
	3/16 deadeyes	.015 "
Topmast stays		.040 "
	3/16 blocks	.025 natural
Topgallant shrouds and backstays		.025 black
	5/32 "	.010 natural
Topgallant stays		.020 black
	1/8 "	.010 natural
Royal backstays		.015 black
	1/8 "	.010 natural
Royal stays		.015 black
	1/8 "	.010 natural
Yard tackles		.040 black
	1/4 "	.020 natural
Slings		.060 black
Lower yard lifts	3/16 "	.025 natural
Lower yard braces	3/16 "	.025 "
Clew garnets	3/16 "	.025 "
Lower sheets and tacks	5/16 "	.040 "
Topsail tyes		.35 black
	1/4 "	.025 natural
Topsail braces	3/16 "	.020 "
Topsail sheets	5/16 "	.035 "
Topsail clews	3/16 "	.020 "
Topsail lifts	3/16 "	.020 "
Topgallant tyes		.025 black
	1/8 "	.020 natural
Topgallant braces	1/8 "	.020 "
Topgallant sheets	3/16 "	.020 "
Topgallant clews	1/8 "	.015 "
Topgallant lifts	bull's-eyes	.015 "
Royal tyes		.015 black
	1/8 blocks	.015 natural
Royal braces	1/8 "	.015 "
Royal sheets	1/8 "	.015 "
Royal lifts	1/8 "	.010 "

Rigging sizes given for masts and yards are for fore and main only.
Parts on mizzen are reduced by one-fifth to one-quarter.

with luff tackles. Falls reeve through holes in the buffalo rails and belay in the pinrails. Main- and mizzen-topmast stays set up on their own ends through bull's-eyes at fore- and mainmast heads, respectively.

Jibstay—Single. Leads over sheave in jibboom and back to gun tackle in bowsprit cap on starboard side. Fall belays as fore-topmast stay falls.

Topgallant and Royal Stay Shrouds Futtocks—Two on each side with bull's-eyes turned in above and secured below as topmast shroud futtocks.

Topgallant Masts

Stay Collar—Collar and bull's-eye fitted to fore-topgallant head.

Shrouds—Two on each side set up on their own ends to the bull's-eyes. Shrouds and futtocks are fitted with ratlines. Bull's-eyes are fitted between the shrouds just below the seizing for yard lifts.

Backstays—Single on each side set up to gun tackles in eyes in the after end of each channel. The fall is rove through the eye and set up on its own end.

Stays—Single on each mast. The fore-topgallant stay reeves over a sheave in the flying jibboom and sets up to a gun tackle in an eyebolt in port bowsprit cap, and the fall belays as the fore-topmast stay. Main- and mizzen-topgallant stays set up on their own ends at the fore-topmast head and main cap, respectively.

Royal Masts

Backstays—Single on each side set up to gun tackles in the main rail just astern of the channels and belay as on topgallant masts. If hammock nettings are fitted, cloth filler must be stopped on each side of these tackles.

Stays—Single on each mast. The fore-royal stay has an eye splice in its lower end which slides over end of the flying jibboom. Stays on main and mizzen set up on their own end to bull's-eyes at the fore-topgallant and main-topmast heads, respectively.

Jibboom & Flying Jibboom

Martingales—One on each side for each spar. Outer ends have eyes which are seized to ends of the spars. They reeve through holes in each dolphin striker and set up in the bow with gun tackles just outboard of fore tack bumpkins and belay as the fore-topmast stays.

Backropes—One on each side for each spar set up outboard like martingales. Each reeves through a staple in the spritsail yard and sets up to gun tackles in eyebolts on forward sides of the catheads. The falls belay as the martingales.

PART 2

Main-Staysail Stay—Put over the head before the mainstays and sets up on its own end to a bull's-eye in a collar around the foremast below the mainstays.

Mizzen-Staysail Stay—Put over the head after the mizzen stay and sets up on its own end to a bull's-eye in a collar around the mainmast at mid-height.

Main-Topmast Staysail-Stay—Put over the head before the main-topmast stay and sets up on its own end to a bull's-eye in a collar around the foremast just below the cheeks.

Upper Main-Topmast Staysail-Stay—Put over the head after the stay and sets up on its own end to a bull's-eye. The bull's-eye traveled on a jackstay rigged from the fore-topgallant crosstree to an eyebolt in the head of the lower mast and was adjusted for height by lines up to the topmast head and down to the fore-top.

Mizzen-Topmast Staysail-Stay—Put over the mizzen-topmast head before the stay and sets up on its own end to a bull's-eye in a collar around the mainmast below the cheeks.

Fore-Topmast Staysail-Stay—Put over the head before the topmast stays and sets up on its own end to a bull's-eye in a collar around the jibboom just aft of the bee seat.

Note: All other staysails set up on regular stays. If sails are not rigged, it is recommended that these stays be omitted.

RUNNING RIGGING

Spritsail Yard

Collar—Secures yard to the underside of the bowsprit. Refer to Chapter XI.

Lift—A single block is stropped to an eye in the bowsprit cap and another to the yardarm. The fall is eye spliced to the strop of the block on the cap, reeves through both blocks and belays as described for the fore-topmast stay.

Foreyard

Slings—Refer to Chapter XI for rope slings.

Truss—Refer to Chapter XI for rope trusses.

Jackstay—Refer to Chapter XI for iron jackstays.

Footrope—Refer to Chapter XI and sail plan.

Brace—An eye splice is lashed to mainstay at the splice. It reeves through a block stropped to the yardarm, to a block stropped to the stay, to a block stropped to an eye on the main trestletree and to the fore fife rail.

Lift—A single block is stropped to the yardarm with the fall spliced to its strop. A double block is stropped to an eyebolt on the cap abreast the topmast. The fall is rove off and belays to the fore fife rail.

Topsail Sheet—An eye splice in the end is toggled to the topsail clew. It reeves through the sheave in the yard, through the quarter block, and belays at the topsail sheet bitt.

Yard Tackle—Rove as shown in sail plan. It hooks to an eyebolt in the fore channel and belays to fore pinrail.

Clew Garnet—Its end is eye spliced to the clew garnet block. It reeves through a block toggled to the sheet and tack blocks, through the clew garnet block, and belays to the fore fife rail.

Tack—An eye splice slides against the shoulder on the fore tack bumpkin. It reeves through a block toggled to the lower clew garnet block, through the block on the bumpkin and belays to pinrail in the bow.

Sheet—An eye splice lashes to a ringbolt in the planking. It reeves through sheet-block on the same toggle as the tack block, through the sheave by the fourth gunport and belays to a cleat just forward of and above port.

Flemish Horse—Refer to Chapter XI and sail plan.

Main Yard

Sling, Truss, Jackstay, Footrope, Lift, Topsail Sheet, Yard Tackle, Clew Garnet, Flemish Horse—Same as on foreyard.

Brace—An eye splice is lashed to an eyebolt in the edge of the arch board outside of davit. It reeves through a block stropped to the yardarm, through forward sheave in the davit, and belays to a cleat on bulwarks just forward of the roundhouse.

Tack—An eye splice is lashed to a ringbolt close to and at mid-height of the chesstree. It reeves through a block toggled to the lower clew garnet block, under sheave in the chesstree, over bulwarks sheave, and belays to a cleat just under the rail between third and fourth gunports.

Sheet—An eye splice is lashed to a ringbolt in the planking over the forward side of eighth gunport. It reeves through a block on the same toggle as the tack block, over the forward sheave by the eighth gunport, and belays to a cleat just under the rail between seventh and eighth gunports.

Crossjack Yard

Sling, Truss, Topsail Sheet—Same as foreyard.

Jackstay, Yard Tackle, Clew Garnet, Tack, Sheet, Flemish Horse—Omitted.

Footrope—Refer to sail plan for number of stirrups. The inner end and stirrup eyes lash to small eyebolts on top of the yard.

Brace—An eye splice is lashed to the after main shroud just below the futtock staff. It crosses the center line to a block stropped to the yardarm, back across the center line to a block stropped to an eye in the after main trestletree, and belays to the main fife rail.

Spanker Boom

Footrope—Refer to sail plan. An eye splice in each end is lashed to a collar on the boom. A stirrup is fitted, common to both footropes, and runs through an eye on top of the yard which is forced into the boom after stirrup is rove through.

Topping Lift—An eye splice in the standing end is worked into the strop of a single block stropped to an eye in the mizzen cap abreast the masthead. It reeves through a single block stropped to end of the boom, back through the block on the cap, and belays to mizzen pinrail.

Sheet—Single with two belaying points. Consists of a double fold purchase. One block is stropped to a ringbolt between the stern chase gunports and the other to the collar around the boom. The fall belays to either cleats on bulwarks above the gunports.

Outhaul (if sails are fitted)—Hitches to clew in the sail, reeves over a sheave in the outboard end, and belays to cleat port side of the boom near sheet collar.

Inhaul (if sails are fitted)—Hitches to clew in the sail and belays to cleat starboard side of the boom near sheet collar.

Spanker Gaff

Throat Halyard—A double purchase with one block stropped through holes drilled between the jaws and spar. The other is stropped to staple in the after crosstree between trestletrees. It belays to mizzen pinrail.

Peak Halyard—Eye splice in the end lashes to eye in after end of mizzen cap. It reeves through a single block stropped to a collar on the gaff, through a double block stropped to a collar just below the mizzen cap, through another single block on the gaff, back through starboard sheave in the double block, and belays in the mizzen pinrail.

Vang—A pendant with a single block below and an eye splice above lashed to a collar around the gaff. The fall has an eye splice lashed to an eyebolt in the rail near davits. It reeves through the single block and belays in the after pinrail.

Fore-Topsail Yard

Parrel—Double row with balls and trucks.

Tye—Hitched to center of yard through a slot in the saddle with a cow hitch and the end seized to the standing part. Refer to topgallant yard tye for *Lexington* in Chapter XIV. It reeves over the sheave in topmast head. The hauling end is a luff tackle or long tackle stropped to an eyebolt in the port channel and belays to pinrail.

Jackstay and Footrope—Same as lower yard.

Lift—An eye splice is lashed to the forward shroud. It reeves through a single block stropped to the yardarm, through lower sister block, and belays to fore fife rail.

Brace—An eye splice is lashed to mainstay at the splice. It reeves through block stropped to the yardarm, through block stropped to an eyebolt in the main trestletrees, and belays to main pinrail.

Topgallant Sheet—Same as topsail sheet except it belays to fore fife rails.

Clew—Same as clew garnet except lower block is toggled to the topsail sheet eye and belays to fore pinrail.

Flemish Horse—Same as lower yard.

Main-Topsail Yard

Parrel, Jackstay, Footrope, Topgallant Sheet, Clew, Lift, Flemish Horse—Same as fore-topsail yard.

Tye—Same as fore-topsail tye except the hauling end is to starboard.

Braces—An eye splice is lashed to mizzen stay at the splice. It reeves through the single block stropped to the yardarm, to the block stropped to the stay, to the block stropped to fore end of the mizzen trestletree, and belays to mizzen fife rail.

Mizzen-Topsail Yard

Parrel, Jackstay, Footrope, Topgallant Sheet, Clew, Lift, Flemish Horse—Same as fore-topsail yard.

Tye—Same as fore-topsail tye except the hauling end is a gun tackle. It belays to port.

Brace—A single block with fall spliced to its strop is stropped to an eyebolt on the main cap. It reeves through a block stropped to the yardarm, back through block at the cap, and belays to main fife rail.

Fore-Topgallant Yard

Parrel—Single row of balls only.

Tye—Same as fore-topsail yard except the hauling end is a gun tackle on the starboard side.

Jackstay and Footrope—Same as lower yard.

Lift—An eye splice in one end fits the yardarm. It reeves through a bull's-eye seized between the shrouds and belays by hitching to a topmast deadeye strop at the cap.

Brace—An eye splice is lashed to the main-topmast stay splice. It reeves through a block stropped to the yardarm, through a block stropped to an eyebolt in the main-topmast trestletree and belays to the main pinrail.

Royal Sheet—Same as topgallant sheet except it belays to fore pinrail.

Clew—Same as topsail clew.

Flemish Horse—Same as lower yard.

Main-Topgallant Yard

Parrel, Jackstay, Footrope, Lift, Royal Sheet, Clew, Flemish Horse—Same as fore-topgallant yard.

Tye—Same as fore-topgallant yard except the hauling end is to port.

Brace—Same as main-topsail yard brace except at mizzen-topmast stay and trestletree.

Mizzen-Topgallant Yard

Parrel, Jackstay, Footrope, Lift, Royal Sheet, Clew, Flemish Horse—Same as fore-topgallant yard.

Tye—Same as fore-topgallant yard except hauling end does not have a tackle. It belays to starboard.

Brace—An eye is slid over the yardarm. It reeves through a block stropped to an eyebolt in the main-topmast trestletrees and belays to main pinrail.

Fore-Royal Yard

Parrel—Same as fore-topgallant yard.

Tye—Same as fore-topgallant yard except hauling end has no tackle and belays to port pinrail.

Jackstay, Footrope, Lift, Flemish Horse—Is not fitted.

Brace—An eye is slid over the yardarm and reeves through a block stropped to an eyebolt in the main-topmast trestletree.

Clew—Same as fore-topgallant except the line is single and toggles directly to the sheet.

Main-Royal Yard

Parrel, Clew—Same as fore-royal yard.

Tye—Same as fore-royal yard except hauling end is to starboard.

Brace—An eye is slid over the yardarm and reeves through a block stropped to heel of mizzen-royal mast. It belays to mizzen pinrail.

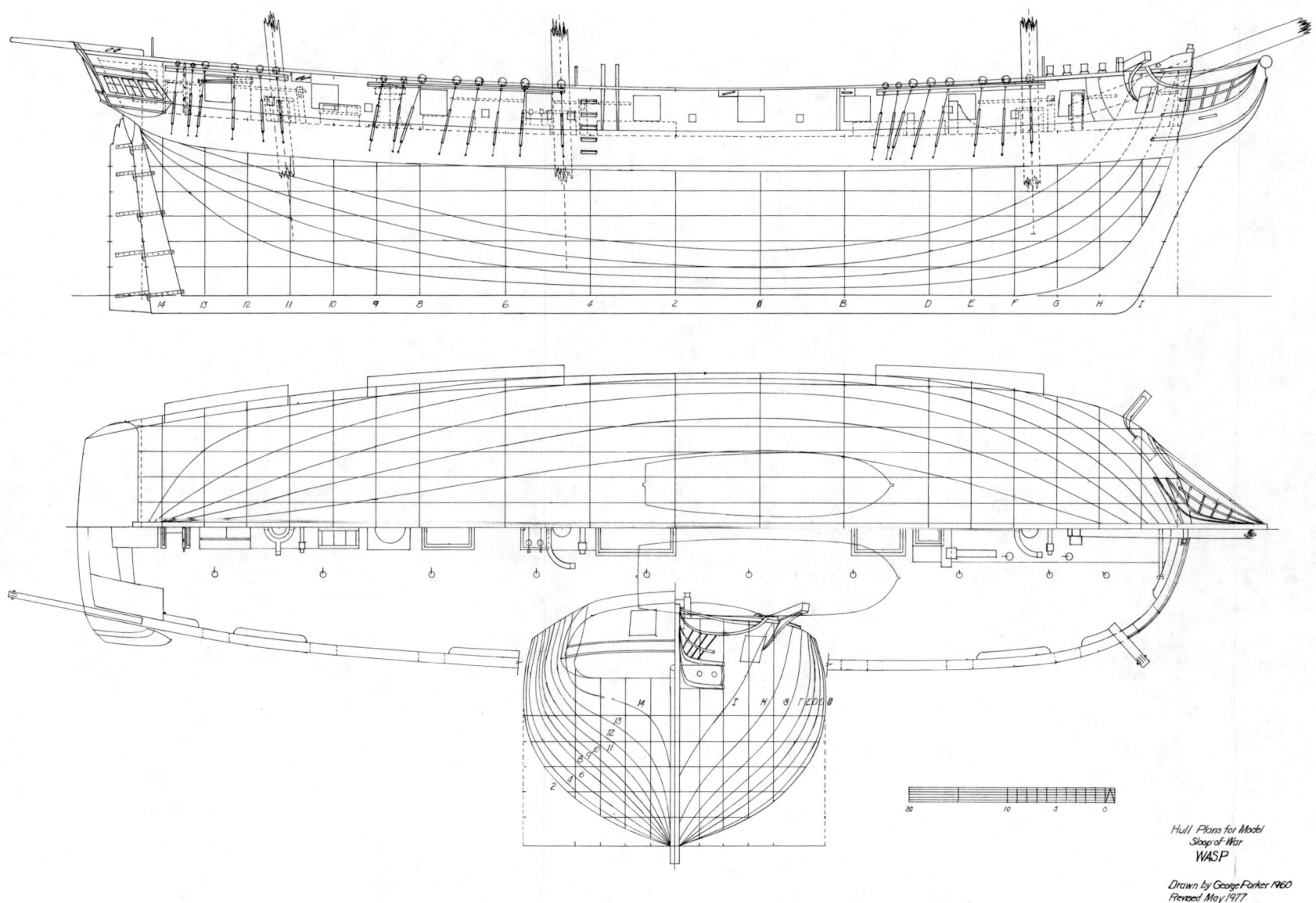

Hull Plans for Model
Sloop-of-War
WASP

Drawn by George Parker 1960
Revised May 1977

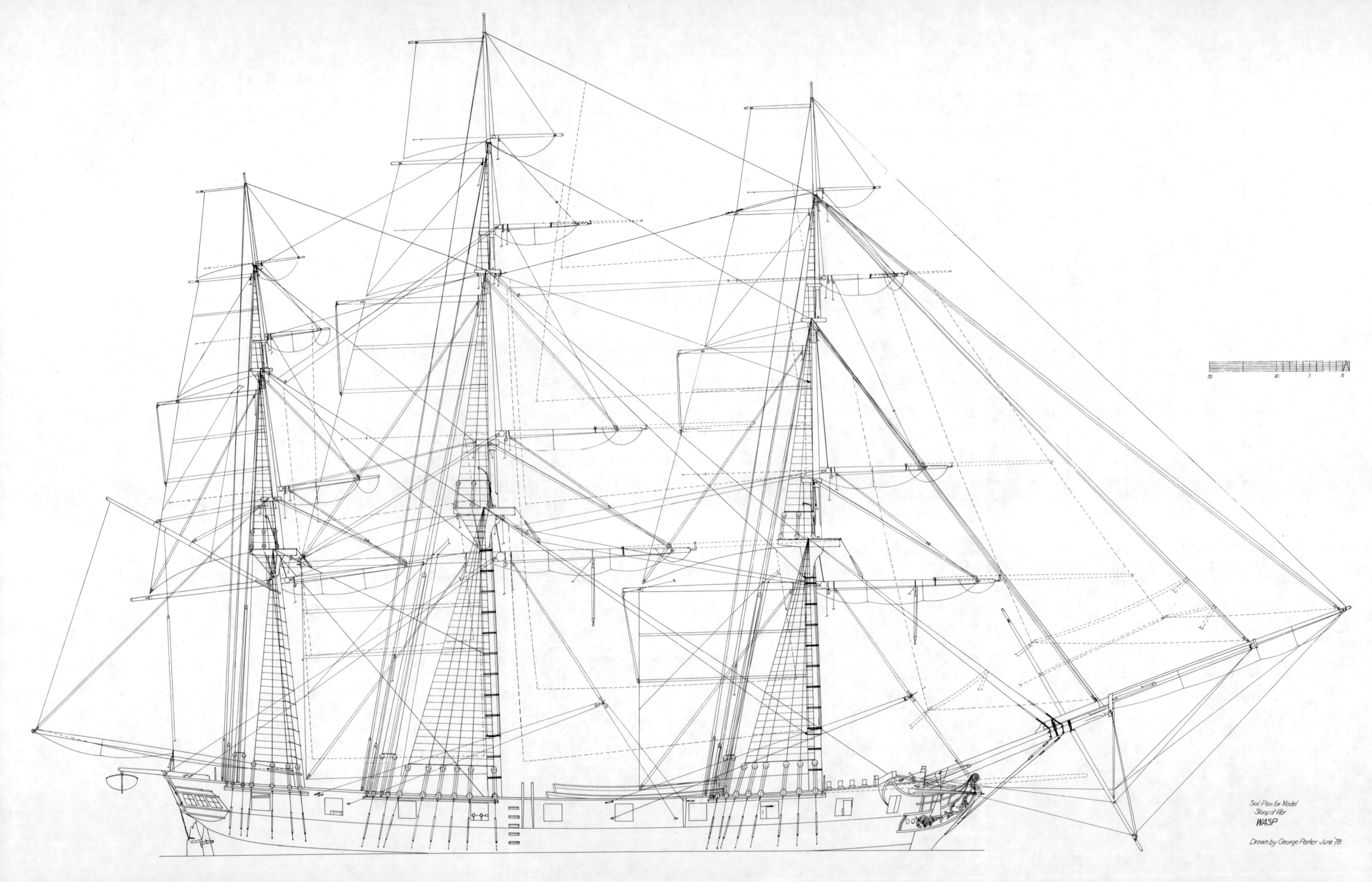

Mizzen-Royal Yard

Parrel, Clew—Same as fore-royal yard.

Tye—Same as fore-royal yard.

Brace—Same as mizzen-topgallant yard.

FINISHING THE MODEL

If sails are to be fitted follow instructions in Chapter XI. Clean deck of all debris and rig the boat in stern davits. It is now ready to install in its permanent mounting and case.

Isaac Webb. Painting by J. Hughes, which clearly portrays many hull and rigging details. Courtesy of The Peabody

Chapter XVI

ISAAC WEBB

Isaac Webb was designed and built by William H. Webb at New York for the Black Ball Line. She was completed in 1850 and entered the packet service running from New York to Liverpool.

The sheer plan closely resembles that of naval frigates. On her sides she even had a white belt and black squares, simulated gunports. The body plan shows deep sides, far wider below than at the rail. Because one of the factors in the registration formula was width on deck, as opposed to maximum beam, this hull form allowed capacity far in excess of registered tonnage. Hence, her registration costs were low.

The entire after section under the long poop deck was cabin class and officers' quarters. Exotic woods such as mahogany, rosewood, and satinwood embellished with gilded carving were commonly used. Food was as good as the storage facilities and a rolling, bucking stove would permit.

Steerage passengers slept in stall-like partitioned-off areas under the main deck. These quarters were unlighted with minimal ventialtion and passengers were not allowed on deck during heavy weather which prevailed for many months of each year. Food was distributed each week. It was weighed out to passengers who stood in line to receive their ration of salted meat, cereal, dried fruit, potatoes, flour, sugar, and common seasoning. Passengers cooked in a separate galley provided forward. Before steerage passengers were allowed aboard, each one had to show the necessary utensils with which to cook their fare. Also, unless they chose to sleep on bunk boards, they had the opportunity to provide their own mattress filled with straw, commonly called "donkey's breakfast" by seamen.

However, rough quarters and all, those steerage passengers on *Isaac Webb* and her sister ships are responsible for today's thousands of families existing in this country, families whose forebears came from Northern Europe, the British Isles, and particularly Ireland. The Black Ball Line was at its zenith when potato crops failed in the 1840s. The resulting famine and poverty drove thousands to seek better conditions in the "New World," and these ships brought a large percentage of them.

Black Ball Line packets sailed as scheduled from New York on the first and sixteenth days of each month. Due to the urgency of holding to schedule, they were driven unmercifully day and night, summer and winter, fair weather and foul. Striving for new records was an obsession with the officers. Large percentages of each crew were recruited from waterfront dives and herded aboard while still drunk just before sailing. Mates drove these men with belaying pins, boots, brass knuckles, and fists. Once these unfortunates returned, the reputation of "bucko" mates was greatly enhanced and lost nothing with each retelling!

Probably, these frigate-like packets were the height of naval architecture in square-riggers. They were unexcelled in cargo carrying capacity and were reasonably fast. But while *Isaac Webb* and her contemporaries were enjoying a monopoly in the North Atlantic passenger trade, British shipwrights were slowly perfecting the steamship. While big packets could outrun early steamers if there was a good breeze, it was the "if" that finally made the difference. Preeminence of the sailing packet was dying even before the Civil War which hastened the process along with America's loss of first place with her international seaborne carriers.

HULL

The work description in Chapter I fits this hull exactly. The block is one piece from the top of the keel to the continuous rail at the top of the bowsprit. Do not attempt to build to the highest continuous rail because the upper works are too fragile to be handled in that manner.

Lumber for this hull consists of pieces 1/2" thick, 25" long, and 6" wide. Since the sheer is nearly straight and the ends very short, Method 1, Chapter I, is best. Time spent laying out and sawing lifts would exceed that required to shape the ends from square stock.

Hints on Shaping

Shaping this hull is more difficult than working with any other described in this book. Following are hints helpful in avoiding errors. When sawing the bow profile to shape, make the cut absolutely square across so the bluff bow at forecastle deck level is not cut into. The first cut on the stern profile is the rabbet followed by sawing down the upper transom to a point below the cross seam. Finish the stern's profile by cutting the lower transoms with a chisel, as demonstrated in Photo 9, Chapter I. When forming sides aft of Stations B or D use particular care to avoid working ripples into the surface. This is far more difficult than on *Margaret Haskell* where sides are of a constant cross section, because they have a very slight curve in the fore and aft direction over a large portion of the hull. It is suggested that the upper sides be formed with a flat *Sur-form* tool worked lengthwise in a slightly rocking motion. Also much of the surface from Station E to the bow above the wales is nearly across the grain. Special attention must be devoted to setting templates in this area; the angle between the templates and the hull is so acute that templates tend to bend out of shape and swing forward. If either condition is allowed to persist the bow will be too full and, indeed, her bow is full enough as designed without exaggerating it.

A similar situation to a lesser degree exists at the underside of the afterbody from Station 16 to the cross seam. When forming the transom curves, the upper transom is formed with sandpaper on a block. The lower transoms are formed with a file worked in a rolling athwartship motion.

When hollowing out this hull leave about 1 1/2" in the bottom and 3/8" around the sides.

Bulwarks—Underlayments

Cutting down the bulwarks is a difficult and far more exacting chore here than for the war vessels. From the break in the deck to Station E the bulwarks are very thin, as described in Chapter IV. The poop deck is at the level of the highest continuous rail. Construction at Stations ⓪ and 6 is drawn in the detail sheet. Construction at deck break is drawn in Fig. 125. Bulwarks for the main deck are cut down from the after surface of the "great beam" to Station E. The builder must decide now how thin the outer skin on the bulwarks will be on the finished model. The thinner the skin the thicker and more realistic the false timberheads will be. When completed the combined thickness of the bulwarks, timberheads, and covering board must be 3/16". Note in the drawings that approximately 1/8" of stock is left outside of the deck beam pockets and underlayment. This allows these parts to be installed while bulwarks are still relatively thick and strong. Deck beams are made of 3/8" wide strips, 1/2" thick, with a 1/8" crown. Main deck beams are placed at Station E, just aft of the foremast, at Station ⓪ and at Station 2 with the last at the break. Poop deck beams are placed under the capstan, at Station 6, just aft of the mizzenmast, and under the wheelbox.

Lay the underlayment on main deck. For construction in the bow refer to detail sheet. Follow through by making and fitting main waterways, decking, and false timberheads; timberheads are important in stiffening thin bulwarks. Make waterways of 3/32" thick birch, by 3/8" wide. False timberheads may be of pine or birch 1/8" thick measured fore and aft and set about 3/8" apart. Set first timberhead with its forward edge coinciding with Station D to support the after edge of the forecastle deck. Set timberheads under the forecastle and follow through by also setting them along the sides. Adjust spacing so a timberhead coincides with the forward edge

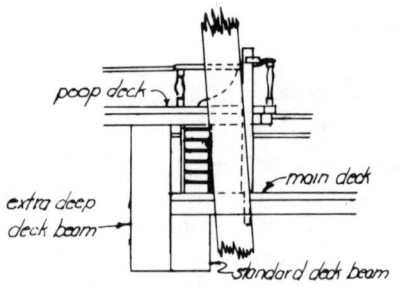

Fig. 125
Deck construction at break

of the poop deck at the side. Refer to Fig. 125 for construction at the break. Similar construction is used at the after end of the forecastle deck, as drawn in detail sheet. Finish bulwarks by installing covering board from the break to the forward timberhead.

Rather than making the forecastle deck underlayment of narrow pieces with the crown formed by heavy deck beams below, it is recommended that the underlayment be made of one piece planed with 1/8" crown and cut to a uniform thickness of 1/8". Its forward edge is cut to fit the hull with an undercut for the bowsprit. The builder may select whether the timberheads and covering board under this deck are to be cut to allow the underlayment to land on them or be notched to allow the underlayment to set inside. Probably the former is preferable. A false beam formed as shown in cross section is fitted across the after end.

When the underlayment is completely fitted, fasten it in place temporarily and bore through both underlayment and main deck for the peg ends of the windlass pawl post and bowsprit heel bitts. See detail sheet for this construction. Make and fit bowsprit temporarily and glue heel bitt in place. Fit stanchions under the after end of the forecastle deck.

Now that the bowsprit can be stepped, fit and attach the stem, keel, and sternpost to the hull. Follow by boring the rudder port. Finish sanding exterior of the hull and mount it in working cradle.

Before attaching the forecastle deck underlayment make the companionway underneath. It may be installed now or a pad which exactly fits its interior can be glued to the deck so it may be installed later. Now the underlayment can be glued in place. Follow by boring the top of the bowsprit heel bitts for the peg on the pawl post and install knees under the after end.

Prepare top of the hull for the main rail by truing up timberheads and covering boards. The rail is made of birch, cherry, or maple 1/16" thick. It is 1/4" wide from the break to the bow and just wide enough to fit outside of the deck beam ends along the poop deck. Fit a piece of the same 3/16" wide stock across the stern and another 1/8" wide piece across the after end of the forecastle deck followed by laying forecastle decking and installing catheads and their bitts.

Refer to cross sections in detail sheet for shape of filler piece between main and monkey rails. This piece has a slight taper from a slack 3/16" deep at the bow to a strong 1/3" at the stern and is 1/8" wide. It is beveled on its lower edge so it continues the shape of the hull from the catheads to the stern. It is beveled to a lesser degree around the bow. The piece across the bow between catheads can be carved from pine and glued in place. Those along sides and across stern are continuous pieces beveled on the bottom as required, glued to the main rail, and held in place with small brads. Make these pieces of pine 1/4" deep so the top surface can be sanded

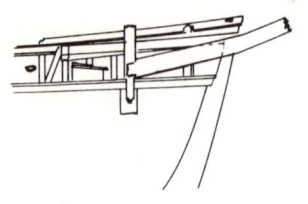
Bow

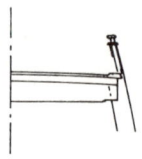
Station Ø

Station 6

Fore end of poop deck

Hull Sections
No scale

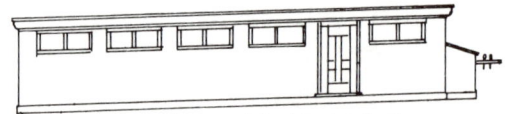
Forward house - st'bd side (port identical)

End view - forward and coach houses. Door, window, and boat skids, fwd house after end only.

Coach house st'bd side (port identical)

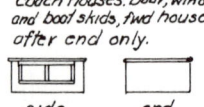
side   end
skylight

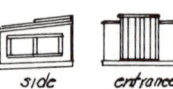
side   entrance end
companionway

Deck structures
No scale

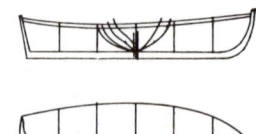
Boats on fwd. house

Quarter boats
(See hull plan for interior layout)

2"   1"   0

ISAAC WEBB
Detail Sheet
Scale for boats only

level athwartships after installation. Before sanding, lay poop deck underlayment. Refer again to Figs. 79 and 125 and to detail sheet for construction on forward end. Except for being curved it is not unlike the after end of the forecastle deck. After the underlayment is installed and sanded, sand down filler piece for monkey rail and carefully cut openings on each side of the overhang for poop deck ladders.

The monkey rail is made of hardwood a scant 1/16" thick, 3/16" wide along the sides, and 1/4" wide across the stern. Fit a piece of the same stock 1/8" wide across forward edge of poop deck, and 1/16" wide borders around both ladder openings followed by decking.

FINISHING THE HULL

Lay out the mast hole openings and bore them. Holes for the mainmast must be located carefully to obtain proper rake. Boring in the poop deck overhang must be done slowly to prevent breaking underlayment. Continue boring and install topsail sheet bitts and fife rails. Refer to Fig. 125, noting that main-topsail sheet bitts pierce the poop deck and extend down into the main deck. Cut snug-fitting slots for them through poop deck with peg ends in main deck. Make and install poop deck bulwarks. Install section across the stern first to help hold sections along the side at the proper angle. Make side sections together so they will be an identical pair. Before fitting them out, shape the mooring pipes, make the bulwarks sheaves, and form ornamentation. It is probably wise at this time to install poop deck ladders and, while at it, also install those on forecastle deck.

After bulwarks are installed, make and install the rail from hardwood, 1/8" wide and a scant 1/16" thick. Add knees to after corners and remember that it crosses the hull on stanchions over the forward edge of the poop deck with metal braces extending ahead of forward corners.

The outside can be finished at this point. Install the false rail followed by boring hawsepipes and installing cheek knees and headrails. Cut opening in the stern and install windows. Install quarter badges, channels, and gangway equipment. Now is as good a time as any to install deadeyes, chain plates, backing links, rudder chains, davit sleeves and sockets. Before turning back to the inside, fit main brace bumpkins which are installed when rigging is started.

Make and install remaining companionways, skylight, houses, steering gear box with its wheel and binnacle. Install capstans with their bars and racks. Lash boats upside down on the forward house after galley stack has been fitted. It is suggested that the galley stack be left long enough to penetrate the main deck to provide ventilation below.

If the buffalo rail has not been fitted do so now. If a piece of ash is available saw it to 1/16" thick and form to shape after steaming over a

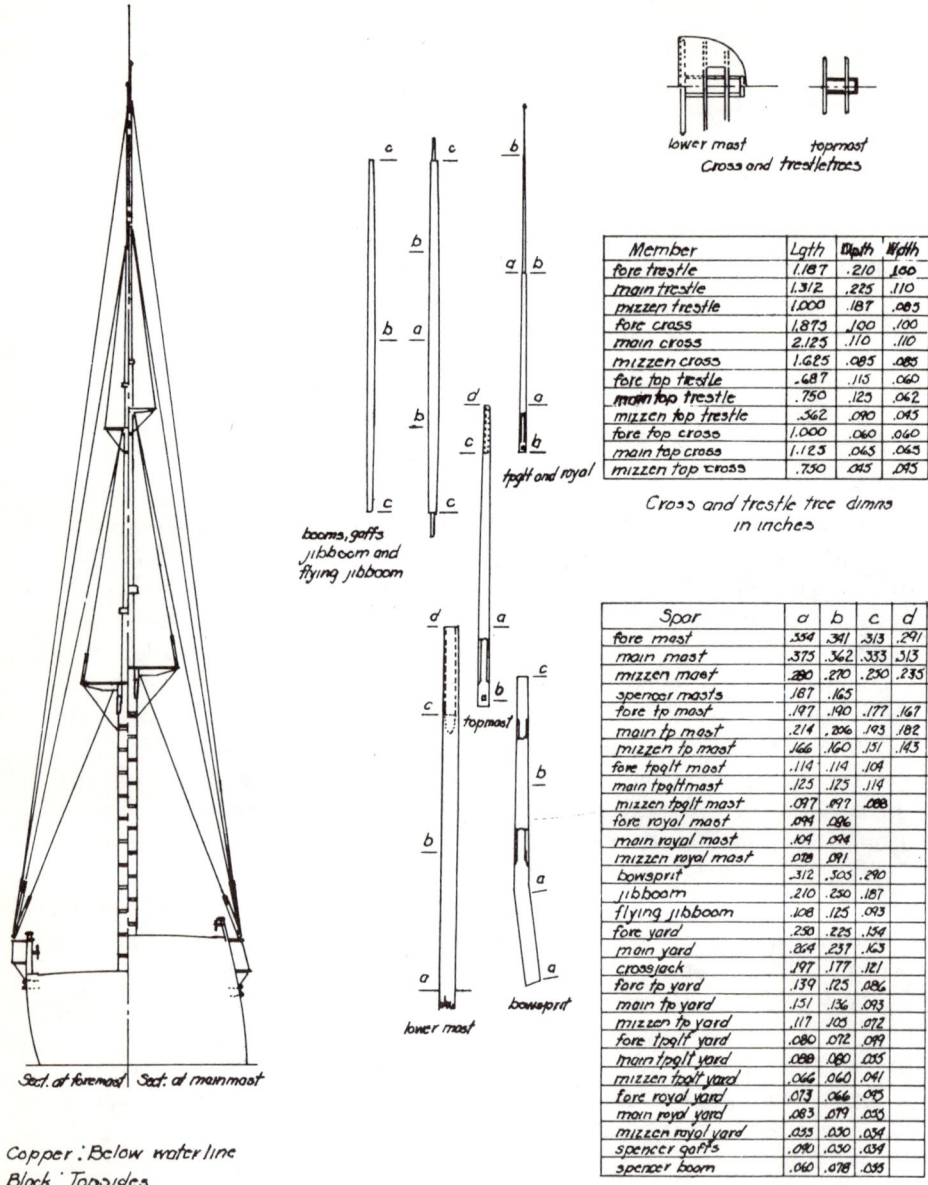

Cross and trestle tree dims in inches

Member	Lgth	Depth	Width
fore trestle	1.187	.210	.100
main trestle	1.312	.225	.110
mizzen trestle	1.000	.187	.085
fore cross	1.875	.100	.100
main cross	2.125	.110	.110
mizzen cross	1.625	.085	.085
fore top trestle	.687	.115	.060
main top trestle	.750	.125	.062
mizzen top trestle	.562	.090	.045
fore top cross	1.000	.060	.060
main top cross	1.125	.065	.065
mizzen top cross	.750	.045	.045

Spar diameters in inches

Spar	a	b	c	d
fore mast	.354	.341	.313	.291
main mast	.375	.362	.333	.313
mizzen mast	.280	.270	.250	.235
spencer masts	.187	.165		
fore tp mast	.197	.190	.177	.167
main tp mast	.214	.206	.193	.182
mizzen tp mast	.166	.160	.151	.143
fore tpglt mast	.114	.114	.104	
main tpgltmast	.125	.125	.114	
mizzen tpglt mast	.097	.097	.088	
fore royal mast	.094	.096		
main royal mast	.104	.094		
mizzen royal mast	.078	.081		
bowsprit	.312	.305	.290	
jibboom	.210	.250	.187	
flying jibboom	.108	.125	.093	
fore yard	.250	.225	.154	
main yard	.264	.237	.163	
crossjack	.197	.177	.121	
fore tp yard	.139	.125	.086	
main tp yard	.151	.136	.093	
mizzen tp yard	.117	.105	.072	
fore tpglt yard	.080	.072	.049	
main tpglt yard	.088	.080	.055	
mizzen tpglt yard	.066	.060	.041	
fore royal yard	.073	.066	.045	
main royal yard	.083	.079	.055	
mizzen royal yard	.055	.050	.034	
spencer gaffs	.090	.050	.034	
spencer boom	.060	.078	.055	

Copper: Below water line
Black: Topsides
Black on white band: False gun port covers (See sail plan)
White: Moldings, inside of bulwarks, sides of steering gear cover, house and companionway sides, skylight sides, ladders, bowsprit, lower masts, doublings, yardarms, and trucks
Light blue: Roofs of houses, companionways, steering gear cover, and skylight
Darkened natural: Decks
Medium brown stain: Balance of spars
Dark brown stain: Bitts and fife rails

Paint Scheme

ISAAC WEBB
Detail Sheet
No scale

teakettle spout. Cut to shape and install. Bore out and finish file the chocklike openings in its upper edge. Make and install mooring line bitts along the bulwarks, cut mooring pipes in the main deck bulwarks, insert fore-sheet sheaves, fit up windlass rocker arm and linkage, install chocks on the stern rail and pinrails, and install cleats for headsail sheets, lower sail sheets, spanker sheet, and main braces.

At this point all that is left is rigging the whaleboats in their davits, rigging the anchor(s), and the ironwork in the deck and hull for rigging. It is suggested that boats, davits, and anchors be held to last.

SPARS

Spars for *Isaac Webb* are made the same as described for the other square-riggers. Spar lengths can be measured directly from the sail plan. Diameters of spars along with their measuring points and dimensions of cross- and trestletrees are tabulated and shown in detail sheet.

Before assembling cheeks onto the masts fit futtock bands and trusses. Before assembling topgallant and royal masts to their respective topmasts, fit bands at each shoulder. When fitting up yards install sling or tye bands first, followed by crance iron bands on the lower yards or clew line block bands on higher masts. If studding-sail boom irons are going to be fitted, install the inner band first, followed by the lift-brace band and the outer studding-sail boom iron last. Bowsprit assembly rigging bands and bands on booms and gaffs should be installed before the wooden parts.

The spar assemblies on this model have many eyebolts for stropping rigging blocks. These can all be located by listing those cited under "Running Rigging" for the model rigged without sails. A few more are needed for leech lines, buntlines, and the like. The locations of these are explained in Chapter XI.

The hull is now ready to rig. Table IV covers the size of major rigging components.

STANDING RIGGING

Bowsprit

Bobstays—Two of chain. One end is slid over bobstay plates and the other into metal strops of deadeyes. Deadeyes at bowsprit are stropped to eyes on bowsprit bands.

TABLE IV
—Isaac Webb—
Main Rigging Component Sizes
(dimensions in inches)

Rigging	Blocks (etc.)	Rigging Dia.
Bobstays		8 link chain
	3/16 deadeyes	.020 black
Bowsprit shrouds		10 link chain
	3/16 ″	.020 black
Lower mast shrouds		.040 ″
	3/16 ″	.020 ″
Lower mast stays	bull's-eyes	.050 ″
Topmast shrouds and backstays		.030 ″
	5/32 deadeyes	.015 ″
Topmast stays	bull's-eyes	.035 ″
Topgallant shrouds and backstays	″	.020 ″
	1/8 deadeyes	.010 ″
Topgallant stays	bull's-eyes	.025 ″
Royal backstays		.015 ″
	1/8 deadeyes	.010 ″
Royal stays	bull's-eyes	.020 ″
Lower yard lifts		.030 ″
	3/16 blocks	.020 natural
Lower yard braces	3/16 ″	.030 ″
Topsail yard tyes		15 link chain
	1/4 ″	.030 black
	3/16 ″	.020 natural
Topsail lifts		.030 black
Topsail braces	5/32 ″	.025 natural
Topsail sheets	3/16 ″	20 link chain
		.035 natural
Topgallant yard tyes		.025 black
	5/32 ″	.020 natural
Topgallant lifts		.025 black
Topgallant braces	5/32 ″	.020 natural
Topgallant sheets	5/32 ″	.030 ″
Royal yard tyes		.020 black
	1/8 ″	.015 natural
Royal lifts		.020 black
Royal braces	1/8 ″	.015 natural
Royal sheets	1/8 ″	.020 ″

Rigging sizes for masts and yards are for fore and main only.
Parts on mizzen are reduced by one-fifth to one-quarter.

Shrouds—One on each side. Hooks on inboard ends are hooked into eyebolts or pad eyes in the bow. Outboard ends have deadeyes similar to bobstays.

Horses—These are ropes with an eye splice in each end and long enough to reach from the cap to the buffalo rail. Small ringbolts in the top of the cap on each side and close to the top of the buffalo rail serve as lashing points and are located so horses parallel sides of the bowsprit. These should not be rigged until all other head rigging has been installed.

Lower Masts

Topmast Futtocks—Three on each side made of wire with deadeyes turned into one end and eyes in the other for attaching to the futtock band.

Shrouds—Six on each side of fore and main, and four on the mizzen. Sheer poles extend across each set. Ratlines on fore and main shrouds cross only the middle four except every sixth which crosses all six. Those on the mizzen cross all shrouds.

Main-Topgallant Stay Collar—Installed before the fore shrouds and consists of a bull's-eye in a collar jammed tightly down on the fore bolsters.

Mizzen-Topmast and Topgallant Stay Collars—Made like topgallant stay collar and installed before the main shrouds, with topmast stay collar below and topgallant stay collar on top.

Forestay—Is made of one part doubled up. Each leg is fed through holes in the top just outside of trestletrees and drawn through. They are seized together over the yard and then passed under the bowsprit from opposite sides. Ends are seized to the standing part of the other leg with three seizings just above bowsprit. Thumb cleats prevent stay from sliding aft.

Mainstay—Is made of one part doubled up and rigged at the head the same as the forestay. Legs are set up on their own ends to bull's-eyes in the bolster just within the fore-topsail sheet bitts.

Mizzen Stay—Single with an eye splice around the head as on *Lexington*'s and *Wasp*'s lower stays. The forward end is set up on its own end to a bull's-eye stropped to a pad eye in the deck just aft of mainmast.

Topmasts

Main-Royal Stay Collar—Same as main-topgallant stay collar except it is fitted at fore-topmast head.

Mizzen-Royal Stay Collar—Same as for main-royal stay except fitted at main-topmast head.

Topgallant Futtocks—Two on each side and similar to topmast futtocks except bull's-eyes are turned into them instead of deadeyes.

Shrouds—Three on each side of each mast set up like lower shrouds with sheer poles on all. Ratlines cross all shrouds and futtocks.

Backstays—Two on each side of each mast with deadeyes and sheer poles below.

Fore-Topmast Stay—Made of one part like the forestay. Each leg reeves through the bees and sets up on its own end to a bull's-eye stropped to an eyebolt or pad eye in the bow alongside bowsprit.

Main-Topmast Stay—Is made of one part like the mainstay. Each leg sets up on its own end to a bull's-eye in the fore-topsail sheet bolster just within the bull's-eye for the mainstay.

Mizzen-Topmast Stay—Single with an eye splice around the head and set up below to the bull's-eye in the collar at the mainmast head.

Jibboom & Flying Jibboom

Martingales—Single with hooks eye spliced into their outboard ends which are hooked into eyes in bands just within the caps. They lead aft under hooks on the lower end of dolphin striker (jibboom to starboard, flying jibboom to port) and set up on their own ends to deadeyes stropped to eyebolts close to those for the bowsprit shrouds.

Backropes—Single with hooks eye spliced into their outboard ends which are hooked into eyes in bands just within the caps. They lead aft to the catheads where they set up on their own ends to bull's-eyes.

Jibstay—Single with an eye splice around the fore-topmast head. It reeves over a sheave in the end of the jibboom and under the higher port hook on the dolphin striker and sets up on its own end to a bull's-eye in the bow on the opposite side from the jibboom martingale.

Topgallant Masts

Shrouds—Two on each side set up on their own ends with ratlines.

Backstays—One on each side with deadeyes below. The sheer pole is extended to include the single royal backstay.

Fore-Topgallant Stay—Same as jibstay except it reeves through a sheave in the flying jibboom and under the lower starboard hook on the dolphin striker and sets up to starboard.

Main-Topgallant Stay—Single with an eye splice over the head and sets up on its own end to bull's-eye in the collar at the foremast head.

Mizzen-Topgallant Stay—Single with eye splice over the head and sets up on its own end to bull's-eye in the collar at mainmast head.

Royal Masts

Backstays—Same as for topgallant backstays except they run singly.

Fore-Royal Stay—Single. Eye spliced over head and end of flying jibboom. This can be tricky to obtain proper tension.

Main- and Mizzen-Royal Stays—Eye spliced over the head and sets up on their own ends to bull's-eyes in next forward topmast head.

RUNNING RIGGING

Foreyard

Sling—Chain attached to band on the yard and a double ended wire loop extending from eyes in the cap to just below the trestletrees.

Truss—Refer to Chapter IX for crance irons.

Jackstay—Refer to Chapter XI for iron jackstays.

Footropes—Refer to Chapter XI and to sail plan.

Lift—A single block is stropped into the pendant with fall spliced into the strop. The other end is spliced into the eye on the band at the yardarm. A double block is stropped to the eyebolt in the cap abreast the topmast. The fall is belayed to the fore fife rail.

Brace—An eye splice is lashed to the mainstay at the seizing. It reeves through the block stropped to band at the yardarm, through the block stropped to the mainstay, through the block stropped to the main cheek, and belays to main fife rail.

Topsail Sheet (optional)—Chain with a rope tailpiece for belaying to topsail sheet bitts. Since it is difficult to obtain chain small enough to reeve through sheave holes and blocks, it is recommended that chain be run only where exposed with wire loops through sheave holes and blocks. A hook is fitted above the yard. The sheet reeves over the sheave in the yard, through quarter block and two-thirds the way to deck where line is spliced into the last link for belaying to topsail sheet bitts.

Flemish Horse—Refer to "Footropes," Chapter XI.

Main Yard

Sling, Truss, Jackstay, Footrope, Lift, Topsail Sheet, Flemish Horse—Same as foreyard.

Brace—An eye splice is lashed to the main brace bumpkin. It reeves through the block stropped to band on the yardarm, over sheave in the poop deck bulwarks, and belays to a cleat.

Crossjack Yard

Sling, Truss, Jackstay, Footrope, Lift, Topsail Sheet—Same as foreyard.

Brace—An eye splice is seized to the after main shroud. It reeves through the block stropped to band on the yardarm, through a block stropped to an eyebolt on the main cheek, and belays to main fife rail.

Main Spencer Gaff

Throat Halyard—A luff tackle. The single block is stropped to the gaff through holes between gaff and jaws. The double block is stropped to the staple under the middle crosstree. The fall belays to the main fife rail.

Peak Halyard—An eye splice is lashed to the eye in the band on the gaff. It reeves through a double block stropped to eyebolt in the after crosstree, through single block stropped to band on the gaff, through the double block again, and belays to main fife rail.

Vang—Has an eye splice in a pendant lashed to an eye in the outer gaff band and a single block in an eye splice below. The hauling part has an eye splice in one end lashed to an eyebolt in the poop deck rail. It reeves through single block on the pendant and belays to main pinrail.

Mizzen Spencer Gaff

Throat Halyard—Same as for main spencer gaff.

Peak Halyard—A double block is stropped to an eyebolt in the mizzen cap with fall spliced to its strop. It reeves through block stropped to outer gaff band, through the double block, through the block stropped to inner gaff band, back through the double block, and belays to mizzen fife rail.

Vangs—Same as for main spencer gaff except the fall belays to a short pinrail aft.

Spanker-Boom

Topping Lift—Pendant with an eye splice in one end and a single block stropped into the other. The eye splice is lashed to an eye in the sheet band. The block is part of a gun tackle with other block stropped to an eyebolt in the mizzen trestletree. The fall belays in the mizzen pinrail.

Sheet—A double purchase with one block stropped to eye on the sheet band. The other is stropped to an eyebolt in the deck. The fall belays to either cleat on the bulwarks across the stern.

Fore-Topsail Yard

Parrel—Double row with trucks and balls.

Tye—Secures to middle of the yard with a cow hitch, as described for *Wasp*. It reeves through sheave in the topmast head with a tye block seized to its end which should hang at mid topmast height when the yard is lowered, refer to Plate VI. Another part has an eye splice lashed to an eyebolt in the starboard channel which reeves through the tye block and has a double block stropped into its other end. The double block is part of a luff tackle with a single block stropped to an eyebolt in the port channel and belays to the fore pinrail.

Jackstay, Footrope, Flemish Horse—Same as for foreyard.

Lift—A single pendant with an eye splice in each end, one lashed to an eye on the yardarm band and the other to topmast head just above the stay.

Brace—An eye splice is lashed to main-topmast stay at the seizing. It reeves through the block stropped to band on the yardarm, through block stropped to the mainstay above the seizing, through block seized to an eyebolt on main trestletrees, and belays to main pinrail.

Topgallant Sheet (optional)—Same as topsail sheet. Reeve this behind the lower yard and belay rope tail to the fore fife rail.

Main-Topsail Yard

Parrel, Jackstay, Flemish Horse, Lift, Topgallant Sheet—Same as for fore-topsail yard.

Tye—Same as for fore-topsail yard except the sides are reversed.

Brace—An eye splice is seized to the mizzen-topmast stay at the seizing. It reeves to a block stropped to band on the yardarm, to block on the mizzen stay, to block on the mizzen trestletree, and belays to main fife rails.

Mizzen-Topsail Yard

Parrel, Jackstay, Flemish Horse, Lift, Topgallant Sheet—Same as fore-topsail yard.

Tye—Attaches to yard same as for fore-topsail yard but the end reeves over sheave in topmast and runs directly to luff tackle in the port channel. The fall belays to the mizzen pinrail.

Brace—An eye splice is lashed to an eyebolt in the main cap. It reeves through a block stropped to band on the yardarm, through block stropped to an eyebolt in the main trestletrees, and belays to main fife rail.

Fore-Topgallant Yard

Parrel—Single row with balls only.

Tye—Attaches to yard with a cow hitch. It reeves over sheave in topgallant masthead and to a luff tackle in the starboard channel. Its fall belays to the fore pinrail.

Jackstay and Footrope—Same as on foreyard.

Lift—A single pendant with an eye in each end, one lashed to an eye on the band on the yardarm and the other to band around heel of the royal mast.

Brace—An eye splice is lashed to the main-topgallant stay. It reeves through block stropped to band on the yardarm, through block stropped to the main-topmast stay, through block stropped to eyebolt on the main-topmast trestletree, and belays to main pinrail.

Main-Topgallant Yard

Parrel, Jackstay, Footrope, Lift—Same as fore-topgallant yard.

Tye—Same as fore-topgallant tye except that a luff tackle is rigged to port.

Brace—An eye splice is lashed to the mizzen-topgallant stay. It reeves through block stropped to eye in band on the yardarm, through block stropped to the mizzen-topmast stay, through block stropped to mizzen trestletree, and belays to mizzen pinrail.

Mizzen-Topgallant Yard

Parrel, Jackstay, Footrope, Lift—Same as fore-topgallant yard.

Tye—Same as fore-topgallant tye except that a gun tackle is rigged into its lower end.

Brace—An eye splice is lashed to eyebolt in the main-topmast trestletree. It reeves through block stropped to eye on the yardarm band, through a block stropped to eye on the main cap, and belays to pinrail.

Fore-Royal Yard

Parrel, Jackstay, Footrope, Lift—Same as fore-topgallant yard.

Tye—Same as fore-topgallant yard except that a gun tackle is used on the portside.

Brace—An eye splice is lashed to eye on the yardarm band. It reeves through block stropped to the royal mast just above topgallant standing rigging, and belays to main pinrail.

Main-Royal Yard

Parrel, Jackstay, Footrope, Lift—Same as fore-royal yard.

Tye—Same as fore-royal yard except it is rigged to starboard.

Brace—Same as fore-royal brace except it reeves through block on the mizzen-royal mast and belays to mizzen pinrail.

Mizzen-Royal Yard

Parrel, Jackstay, Footrope, Lift—Same as fore-royal yard.

Tye—Same as fore-royal yard except that a single block is stropped in its lower end. The fall has an eye splice lashed to eye in the port mizzen channel and belays to mizzen pinrail.

Brace—Same as fore-royal brace except it reeves through block stropped to eyebolt in the main-topmast trestletree and belays to the main fife rail.

Builders must decide how much running rigging is wanted if sails are not fitted. That just described is the amount still left aloft when the vessel arrived at a safe port, by which time rigging with all sails had been sent below.

Since the amount rigged is minimal and may appear to be very sparce when compared to the other two square-riggers, modelers may wish to rig staysail halyards and downhauls. Halyards consisting of gun tackles can be fitted on the mizzen stay, all topmast stays, jibstay, fore-topgallant stay, and main-topgallant stay. Single part halyards are appropriate for the mizzen-topgallant stay and both the main- and mizzen-royal stays. The upper blocks are stropped to the upper end of the stays and lower blocks to the lower ends of stays unless downhauls are fitted. Downhauls are appropriate on all staysails except for those on the main-topmast and mizzen stays. Downhaul blocks are secured to the lower ends of the appropriate stays. They hook to the strop of the lower halyard blocks (eye splice if single parts), reeve through the downhaul block, and belay along with the halyards where shown in the belaying pin plan.

Some modelers prefer to rig head-staysail sheet-blocks to increase the amount of rigging on the bowsprit assembly. If this is to be done, strop a single block in each end of a short pendant with a hook in its middle attached to the eye in the downhauls so a block can be rigged on each side. The sheets have an eye splice in one end lashed to the eyebolt on the inboard end of the cathead. They are rove through the blocks on the pendant and back to cleats near the after edge of the forecastle deck where they are belayed.

FINISHING THE MODEL

Upon completion of the rigging, clean up the deck. Rig whaleboat davits and stow the boats in them. Rig anchor(s) as described in Chapter VI. The model is now ready for its permanent mounting and case.

Helen B. Thomas. **Photograph by W. B. Jackson during a race for the Lipton Cup,** *Helen B. Thomas* **with all sails set except for the fore topsail. Many details of deck structures and rig are very clear. Courtesy of The Peabody Museum, Salem.**

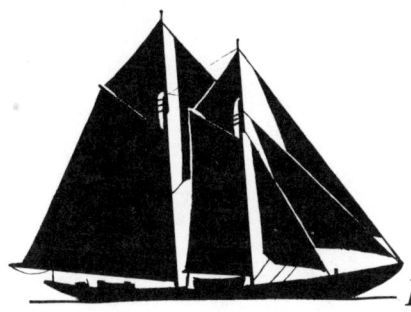

Chapter XVII
HELEN B. THOMAS

Helen B. Thomas was an experimental vessel designed by Thomas F. McManus of Boston in 1901. The idea for this bowspritless design stemmed from his desire to reduce loss of life aboard fishing schooners. Many men were washed away while handling sail on the bowsprit. In Massachusetts fishing towns the condition was so bad that a bowsprit was commonly referred to as a "widow-maker."

This schooner and later bowspritless vessels were known to fishermen as "knockabouts" after the term used to designate sloops and other small craft without bowsprits, used in congested areas. Some fishermen, usually a conservative people, believed this idea was too radical for immediate acceptance, but Captain William Thomas of Portland, Maine, nonetheless had the vessel built.

She was built by the noted firm of Oxner and Story at Essex, Massachusetts, during the winter of 1902. Her lines were for a vessel 105'6" long, by 20'11" in beam, and 10'6" in depth. According to authoritative reports, changes were made by the builder. These changes slightly altered and modified her appearance. The drawings for this model were not changed in an attempt to fit these deviations.

Her rig was that of contemporary fishing schooners except that the masts were closer together and a little farther aft than normal, to allow headstays to be attached to the hull and still retain the customary configuration.

The hull design had one serious drawback for a working vessel. By necessity her long slim bow created a very small hull in terms of capacity. Because initial cost is governed to a large extent by hull length, her cost per ton of capacity was relatively high. Consequently, this experiment was not repeated and all later knockabouts were built with deeper hulls in the forward parts.

She was a smart sailer and it is claimed that she could complete a tack in twenty to twenty-five seconds on relatively smooth seas. She was raced in at least one annual fisherman's race with mediocre results, but there is some question about how well she was handled. Annual races between individual vessels or vessels from rival fishing towns allowed fishermen a

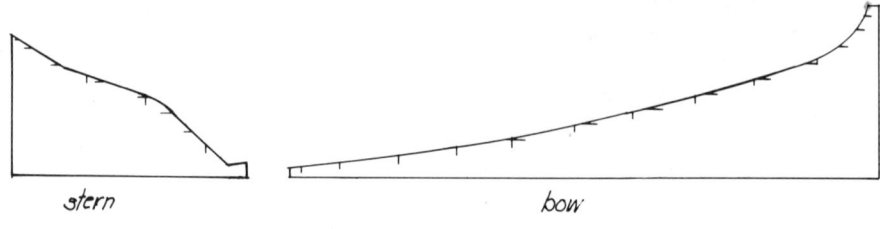

Fig. 126
Templates for bow and stern

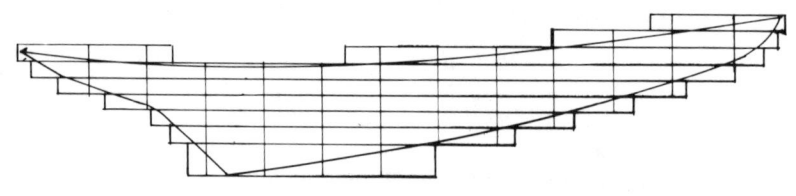

Fig. 127
Hull block for construction
under Method 1 as modified

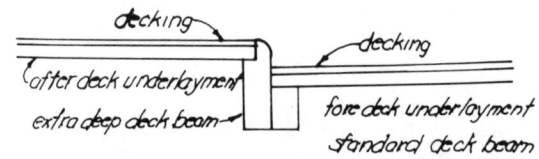

Fig. 128
Cross-section of "great beam" and
deck construction at deck break

little diversion from the grinding toil and constant dangers associated with their work. Customarily they raced with almost a vengenance, with all sails set, regardless of weather. These races were held in the fall when stiff breezes are common, and no sail was removed unless the wind blew it away.

Her size was quite ideal for a fishing schooner. She normally carried two nests of five dories each when engaged in trawling on the fishing banks. She also spent part of her career seining, but equipment for seining is very difficult to miniaturize so it is better to fit the model for trawling.

Helen B. Thomas plied her trade for twenty years with few mishaps and little loss of life—both events all too common with and aboard these schooners. She was a profitable vessel whether seining or trawling. Although never repeated, her design influenced the design of later craft, especially that of the knockabout. After her successful twenty years service she sailed away from Gloucester for the last time to finish her days as a Bermudian pilot boat.

HULL

Methods described in Chapter I must be modified for this hull. Because of the hull's underbody profile shape, the bow template must be extended to include the whole profile from sternpost to stemhead. Also, neither of the methods described in Chapter I provide an easy method for building this hull. Method 1 requires far too much shaping and Method 2 requires very careful measuring to obtain a hull of proper depth.

The drawing, Fig. 126, of both bow and stern profile templates is suitable for this hull. Fig. 127 is a side view of a suitable hull block for construction under a modified scheme following Method 1. Each lift is 5 3/4" wide. The lowest lift is 15/16" thick by about 9" long. The other pieces are 1/2" thick and of various lengths. Success in this operation is obtained by carefully locating each station on every lift and by gluing lifts on one at a time, as described under Method 2. When gluing is completed, plane one side clean, straight, and square with lift surfaces to use as reference when establishing the fore-and-aft, vertical, center line plane. Reestablish station lines on this side. Then locate the point where the sheer crosses the stem profile and where the keel crosses Station 9 on each side of the block. With the aid of the template, draw the shape of the underbody profile on each side. Follow up by drawing the stern profile and that of the sheer. Shape the profile completely. Then draw the center line all around, draw the rabbet offsets and reestablish the stations on the profile surfaces just cut.

Shaping this hull is the easiest of any described in this book. There are no areas where the shape changes rapidly and all cuts are on a favorable cutting angle with the wood grain.

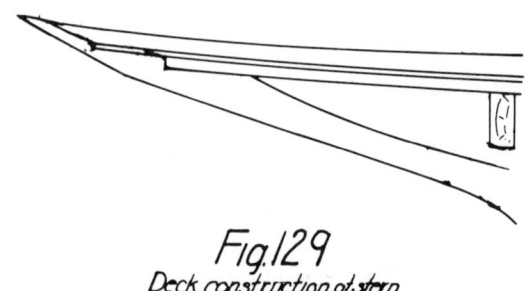

Fig. 129
Deck construction at stern

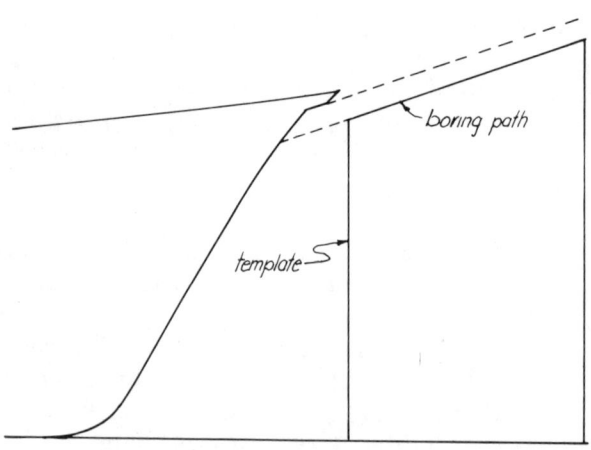

Fig. 130
Boring template for bowsprit hole

Hollowing out the hull is somewhat difficult. There is little chance of satisfactorily holding the hull in a vise, so hold it on the lap and work towards the middle from each end with a curved bit gouge. Leave about 1" in the lower part of the hull and 1/4" along the sides. When cutting down the sides for the deck allow 1/8" for underlayment and 1/16" for decking. Like *Isaac Webb*, the bulwarks width is outside planking thickness. Cut them down so they are 3/32" thick around the sides and thick enough across the stern so the fore-and-aft dimension on deck is 3/16". Fair this surface into the sides, as shown in deck plan. Do not forget that there is a break in the deck just aft of Station 7.

Deck beams are located midway between Stations 2 and 3, under the windlass, under the galley stack, at Station 8, under the forward end of the afterhouse, and under the after end of the afterhouse. They are made of stock 1/2" thick and stripped into pieces 1/4" wide with a crown of 3/32" at the widest part of the hull. Refer to Fig. 128 for construction at the break. Note that underlayment and decking both fit in a rabbet on the after side of the extra-deep deck beam. The forward corner is rounded off in a neat radius. Cut the fit for the after end of the underlayment about 1 1/4" aft of Station 12 and fit for the decking all the way aft to the bulwarks across the stern. See Fig. 129. Finish this phase of the work by setting the underlayment on each deck.

At this point in its construction the hull is in the same condition as that for the "Merchant Vessel of 1800" and *Margaret Haskell* at the close of Chapter I.

FINISHING THE HULL

Make and install sternpost after rudder port has been bored followed by the completed stem-keel assembly. Shape the rudder, bevel the sternpost, and fit the pintles and gudgeons so rudder can be fitted as soon as bulwarks and rail are completed.

Carve bulwarks from bow to stern to a uniform thickness of 1/16" from sheer to top of underlayment. Cut inside of transom down to 1/8" and fair the quarters into the bulwarks. Cut a rabbet across stern to receive the after end of deck planking. See Fig. 129. Make and install waterways 1/16" thick by 3/16" wide followed by false timberheads along the sides from transom to just aft of the hawsepipes. Timberheads are 1/8", fore and aft spaced at 1/2" on centers, and of suitable thickness to accommodate a 3/16" wide main rail. From just aft of the hawsepipes to the bow, bulwarks are padded out on the inside to the same thickness as timberheads. The padding is carved from pine to shape and glued in place.

Now that timberheads are installed, form the thin section of planking just below the rail and cut the cove. Bore the hawsepipes starting with a

Main sheet equipment
No scale

Galley
Chimney
No scale

Headsail furling and stowing plank
No scale

Foot of main mast
No scale

Hull sections at each
mast showing chainplates
No scale

Smoke hood-after house
No scale

Boom and gaff end fittings
No scale

Dory nest

Hollowing out templates

end view
Anchor chain box

After house

Companionway

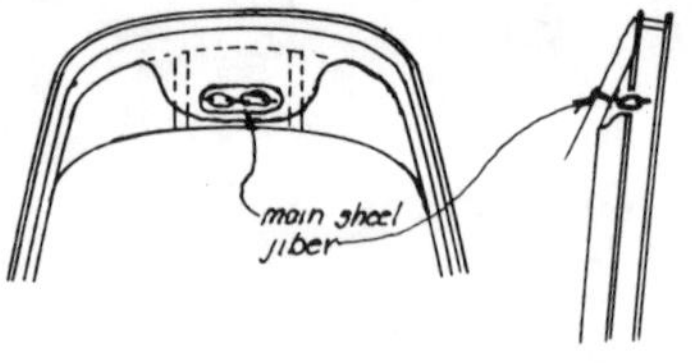

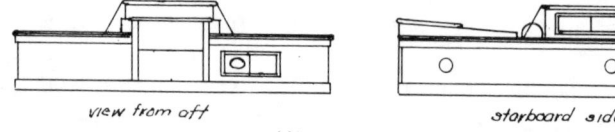

Reddish brown: Below waterline
Black: Topsides including top of highest rail
White: Inside of bulwarks, bitts, hatches, furling plank, furling plank, companionway sides, house sides, steering gear box, masts from deck to boom, doublings, poles, trucks, gaffs, booms, and blocks
Yellow: Coves and ornamentation
Vermillion: Hawse pipes
Medium grey: House and companionway tops
Light grey: Decks
Medium brown stain: Balance of spars

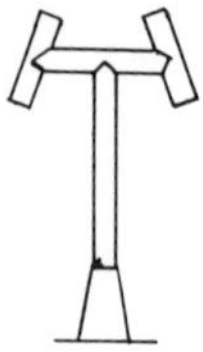

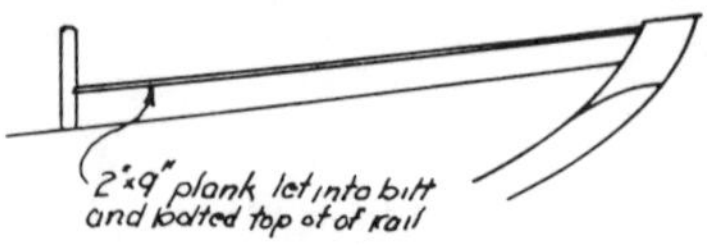

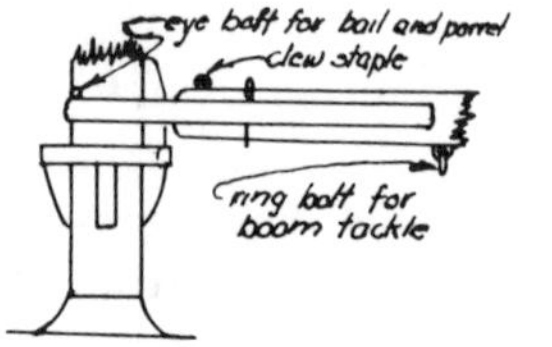

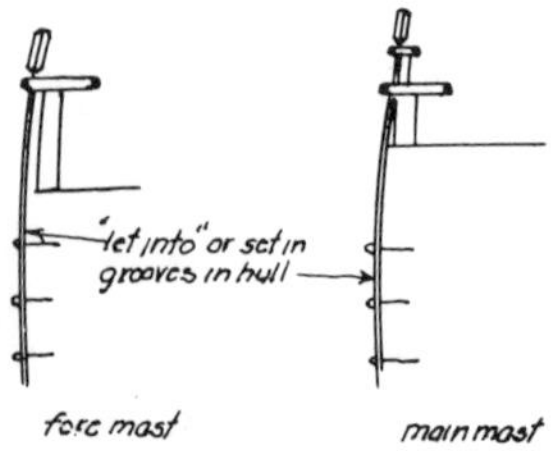

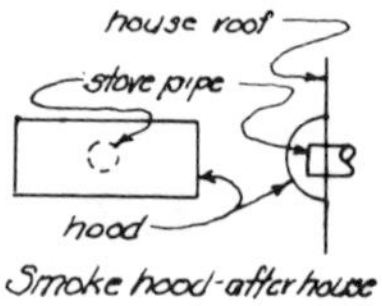

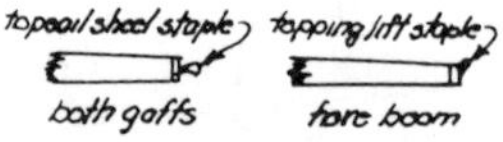

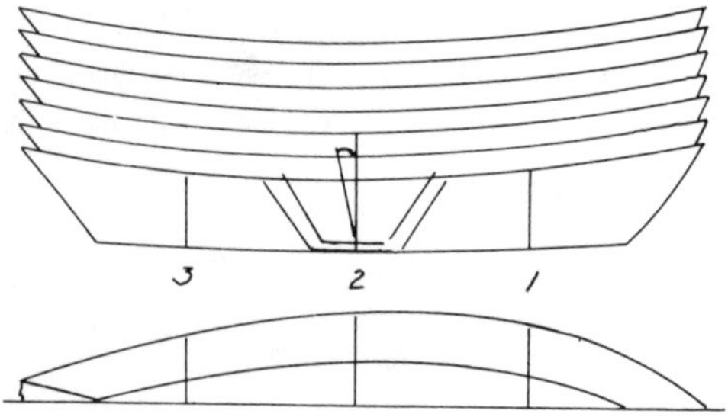

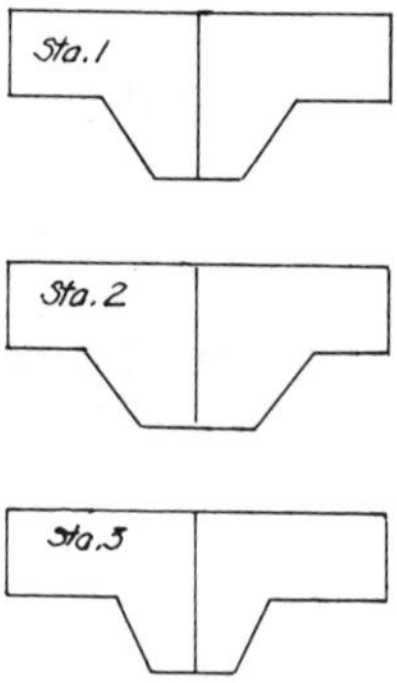

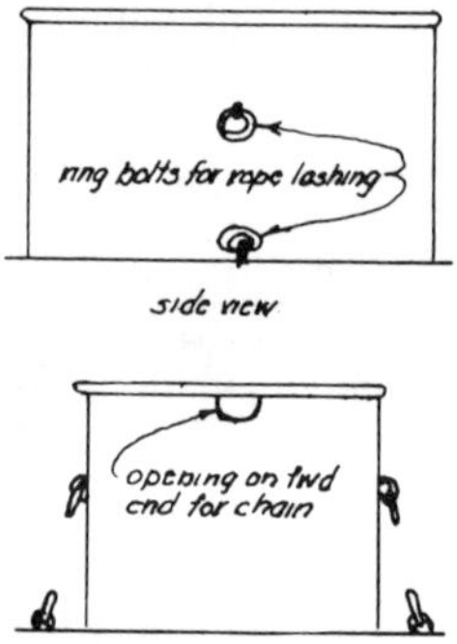

Paint scheme

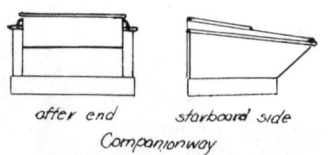

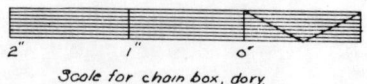

Scale for chain box, dory, companionway, and after house

HELEN B THOMAS
Detail Sheet
Scale as noted

fine drill and increase their size to 5/32" by using successively larger drills. Then install the deck including padding. Before installing main rail, make and install brackets on each side of the mainsheet jiber, and follow with the jiber itself. Then fit and install the main rail including pinrails abreast the mast, the long breasthook forward, and the jiber aft. Make and fit hawse blocks and glue the lips in place. Finish rails by making and installing the buffalo rails forward and the monkey rail aft. Buffalo rails are just 1/16" stock edge-fastened to the main rail. Monkey rails rest on filler pieces edge-fastened on the main rail. See construction and cross section at the main mast in detail sheet. Carve a piece 1/16" thick to fit across the stern which is neatly butted to 1/16" thick pieces that run forward to the deck break. These pieces terminate with a radius. After these pieces are installed, fit the surmounting rail. The portion across the stern and those over the radii must be carved to shape.

Main-topmast bitts and fife rails are made as shown in deck plan. Note that the foresheet cleat and the foreboom crotch are integral parts of this unit and that a hand-operated winch was incorporated in the construction. Mainsheet bitts are shown in the deck and sheer plans with two sets of arms on each. The only other bitt is located forward of the forestay and supports the after end of the headsail furling and stowing plank.

This work completes the hull through Chapter IV, except for hatches covered in the next section.

FITTING OUT THE DECK

Make and install the furling plank from beech or maple 3/16" wide and a strong 1/32" thick, fitted from the forward bitt to the stem on top of the main rail. Refer to detail sheet. Make and install galley hatch, described in Chapter V. Make and install jumbo sheet horse, eyes for the jib sheet, and the stropped bull's-eye leads in pad eyes. Install windlass and stow the heavers. All work forward of the foremast is completed when the eyes for the three headstays are installed.

Make and install hatches for the main and after decks. Coamings are 1/4" high. There are athwartships covers on each with a narrow strap fore and aft which can be simulated by a narrow strip of paper extended down each end 1/8".

Make and install the companionway, the afterhouse, and the wheelbox. Construction of each is as described in Chapter V. Note that the companionway has an extension to support the forward ends of slide rails, but the forward end of the trunk is vertical. The companionway slide on the afterhouse is like any other with sliding boards on the end like the companionway. This slide is amidships, so the compass window and its cover

Spar	a	b	c	d
fore mast	.375	.312	.291	.281
main mast	.395	.333	.312	.300
fore topmast	.229	.229	.166	
main topmast	.250	.250	.187	
fore boom	.145	.166	.120	
main boom	.187	.229	.166	
fore gaff	.140	.160	.120	
main gaff	.155	.176	.135	
staysail club	.030	.045	.032	

Spar diameters in inches

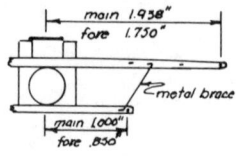

Cross & trestle trees

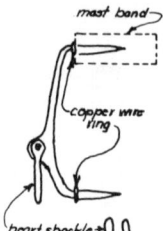

Throat halyard crane

Throat halyard connections on gaffs

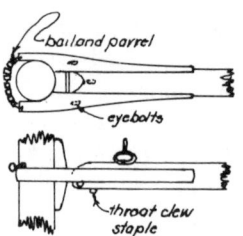

Gaff throat end construction

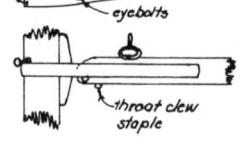

Schematic of throat halyards

Sheet band and bail

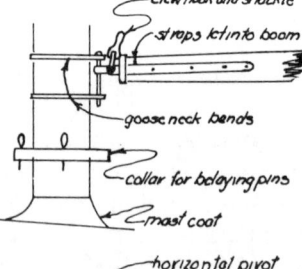

Lower foremast and gooseneck

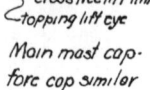

Main mast cap — fore cap similar

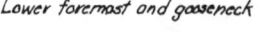

gaffs & booms

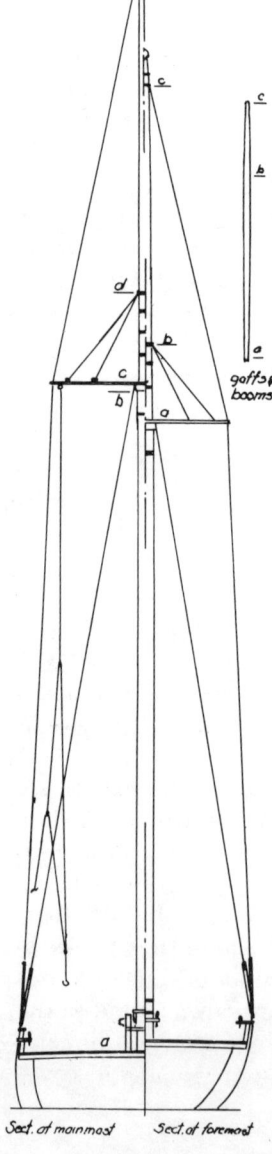

Sect. of mainmast   Sect. of foremast

HELEN B. THOMAS
Detail Sheet
No Scale

are to starboard. The skylight on the afterhouse has windows on each side with vertical rods. Straps on each corner hold it down. The hood is described in Chapter IX and shown in detail sheet. The wheelbox is shaped as shown with a flush-edged, slightly crowned roof. The roof was removable and held down with an athwartship steel strap. The wheel is mounted by gluing its shaft into a hole bored in its forward end.

Make galley stack as described in Chapter IX and shown in detail sheet. Its shank fits in a snug-fitting hole on the starboard side of the companionway.

Make chain box. It is made hollow with a hole just under the cover on its forward end and a very thin, slightly overhanging cover. Ringbolts in each side are lashed to ringbolts in the deck. Try a dory nest on deck with the stern just forward of the break and locate the chain box abreast of the foremast so it clears dories and allows space to work at the fore pinrail and pin rack. After it is lashed down, feed some chain, eight or ten links per inch, into the hole. Stretch chain along deck and wrap two turns around the port windlass barrel in a counterclockwise direction, as viewed from portside. The end is led aft an inch or so and lashed to the other part.

Deck work is finished when the foresheet horse, its bull's-eye lead, the eyes in the pinrails (as shown in deck plan), and the four dory nest hold-down ringbolts on each side are installed. Ringbolts are located in deck abreast the forward and after stations. Make hooks to fit over top dory gunwales. Lashings between hooks and ringbolts hold the nests down. It is suggested that dory nests be fitted after rigging is completed.

Finish work on the hull by fitting chain plates and deadeyes. This work is best done just after rails are completed.

SPARS

Directions for making spars are given in Chapter XI. For fittings see Chapter XII. Ironwork is described in Chapter IX and shown in detail sheet.

Spar lengths are taken directly off the sail plan; diameters are given in detail sheet. For lower masts (a) is the diameter at deck, (b) at the cheeks, (c) above the shoulder at the trestletrees, and (d) at the cap. For topmasts (a) is at the heel, (b) at the cap, and (c) just below the shoulder at the head. For other spars (a) is at the forward end, (b) at two-thirds the way aft, and (c) at the after end.

Rig the masts first. Make and fit the cheeks followed by trestletrees and crosstrees. Insert eyes for crosstree lifts and dory tackles. Drill ends of the foward crosstrees for topmast backstays and install brace between crosstrees. Make and install all bands on mastheads. Those for peak halyard blocks are fitted with ears and rings. Bands for throat halyard cranes are bored to receive upper horns. The highest band on the foremast has holes athwartships to receive horns on the jibstay bail. Make and install caps with a bail for mainstay on the main cap and two bails on the fore cap. One is for the mainstay, the other for the main-topmast stay. An elongated link is fitted next to the caps on each side under the bails with their lower ends turned outward for crosstree lifts. Make and fit eyes in the fore trestletrees for jumbo halyard blocks and a link on the fore side of the mainmast in line with the lower-throat-halyard crane horn for the fore-boom topping lift. Rig wire rods with eyes in each end for the crosstree lifts.

The jumbo stay bail can be made now but it should not be fitted until the mast is stepped. Slide lower mast hoops onto their spars and make the main boom saddle, the fore boom gooseneck bands, and the collar for the belaying pins under the gooseneck. The masts so rigged are ready to receive their topmasts and be stepped in the hull.

Topmasts are fitted in place from below; so make fid holes and fids. Slide them up through and fit them followed by installing the gates on both pairs of trestletrees. Then feed the topmast hoops on followed by eyes or bands at their heads. Now the spar assemblies can be stepped.

Booms and gaffs are rigged as shown in sail plan and detail sheet. Make jaw and clappers for gaffs and main booms. While fitting clappers on the gaffs cut away enough stock on the upper fore part of the spar to allow them to be peaked up without binding. Refer to detail sheet for drawing of the three-link assembly in eyes on the upper sides of the jaws for the throat halyard blocks. The upper link on the fore gaff is just a ring, but that on the main has eyes on each side so two blocks could be hooked to it. Bands for peak halyard blocks have ears for attaching blocks. Bands with bails are fitted on the booms for attaching sheet-blocks. Bands with eyes are fitted just inboard of the outer ends on both booms and gaffs for securing sail clews.

Outboard ends have ferrules to prevent ends from cracking. The ferrule on main boom has an eye for attaching the lift. Ferrules on the others had staples welded on their insides for attaching topsail sheet-blocks on the gaffs and topping lift on the fore boom. These can be miniaturized or simulated by eyes with their shanks driven into the booms.

Gaffs are complete when eyes are fitted to the underside of the port fore jaw and the starboard main jaw for the topsail sheet-lead-blocks and when very small eyes are fitted on the upper fore end of each jaw for the bail and parrel. The fore boom is complete when gooseneck is fitted, as described in Chapter IX. The main boom has two sheaves in its outboard end for the topping lift. Two small eyes evenly spaced along the boom on the lower starboard side are driven into the boom, and the topping lift tackle is rove through them to a pin in the starboard jaw. A band with an eye and an eyebolt provides securing points for the boom tackle under the boom and

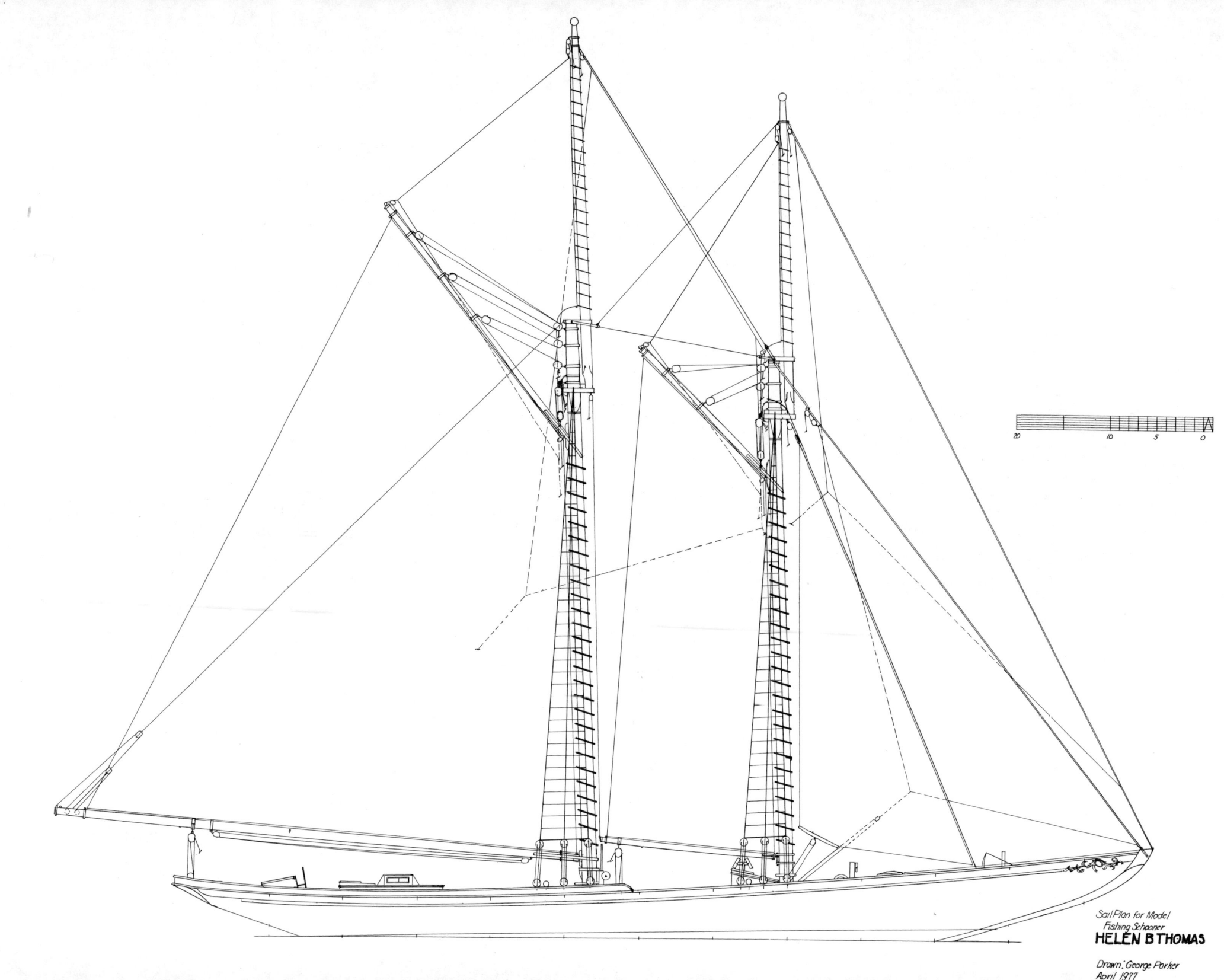

Sail Plan for Model
Fishing Schooner
HELEN B THOMAS

Drawn: George Parker
April 1977

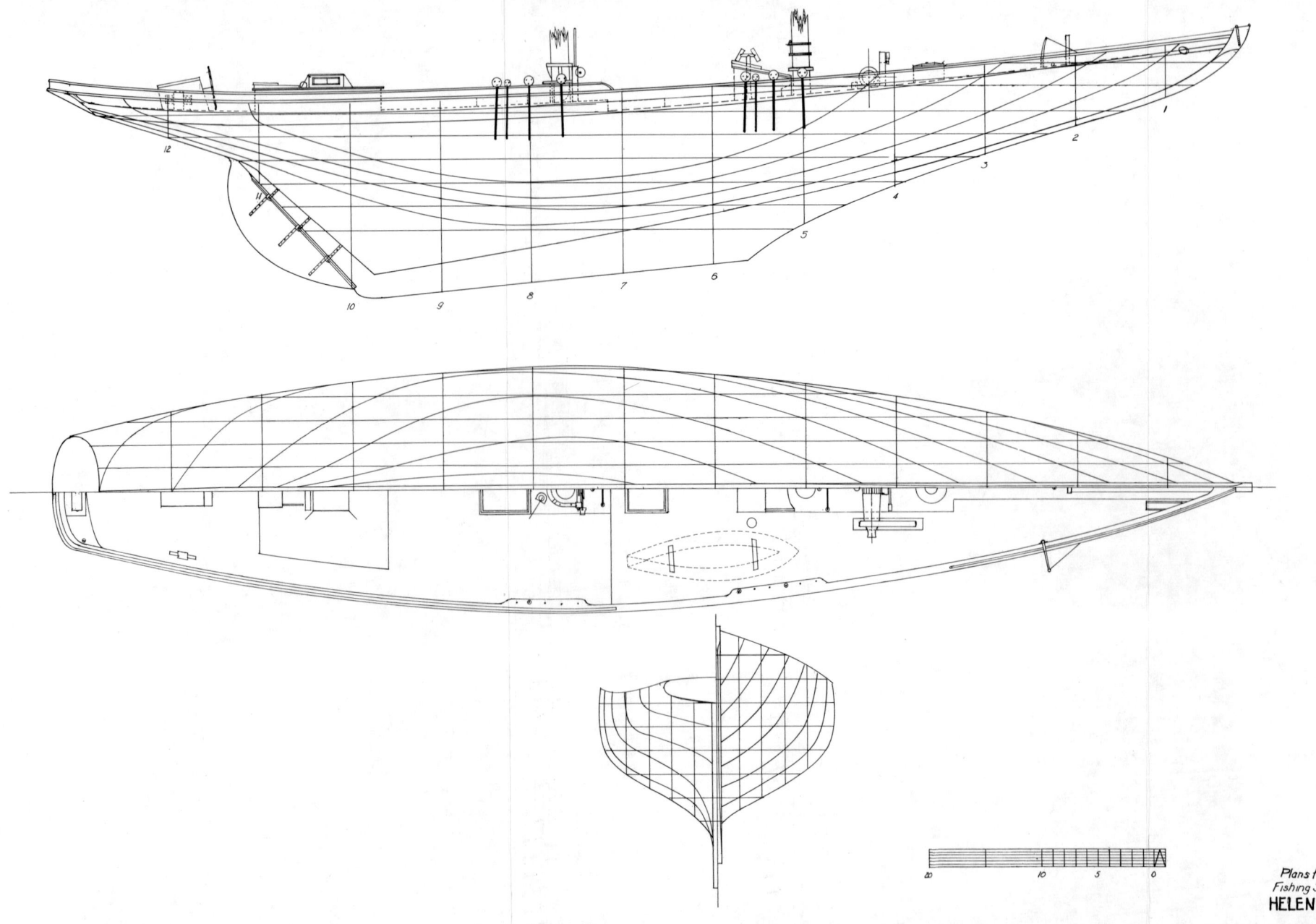

TABLE V
—Helen B. Thomas—
Major Rigging Component Sizes
(dimensions in inches)

Rigging	Blocks (etc.)	Rigging Dia.
Headstays on foremast		.020 wire
Fore-topmast stay		.015 "
Lower shrouds		.020 "
	5/32 deadeyes	.020 black thread
Topmast backstays		.013 wire
	1/8 deadeyes	.015 black thread
Mainstay		.020 wire
Main-topmast stay		.015 "
Headsail halyards	3/16 blocks	.015 natural thread
Throat halyards	1/4 "	.020 " "
Peak halyards	1/4 "	.020 " "
Jumbo sheets	3/16 "	.015 " "
Foresheets	1/4 "	.020 " "
Mainsheets	1/4 "	.020 " "
Boom tackle	3/16 "	.015 " "
Main-boom topping lift		.020 black thread
	3/16 & 1/8 blocks	.015 natural thread
Topsail rigging	1/8 blocks	.015 " "

its fall belays to pin in the port jaw. Similar small eyes are installed in the main boom jaws, as was described for the gaff for the parrel bail. Parrels are a string of very small wooden beads, as described for the upper yards on square-riggers, but a fine wire bail with an eye in each end attached to the jaw eyes was used instead of rope. Before setting the boom aside as complete, rig two footropes from the eyes above the bail on the main sheet band to the topping lift eye in the ferrule. They should hang about 1/2" below the top of the boom. This scales up to 2' and would be about right for a man to stand on while straddling the boom as he was securing the reef earing. If sails are going to be fitted the jib sprit has to be made and rigged. A fine band with an eye is fitted for its sheet. Athwartship holes on each end allow a seizing to the sail with a spiral lacing between.

The hull is now ready to rig. See Table V for sizes for rigging, blocks, etc.

STANDING RIGGING

Shrouds—Three on each side with deadeyes below and a sheer pole across all three with ratlines on all from sheer poles to trestletrees. Before putting ratlines on the fore shrouds install the running-light boxes. If the boxes are in the way of ratlines, drill small holes through the chocks close to the shrouds for reeving them through.

Jumbo Stay—Single between the wire bail over the masthead and the link in a pad eye on deck.

Jibstay—Single between the bail on the mast band just below the fore cap and a link in the inboard eyebolt or pad eye on the stemhead.

Mainstay—Single between bails on each mast cap.

Backstays—Single on each side. A tight-fitting eye is slid over the head and jammed onto the band. Each is fed through a hole in the outboard end of the long crosstree to a deadeye in the lower end.

Ballooner Stay—Single with eye over fore-topmast head and to link in the outboard eyebolt or pad eye on the stemhead.

Main-topmast Stay—Single with eye over the main-topmast head to a bail in the foremast cap.

Counter Stay—Single and opposite to main-topmast stay.

Pin Racks—Although these cannot be considered rigging they cannot be installed until the shroud deadeyes lanyards are installed. They are made of maple 1/16" thick and wide enough to be a fit between lanyards. They are long enough to cross all shrouds and are lashed to the lanyards for each shroud with an X-shaped lashing being careful to keep all at the same height above the lower deadeyes and parallel to the sheer. Two pinholes between the shrouds are drilled through.

RUNNING RIGGING

Ballooner

Halyard—Single. Reeves through block hooked to the eye in band on fore-topmast head and belays to starboard. If sails are set, the standing part hooks to clew in upper corner of sail. If not, it hooks to ballooner downhaul.

Downhaul—Single. Reeves through block hooked to ballooner stay in stemhead. The standing end reeves up through the hanks and hooks into halyard. It belays to pin in starboard side of rail breasthook.

Sheets—One on each side made of one length of rigging rove through the sail's clew so legs are of equal length and seized together. The legs reeve outboard of backstays of both masts on each side and belay to cleats on a timberhead abreast the after end of the afterhouse. Sheets are not rigged without sails.

Jib

Halyard—A gun tackle with the higher block hooked to the jibstay bail and belays to port. If sails are set, the lower block hooks to the sail; if not, it hooks to the downhaul.

Downhaul—Same as for ballooner except it belays to port.

Sheet—Double. Reeve a short length of line, as described for the ballooner, and splice a bull's-eye in each end. Insert an eye in each waterway abreast the foremast with a line spliced into it. Reeve each through the bull's-eyes on the sheet pendant, through the lead bull's-eye, and belay in fore pin racks. As before, these are not rigged without sails.

Jumbo

Halyard—One end belays on starboard pinrail. It reeves through a block hooked to the starboard trestletree, to a block hooked to the sail, to a block on the port trestletree, and to the port pinrail.

Downhaul—It is not certain if a downhauler was used for jumbos on knockabouts but, since they were inboard, it seems that they would not be necessary, so the lower jumbo halyard block can be hooked to the stay pad eye on deck if sails are not rigged.

Sheet—A gun tackle with one block hooked to an eye in a band on the sprit and the other block to a ring on the horse. The fall leads to a bull's-eye stropped to an eye on the center line astern of the horse and up to a pin on the foremast. This is not rigged without sails.

Foresail

Throat Halyard—Has a treble block hooked to a ring in the crane and a double block hooked to a ring on the gaff jaws. See detail sheet. One end of the halyard belays at the mast on portside. It reeves off as sketch shows and ends starboard side with a double block hooked to a small eye splice. The double block is part of a luff tackle with a single block in the starboard waterways, and the fall belays at the starboard rail.

Peak Halyard—Has a double and a single block hooked to rings in bands on the mast and two single blocks hooked to eyes in bands on the gaff. See sail plan. One end of the halyard belays at mast on starboard side. It reeves up through starboard sheave of the double block and so on until it reeves down through the single block on the mast and ends portside with a double block hooked to a small eye splice. It in turn is part of a luff tackle, as described for throat halyard, except to port.

Sheet—A luff tackle with the double block hooked to the sheet band bail and the single block to a ring on the horse. Its fall leads to a bull's-eye, as described for the jumbo, and belays to the cleat on the foreside of the main-topmast bitt bolster.

Boom Topping Lift—A whip purchase hooked to the eye in the end of the boom. It reeves through a single block hooked to an eye on the foremast under the trestletrees and belays to starboard.

Mainsail

Throat Halyard—Has two double blocks hooked on either side of a heart iron in the crane and a double and single to the spectacle iron on the gaff jaws. See detail sheet. One end of the halyard belays at the fife rails on portside. It reeves off, as shown in sketch, and ends starboard side with a luff tackle, as described for the fore throat halyard.

Peak Halyard—Has a double and two single blocks hooked to rings in bands on the mast and three single blocks hooked to eyes in bands on the gaff. See sail plan. One end of the halyard belays at the fife rails and reeves off with a luff tackle in the other similar to the fore peak halyard.

Sheet—Has a treble block hooked to the sheet band bail and a double to the ring on the jiber. Its fall leads to a bull's-eye, as described for the jumbo sheet, and belays to either mainsheet bitt.

Boom Topping Lift—Refer to sail plan. The main part consists of a line spliced to the eye in the mainmast cap and a single block hooked to a small eye splice in the lower end. The second part reeves through the block in the main part with an eye splice in the eye on the after boom band and a block hooked to an eye splice in the other end. The third part is a gun tackle using the last mentioned block and the outboard sheave. The tackle fall leads over the inboard sheave and reeves through a couple of small eyes on the starboard side of the boom to hold it up and belays to a pin in the starboard boom jaw.

Boom Tackle—Consists of a luff tackle with the double block hooked to the eye of the boom band and the single hooked to an eye in the boom. The fall belays to a pin in the port boom jaws.

Crotch Tackle—When the mainsail was lowered the boom crotch was fitted in its deck socket and the topping lift slacked off until the boom rested in its crotch. Because of the deck socket's construction and the heavy weight of boom, gaff, and sail the crotch could not be relied upon to constrain the boom while the vessel rolled. To counteract sidewise forces, tackles were rigged from the boom to the waterways. These are rigged on the model only when sails are not set and consist of two luff tackles with double blocks hooked to the sheet bail, the singles to eyes in the waterway, and the falls belayed to cleats on timberheads.

GAFF TOPSAILS

Halyards—Consist of gun tackles hooked to topmast bands, where shown in sail plan. When sails are set the tackle hooks to the clews of the sails; when sails are removed tackle hooks to any handy eye at the mast caps. They are belayed to port pin racks.

Sheets—Hitch to sail clew. It reeves through a block hooked to an eye in the end of the gaffs and through a block hooked to an eye in the underside of one gaff jaw. The eyes are in the port jaw on the fore gaff and belay at the mast, opposite on main. When sails are not fitted, sheets are not rigged.

Tacks—Hitch sail to clew and belay to pin in opposite side from sheets, not rigged without sails.

Clews—Small single blocks are hooked to three corners of the sails with a double block seized to lowest topmast hoop. The fall is rove through one sheave in the double block and around through each single block and back through the other sheave. Both parts lead to port pin racks. Evenly spaced thimbles on foot and luff of each sail contained the clew lines and prevented them from sagging. These can be simulated by seizing the clew line to the edge of the sail.

Note: Fore-topsails were set to port of peak halyard and to starboard of gaff so they set as flat as possible. Main-topsails were set on opposite sides.

Fisherman's Staysail

Halyards—Peak halyard blocks are hooked to band at main-topmast head and throat halyard block to bail for the main-topmast stay. Each halyard is long enough to belay to pinrail on each side and through block above. This allowed the sail to be hoisted outboard of the leeward fore gaff.

Tack—Hitches to clew iron and belays to pin on lee side of jumbo sheet pin.

Sheets—Secures to clew iron, same as sheets on ballooner. They lead aft outside of main-topmast backstays and belay to cleats on timberheads.

Dory Hitches

They are rigged as shown in detail sheet. The hook is engaged to eye in the rail and the fall belayed where shown.
Plate XIII shows the location of each belaying pin, cleat, and bitt with a number code for use of each. Where pins are not coded they are spares.

FINISHING THE MODEL

If sails are to be rigged, follow instructions in Chapters II and XII. If they are not fitted, lower fore and main booms into their crotches. Then lower their gaffs onto booms and tie them in place with two lines neatly knotted with ends cut short. Clean deck of all construction debris and lash dory nests, as described previously, to the deck. It is now ready for its permanent mounting and case.

Chapter XVIII

MARGARET HASKELL

Margaret Haskell was built in 1904 by H.M. Bean of Camden, Maine, for the Coastwise Transportation Company. She was designed by B.B. Crowningshield for the coastal coal trade. Her first runs were from Chesapeake Bay, Maryland, and Virginia coal ports to Boston, Massachusetts, ports. Apparently her trips were uneventful with the exception of two collisions within a period of two hours and having to be towed into Boston for repairs.

When she was built it was the latter part of the era of large schooners, although they were built in diminishing numbers until after World War I. This era started modestly in 1880 with the building of a four-master. Hulls were built longer and longer and by 1888 a five-master was built. Soon thereafter a six-master appeared and ultimately a single seven-master was constructed.

This schooner is representative of a very important though short-lived class of merchantmen. Unfortunately the history of the design aspects of these schooners has received too little attention. Because of the scarcity of information about them existing models are frequently poor examples. Yet, as hundreds of thousands of tons were built over a thirty-year span, they deserve recognition comparable to that given other types for which excellent models have been built and displayed.

These schooners were essentially an outgrowth of two-masted coasters in use for two centuries. As the need for greater capacity grew, hulls were lengthened until sails became too large to handle; three-masters were the result and were well established along the coast soon after the Civil War. Further increases in size made the addition of more masts necessary. Vessels increased to the six-masted, 3,730 ton, wooden *Wyoming* and the seven-masted, 5,218 ton, steel *Thomas W. Lawson*.

Large schooners were built after steam had nearly driven commercial sail from deep water and packet services. They were the last glorious burst in sail but were pushed hard by unsettled labor and economic conditions and long strings of coal barges being towed by a single tug. Ultimately the barges along with the newly introduced steam colliers won, and the big schooners also disappeared.

While *Margaret Haskell* was operating in the coal trade, many problems existed at the loading end. Schooners were frequently obliged to seek

Margaret Haskell. Photograph of the nearly-completed vessel shortly after leaving the launching ways. The people on deck and the houses in the background give an idea of the size of the vessel. From the Collection of Paul C. Morris, Nantucket.

cargos elsewhere as is exemplified by her loss; she was carrying five thousand barrels of rosin and a million board feet of heavy timber from Pensacola, Florida, to Genoa, Italy, when before leaving the Gulf of Mexico she encountered severe weather and because clogged pump suction prevented pumping her out, she was abandoned in sinking condition.

These big schooners were not developed in the traditional sense. As has been intimated, they were overgrown small schooners. Depth of water in areas where these vessels had to travel placed severe constraints on the depth of hull. Hence, they were much narrower and shoaler in proportion to length than the smaller schooners or large square-riggers. These narrow, shallow hulls as designed did not offer adequate longitudinal strength required by the then contemporary practices. The ends were long and fine so they were virtually unsupported by their own buoyancy, particularly when light. Through these weaknesses their hulls soon became limber and leaky. Ends sagged and the sheer tended to straighten, a process known as "hogging."

The rig was strong, heavy, and durable. Given power to hoist sail and anchors these vessels were manned by a very small crew. By rule of thumb their entire compliment consisted of two men per mast plus two, making these large coasting schooners the most economical carriers in the history of commercial sail.

HULL

The description under either Method 1 or 2, Chapter I, fits this hull exactly. The block is one piece from the keel's upper surface to the sheer. Recall also that the last section in Chapter I is a description with accompanying photos of this hull's construction.

Lumber for it is 6 1/2" wide and a full 1/2" thick. Eight pieces 36" long are required along with two short pieces to bring up the height forward. The hull is 4 1/16" deep at the stern, and if the stock plus the glue joints do not suffice a short thin piece can be added there to make up the difference.

It is a relatively easy hull to build by either method described, but there are two areas in need of explanation. One area is the break in the hull's profile over the bowsprit, as shown in her hull plan and in Photo 7. The other area is the shape of the stern above the transom. Although the break in the upper part of the bow's profile appears doubtful, the combination of the bowsprit piercing the hull and the fact that the hull goes through a transition from terminating at stem width below to a point above does, indeed, create this shape. The upper stern is another matter. Its shape does not come automatically and is not adequately shown if the modeler is a novice. When cutting down the sides, do not cut down curve around the stern. While shaping the afterbody, carry hull form aft to the end of the hull block. When sides are done, lay out and shape the transom's curvature. Then make a template of the transom's shape from the detail sheet and transfer this shape to the transom surface. Refer to body and half-breadth plans. It is clear that the upper edge of the transom is outside of the hull's shape on deck from the transom's outboard end to Buttock #3. Starting at Buttock #3, where the sheer and transom converge, the area is flat and tilts forward in the fore and aft direction. This flat area is continued to the side where it blends into the shape of the hull at the side. This shaping is done most easily with a sanding block using medium paper.

While hollowing out the hull leave 1 1/2" in the bottom and 3/8" around the sides. Refer to detail sheet for a cross section of the hull hollowed out and deck installed. The cut for decking is 3/16" deep, 1/8" for underlayment, and 1/16" for decking. This cut is 3/16" in from the edge with slightly more allowed for underlayment forward and across stern to prevent breaking through outside surfaces.

Deck beams, except the most forward one, are made from 5/8" stock stripped into pieces 5/16" wide and cut on top for a crown of 3/32" in the longest beams. The forward one is 1 1/4" deep. These beams are set at Stations 2, 6, and 10, just forward of Stations 14, 18, and 21, and just aft of Station 24. Refer to Photo 9 which shows these beams in place; this photographed step is described in Chapter I and mentions that the bowsprit must be fitted before installing the underlayment.

The bowsprit is 5/16" square. It pierces the hull so its upper surface coincides with the break in the bow profile. Laying out work must be done carefully to assure that bowsprit is absolutely centered with the hull and that its steeve is correct. Start laying out by accurately locating center line on the forward deck beam. This is done by aligning the straightedge with center lines on bow and stern to draw the center line on its top surface. Finish center line by laying a parallel-sided piece of wood across hull and, with an adjustable square or bevel set square, extend center line down its forward face. Refer to detail sheet for dimensions to establish steeve. If forward deck beam is not exactly centered on Station 2, adjust vertical dimension accordingly.

It will be advantageous when boring through the hull to use a template like that in Fig. 130. Bore hole with a #4 auger bit close up under the break. If after boring through the hull the auger's worm cannot be made to center on the point on the forward beam, ease the hole with a round file before boring through the beam. Square up the hole in the hull with a square rasp. When starting, aim the rasp toward the hole in the deck beam until the hole is 5/16" square on the outside, symmetrical with the rabbet, and tight up under the break. Then square up the inside of the hole with parallel sides through the hull. Plane up a piece of 5/16" square stock with a 1/4" peg on its end to use as a gauge while working. Work out the square hole until stock fits snugly and peg end readily enters deck beam. There is a possibility that the lay out work and boring will not produce exact results; in which case the peg can be cut off and a new one formed slightly off-center as required.

When work in the hole is done, install underlayment. Recall that slightly more than 3/16" was allowed forward and across the stern to avoid breaking through. Cut these areas down now while using the underlayment as a guide for depth.

With the exception of the bowsprit fitting being done, this hull is at the same point in its construction as that of our "Merchant Vessel of 1800" at the close of Chapter I.

FINISHING THE HULL

Make and install sternpost after rudder port has been bored and follow with stem and keel. The rough bowsprit mentioned in previous section should be inserted in the hull when fitting stem so it will fit snugly up under the bowsprit. Refer to Photo 19; note that the keel extends aft of the sternpost. The rudder port or rudderpost may have to be eased slightly to allow insertion. Since this rudder is quite well protected it can be made and installed now. Lay out the location of and bore hawsepipe holes. Before boring cut shackles of each anchor shank and point the ends so the depth of each bore can be determined. Glue on hawsepipe lips. Make and install trail boards. Refer to detail sheet for cross sections of hull. The waterways are 1/16" thick and wide enough so their inboard edges are 1/2" from the outside surface of the hull all the way around. Lay deck of 1/16" square stock and sand the whole surface smooth. The main rail is continuous from bow to stern on each side and cross stern. It is 1/16" thick and a slack 1/2" wide set to extend 1/32" outboard of the hull's side so there is 1/16" between rail and waterway. The rail can be made by laminating 1/32" stock with well-spaced butts. Then the rough rail piece is fastened to the hull and marked around the outside. After outboard shape is formed and faired, the inner shape is scribed and cut. After cutting, the upper inboard corner is rounded slightly, along with both outboard corners, and the finished piece is glued to the hull.

The work that follows on the rail is the most exacting of any on the model. It consists of making the rail assembly above the main rail. A log rail rests on the main rail 3/16" from the edge of the hull surmounted by dozens of stanchions which support the monkey rail. The log rail is 1/8" wide and 1/8" deep on its outboard side. The stanchions are turned, 1/4" long, and have integral pegs on each end. Model supply houses have these

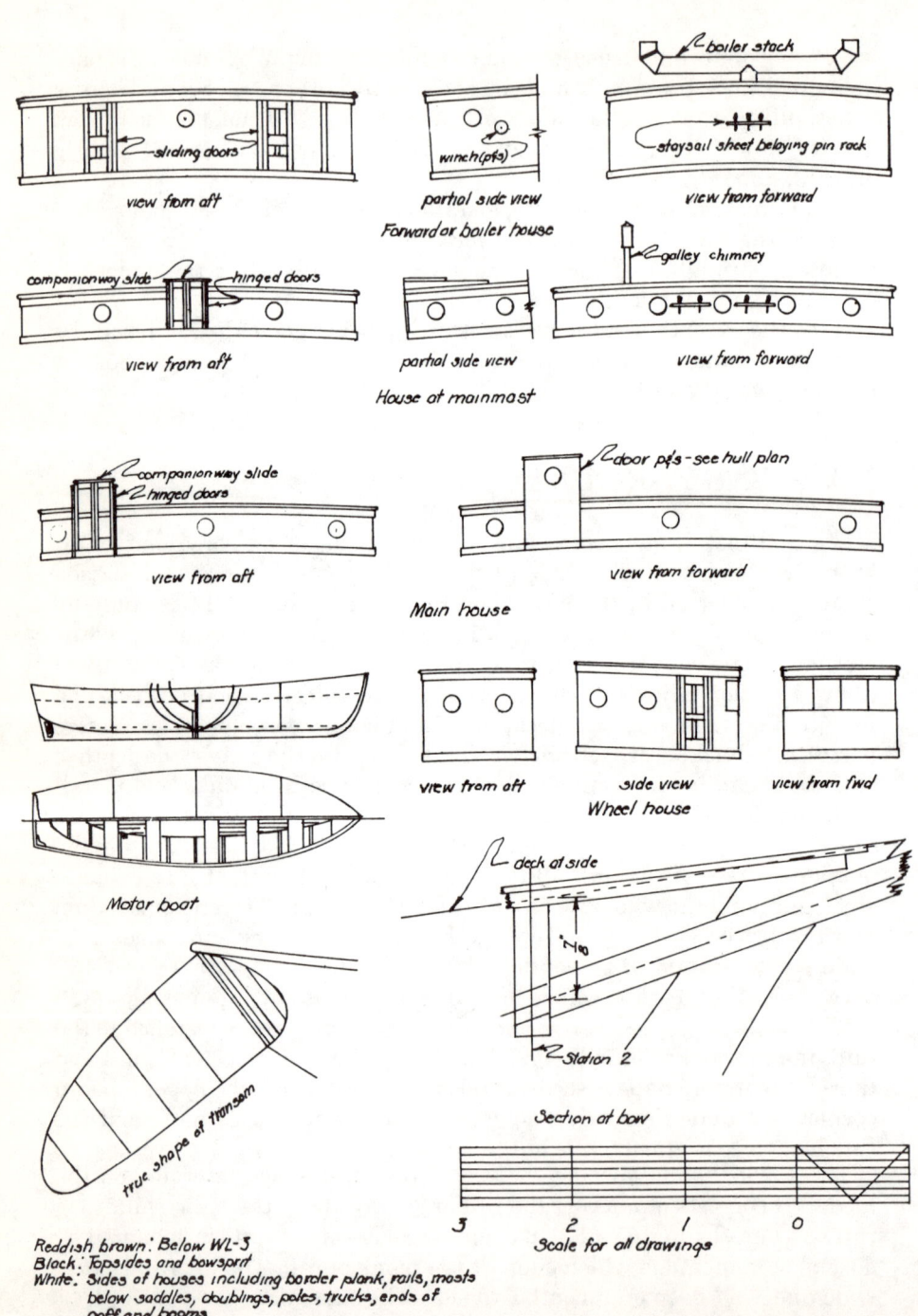

stanchions. They are all alike and should be used rather than trying to make them (thirteen dozen were used on the *Margaret Haskell* model).

The monkey rail is 1/8" wide by a scant 1/16" thick. This assembly is made so it is an extension of the hull's shape. Over most of the hull the assembly tilts inward at the top, as shown in the half-section at Station 10 in detail sheet. Note that the log rail is beveled on its lower surface to create tilt and the upper edge is left square. The stanchions stand perpendicular to the upper edge. The rail assembly stands plumb across the stern. At the bow it tilts outward at an ever increasing angle as it approaches the stem, but to a lesser degree than the flare of the hull.

Make and install the log rail first. Since the curve around the quarters is very severe it is recommended that the part aft of Station 26 1/2 be carved from one piece. The center portion, 3 1/2" long, is perfectly plumb and the ends gradually tilt inboard. The log rail is completed with single, long pieces on each side which run all the way to the bow. Make them of 3/16" by 1/8" pine set on edge. The bevel can be sanded by eye and checked by fitting the rail in place. When the bevel is satisfactory throughout on each, they are glued in place and held there with fine brads set slightly more than 1/16" below the surface. Miter pieces at the bow so the joint is perfect and on the center line. After both pieces are in place, sand top surfaces square with the sides until outboard edges are 1/8" high over their entire length. It is very important that the log rail be stepped back the 3/16" and that it tilt inboard in the way of the shrouds or else rigging screws will rub on the monkey rail.

Because the monkey sets on stanchions that tilt at changing angles over hull's length there is no direct relationship between its shape and that of the log or main rail. Consequently, there is no readily obtainable shape from which this rail can be carved. Rather than try to generate this shape it is easier to carve a section over the stern and a section on each side forward of Station 4 with straight strips along each side.

Start by carving the stern piece similar in shape to log rail with arms extending forward to Station 26 1/2. Make the center section 3/16" wide and taper arms to 1/8". After carving, saw 1/8" off each end on an angle parallel to sides of the hull at Station 26 1/2. Side rail pieces are glued to sawed surfaces and original shape restored. Before gluing, hold this assembly in place to check the angles and adjust if necessary.

Before proceeding draw a line centrally full length of the tops of both monkey and log rails for aligning drill holes. Stanchions are spaced 1/2" apart starting on the center line at stern. Measure carefully to locate five stanchions on each side and drill holes for their peg ends. Holes in the monkey rail are drilled through. Those in the log rail are drilled 1/8" deep. Acetone cement, epoxy, or urethane are suitable glues. If cement is used, holes should be a snug but easy fit. If either epoxy or urethane is used, the holes should be slightly larger.

Spar	a	b	c	d
fore mast	.312	.292	.272	.230
other masts	.300	.280	.260	.240
fore topmast	.250	.250	.176	
other topmasts	.240	.240	.166	
bowsprit	.312 square			
jibboom	.125	.187	.093	
jib boom	.062	.083	.030	
staysail boom	.083	.125	.070	
spanker boom	.145	.187	.125	
other booms	.125	.145	.104	
spanker gaff	.125	.145	.104	
other gaffs	.093	.104	.080	

Spar dimensions in inches

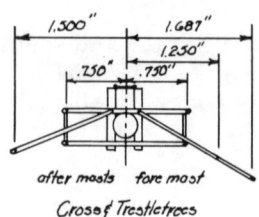

Cross of Trestletrees

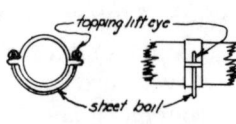

Half-Section Station 10

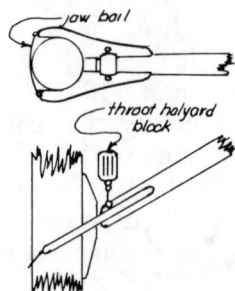

Sheet band and bail

Typical gaff jaw assembly

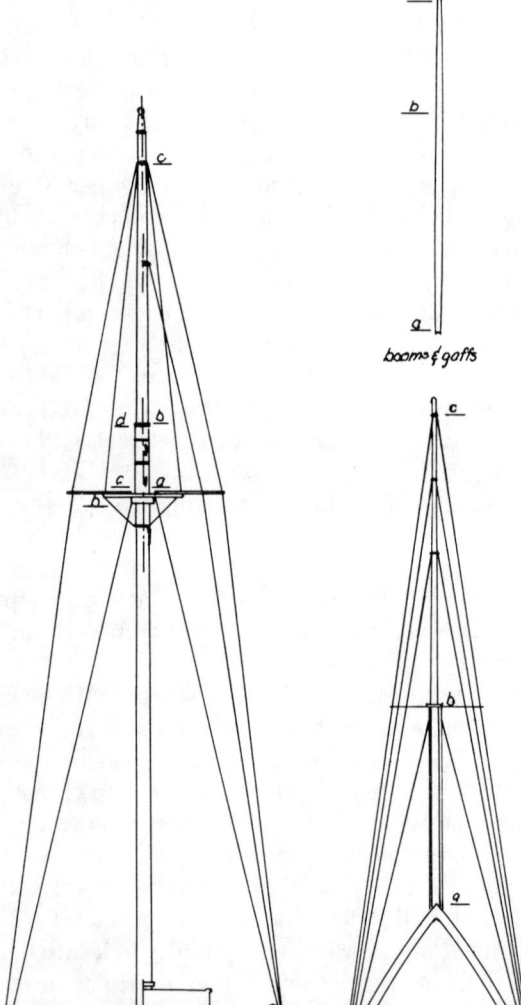

booms & gaffs

Sect. at mizzenmast   Sect. at fore mast

Top view - bowsprit & jibboom

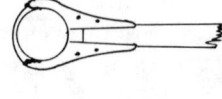

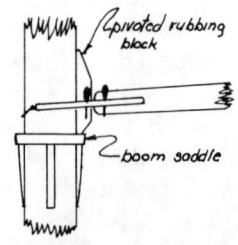

Typical boom jaw assembly

MARGARET HASKELL
Detail Sheet
No Scale

Before starting to glue insert stanchions in the eleven drilled holes and fit the rail in place. Some adjusting of the peg holes may be required by reaming them oversized until all stanchions stand plumb. Refer to Photo 26 for arrangement and appearance of the rail. Note chock on log rail. After the rail fits measure off six more spaces along each side and through drill from above. To hold the rail in place while drilling, weight the section across the stern, insert a 1/4" thick block under unsupported sections, and bend the rail into place.

After this is done remove the rail, apply glue to peg ends, and replace the rail. It will not follow the stern horizontal curvature, but proceed by inserting three stanchions on each side with glue applied followed by three without glue. Place sufficient weight on each side to force the rail onto the pegs, and allow the glue to dry. If rails tend to spread, tie them together.

After the glue is dry holes can be located and drilled as far forward as Station 5. Crosspieces can be fitted at critical points that fit snugly inside of the log rails to establish widths. Ends must be cut on an angle to allow for inward tilt. Blocking under each rail provides support, and a lashing between forward ends provides proper curvature.

After all holes are drilled, stanchions can be inserted. Recall that three stanchions were inserted without glue on each side. This allows the rail to be lifted so the next stanchions can be inserted. If the operation must be stopped for any reason, three unglued stanchions must be inserted to allow resuming without risking damage to completed work. From this point onward stanchions are graspd in smooth-jawed, narrow nosed pliers. Each peg end is coated with glue and inserted. As the work proceeds, check for lifting and weight as necessary to hold the rail down.

The rail sections from Station 4 forward are carved using the log rail as a guide but allowing the curve to fan out slightly so they project slightly beyond the log rail. They are joined to side sections by halving joints. A breasthook ties forward ends together. After the joints are completed, draw center lines on the bow sections and continue drilling. As the bow is approached adjust spacing so end stanchions are about 1/2" from the bow. See Photo 27. After all stanchions are set and the glue dry file away any projecting peg ends and fill all holes.

With the rails out of the way, make and install hatches using a straightedge to obtain exact alignment on deck followed by the houses and including the wheelhouse. Because fore- and mainmasts pierce the forward house roofs and it is virtually impossible to locate holes in the house roof and deck to obtain perfect rake, rebore the holes in the deck 1/8" oversize to allow some play with respect to the holes above. Carefully locate holes on each roof and locate houses on deck so mast spacing is proper and fore-and-aft alignment maintained. Make and install fife rails, jib sheet bitts, spanker sheet bitts, sheet cleats, and bollard pads to essentially complete the woodwork.

Make and install the six sheet horses with their lead bull's-eyes along with pad eyes, etc., for headsail sheets, preventer stays, lower sail halyards, and crotch tackles. Davits, boats, pumps and hoisting engine finish deck work and the model is ready to rig.

There is a possibility that a house was built over the hoisting engine just aft of the jiggermast fife rails since one seems to be evident in the photograph. Its shape is not very clear but one can speculate that it was a structure about 7' long by 6' wide and no more than 4' high so the boom does not have to be elevated. The floor was probably somewhat below the deck line. House construction would be the same as that for the others. A hinged door about 2 1/2' wide in each side with a companionway slide above would be adequate to allow entrance and light to the engine space. Winch heads about 2 1/2'' above deck should be mounted on each side near the after end. At least one porthole should be located in each end. In all likelyhood the pumps were still exposed and driven by chain through a slot in the forward end of the house. The existence of this house is not wholly certain and was not included in the original design. However, it is far easier to construct than the very small scale engine, and departures of this nature resulting from ideas of the owner or captain were not uncommon, so it is a perfectly valid deviation in terms of the model.

SPARS

Directions for making spars are given in Chapter XI and fittings for them are described in Chapter XII. Ironwork is explained in Chapter IX and shown in detail sheet.

Spar lengths are taken directly off the sail plan and diameters are given in detail sheet. For lower spars (a) is the diameter at deck, (b) just below the trestletrees, (c) at the trestletrees, and (d) at the cap. For topmasts and the jibboom (a) is at the heel, (b) at the cap, and (c) at the upper or outer ends. For gaffs and booms including those on staysails (a) is at the heel, (b) at two-thirds the way aft, and (c) at the after ends.

Fit up the masts first. Make and fit cheek and trestletree assembly on the foremast followed by trestletrees and crosstrees on the lower ends of the mastheads. Before installing them fit futtock bands with eyes on each side and a band below each trestletree. Fit chocks for the forestay bail followed by the lower peak halyard band. Fit chocks for the jibstay bail followed by the upper peak halyard block band. Then fit bands for the peak halyard blocks on the other masts. Each band has an eye and ring for the blocks and eyes are fitted on the sides of the upper bands on the mizzenmast and jigger mast for the preventer stays. Fit eyes in each after crosstree above the trestletrees for double topping lifts and a staple between trestletrees for the throat halyard block. Attach eyes under the fore trestletrees to attach the staysail and jib topping lifts, staysail to starboard. Make and fit caps with bails, as shown in sail plan.

If the builder elects to fit heel chains, solder ears on the lower rim on each side of the caps and rig the chains from them to staples in the fore ends of the trestletrees. Drill outer ends of crosstrees to receive futtocks and glue in fore-and-aft pieces between outer ends of the crosstrees followed by the spreaders. Note that the forward spreader has two backstay holes along its length instead of just one in the outer end as on other masts and that it is longer than the others. Turn rigging screws into upper end of futtocks, reeve futtocks through crosstree holes, and attach them to futtock bands with small eyes in their lower ends. Slide lower mast hoops into their spars and make the boom saddles for each mast. Four chocks for each are shown for the three aftermasts only, but short ones were probably fitted on the two forward masts with slight clearance between them and the roofs of the houses. The masts so rigged are ready for receiving their topmasts.

Topmasts are fitted in place from below, so have the fid holes and fids made. Remember that the fore-topmast has a fid at both sets of trestletrees. Slide them up through and fit the fids followed by gates on each pair of trestletrees. Then feed the topmast hoops on followed by the bands. Note that no hoops are fitted above the mid-height band on the fore-topmast. Now the spar assemblies are ready to be stepped.

Booms and gaffs are rigged, as shown in sail plan and detail sheet. Jaws and clappers are fitted on the fore ends of each boom and gaff for the five quadrilateral sails with belaying pins in each boom jaw. Gaff jaws have an eye on each side with two links to a ring in the middle for hooking on the throat halyard block and an eye below on the starboard side for a topsail sheet-lead-block. Staples on the under lower sides of gaff and upper sides of booms close to the mast are driven for connecting sail clews. Each gaff has four bands with ears or eyes for hooking on the peak halyards and a fifth band on the end with an eye above for the topsail sheet-block and one below for the sail clew. Boom tackles are hooked to bands with eyes outboard and an eyebolt on forward ends. Sheet bands and bails are made, as shown in the detail sheet. Note that spanker boom has two and that all bands, except the forward one on the spanker boom, have eyes above the bails for attaching topping lifts. Bands with eyes on the end of each boom provide attaching points for sail clews. Eyes on each side of the spanker boom band provide attaching points for footropes.

Staysail and jibbooms have eyes in their forward ends. The staysail boom eye fits on the stay fitting. That on the jibboom is bent 90° to fit on the

TABLE VI
—Margaret Haskell—
Major Rigging Component Sizes
(dimensions in inches)

Rigging	Blocks (etc.)	Rigging Dia.
Lower shrouds	3/4 rigging screws	.015 wire
Bobstays		18 link chain
Bowsprit shrouds		25 " "
Topmast shrouds	5/8 rigging screws	.012 wire
Backstays	3/4 " "	.014 "
Preventer stays		.014 "
Preventer stay tackle	1/8 blocks	.012 natural thread
Staysail stay		.017 wire
Jibstay	3/4 rigging screws	.017 "
Jib-topsail stay	5/8 " "	.010 "
Aftermast stays		.017 "
After-topmast stays		.012 "
Throat halyards	5/32 blocks	.015 natural thread
Peak halyards	5/32 "	.015 " "
Lower sail sheets	5/32 "	.015 " "
Boom tackles	1/8 "	.010 " "
Headsail halyards	1/8 "	.010 " "
Topping lifts	1/8 "	.010 " "
		.008 wire
Topsail halyards	1/8 "	.010 natural thread
Topsail tacks and sheets	1/8 "	.010 " "

jibboom horse. Bands with eyes above are fitted on each end for attaching sails. The after bands have two eyes, the second for topping lifts. Each has sheet bands with bails but no eyes above.

See Chapter XII for a description of the bowsprit assembly.

At this point bails must be made for staysail and jibstays and slid down over their cleats. The staysail bail will probably have to be bent where it crosses the crosstrees so the lower part will align with its stay.

The model is now ready to rig. Table VI covers sizes of major rigging components.

STANDING RIGGING

Topmast Shroud Futtocks—Two on each side with lower shank eye of rigging screws turned in and fed through outer ends of the crosstrees. Eyes in their lower ends are turned into eyes on the futtock bands.

Lower Shrouds—Five on each side of the foremast and four on each side of the others. They are connected to rigging screws below with heads seized into the bight around the mast above. Sheer poles cross all shrouds. Ratlines cross only second and third shrouds. Refer to previous chapter for method of installing light boxes.

Staysail Stay—Single between the wire bail over cleats on the lower part of the fore-masthead to the forestay fitting on deck.

Jibstay—Double between the wire bail over upper cleats on the fore-masthead to holes in the bees and to rigging screws on plates on the stem just above bobstay plates. The two stays are seized together 1/2" above the bees with fine wire and are soldered.

Aftermast Stays—Single between bails on the aftermast caps to eyes in the caps of the next masts forward.

Bobstays—Two of chain between eyes in the bee bands and the bobstay plates.

Bowsprit Shrouds—One of chain on each side between eyes in the inner bee band and plates in the bow.

Flying Jibstay—Single secured to bail on the fore cap and reeves over the inboard sheave in the jibboom. It leads aft under the starboard hook at mid-length of the dolphin striker and sets up to a plate in the starboard bow.

Topmast Shrouds—Two on each side from the lower bands on the topmast heads to rigging screws on the crosstrees. Ratlines are fitted up to the height of the lower mast cap.

Fore-Topmast Lower Backstay—Single on each side connected to band at mid-height of fore-topmast. It reeves through hole in the middle of the spreader and to a rigging screw below.

Outer Jibstay—Single connected to band at mid-height of fore-topmast. It reeves over the second sheave in the jibboom. It leads aft similar to the flying jibstay but to port.

Jib Topsail Stay—Single connected to lower band at fore-topmast head. It reeves over third sheave in jibboom and leads aft similar to flying jibstay.

Fore-Topmast Stay—Single connected to upper band on fore-topmast head. It reeves over outer sheave in jibboom and leads aft similar to outer jibstay.

After-Topmast Stays—Two per topmast. Each is secured to the bands at the topmast heads on their after end and to bails on the caps of the next forward masts.

Topmast Backstays—One on each side connected to the upper band on the topmast head. It reeves through the outer hole in the spreader to a rigging screw below.

Mizzen- and Jiggermast Preventer Stays—One on each side secured above to the highest peak halyard mast band and sets up below to a pad eye in the waterways athwartships of the next forward mast. Pad eyes are also set abreast the forward mizzen- and jiggermast shrouds on the waterways or main rail so the lee preventers could be secured there and be clear of the spars on the next forward sail.

Martingales—Three set up at bands on the jibboom with their lower ends connected to rigging screws fastened to the lower band on the dolphin striker. Two lead aft from this band to plates in the bow.

Note: Refer to Chapter XII for an alternate method of leading headstays from the jibboom and martingales.

Backropes—Three on each side fastened outboard to each of the bands on the jibboom. They lead aft to the whisker booms and to plates in the bow.

RUNNING RIGGING

Jibboom Footropes

One on each side. Eyes are spliced in each end. Inboard ends are seized to the eyes on the whisker booms and outboard to the eyes for outer backropes on the end of the jibboom. The middles are lashed to backrope eyes on the inner jibboom band to form two spans. Each span hangs 3/8" below the top of the jibboom. Knots at 3/8" intervals should be worked in through the length of each to prevent a sailor's feet from slipping inboard while furling outer jibs.

Jib Topsail

Halyard—A gun tackle with higher block hooked to the band at the fore-topmast head and belays to starboard. If sails are set, the standing part hooks to clew in sail. If not, it hooks to downhaul.

Downhaul—Single. Reeves through block hooked to staple in jibboom just aft of the stay and belays to pin in jib sheet bitts.

Sheets—Double with bull's-eyes in pendants as described for jib on *Helen B. Thomas*. Insert an eye in the waterways or main rail on each side with another stropped to a bull's-eye just aft. Splice the end of a line to the pad eye on each side, reeve the lines through the bull's-eyes on the pendants and through the lead bull's-eye in the waterways, and belay them to pins in the rail on each side. These are not rigged if sails are omitted.

Outer Jib

Halyard—Same as jib topsail except belays to port.

Downhaul and Sheets—Similar to jib topsail.

Flying Jib

Halyard—A gun tackle with the higher block hooked to the stay bail and belays to starboard. Lower block same as for jib topsail.

Downhaul and Sheets—Same as jib topsail.

Jib

Halyard—Similar to flying jib except belays to port.

Downhaul—Same as for outer jibs.

Sheet—A gun tackle with its higher block hooked to boom band bail and the other to a ring on the jib horse. It belays to a pin in the jib sheet bitts.

Topping Lift—Reeves through a block hooked to the port trestletrees. One end hooks to the boom band eye and the other belays to port.

Forestaysail

Halyard—Similar to jib except it belays to starboard.

Downhaul—Since the stay is inboard the crew could haul the sail down by its hanks so a downhaul need not be fitted.

Sheet—Same as for jib except it belays to a cleat on the forward end of the house.

Topping Lift—Same as for jib except block and belaying is to starboard.

Lower Sails

Throat Halyards—Two treble blocks with standing end of its fall spliced into the strap of the higher block. Higher blocks hook to staples in the crosstrees and the lower to rings in the gaffs. The falls are rove so they belay to port. Throat halyards for fore- and mainsails to belay to pins in the rail, the after ones to the fife rails.

Peak Halyards—One double and one treble hooked to mast bands (double higher) with four singles hooked to bands on the gaff. Falls are double, one belays to port and the other to starboard. On fore- and mainsails they belay to pins in the rail, on aftermasts to the fife rails.

Note: Since both throat and peak halyards were led away to winch heads while hoisting sail, lead blocks hooked to pad eyes in the deck alongside the belaying pin are appropriate. The halyards can then be led through these blocks to belaying pins.

Topping Lifts—One on each side consisting of a long pendant hooked to the eye in the sheet band and above to the single block of a luff tackle. The double block is hooked to an eye in the trestletrees and led below the same as the halyards.

Sheets—Are luff tackles on the four forward sails with the double blocks hooked to bails on the booms and the others to rings on their horses. The hauling ends reeve through bull's-eyes stropped to pad eyes in the deck just aft of the horses. The foresail sheet belays to a cleat on the forward side of the middle house and the others to pins in the bolsters on the fife rails. The spanker sheet has a treble hooked to a ring on the horse with a double hooked to the outer bail and a single to the inner. The standing end is spliced into the strop of the treble block and rove off as shown. The hauling end is led through a block hooked to a pad eye just forward of the horse and belays to either bitt.

Boom Tackles—Luff tackles with the double block hooked to the band and the single to an eyebolt. Their falls were belayed to a pin in the port boom jaw.

Topsails

Halyards—Gun tackles hooked to topmast bands, where shown in sail plan. When sails are set the tackles hook to sail clews; when not set to any handy eye at the mast cap, they belay to pins in the port rail.

Note: Staysails are usually fitted on new vessels but were seldom replaced when they wore out. When gone their blocks and gear were removed. Therefore, it is entirely proper to fit this model without any of this gear.

Spanker Boom Footropes

One is fitted on each side with a small eye splice in each end that is lashed to the topping lift eyes on the sheet band and to eyes on the outboard boom band. They hang about one-quarter inch below the top of the boom.

Spanker Crotch Tackles

Because coasters were rigged with heavy, double topping lifts on each boom, no boom crotches were used, so when sails were lowered their sheets were hauled taut to hold the booms amidships. This was not adequate for the main boom because of its extra length and weight, so crotch tackles were rigged between the forward sheet bail and pad eyes in the waterways on each side. They were also rigged while reefing to steady the boom. They consisted of a luff tackle with the double block hooked to the bail and belay to pins in the rail.

Lazyjacks

Description of this equipment has been held to the end because those shown in the sail plan are total reconstructions. If fitted, each one was a continuous line secured to the topping lift on each side and rove through a hole in a small batten under the boom. Their function was to contain sails while being lowered. However, it has not been determined with certainty whether they were used on all vessels. Since the crew was extraordinarily small for the size of hull and sail area, it seems inconceivable that the sail furling operation could have been done without lazyjacks in a reasonable time period.

If the modeler decides to rig them, it must be done before the topping lifts are belayed. Very fine line is spliced along the topping lifts and rove through nearly flush staples under the boom. They should be tight enough to appear taut and require careful measuring and fitting to look right.

FINISHING THE MODEL

If sails are to be rigged, follow instructions in Chapters II and XII. If they are not fitted, set topping lifts so all booms hang at the same angle with the waterline (the same angle as when sails are set). Then lower their gaffs onto the booms and tie them in place with two lines about both gaffs and booms neatly knotted with ends cut short. Clean deck of all debris. Rig davits and stern boat. The model is now ready for its permanent mounting and case.

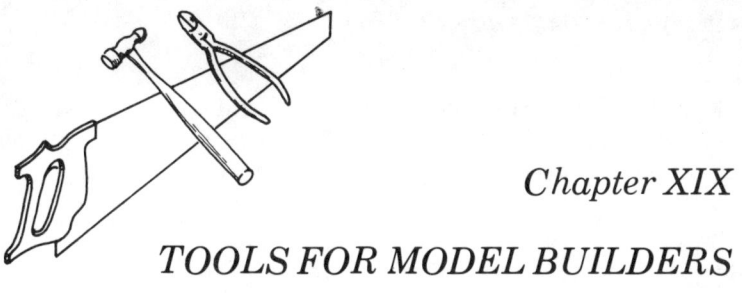

Chapter XIX
TOOLS FOR MODEL BUILDERS

Beautiful models have been built with little more than a jackknife by seamen on long voyages and while prisoners of war. Probably many models were built to while away hours of shipboard inactivity or to relieve monotony of seemingly endless hours. The potential model maker, preparatory to attempting any of these models, should have selected only *good* appropriate tools.

It is no simple matter to advise on tool purchase requirements because the extent of the compliment has to be matched both to the space available for work and to the builder's pocketbook. There is one small comfort, however, in terms of cost. Materials for any model represent a very small investment when compared to most other hobbies and, with few exceptions, the tools needed should last through many generations of model builders. Unless the builder has a large shop area and unlimited finances, it is suggested that tools be purchased as the need requires.

Storage for tools is very important for those working in limited space where everything must be put away when not actually being used. Edged tools, such as files and chisels, should be protected while stored or they may become nicked and will dull continuously. In general this can be achieved by rolling them up separately in cloth. Most iron or steel tools should be wiped off occasionally with a lightly oiled rag to preserve finish. The wrapping cloth should not be oiled—oily rags promote spontaneous combustion!

Most tools should be the best obtainable because their performance is usually directly proportional to their cost and it is almost impossible to do fine work with substandard equipment. It is even recommended that also the novice purchase top quality, American-made tools at first. There are very fine imported tools but there are also some poor ones and money spent on less than the best is money thrown away. Thus, unless the modeler has experience in judging quality, tools should be made by well known manufacturers. Most reliable dealers in hand tools will advise the modeler on selection to suit requirements specified.

It is essential while building the hull that the workbench be sturdy and a vise be at hand. Several large C-clamps, large chisels and gauges, and large planes are needed among the tools which, in general, will be used while making the hull. Apartment dwellers might avail themselves of adult education classes with their facilities—space, machinery and tools with experienced instruction and opportunities for consultations.

Tool List

Boring Equipment
　Bit brace with #4, #5, #6, #7, #8, #16 bits
　Hand drill with assorted drills (purchase as needed)
　Pin vise with assorted small drills
　(No.'s 60, 65, 70, and 75 for starters)

Hammers
　12 or 16 oz. claw
　4 oz. jeweler's

Pliers
　5" diagonals
　4" round nosed
　6" flat nosed

Shaping Tools
　Smoothing plane
　Block plane
　Chisels with 1/4", 3/8", and 1/2" bits
　Spokeshave
　Drawknife
　Assorted rasps (purchase as needed)
　Assorted files (purchase as needed)
　Assorted needle and diesinker's files (purchase as needed)
　Set of small carving tools

Soldering Tools
　Soldering iron, solder, and flux
　High temperature torch, silver solder, and flux
　Charcoal blocks for silver soldering
　Alcohol lamp

Sawing Tools
　12 tooth cutoff saw
　Dovetail saw
　6" stiff backsaw for miniature miter box
　Jeweler's saw with assorted blades
　Coping saw

In addition, the modeler will need small C-clamps, a square, marking gauges, and a carving knife as well as equipment which can be made, like the miter box and sparmaker's jig. Dentist tooth-cleaning tools can be reshaped for certain work. Even crochet needles can be reshaped with forked ends to guide and twist lines onto belaying pins. Good quality needles with large eyes are a must; three identical ones with slightly blunt points are perfect for splicing. This list can be expanded upon but should first include only those tools needed.

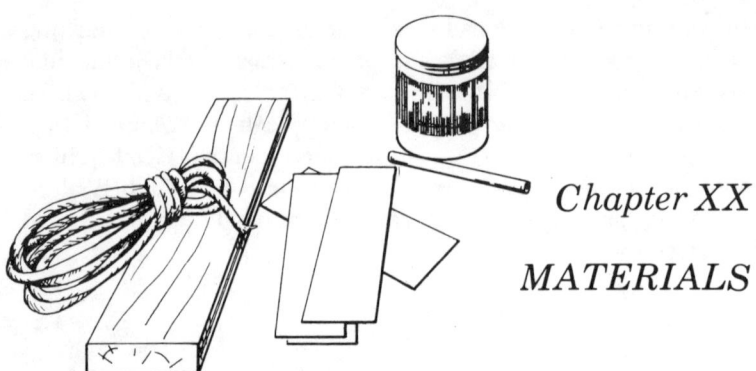

Chapter XX

MATERIALS

Materials have been indicated where necessary or important throughout the text. Many favorite shipbuilding woods, such as elm, hackmatack, maple, and oak do not scale-down well and others are either not available or would be totally unsuitable. Therefore, the modeler should select woods suitable to the needs irrespective of the kinds of materials used in the ship's actual construction. For example, ironwork on vessels was normally of wrought or cast-iron except for some machined equipment which was steel or brass on later craft. But on models, these parts are all made of brass or copper. Natural fiber rigging was hemp or Manila which is stranded linen twine on models. Steel-stranded wire rope is simulated with clean, stranded copper wire.

WOOD

There are many woods which can be used for the various parts of models. Some suitable ones are, as follows:

Ash—An excellent wood for bending when either cold or steamed, but its coarse grain excludes it for most other purposes. It is ideal for buffalo rails and monkey rails.

Beech—A hard, fine-grain, light brown wood. It is excellent for bitts, bolsters, fife rails, pinrails, cheeks, trestletrees, crosstrees, and similar applications.

Birch—Similar to beech except that the grain tends to be coarser and there is variation in color.

Black walnut—A dark brown, medium-grain wood ideal for bitts, etc., where a few coats of olive oil provide a finish with the appearance of age.

Boxwood—A yellow, hard, almost grainless wood. It warps readily so has very limited usefulness but is unexcelled for blocks, deadeyes, hearts, etc.

Cherry—Similar to black walnut except that it is reddish brown in color and somewhat harder. It is excellent for deckhouses, hatch coamings, and rails.

Mahogany—A reddish brown, heavy wood with various color and grain structures. Most varieties are fine for bitts, rails, etc. Do not use the variety known as Philippine mahogany—it is too soft and has ribbon figure or ribbon grain which makes working and finishing difficult.

Maple—A heavy, hard, fine-grain wood. It ranges from very light to light brown depending upon variety. It is excellent for bitts, bolsters, cheeks, trestletrees, crosstrees, etc. It is not recommended for deckhouses because when painted the surfaces tend to look like painted metal.

Port Orford cedar—Similar in appearance to white pine, it is used for making the finest arrow shafts and is one of the best woods for spars.

White holly—An almost snow-white wood, close-grained, with a hard texture. It is excellent for gratings, ladders, etc.

White pine—Light in weight, relatively soft, easily worked, and takes an excellent finish either for staining or painting. It makes excellent stock for hulls, spars, and decking.

Whitewood, basswood, yellow poplar—Under any of these names it is light colored, a softwood which carves well, and can be obtained in sizes which make excellent deck stock. Large sizes are good for hull blanks.

Many other woods can be used but the selection here is more than adequate for the model builder. Unless a supply of patternmaker's pine or similar quality is not available, pine should be eastern white. If not, that obtainable elsewhere will have to do. Most woods cited are available from suppliers of cabinet grade or exotic woods or from suppliers of marine grade lumber, usually from any lumberyard. Boxwood is available from suppliers of jewelers' tools and materials. Thin wood can be obtained from houses specializing in veneer. Port Orford cedar is available from dealers in archery supplies and is normally furnished as round shafts either 5/16" or 3/8" in diameter and 30" long. White holly and basswood are available from model supply houses.

GLUE & ADHESIVES

There are several varieties of glue suitable for model construction. Any of the white or cream-colored premixed glues are satisfactory. There are also varieties of powdered glue which work equally well. Each of these types is reasonably water-resistant. Stay clear of animal glues, they are affected by moisture, and the waterproof varieties are too hard to handle.

Epoxy and urethane adhesives are recommended where metals are bonded to wood and for wood-to-wood joints where clamping is impossible. Urethane is used directly from its tube. Epoxy must be mixed according to directions. The easiest type to use comes in a double-barreled, hypodermic-like container with joined pistons so equal amounts are forced out. Neither product is recommended for clamped joints because clamping pressure is very critical.

Contact cement has desirable qualities for laminating rails. Edges of each lamination can be rounded and cement applied to each mating surface. Since the cement must be allowed to dry before assembly, it is not squeezed out into the rounded seam.

Acetone-based cement is useful to secure splices, knots, etc., in rigging.

METAL

Because a modeler must make joints in metal parts with either hard or soft solder, the selection is limited to brass and copper. This is not a handicap, however, because both are easily worked, are durable, and turn dark with age.

Sheet copper can be obtained in all necessary thicknesses from hardware stores, roofing material suppliers, automotive supply shops, and model supply houses. Solid copper wire can be obtained from model supply houses, jewelry manufacturer's supply houses, and hardware stores. Stranded wire along with solid wire can be purchased as electrical conductor cable. The insulation has to be removed by stripping it off but the wire revealed is clean and ready to solder. Tubing for galley stacks can be obtained at plumber's supply stores.

Sheet brass in various thicknesses, brass rod in several diameters, and brass strips in some sizes can be obtained from model supply houses. Also, a limited variety of both hard and annealed brass wire is carried by model supply houses. Heavier brass rod suitable for gun barrel stock is carried by some hardware stores or, if not, it can be ordered.

Soldering acids, fluxes, and solder must come from plumber's suppliers dealing in these materials. Soft solder must be of composition known as "50-50" to obtain required strength. Varieties sold in rolls with or without flux cores are unfortunately too weak to withstand the continuous stress many model parts set up.

Much of the required metals can be obtained in scrap metal yards. Frequently separate areas are set aside for nonferrous metals where sheet, tubing, and solid rod stock can be found. Also, relatively heavy stock can be found for such parts as anchors and crance irons. Junkyard prices fluctuate with the market but are normally substantially cheaper than the cost of new materials.

ROPE

If available, only three-stranded linen should be used. It looks and handles like rope; it dyes well, is dimensionally stable, and is resistant to rot. Cotton is the next best material, but it shrinks and stretches with changes in humidity and is not rot resistant. Nylon or other synthetic fibers have too many undesirable features to be seriously considered.

PAINT

Paint for models must dry to a flat, hard finish without excessive buildup. Several varieties sold by model supply houses appear to provide a satisfactory result. Signwriter's paint is quite practical. It is made by grinding the pigment in japan drier, known to sign painters as "coachmaker" or japan paint. It can be thinned to any consistency and when dry it sands well, providing a good surface for another coat.

SAILCLOTH

For the modeler who wishes to make and bend sails, Egyptian cotton sailcloth is the thinnest, most suitable material available. It is a hard, woven material intended for working model sailboats and is usually available at model supply houses.

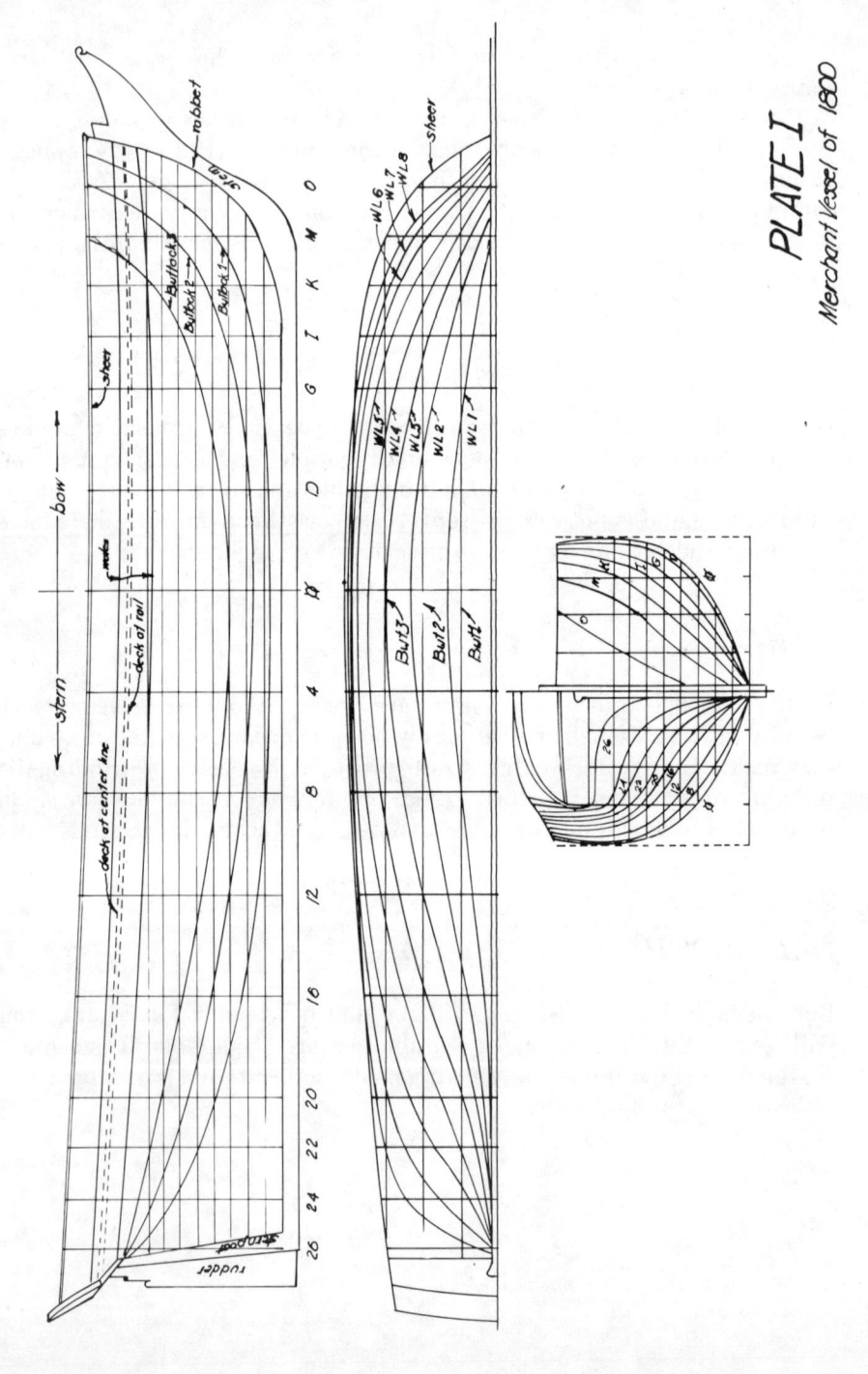

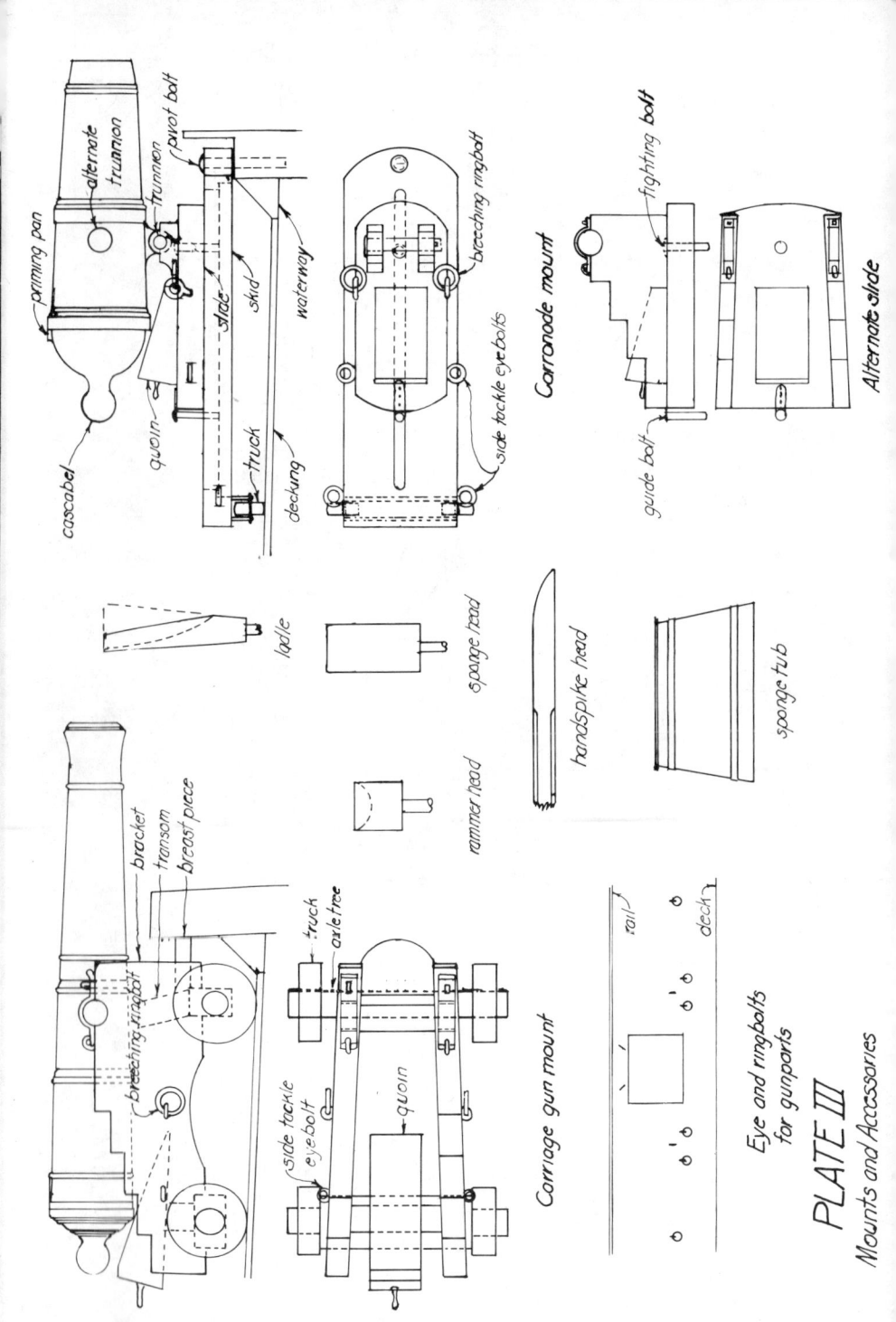

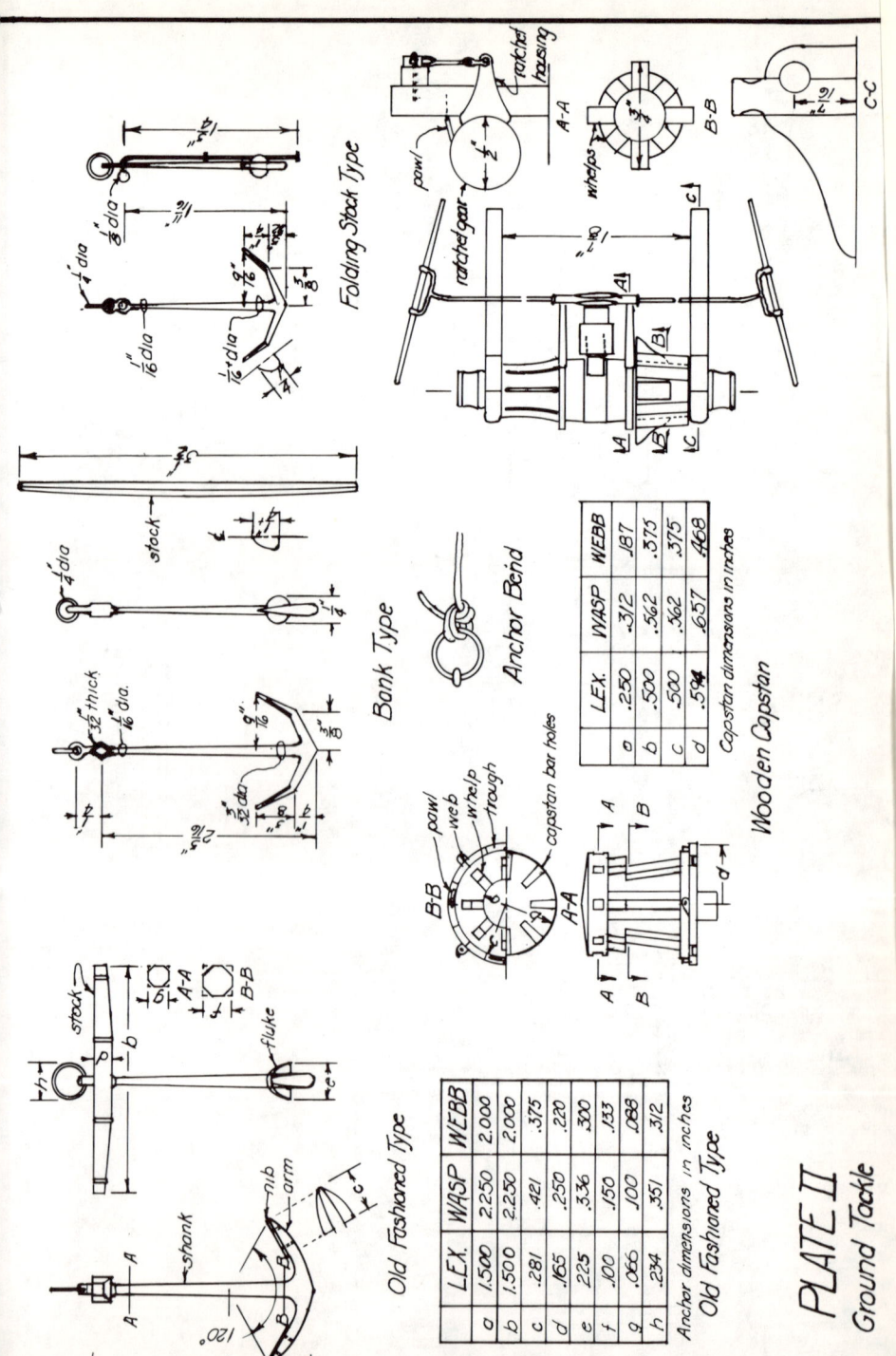

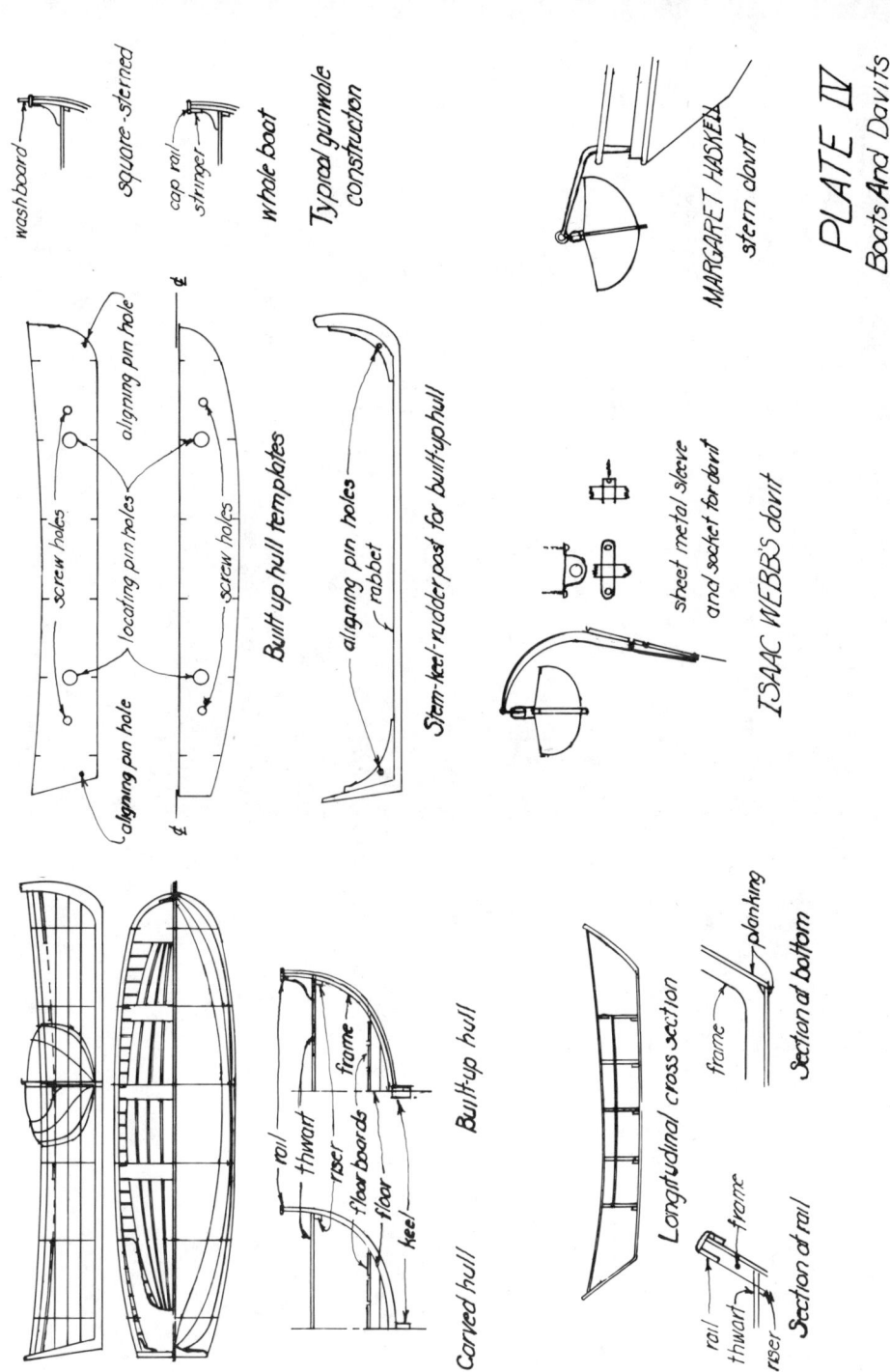

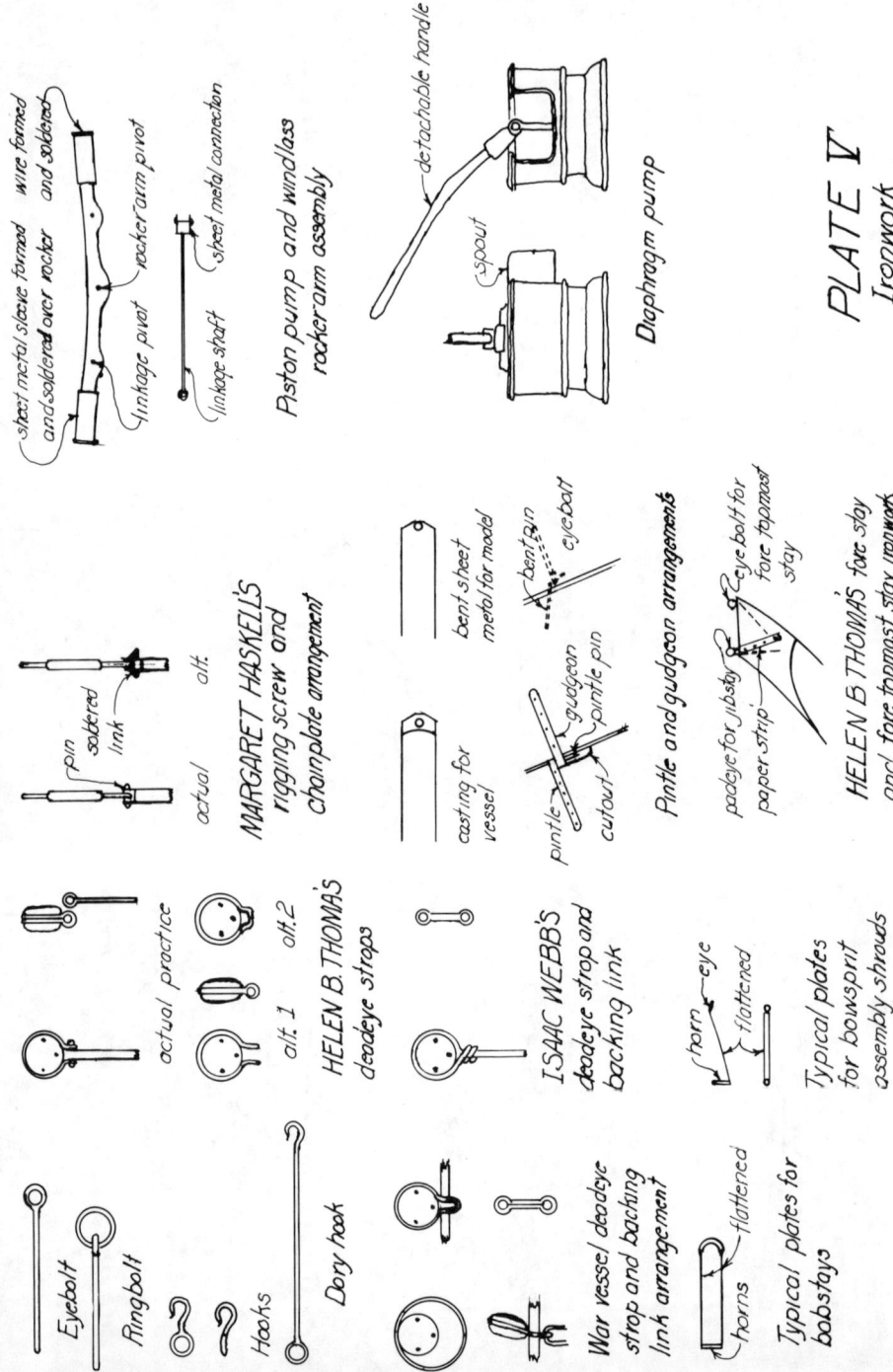

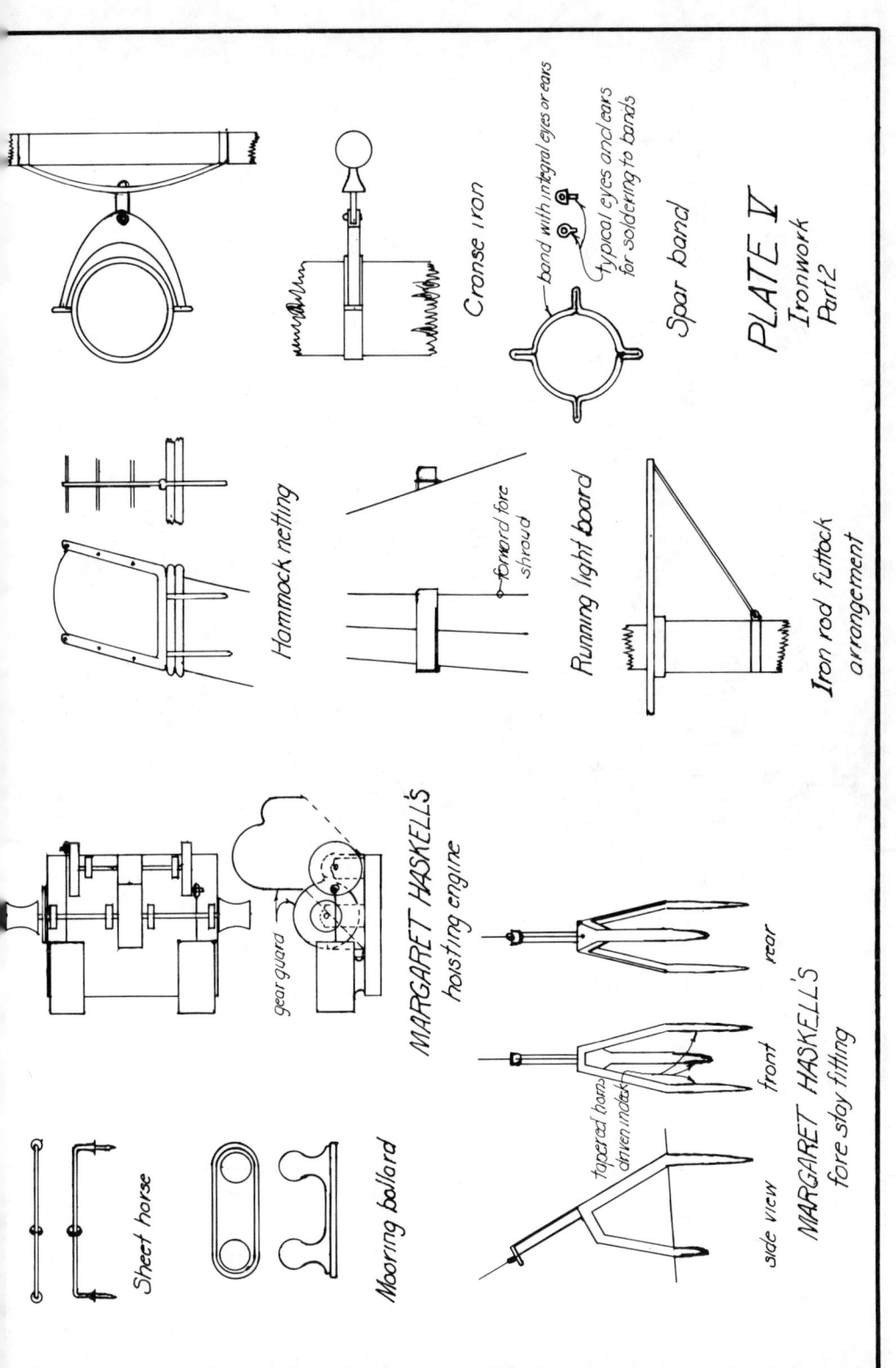

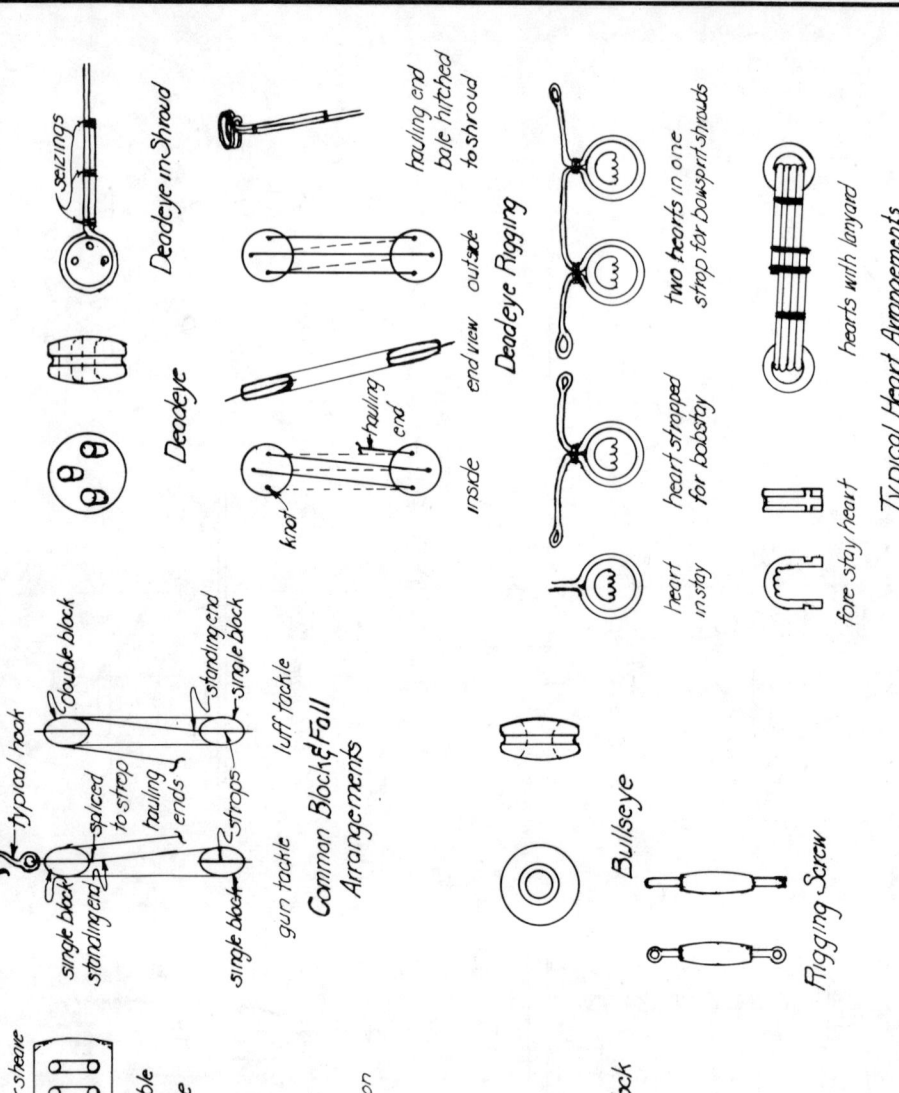

PLATE VI

Blocks, Bullseyes, Deadeyes
Hearts And Rigging Screws

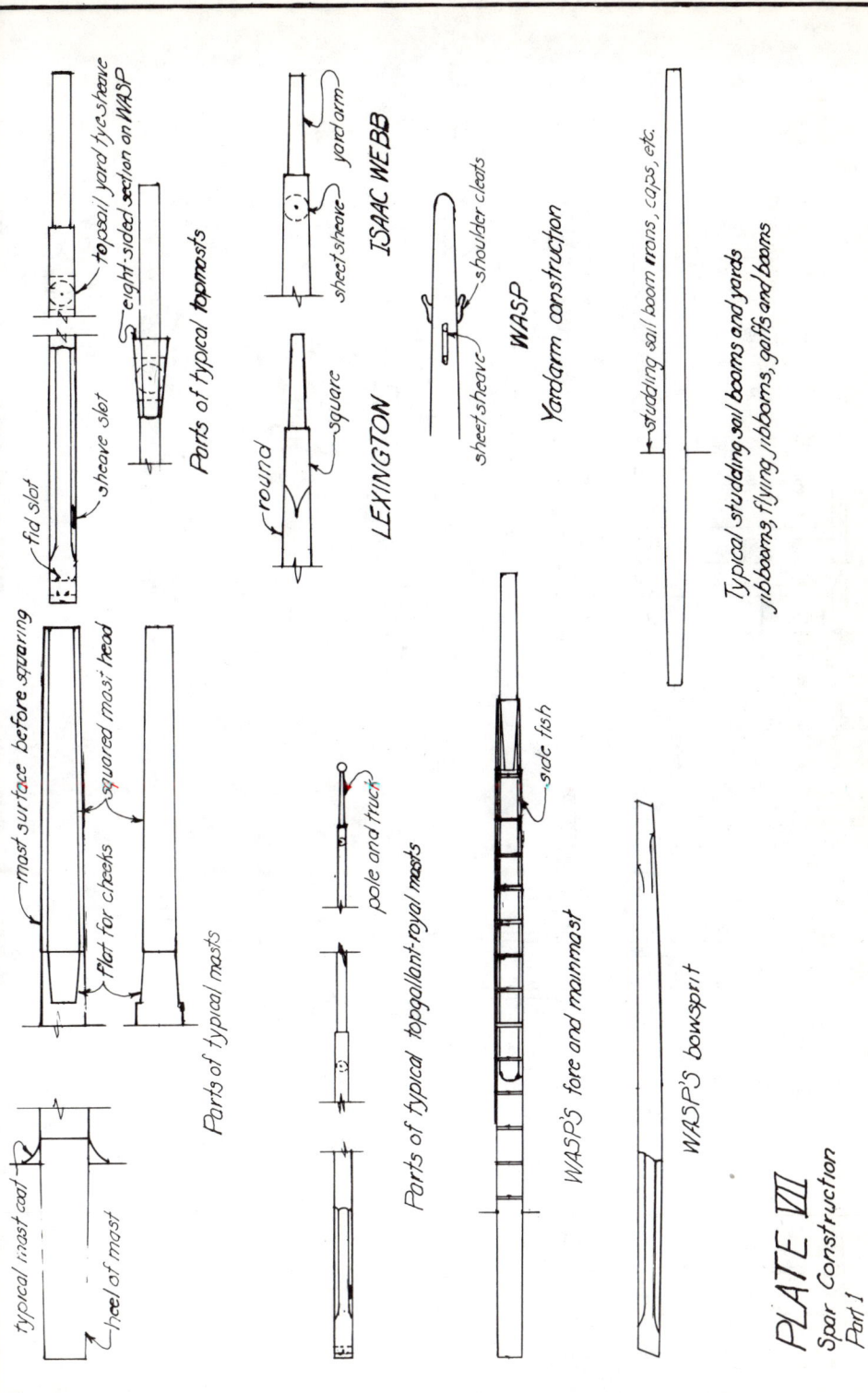

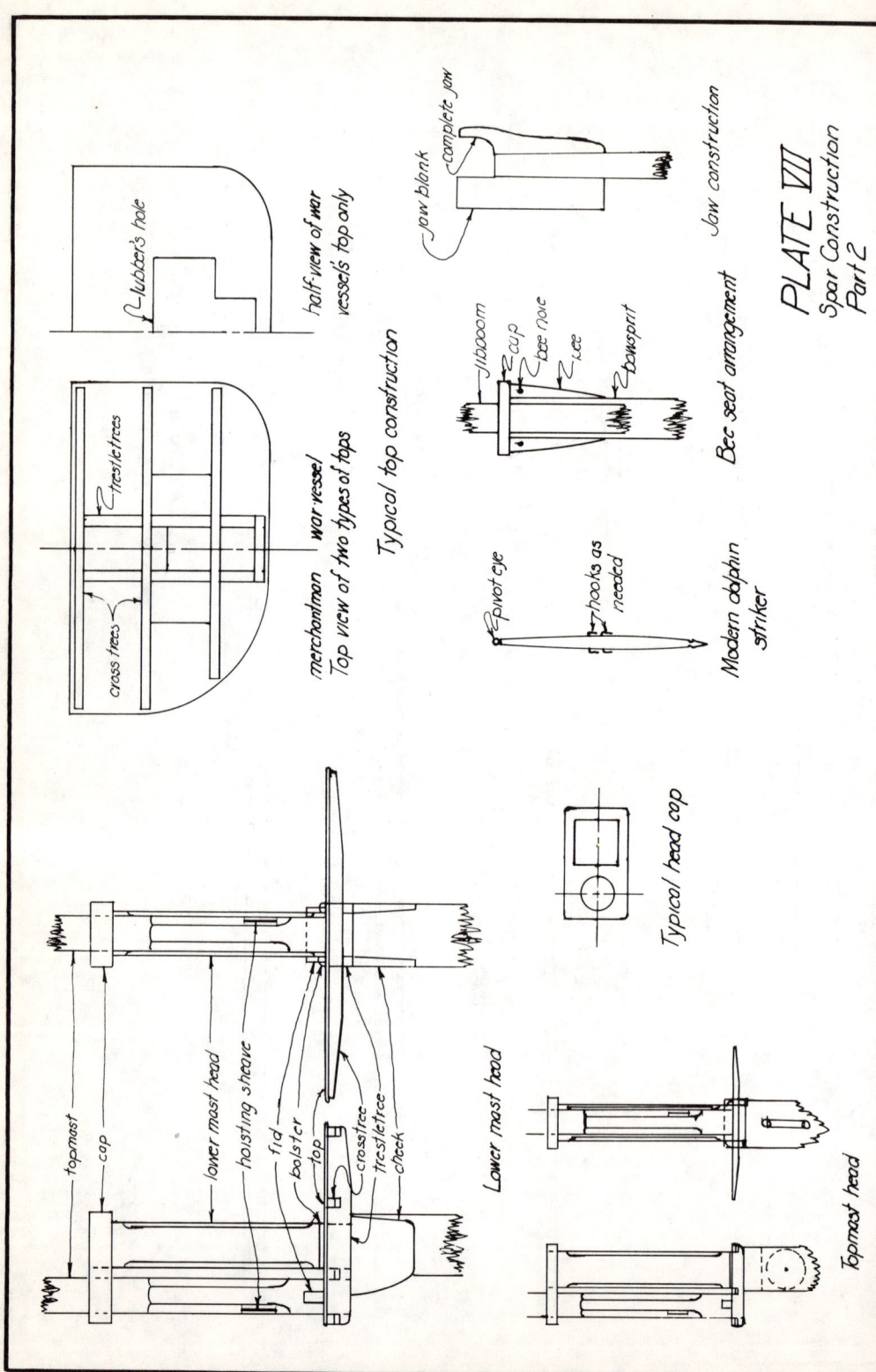

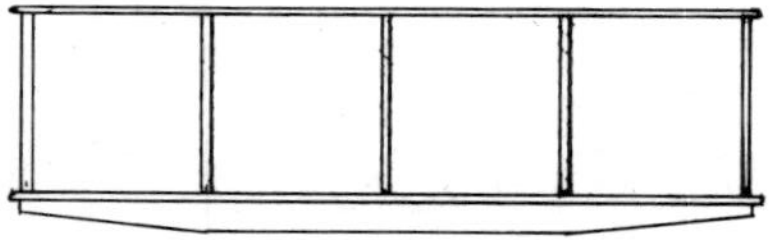

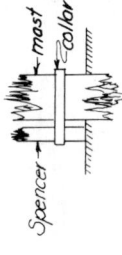

PLATE VIII
Miscellaneous rigging

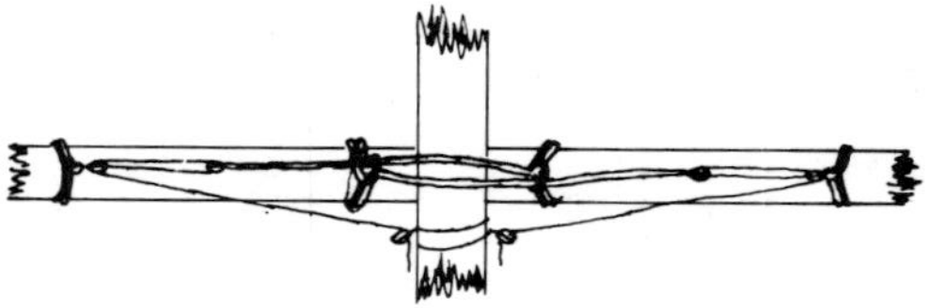

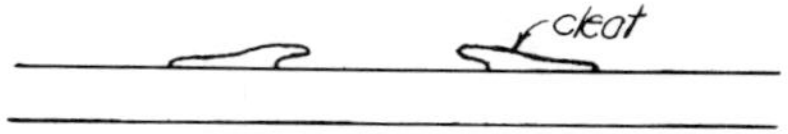

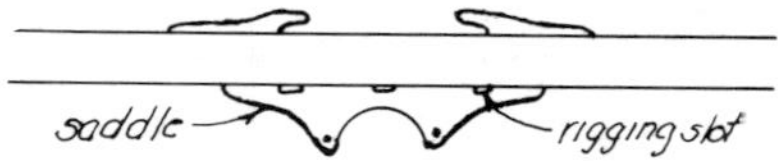

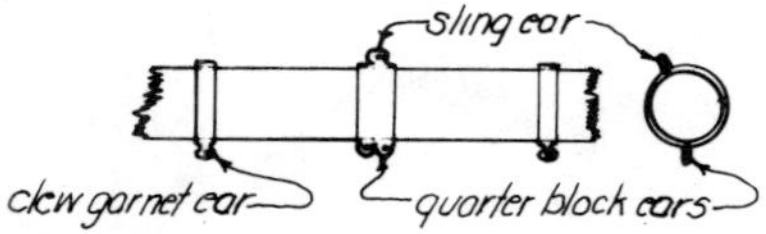

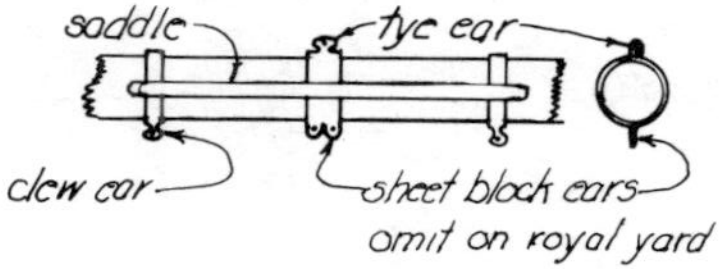

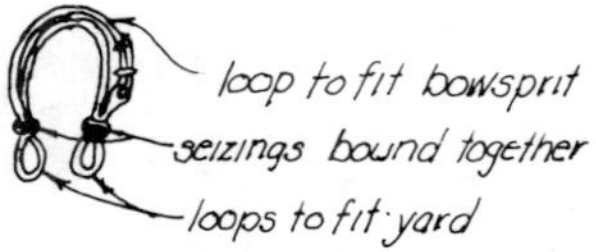

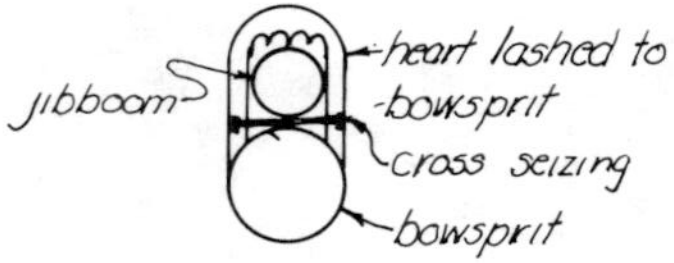

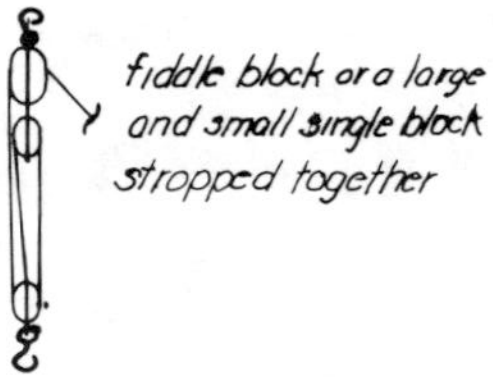

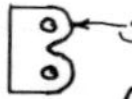

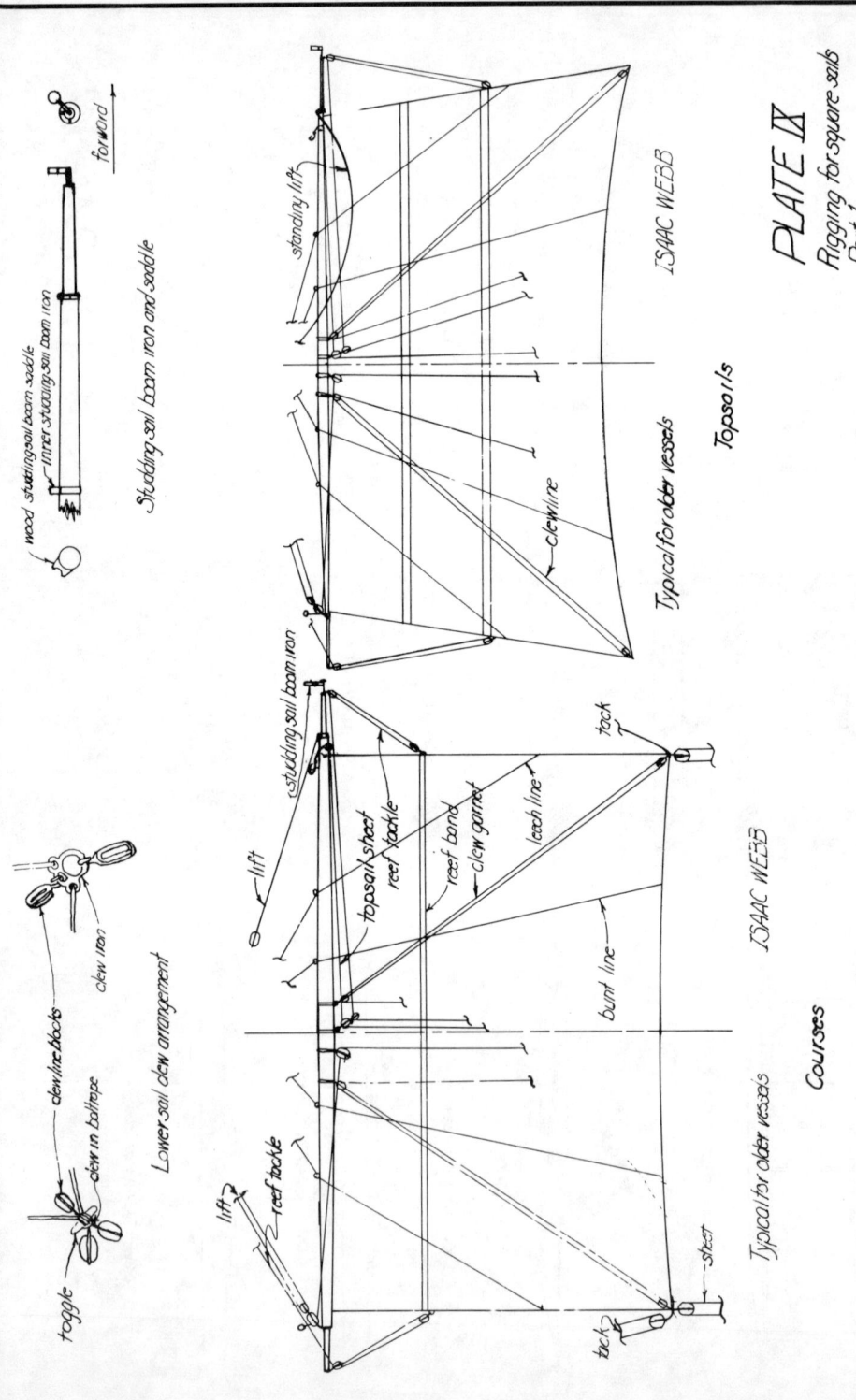

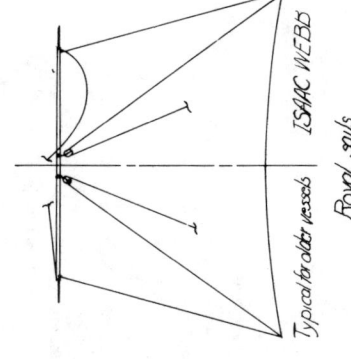
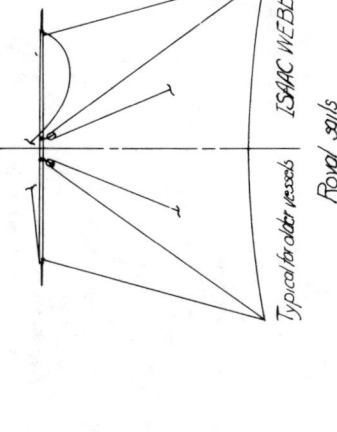

PLATE IX
Rigging for square sails
Part 2

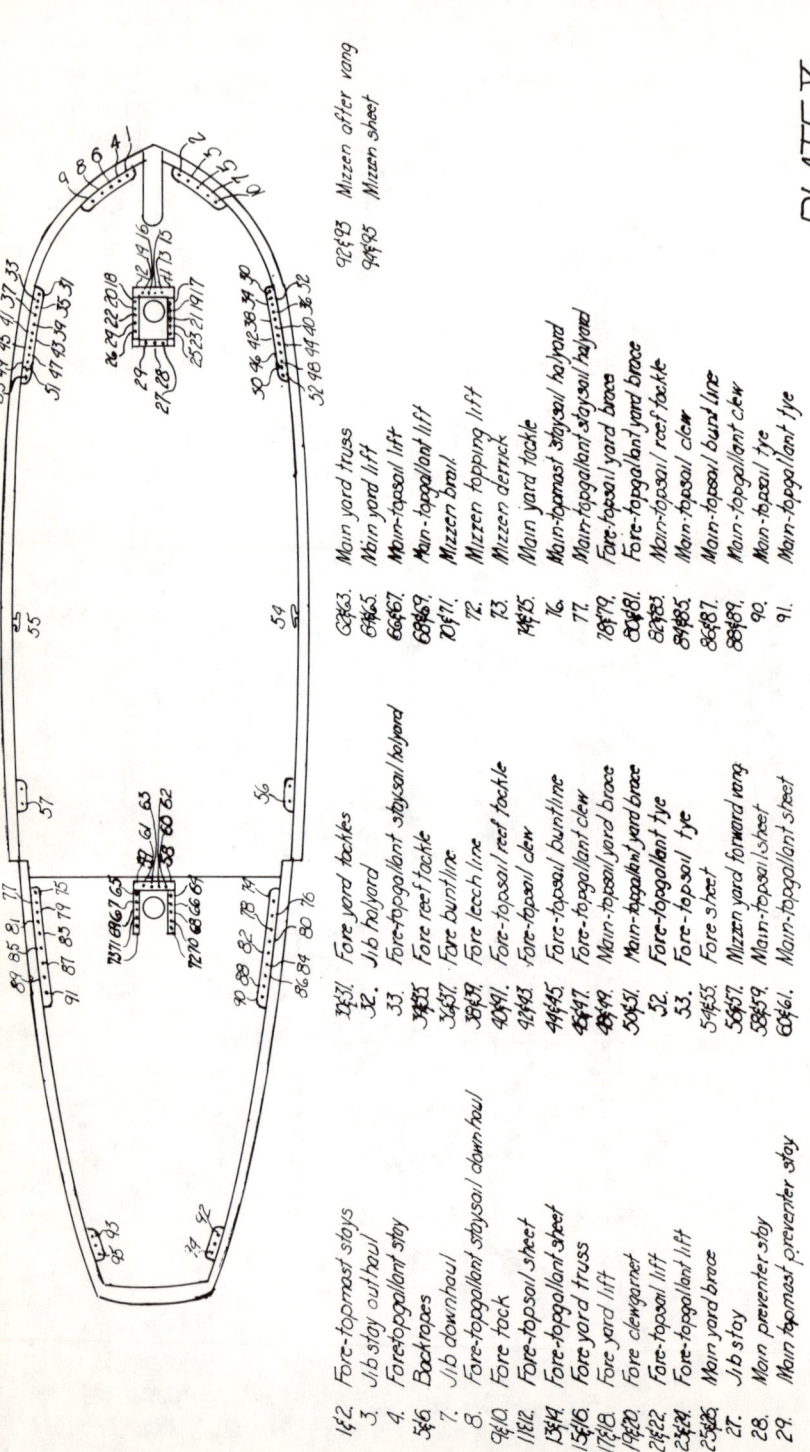

PLATE X
Belaying pin plan
LEXINGTON

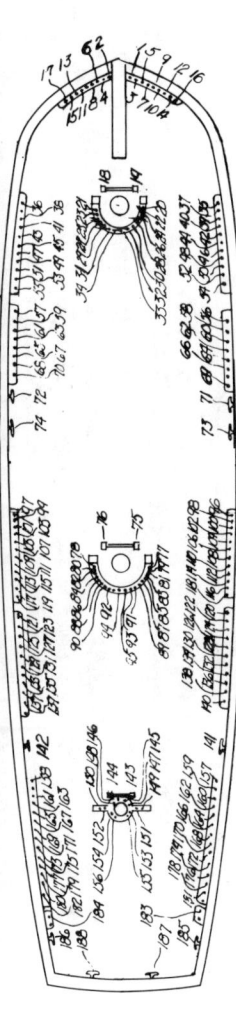

1&2.	Fore-topmast stay	41&43.	Fore bunt line
3.	Jib stay	44&45.	Fore leech line
4.	Fore-topgallant stay	46&47.	Foretopsail lift
5&6.	Spritsail yard lift	48&49.	Foretopsail reef tackle
7.	Fore-topmast staysail downhaul	50&51.	Fore-topsail bunt line
8.	Jib downhaul	52&53.	Foretopsail clew line
9.	Fore-topgallant staysail downhaul	54&55.	Fore-topsail leech line
10.	Jibcoom martingale	56&57.	Fore-topgallant lift
11.	Flying jib martingale	58&59.	Foretopgallant reef tackle
12&13.	Jibcoom backropes	60&61.	Foretopgallant bunt line
14&15.	Flying jibcoom backropes	62&63.	Fore-topgallant clewline
16&17.	Fore tack	64&65.	Fore-royal lift
18&19.	Fore-topsail sheet	66&67.	Fore-royal clewline
20&21.	Fore yard lift	68.	Fore-topsail tye
22&23.	Fore clew garnet	69.	Fore-topgallant tye
24&25.	Fore truss	70.	Fore-royal tye
26&27.	Fore-topgallant sheet	71&72.	Main tack
28&29.	Fore-royal sheet	73&74.	Fore sheet
30.	Main-topmast staysail downhaul	75&76.	Main-topsail sheet
31.	Maintopgallant staysail downhaul	77&78.	Main yard lift
32.	Main-royal staysail downhaul	79&80.	Main clew garnet
33&34.	Fore yard brace	81&82.	Main truss
35&36.	Fore yard tackle	83&84.	Main-topgallant sheet
37.	Fore-royal sheet	85&86.	Main-royal sheet
38.	Jib halyard	87&88.	Crossjack sheet
39.	Fore-topgallant staysail halyard	89&90.	Mizzen-topsail brace
40&41.	Fore reef tackle	91&92.	Fore-topsail brace

93.	Mizzen-topsail downhaul	139.	Main-topgallant tye
94.	Mizzen-topmast staysail downhaul	140.	Main-royal tye
95.	Mizzen-topgallant staysail downhaul	141&142.	Main sheet
96&97.	Main yard tackle	143&144.	Mizzen-topsail sheet
98.	Main-staysail halyard	145&146.	Crossjack yard lift
99.	Main-topmast staysail halyard	147&148.	Crossjack truss
100.	Main-topgallant staysail halyard	149&150.	Mizzen-topgallant sheet
101.	Main-royal staysail halyard	151&152.	Mizzen royal sheet
102&103.	Fore-topgallant brace	153.	Spanker throat halyard
104&105.	Fore-royal brace	154.	Spanker peak halyard
106&107.	Main reef tackle	155&156.	Spanker topping lift
108&109.	Main buntline	157.	Main-staysail halyard
110&111.	Main leech line	158.	Mizzen-topmast staysail halyard
112&113.	Main-topsail lift	159.	Mizzen-topgallant staysail halyard
114&115.	Main-topsail reef tackle	160&161.	Mizzen-topsail lift
116&117.	Main-topsail bunt line	162&163.	Mizzen-topsail reef tackle
118&119.	Main-topsail clewline	164&165.	Mizzen-topsail bunt line
120&121.	Main-topsail leechline	166&167.	Mizzen-topsail clew line
122&123.	Main-topgallant lift	168&169.	Mizzen-topsail leech line
124&125.	Main-topgallant reef tackle	170&171.	Mizzen-topgallant lift
126&127.	Main-topgallant bunt line	172&173.	Mizzen-topgallant reef tackle
128&129.	Main-topgallant clew line	174&175.	Mizzen-topgallant bunt line
130&131.	Main-royal lift	176&177.	Mizzen-topgallant clew line
132&133.	Main-royal clewline	178&179.	Mizzen-topgallant leech line
134&135.	Main-royal sheet	180.	Mizzen-topsail tye
136&137.	Mizzen-royal brace	181.	Mizzen-topgallant tye
138.	Fore-topsail brace	182.	Mizzen-royal tye
		183&184.	Spanker vangs
		185&186.	Main brace
		187&188.	Spanker sheet

PLATE XI

Belaying pin plan for WASP

1. Fore-staysail downhaul
2. Flying jib downhaul
3. Fore-topgallant staysail downhaul
4&5. Fore tack
6&7. Fore-staysail sheet
8&9. Flying jib sheet
10&11. Fore-topgallant staysail sheet
12&13. Fore-topsail sheet
14&15. Fore yard lift
16&17. Fore clew garnet
18&19. Fore-topgallant sheet
20&21. Fore-royal sheet
22. Main-topgallant staysail downhaul
23. Main-royal staysail downhaul
24. Fore-royal staysail halyard
25. Jib halyard
26. Fore-topmast staysail downhaul
27&28. Fore reef tackle
29&30. Fore buntline
31&32. Fore leechline
33&34. Fore-topsail reef tackle
35&36. Fore-topsail buntline
37&38. Fore-topsail clewline
39&40. Fore-topgallant clewline
41&42. Fore-royal clew line
43. Fore-topsail tye
44. Fore-topgallant tye
45. Fore-royal tye
46&47. Main tack
48&49. Fore sheet
50&51. Main-topsail sheet
52&53. Main yard lift
54&55. Main clew garnet
56&57. Fore brace
58&59. Main-topgallant sheet
60&61. Main-royal sheet
62. Mizzen-topmast staysail downhaul
63. Mizzen-topgallant staysail downhaul
64. Main-spencer throat halyard
65. Main-spencer peak halyard
66&67. Crossjack brace
68&69. Mizzen-topsail brace
70&71. Mizzen-topgallant brace
72&73. Mizzen-royal brace
74. Main-royal staysail halyard
75. Main-topgallant staysail halyard
76. Main-topmast staysail halyard
77&78. Fore-topsail brace
79&80. Fore-topgallant brace
81&82. Fore-royal brace
83&84. Main reef tackle
85&86. Main buntline
87&88. Main leechline
89&90. Main-topsail reef tackle
91&92. Main-topsail buntline
93&94. Main-topsail clew line
95&96. Main-topgallant clewline
97&98. Main-royal clewline
99. Main-topsail tye
100. Main-topgallant tye
101. Main-royal tye
102&103. Main spencer vang
104&105. Main sheet
106&107. Mizzen-topsail sheet
108&109. Crossjack yard lift
110&111. Mizzen-topgallant sheet
112&113. Mizzen-royal sheet
114. Mizzen-spencer throat halyard
115. Mizzen-spencer peak halyard
116. Mizzen-topgallant staysail halyard
117. Mizzen-topsail staysail halyard
118. Mizzen-staysail halyard
119&120. Main-topsail brace
121&122. Main-topgallant brace
123&124. Main-royal brace
125&126. Mizzen-topsail reef tackle
127&128. Mizzen-topsail buntline
129&130. Mizzen-topsail clewline
131&132. Mizzen-topgallant clewline
133&134. Mizzen-royal clewline
135&136. Mizzen-boom topping lift
137. Mizzen-topsail tye
138. Mizzen-topgallant tye
139. Mizzen-royal tye
140&141. Mizzen gaff vang
142&143. Main brace
144&145. Spanker sheet

PLATE XII

Belaying pin plan
for ISAAC WEBB

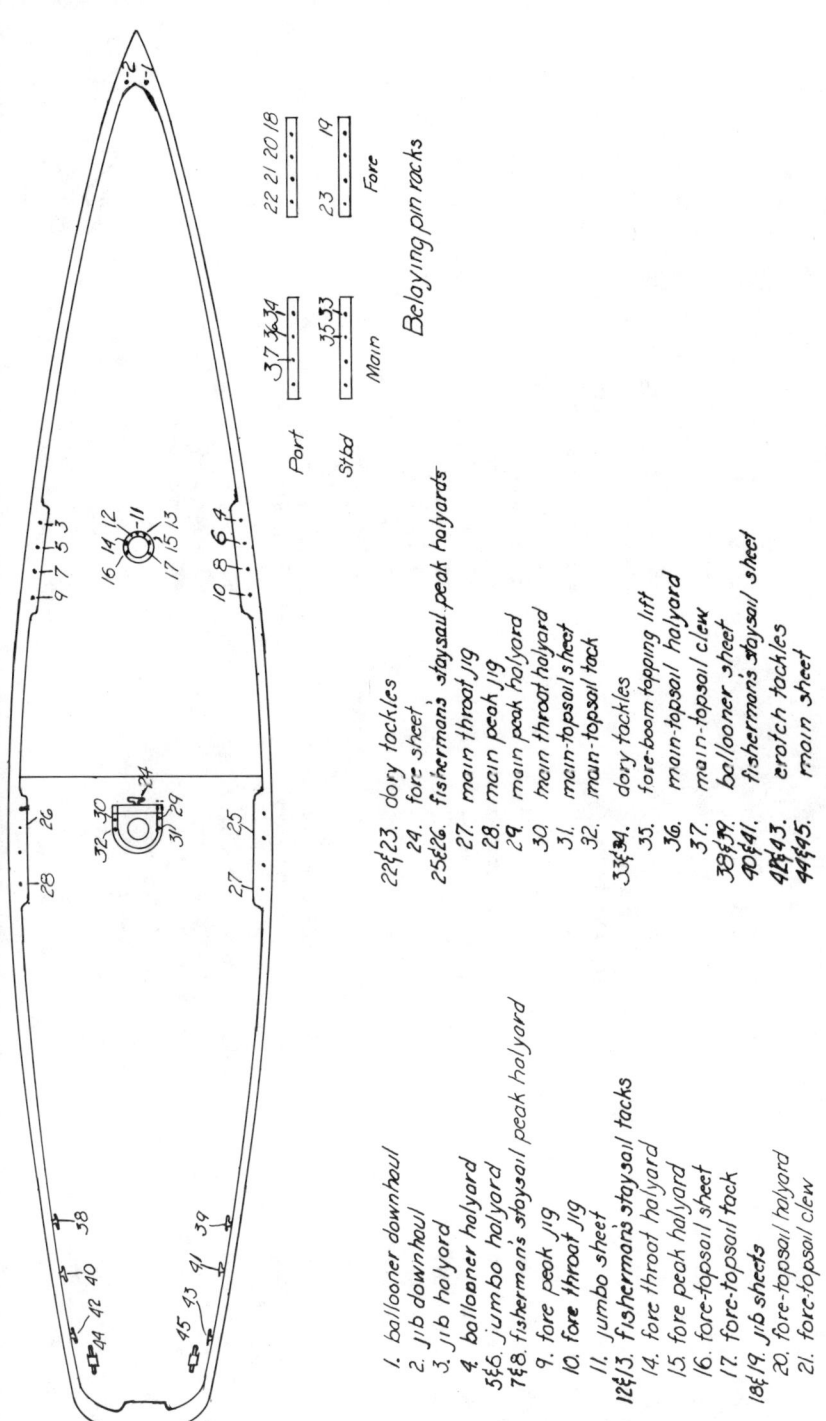

PLATE XIII
Belaying pin plan
for HELEN B. THOMAS

1. jib sheet
2. flying jib downhaul
3. jib downhaul
4. jib topsail downhaul
5. outer jib downhaul
6. fore staysail sheet
7&8. jib topsail sheets
9&10. outer jib sheets
11&12. flying jib sheets
13. fore staysail topping lift
14. jib topping lift
15. jib topsail halyard
16. outer jib halyard
17. flying jib halyard
18. jib halyard
19. fore staysail halyard
20. fore throat halyard
21&22. fore peak halyard
23&24. fore boom topping lift
25. fore-topsail clew
26. fore-topsail halyard
27. main staysail downhaul
28. fore boom tackle
29. fore-topsail tack
30. fore-topsail sheet
31. fore sheet

32. main-topmast staysail halyard
33. main-topmast staysail sheet
34. main throat halyard
35&36. main peak halyard
37&38. main boom topping lifts
39. main-topsail clew
40. main-topsail halyard
41. mizzen staysail downhaul
42&43. mizzen-preventer stay tackles
44. main boom tackles
45. main-topsail tack
46. main-topsail sheet
47. main sheet
48&49. mizzen-preventer stay tackle (unrigged position)
50. mizzen-topmast staysail halyard
51. mizzen-topmast staysail sheet
52. mizzen throat halyard
53&54. mizzen peak halyard
55&56. mizzen boom topping lifts
57. mizzen-topsail clew
58. mizzen-topsail halyard
59. jigger topmast staysail downhaul
60&61. jigger preventer stay tackles
62. mizzen boom tackle
63. mizzen-topsail tack
64. mizzen-topsail sheet

65. mizzen sheet
66&67. jigger preventer stay tackles (unrigged position)
68. jigger topmast staysail halyard
69. jigger topmast staysail sheet
70&71. jigger boom topping lifts
72. jigger topsail clew
73. jigger topsail halyard
74. spanker topmast staysail downhaul
75. jigger throat halyard
76&77. jigger peak halyard
78. jigger boom tackle
79. jigger topsail tack
80. jigger topsail sheet
81. jigger sheet
82. spanker topmast staysail halyard
83. spanker topmast staysail sheet
84&85. spanker boom topping lifts
86. spanker topsail clew
87. spanker topsail halyard
88. spanker throat halyard
89&90. spanker peak halyard
91. spanker boom tackles
92. spanker topsail tack
93. spanker topsail sheet
94&95. spanker sheet
96&97. spanker boom crotch tackles

PLATE XIV

Belaying pin plan for
MARGARET HASKELL

BIBLIOGRAPHY

This list consists of two sections. The first includes those books which proved most helpful to the writer in gathering information used for the present work.

The second listing is intended to serve as a valuable guide to the various craft techniques (e.g., rope work, model metalwork, hard and soft soldering, use of tools, and woodworking) for those seeking to improve their proficiency in ship model building.

Items in both sections are generally available in ship model supply houses, book stores, and public libraries.

SOURCES CONSULTED

Biddlecombe, Captain George, R. N. *The Art of Rigging.* Reprint. Salem: Marine Research Society, 1925.
> A reprint of a book published around 1850 for Naval Academy students in England. In simple language, it describes the sequence and method of rigging contemporary vessels.

Brady, William N. *The Kedge Anchor.* 1876. Reprint. New York: Library Editions, Ltd. 1970.
> An excellent reference covering marlinespike seamanship, rigging, and handling the vessel as well as pertinent tables covering rigging, blocks, spars, anchors, etc.

Chapelle, Howard I. *The American Fishing Schooner 1825-1935.* New York: W. W. Norton, 1973.
> The first part of this book provides a thorough discussion of hull and sail plans for vessels built and used over the last 110 years of sailing banks fishing vessels. The second part contains notes and sketches relating to the hull and rigging of these craft.

―――. *The History of the American Sailing Navy.* New York: Bonanza Books, 1949.

The development and design aspects of several types of American commercial and naval craft are emphasized. Many hull and rigging plans are included providing pertinent information for the model builder.

Davis, Charles G. *The Built-up Ship Model.* 1933. Reprint. New York: Caravan Book Service, 1960.
A step-by-step description with supporting plans and figures for building a built-up model of a single-decked-brig-of-war, *Lexington.* The disparity between this plan and the one used in the present volume is discussed in the text. However, many of the items described and the figures included relate to the model discussed in the present volume.

———. *The Ship Model Builder's Assistant.* 1926. Reprint. New York: Edward W. Sweetman, 1955.
Written for the builder of the square-rigged ship model. Considerable information amplified with sketches and an appendix with a set of tables are included.

———. *Ship Models, How to Build Them.* Salem: Marine Research Society, 1925.
Step-by-step instructions for building a model of the celebrated clipper ship *Sea Witch.* Hull and deck structure construction and fittings and rigging are very similar to that for *Isaac Webb.*

Lever, Darcy. *The Sheet Anchor.* 1808. Reprint. New York: Edward W. Sweetman, 1955.
Published originally in London as a text in rigging and seamanship for young sea officers, this reprint includes the Appendix from the second edition published in London in 1819. It is an excellent reference for those building models of ships constructed around 1800.

Reisenberg, Felix. *Standard Seamanship for the Merchant Service.* 2d ed. Princeton, New Jersey: Van Nostrand, 1936.
A text for sailors in sail and steam vessels, Chapter III, "Ropes, Knots, Splices," is very informative about handling fiber and steel wire rope. Chapter VI, "Sailing Ship-Rigging—Sails-Canvas," contains excellent drawings of a multimasted schooner's bowsprit and mast rigging.

Steel's Elements of Mastmaking, Sailmaking and Rigging. London, 1794. Reprint. New York: Edward W. Sweetman, 1932.

Similar to *The Sheet Anchor* cited above, this text also contains tables showing sizes of rigging with species, size and number of blocks, deadeyes, etc., for various sizes of commercial and war vessels.

Underhill, Harold A. *Masting and Rigging the Clipper Ship & Ocean Carrier.* Glasgow: Brown, Son and Fergueson, 1946.

A description of English sailing ship spars and rigging in the nineteenth and twentieth centuries illustrated with well-executed drawings. Since the difference between English and American rigging methods and hardware were minor, the sketches can be applied to models of contemporary American vessels.

———. *Plank On Frame Models.* Vol. II. Glasgow: Brown, Son and Fergueson, 1960.

A step-by-step description for rigging a built-up model of a merchant brigantine. Perspective drawings of the author's methods for building and assembling the metal parts are very informative for any model builder.

U.S. Navy, Bureau of Constructions and Repair. *United States Frigate "Constitution."* Washington, D.C.: Government Printing Office, 1932.

A brief history of the *Constitution* along with an account of the 1927-1931 restoration as well as drawings of guns, carriages, rigging, and deck plans make this publication an excellent reference for the model builder.

Wales, George C. *Etchings & Lithographs of American Ships.* Boston: Charles E. Goodspeed, 1927.

A "Catalogue of the Etchings" by Mr. Wales is included along with many etchings reproduced in the text. Several of these etchings are worth careful study because they are authentic and well-executed showing details of the vessels and their rigging.

Webb, William Henry. *Plans of Wooden Vessels Selected as Types...Built by William H. Webb, In the City of New York From the Year 1840 to the Year 1869....* New York: Published by the author.

A book of large scale hull and sail plans including those of *Isaac Webb.*

CRAFT BOOKS

Ashley, Clifford W. *The Ashley Book of Knots.* Garden City, New York: Doubleday, 1944.

    An excellent reference including descriptions and figures for 3,854 knots and pieces of rope work. All operations with Manila rope needed by the model builder are contained in this book.

Fryklund, Verne C., and LaBerge, Armand J. *Bench Woodworking.* 4th ed. Bloomington, Illinois: McKnight and McKnight, 1955.

    A textbook covering care, maintenance, and use of hand tools with descriptions of bench woodworking operations.

Hardy, R. Allen, and Bowman, John J. *The Jewelry Repair Manual.* 2d. ed. Princeton, New Jersey: Van Nostrand, 1967.

    Contains valuable information about methods of working with small metal parts.

Shea, John Gerald. *Woodworking for Everybody.* 4th ed. Princeton, New Jersey: Van Nostrand, 1970.

    An excellent discussion of woodworking which includes hand tools, woodworking processes, power tools, tool sharpening, and shop safety.

Weiner, Louis. *Hand Made Jewelry.* 2d ed. Princeton, New Jersey: Van Nostrand, 1960.

    An excellent reference for work on small metal parts made from sheet metal with directions for both hard and soft soldering.

INDEX

Adhesive, 336
Anchor, 146-147
  chain, 148
  rode, 148
  stowage, 148-149
Arch board, 102-105

Ballooner, 308-309
Billboard, 111
Binnacle, 131
Bitt, 127-129
Block, 194-196
Boat, 167-170, 245, 261
Bobstay plate, 179-181
Bollard, 183-184
Boom, 70, 85, 203, 204, 207-208, 225-227
  jibboom, 63, 203, 206, 225, 268, 288
  jibboom, flying, 203, 206, 268, 288
  spanker, 271, 291
Bowline, 217, 218
Bowsprit, 63, 83, 203, 225, 247, 249, 263, 285-287, 316, 317
Bowsprit shroud plate, 181
Breasthook, 91
Bull's-eye, 196-197
Bulwarks, 43, 115-117
  construction, 43, 115-117, 279
  sheave, 120
Bumpkin, 101

Capstan, 149-151
Case, 235-236
Cathead, 113-115
Chainbox, 305
Chain plate, 176-178
Channel, 99-101
Cheek knee, 97-98
Chesstree, 99
Cleat, 129
Companionway, 143-145
Crance iron, 188-189
Crosstree, 61, 205, 206, 222-223, 305

Davit, 171-174
Deadeye, 197-198
Deadeye strop, 176-177
Deck construction, 43, 44, 121-125
Deck structures, 243-245
  house, 137-145
  galley hatch, 145
Dory, 170, 171
  hitch, 312

Engine, hoisting, 184-185
Eyebolt, 176

Fife rail, 130-131
Footrope, 212-213
  jibboom, 327
Foreboom gooseneck, 191
Foresail, 310

Forestay, 187-188
  fitting, 187-188
Futtock, 188

Gaff, 70, 85, 203, 204, 207-208, 225-227
  main spencer, 291
  mizzen spencer, 291
  spanker, 271-272
Gammoning, 208
Gangway, 125
Glue, 336
Ground tackle, 245, 261
Gudgeon, 178-179
Gun, 245, 261
  accessories, 162-164
  carriage, 159-161, 164
  carronade mount, 162, 164
  gunport, 164, 165

Hammock netting, 185-186
Hatch, 125-127
Hawse block, 113
Hawsepipe, 111, 113
Headrail, 98
Headstay ironwork, 181, 182
Heart, 198
Hitch, dory, 312
Hook, 176
Hull
  building methods, 17-43
  built-up, 3, 4
  carved, 3, 4-5
  material, 17, 91-93
  plans, 5-17

Ironwork, 245-247, 261-263

Jackstay, 211-212
Jibboom, 203, 204, 225

Jibboom, flying, 203, 204
Jumbo, 309

Keel, 93
Knee, 91
  cheek, 97-98, 99

Ladders, 133
Lantern, stern, 191
Lazyjack, 330
Light box, 187
Link, backing, 177-178

Mainsail, 310-311
Mainsheet buffer, 190-191
Mast, 59
  lower, 61, 81, 200, 201, 221, 249, 265, 287
  royal, 203, 267, 289
  topgallant, 61, 203, 267, 289
  topmast, 61, 83, 201, 221, 222, 249-252, 265-267, 288
Masthead cap, 61, 192, 205
Metal, 336-337
Mooring pipe, 111, 113
Mounting, 230-233
  permanent, 233-235
  working, 233

Ornamentation, 105-111

Paint, 337
Pinrail, 130-131
Pintle, 178-179
Plans, 5-11
Plates
  bobstay, 179-181
  bowsprit shroud, 181
  chain, 176-178
Pump, 182-183

Quarter badges, 102
Quarter gallery, 102-105

Rails, 119-120, 317-321
  fife, 130-131
  headrail, 98
  pinrail, 130-131
Ratline, 211
Rigging, running, 65-71, 85-87, 213-214
  fore-and-aft sail, 216, 228, 229, 253, 271, 272, 291, 308-312, 327, 330
  lower yard, 214, 215, 252, 253, 269, 270, 271, 289, 290
  studding sail, 216
  topgallant yard, 215, 216, 254, 255, 273, 274, 293, 294
  topsail yard, 215, 253, 254, 272, 273, 292, 293
Rigging, standing, 59-65, 81-83, 208
  bowsprit, 208, 209, 225, 249, 263, 265, 285, 287, 325
  flying jibboom, 268, 288
  jibboom, 251, 288, 326
  lower mast, 209, 210, 227, 228, 249, 265, 287, 307, 308, 325, 326
  royal mast, 210, 267, 289
  topgallant mast, 210, 250, 251, 267, 289
  topmast, 210, 249, 250, 265, 267, 288, 308, 326
Ringbolt, 176
Rope, 337
Rudder, 95
  chain, 179
  gudgeon, 178-179
  pintle, 178-179

Sail, 73-78, 89-90, 229
Sailcloth, 72, 73, 337
Scale, 11-13, 16, 17
Scupper, 117
Sheet band, 191-192
Sheet horse, 183
Skid beam, 99
Skylight, 143
Smokestack, 190
Spar, 199-204, 221-222, 247, 248, 263, 285, 305-307, 322-324
Spar band, 189-190
Steering wheel, 134
Stem, 93
Sternpost, 93
Studding, 216
Studding sail boom iron, 192-193
Studding sail boom saddle, 193

Tackle
  ground, 146, 245, 261
  spanker crotch, 311, 330
Template, 15-17, 46, 47
Trail board, 99
Trestletree, 222-223
Trusses, *see* Crance iron

Wale, 95, 97
Water cask, 135
Winch head, 184
Windlass, 151-154
Wood, 334-335

Yard, 65, 66, 203, 207

FIVE HISTORIC SHIPS
From Plan to Model

has been composed by Cornell Maritime Press in Linoterm Century Schoolbook, a modern version of a typeface designed about 1890 by L.B. Benton for American Typefounders for use in *Century Magazine*, for which it was named. All of the drawings and photographs in the book, unless otherwise indicated, are by the author. It has been printed and bound by The Maple Press Company in York, Pennsylvania.

Cornell Maritime Press
Centreville, Maryland